Roman Catholicism
in Fantastic Film

Roman Catholicism in Fantastic Film

Essays on Belief, Spectacle, Ritual and Imagery

Edited by REGINA HANSEN

McFarland & Company, Inc., Publishers
Jefferson, North Carolina, and London

LIBRARY OF CONGRESS CATALOGUING-IN-PUBLICATION DATA

Roman Catholicism in fantastic film : essays on belief, spectacle, ritual and imagery / edited by Regina Hansen.
    p.   cm.

Includes bibliographical references and index.

ISBN 978-0-7864-6474-6
softcover : 50# alkaline paper ∞

1. Fantasy films — History and criticism.   2. Horror films — History and criticism.   3. Science fiction films — History and criticism.   4. Catholic Church — In motion pictures.
5. Motion pictures — Religious aspects — Catholic Church.
6. Catholics in motion pictures.   I. Hansen, Regina.
PN1995.9.F36R56   2011
791.43'615 — dc22   2011007859

BRITISH LIBRARY CATALOGUING DATA ARE AVAILABLE

© 2011 Regina Hansen. All rights reserved

No part of this book may be reproduced or transmitted in any form or by any means, electronic or mechanical, including photocopying or recording, or by any information storage and retrieval system, without permission in writing from the publisher.

On the cover: Keanu Reeves as the title character in the 2005 film *Constantine* (Warner Bros./Photofest)

Manufactured in the United States of America

McFarland & Company, Inc., Publishers
  Box 611, Jefferson, North Carolina 28640
    www.mcfarlandpub.com

To Michael Joseph Cremin II
"Defend us…"

Table of Contents

Preface ... 1

Introduction ... 2

Section One:
Marvelous Catholicism

"When the Saints Go Marching In": Saints, Money and the Global Marketplace in Danny Boyle's *Millions*
    JOHN REGAN ... 17

Blasphemy in the Name of Fantasy: The Films of Terry Gilliam in a Catholic Context
    CHRISTOPHER MCKITTRICK ... 29

Sacramentality Between Catholicism and the New Age in *The Lord of the Rings*
    EM MCAVAN ... 41

"The Devil Made Me Do It": Catholicism, Verisimilitude and the Reception of Horror Films
    RICK PIETO ... 52

"The Power of Christ Compels You": Moral Spectacle and *The Exorcist* Universe
    ALEXANDRA HELLER-NICHOLAS ... 65

Our Lady of Fátima and Marian Myth in Portuguese Cinema
    PAULO CUNHA *and* DANIEL RIBAS ... 81

Section Two: Uncanny Catholicism

Music That Sucks and Bloody Liturgy: Catholicism in Vampire Movies
  ISABELLA VAN ELFEREN — 97

"The Blood Is the Life": Roman Catholic Imagery in Vampire Films of the 1930s
  ANN KORDAS — 114

House of Horrors: *Brideshead Revisited* at the Movies
  KATHLEEN E. URDA — 126

Drying Blood: De-sexualization and Style in Paul Schrader's *Cat People*
  MARCO GROSOLI — 140

Something in the Dark: Race, Faith, Horror and the Other
  RALPH BELIVEAU — 152

Section Three: Ridiculous and Monstrous Catholicism

Reversing the Gospel of Jesus: How the Zombie Theme Satirizes the Resurrection of the Body and the Eucharist
  JANA TOPPE — 169

Kin Dza Dza! Christianity and Its Transformations Across Space
  MARGARITA GEORGIEVA — 183

Murder Mystery Meets Sacred Mystery: The Catholic Sacramental in Hitchcock's *I Confess*
  BARRY C. KNOWLTON and ELOISE R. KNOWLTON — 196

Catholic Moral Teaching as a Fantastic Element in *Gone Baby Gone*
  BRETT GAUL — 209

The "Fantastic" Roman Catholic Church in Italian Cinema
  VICTORIA SURLIUGA — 219

The Satanic Saint in Maurice Pialat's *Sous le soleil de Satan*
    CHRISTA JONES   232

Dark Imperative: Kant, Sade and Catholicism in
Jess Franco's *Exorcism*
    DAVID ANNANDALE   244

Killer Priests: The Last Taboo?
    SHELLEY F. O'BRIEN   256

Mad Drunken Exorcists: The Decline of the Hero Priest
    REGINA HANSEN   268

Otherness in *The Others:* Haunting the Catholic Other,
Humanizing the Self
    ANABEL ALTEMIR GIRAL *and* ISMAEL IBÁÑEZ ROSALES   275

About the Contributors   287

Index   291

Preface

This volume combines two fields of inquiry, the study of film — particularly in the "fantastical" genres of horror, fantasy, science fiction and the supernatural — and the study of a particular religious tradition, Roman Catholicism. Catholic themes are widespread in Western film traditions, particularly in films dealing with fantastic subject matter — from saints and angels to vampires and zombies — or even as an element of the fantastic in films that are otherwise presented as realistic. There have been some books dealing with filmic portrayals of Catholicism and Catholic believers — including Peter Malone's *Through a Catholic Lens: Religious Perspectives of Nineteen Film Directors from Around the World* (2007) and collection *Catholics in the Movies* (2008), edited by Colleen McDannell. Catholic subject matter also appears in *Christians in the Movies: A Century of Saints and Sinners* (2009) by Peter E. Dans. What this book does differently is to posit Catholicism as one of the central elements of fantastic narrative in North American and European film, and to look at the ways in which Catholicism appears and reappears in films dealing with magical, marvelous and uncanny themes.

The contributors to this book come from various scholarly backgrounds — some are film scholars, some are theologians and philosophers, while others are interested in cultural history — and represent a wide range of attitudes toward Catholicism as a belief system and the Catholic Church as an institution. What we share is a fascination with the ways in which the stuff of Catholicism — its supernatural claims, its rituals and artifacts, its moral exigencies and contradictions — have appealed and continue to appeal to filmmakers in the fantastic genres. Chapters range from direct discussion of the supernatural elements of Catholic belief — such as saints, and practices such as exorcism — to the metaphorical Catholicism in films featuring zombies and vampires, among others, and the use of Catholic tropes to enhance the fantastic, marvelous or uncanny atmosphere of a film. The intent is to give as complete as possible an understanding of the ways in which Catholicism and the fantastic intersect in film. Although a couple of the chapters deal with so-called realistic films, the focus is always on the way a film's portrayal of Catholicism is meant to invoke the fantastic. With that in mind, not included are narratives dealing chiefly with the everyday lives of Catholic believers or the sociopolitical aspects of Catholicism, or films in which the protagonists just happen to be Catholic. *Shoes of the Fisherman*, *Doubt*, *Going My Way*, *A Change of Habit*, *Sister Act* and *Gran Torino* might be among these.

As editor, I am grateful for the support and enthusiasm of my colleagues and students at Boston University's College of General Studies, and for the excellent resources provided by Boston University's Mugar Library and the Somerville Public Library in Somerville Massachusetts. Many thanks, as always, to my family — especially my mother, as well as Brian Kemmett, and Dominic, Angelina and Veronica Kemmett. The idea for this volume came out of discussions with friends at the International Conference for the Fantastic in the Arts. The good work of some of the Conference's members is on display in these pages.

Introduction

The articles in this collection examine the intimate link between a religious tradition, Roman Catholicism, and an artistic/literary genre, the fantastic, as conveyed in North American and European film. In film, representations of Roman Catholicism, its symbolism and ritual, are often meant to evoke an experience of the fantastic, what Tzvetan Todorov calls "that hesitation experienced by a person who knows only the laws of nature, confronting an apparently supernatural event" (25), and existing between "two tendencies: that of the supernatural explained (the 'uncanny')...; and that of the supernatural accepted (the 'marvelous')." (41) In Todorov's understanding of the uncanny, "events are related which may be readily accounted for by the laws of reason, but which are, in one way or another, incredible, extraordinary, shocking, singular, disturbing or unexpected" (46). Sigmund Freud described this sense as "*unheimlich*" or un-homely, "the opposite of what is familiar" (195), but without the appeal of the unfamiliar, invoking instead secrecy, strangeness and the occult, the hidden, that which cannot be trusted (195). To go further, in film, the uncanny often translates into an experience of the monstrous — something so strange, so *unheimlich,* as to repel both the film's protagonist and the viewer. The uncanny can also be perceived as the ridiculous, too strange, we might say too "fantastic" to be believed, and thus laughable. On the other hand, the "marvelous," what Todorov calls "the class of narratives that are presented as fantastic and that end with an acceptance of the supernatural" (52), is experienced by the filmgoer as a sense of wonder, an acceptance and even embrace of mystery.

While Todorov locates the fantastic on "the frontier of two genres" (41), the filmgoer's experience of the fantastic could be said to encompass both. A constantly shifting sense of the fantastic as marvelous and uncanny, monstrous and wondrous, mysterious and ridiculous, is part of the experience of watching the many subgenres of fantastic film — from horror to fantasy, science fiction to ghost stories — and understanding the Catholicism presented in those films. Filmic portrayals of Catholicism can serve to evoke any or all of the above permutations of the fantastic, or may simply reflect the "hesitation" of which Todorov speaks. The representation of Catholicism in film is as varied as the ways in which the fantastic itself is expressed, and appears both overtly and in subtext, as both central and tangential to a film's main concerns.

Film history is filled with explicitly Catholic subject matter, in which the ritual, iconography and stories of Catholicism — the fantastic claims of Catholicism itself— form the central focus: *The Passion of the Christ* tells a story shared by all Christians but in a way that specifically reflects the Catholic practices of the Passion Play and the Stations of the Cross. Marian apparition stories like *Song of Bernadette* or *Miracle of Our Lady of Fatima* are also common film subjects, as are retellings of the lives of the saints, people who are believed in Catholic tradition to have miraculous powers. Other fantastic films evoke Catholic belief and ritual in a modern context, portraying the protagonists' interactions with these beliefs as either marvelous or uncanny, depending on point of view. In this category are films of everyday interaction with the miraculous — Danny Boyle's *Millions* in which the protagonist interacts with saints out of his childhood storybooks — as well as the many horror films which make use of Catholic rituals as ways to combat evil — *The Exorcist* and its many imitators — or that show the Church itself as the seat of such evil.

In part because of Catholicism's own claims as a locus of authentic supernatural experience, Catholic symbolism and ritual can appear as the sole reference to the fantastic in otherwise realistic films. In such cases, references to saints, incense, Mass or the Virgin Mary may be meant to evoke a sense of either wonder or uncanny dread — this last being evident in any film based on a book by Dan Brown. Even when Catholicism is not in itself the subject of the film, Catholic rites and beliefs can be seen as subtext in numerous films with fantastic themes — such as the ever-growing vampire and zombie corpus, in which eternal life is promised through the literal consumption of flesh and blood. As portrayed in film, the diverse and multi-faceted nature of what might be called "the Catholic fantastic" reflects, and is intertwined with, Western culture's relationship to Catholicism, the ways in which that particular religious tradition has been portrayed in art and literature throughout Western history.

Marvelous Catholicism

Like the art forms that preceded it, film portrays Catholicism, and its connection to the fantastic, both from the outside and as they are experienced by the faith's adherents. Depending in part on point of view, depictions of the fantastic elements of Catholicism — the miracles and sacred objects, the stories of saints and the ritual of the Mass — have veered toward either uncanny or marvelous interpretations or remained in Todorov's mode of hesitation. Catholicism itself has always made claims to the marvelous, to being marvelous in the very nature of its beliefs and practices, as can be seen in art back to the Middle Ages and the Renaissance. Catholicism presents the fantastic events and powers it relates as real, locating the supernatural in everyday life, in rituals that recur sometimes daily, sometimes according to a calendar steeped in the seasonal cycles of nature. The poet Seamus Heaney recalls his childhood experience of Catholicism as giving him "the sense of eternity and the sense of grace and god-filled space ... inner expansiveness of consciousness and the supernatural sense of a universe drenched in radiance" (*Charlie Rose*). This is certainly Catholicism's narrative about itself, both in the way this particular faith reflects beliefs held by all Christians — the virgin birth, Jesus's death and resurrection — but also through the investment of fantastic/marvelous power and significance in Catholicism's personnel and material culture.

Catholics, at least in theory, believe in the reality of everyday marvelous occurrences and powers, and also enact their beliefs in an innately theatrical manner, enhancing, or attempting to enhance, people's experience of the marvelous through the use of showmanship and spectacle. Later in this volume, Alexandra Heller-Nicholas suggests that "the phenomenon of the spectacle has a privileged position in Roman Catholic faith, as it hinges so fundamentally upon belief in the unseeable." That "privileged position," that centrality of spectacle, is also part of what so intimately links Catholicism and film. Historically, both Catholicism as a religious tradition and film as an art form have used spectacle to evoke a sense of the fantastic-marvelous. In the case of Catholicism, this practice is centuries old. We see it in the rituals of the faith, especially the central ritual of the Mass, in which priests are believed to be invested with the power to turn bread and wine into Christ's actual body and blood, but in other daily practices, too. Statues of saints are everywhere in Catholic churches, and while they are not meant to be worshipped as such, represent people who have done fantastic-marvelous things (or who are believed to have done them) and also, by calling to mind images of the gods of polytheism, remind us of the pagan roots of much of Catholic practice and add to the sense of spectacle by evoking ancient, even pre-historic rituals. Moreover, the stories of these saints have been represented in art through the centuries and assiduously studied by the Vatican to determine the potential truth of the spectacular, fantastic, marvelous events they recount. Catholics also carry sacred objects, such as blessed crucifixes and medals, and perform everyday ritual gestures like the sign of the cross. Use of these objects and gestures creates a small spectacle in its own right, since both invoke "unseeable," potentially marvelous spiritual protection, and also call attention to the person wearing the medal or performing the gesture as belonging to a particular faith.

Catholicism is not the only faith to evoke the marvelous through spectacle, or whose adherents purportedly believe in marvelous occurrences — even the specific gestures, objects and rituals mentioned above are not necessarily unique to Catholicism, but are present in the Orthodox, and to some extent, the Anglican religious traditions. At the same time, the spectacle of Catholicism is still the most familiar, certainly to the North American and European filmmakers to be discussed in this book. The largest single Christian denomination, with a network of churches, schools and other cultural institutions throughout the world, the imagery and ritual of Catholicism are as common and recognizable as they are supernaturally evocative, at least to Westerners. In a sense, for filmmakers, Catholic spectacle presents a sense of the marvelous that is both exotic in its supernaturalism and, through its very ubiquity, familiar and accessible. In turn, by so frequently using Catholic imagery and ritual as tropes through which to represent the supernatural acting or believed to be acting in the world, North American and European filmmakers perpetuate the identification of Catholicism with the fantastic as marvelous, as uncanny, and in all its other iterations as well.

Uncanny Catholicism

If Roman Catholicism represents its beliefs and practices in terms of the fantastic-marvelous, historically these same have often been seen in a more uncanny light. Film reflects this tension. The association of Catholicism with more problematic issues related to the fantastic, with the uncanny interpretation of the fantastic, can probably be dated the 17th century as the Protestant Reformation discarded elements of Christian religious practice that were deemed idolatrous, or rooted in a pagan past, such as the veneration of the Virgin Mary and the Saints, or the celebration of certain holidays. Such practices were seen both to needlessly mystify religious experience, alienating the believer from a direct connection to God, while also investing too much mystical power in the Church's human representatives — as evidenced in the Catholic doctrine of transubstantiation, in which the priest is seen as literally having the power (albeit from God) to turn bread and wine into the body and blood of Christ. The 18th-century Enlightenment belief in the supremacy of human reason led to further association of Catholicism with the uncanny. In an intellectual climate that prized rationalism and thinking for one's self, Catholicism represented the irrational, blind faith not only in a supernatural God, but also in his earthly representatives. In England and later America, Catholicism stood for outmoded supernatural beliefs at odds with a rational world, as well as an untrustworthy, too powerful clergy. The latter concern was also part of literary representations of the faith in countries such as Spain and Italy, where Catholics were an overwhelming majority.

The Church's use of spectacle as a vehicle for the delivery of its marvelous claims, discussed above, was also a matter of deep distrust among those who did not practice the faith. In *Anti-Catholicism and Nineteenth Century Fiction*, Susan Griffin refers to descriptions of Catholicism, "as a religion of forms and surfaces: gilded decorations, ritualized behaviors, and mediated (through clergy or saints) relations with God," Catholicism as "a religion which is theatrically performed" (5)—rather than authentically experienced. That condemnation of the use of spectacle, not to inspire belief in the marvelous, but rather to underscore the Church's claims to earthly power, remains a prevalent criticism of Catholicism to this day, and will be addressed in this volume by Victoria Surliuga, Rick Pieto and others. Still, during the 18th and into the 19th centuries, the spectacular strangeness of Catholic ritual was as aesthetically and thematically attractive to many non–Catholic artists, especially authors, as it might have been spiritually appalling. The 18th century Gothic novel, the progenitor of the modern fantastic subgenre known as horror, dramatized this distrust of the irrational in general and of the supposedly occult and uncanny nature of Catholicism in particular, by making what for many readers was a tantalizing use of narrative tropes that suggested Catholic ritual and iconography. Novels like Hugh Walpole's *Castle of Otranto* (1764) and Ann Radcliffe's *Mysteries of Udolpho* (1794) portrayed a Catholicism of ruined abbeys, dark-skinned lecherous priests and monks with seemingly supernatural powers to enslave women, and nuns walled up in convents, as well as purportedly superstitious practices such as the telling of beads and the implied "worship" of the Virgin Mary. Much like the modern horror films that they eventually inspired, such novels were simultaneously fascinating and repellent to readers, who experienced them both as lessons against indulging in superstition and mysticism and as thrilling stories of transgression.

Nineteenth-century fiction continued the Gothic fascination with uncanny Catholicism, often in the service of religious intolerance and ethnic bigotry. Mass Irish immigration to England, where Catholics had long been a distrusted religious minority, as well as immigration to America from Ireland and the majority Catholic countries of Southern and Central Europe led many British and American writers to associate Catholicism with foreignness and the "racialized Other" (Griffin 210). Thus we find a continuation of certain Gothic archetypes — the swarthy Spanish priest with the power of mesmerism, the mad Italian countess, the superstitious Hungarian peasant warning of vampires. In America, not only did Catholics represent the ethnic other, but their beliefs and rituals also recalled an archaic irrationality that was seen as threatening in a country founded on the values of the Enlightenment. In the 19th Century, and to a lesser extent into the 1920s and 30s, Gothicized representations of Catholicism and Catholics as unnatural and uncanny threats were found not only in the overtly anti–Catholic American "nativist" tracts like *The Awful Disclosures of Maria Monk*, but also in many of the mainstream British and American novels of the period, most famously Charlotte Bronte's 1853 novel *Villette* (Griffin 12), as well as in early film, such as the vampire and zombie movies Ann Kordas will discuss in this volume.

Catholicism: Ridiculous, Monstrous and "Faux"

The writers above used the medium of the irrational, the strange, the uncanny, to critique a religious tradition they thought of in those terms, but as Susan Griffin reminds us, works like those just mentioned represent "only partially the range of nineteenth-century attitudes toward the Catholic Church" (12), not to mention, for our purposes, the Catholic fantastic. The Medievalist artistic and literary movements that developed during the mid and late 19th century veered more toward the marvelous in their portrayal of the Catholic fantastic, as poets and artists like the Pre-Raphaelites used images of female saints and the Virgin Mary to evoke a more beneficent supernatural atmosphere. The work of these artists and writers, as taken up by people like C.S. Lewis and the (perhaps not coincidentally Catholic) J.R.R. Tolkien, was the foundation for modern fantasy literature and film, another of the subgenres of the fantastic to be discussed here. Moreover as the Gothic developed into the basis for modern horror, writers and later filmmakers would find many narrative uses for Gothic tropes, some of which offered intelligent critiques of Catholicism, others that elevated the faith to a heroic force, and still others that used Catholicism's ritual and symbolism as merely aesthetic signifiers, or even not at all, choosing instead to locate the uncanny and marvelous in the practices of Evangelical Protestantism, Judaism or Native American religion among others.

In America, the fading away of blatant anti–Catholicism throughout the early decades of the 20th century coincided not only with the beginning of assimilation and growing social power among Catholic immigrants and their children, but with the rising to primacy of film as an art form. As Colleen McDannell tells us, there has been a "sustained cinematic attention to Catholicism" (3) since the very beginning of moviemaking. As film became central to European and North American culture, Catholicism and Catholic spirituality were frequent subjects, or at least common elements, of many movies, especially in fantastic subgenres such as horror, supernatural or fantasy. While some of this book's contributors make the case that early American films continued to reflect the fear of the mass immigration of Catholics, it is also true that American Catholics, as an urban populace, were among the most likely consumers of films (17) and that Catholic social institutions of all kinds were growing in such prominence (18) as to have influence on what films people saw and how they were presented. In fact, from 1930 to 1966 the Motion Picture Production Code, also known as the Hays Code, originally enforced by William Hays and eventually presided over by lay Catholic Joseph Breen (92) ensured that films maintained conservative moral standards but also made it so that the anti–Catholicism of the nativists or any inaccurate representation of Catholic practice — as well as perhaps any fair critique of the Church — could not be overtly detected in American films throughout the 1930s through the early 60s. (19) As Paulo Cunha and Daniel Ribas will argue later in this volume, this was also true in many parts of Catholic Europe, where Church and state remained historically intertwined. The manifold social changes of the 1960s brought with them an opening up of Catholic religious practices with the Second Vatican Council, as well as the abolishment of the Hays Code and eventually the loosening of censorship standards in parts of Europe as well.

Throughout the late 20th century and into the 21st, filmmakers gained freedom to represent Catholicism in any way they chose, to utilize its ritual and imagery in the furtherance of a rich variety of narratives. Depictions of Catholicism and its relationship to the fantastic could call up the uncanny, could celebrate the marvelous or critique the ridiculous. Starting in the late 1980s, events in the Catholic Church led to a filmic revisiting of older narrative tropes, as the ongoing child sexual abuse scandal and its attendant cover-up by the religious hierarchy, fed into, and often justified, newly Gothicized representations of Catholics and Catholicism. In recent years, many filmmakers have reintroduced the theme of Catholic clergy as Gothic monsters, or as Christa Jones and David Annandale will argue here, have employed the fantastic, in its monstrous and uncanny iterations, as a vehicle through which to critique the ideas and practices within the Church that many would say may have led to the scandal. In other films, of course, narrative and visual use of the Catholic fantastic, its iconography and rituals, its theatricality and spectacle, have had more to do with aesthetic and entertainment value than with any comment on Roman Catholicism itself.

As discussed before, Catholic churches and rituals provide a background that both is familiar and appears genuinely supernatural. Indeed, as Rick Pieto and Alexandra Heller-Nicholas will suggest here, the violence of some of Catholic spectacle — including references to the martyrdom of the saints, books and images about them and loving recreation of Christ's death during the Passion and the Stations of the Cross, link the spectacle of Catholicism to theatricality in a way that has well served the fantastic sub-genre of horror. This is true whether or not the Catholicism represented is authentically realized on screen. In many films, the Catholic fantastic has been transmuted into what Victoria Nelson calls "faux Catholicism ... an exoticized, patently fictional, and some would say anti-clerical fantasy of Catholicism" (88). Whether exemplified through pre–Vatican II images of nuns in full habit, the well placed Latin chanting discussed by Isabella van Elferen in this volume, or the labyrinthine Vatican conspiracies posited by Dan Brown and the films of his books, faux Catholic tropes have entertainment value as sure signifiers of fantastic, usually uncanny goings on within a film. According to Nelson, "faux Catholic" films, or elements within films, posit the Catholic Church as both the uncanny supernatural villain of the narrative and the "only effective defense" against an even greater evil that must be vanquished through secret power and ritual known to Catholics alone, and the use of their "perceived magical talismans" (91). Like the Gothic tradition in which it is partially rooted, faux Catholicism is both attractive and repellent, both intriguing and frightening, and reflects the inherent tensions — Todorov's "hesitation" again — within filmic representations of the Catholic fantastic. This tension and hesitation exists between belief and skepticism, between the strangeness of Catholic mysticism and the familiarity and ubiquity of the Catholic Church as an institution, between the faith's "marvelous" self-representation and perceptions of its practice and teaching as uncanny, ridiculous, even monstrous, and has been represented over and over in the text and subtext of fantastic film.

Content and Contributors

The chapters in this volume will deal with the many overt and metaphorical representations of the Catholic fantastic, whether marvelous or uncanny, monstrous or ridiculous. So, there are saints, relics, priests, nuns, angels, and the Virgin Mary, along with sub-textual vampires, zombies and haunted houses. Contributors will explore the fantastic subgenres of horror, fantasy, ghost story, and science fiction as well as showing how references to Catholic ritual and imagery provide the fantastic element in otherwise realistic film. Like the films they discuss, the chapters in this collection run the gamut from reflection of Catholic beliefs and practices through critique and rejection of Catholicism to aesthetic appreciation of how Catholic narrative and iconography are used to promote a filmgoer's experience of the fantastic. The chapters are arranged into three sections.

Section One includes articles that examine Catholicism within filmic representations of the marvelous or belief in the marvelous. Many of the chapters focus on Catholicism's representation of itself as fantastic-marvelous and the extent to which the film's protagonists believe these claims. In "'When the Saints Go Marching In': Saints, Money and the Global Marketplace in Danny Boyle's *Millions*," John Regan analyzes a boy's attempts to reconcile his true belief in Catholicism — both its supernatural stories of saintly miracles and the exigencies of its moral call to charity — with the lure of wealth and capitalism exemplified by his discovery of a bag full of "millions" of British pound notes. Christopher McKittrick's "Blasphemy in the Name of Fantasy: The Films of Terry Gilliam in a Catholic Context" explores the ways in which Gilliam employs Catholic imagery as part of the parade of marvels in his already supernaturally rich films. Partly echoing Regan's chapter, McKittrick focuses in great measure on *The Fisher King* and its use of medieval Catholic religious symbols to critique modern capitalism. Em McAvan's chapter "Sacramentality Between Catholicism and the New Age in *The Lord of the Rings*" portrays the relationship between the Catholic fantastic and capitalism and also between the Catholic fantastic and New Age spirituality, discussing how the elements of fantastic-marvelous Catholicism in Tolkien's books are diluted in the films in favor of a more marketable New Age philosophy.

While the authors above examine the intersections of Catholicism and the fantastic-marvelous as social critique, Rick Pieto focuses his discussion on the filmgoer's experience of Catholicism as spectacle. His study, "'The Devil Made Me Do It': Catholicism, Verisimilitude and the Reception of Horror Films," examines the ways in which being raised Catholic and believing in Catholicism's marvelous claim, affects a viewer's understanding of certain horror film narratives as true, having the potential to actually occur. In "'The Power of Christ Compels You': Moral Spectacle and *The Exorcist* Universe," Alexandra Heller-Nicholas examines the many films based on or inspired by William Peter Blatty's novel *The Exorcist*. She suggests that all such films make use of Catholic spectacle to frighten their audiences, thus implicitly counting on a certain degree of belief in both the film's supernatural marvels as well as the moral system they uphold. The combination of filmic and Catholic spectacle can facilitate both viewers' belief in marvelous supernatural occurrences and acceptance of a particular Catholic moral viewpoint, but can also be used to support a more secular agenda. In "Our Lady of Fátima and Marian Myth in Portuguese Cinema," Paulo Cunha and Daniel Ribas survey the group of films featuring the purported apparitions of the Virgin Mary at Fatima, Portugal, and look at the ways in which the Fatima story — and thus the Catholic fantastic — has been used to serve various political perspectives and groups throughout the country's history.

Section Two examines films that represent or critique uncanny Catholicism, starting with two chapters that examine the specifically Catholic subtext of the vampire mythos. Isabella van Elferen's "Music That Sucks and Bloody Liturgy: Catholicism in Vampire Movies" neatly portrays the specifically Roman Catholic (as opposed to Protestant Christian) subtext of a modern vampire film, Coppola's *Bram Stoker's Dracula*, particularly as expressed in the film's music. In "'The Blood Is the Life': Roman Catholic Imagery in Vampire Films of the 1930s," Ann Kordas draws connections between the figure of the vampire in early horror movies and Catholic ritual and belief, in order to discuss the anti–Catholic sentiments arising from continued immigration to the United States in the 1920s and 30s. In "House of Horrors: *Brideshead Revisited* at the Movies," Kathleen E. Urda builds on Kordas's ideas. In a critique of the most recent film interpretation of Evelyn Waugh's novel, Urda examines the filmmakers' reversion to Gothic narrative tropes to create an uncanny and threatening image of the Catholicism of the film's main characters.

While films like the ones Kordas and Urda discuss may reflect a distrust of Catholic ritual and belief, an understanding of them as uncanny and threatening, Marco Grosoli's chapter suggests that there may in fact be something uncanny in Catholic teaching. In "Drying Blood: De-sexualization and Style in Paul Schrader's *Cat People*," Grosoli asserts that Schrader uses uncanny imagery and references to shape shifters and vampires to comment on Catholicism's understanding of sexuality. If Catholicism can be viewed in an uncanny light, Catholics themselves may experience the uncanny when confronted with the rituals and beliefs of other cultures. In "Something in the Dark: Race, Faith, Horror, and the Other," Ralph Beliveau discusses how the fantastic-uncanny presents itself in films in which Catholicism as a representative of the West encounters religious practices that mix Catholic and African or indigenous beliefs — specifically Haitian Voudoun and Latin American Santería. According to Beliveau, such films portray "a conflict between two supernatural systems," with Catholicism as a representative of European religious and cultural hegemony.

Section Three encounters the Catholic fantastic in its ridiculous and monstrous iterations, with many articles examining the use of the fantastic to satirize or critique Catholic beliefs and practices. In "Reversing the Gospel of Jesus: How the Zombie Theme Satirizes the Resurrection of the Body and the Eucharist," Jana Toppe considers the ways in which zombie movies satirize and subvert both the Christian doctrines of the resurrection and the Eucharist and the specifically Catholic idea of the resurrection of the body. Margarita Georgieva's "*Kin Dza Dza!* Christianity and Its Transformations Across Space" examines a space travel comedy that parodies doctrinal conflicts between Christianity and Communism but also among Christians, specifically Roman Catholics and Russian Orthodox. Other chapters feature characters that openly view Catholicism and Catholic teaching in a fantastic-ridiculous light. In "Murder Mystery Meets Sacred Mystery: The Catholic Sacramental in Hitchcock's *I Confess*," Barry C. Knowlton and Eloise R. Knowlton portray how the Catholic core of Hitchcock's film, its portrayal of the sacrament of confession, makes the film fantastical. Brett Gaul's "Catholic Moral Teaching as a Fantastic Element in *Gone Baby Gone*" focuses not so much on the ritual and symbolism of Catholicism as fantastic, but on the ways in which the central character's moral and ethical belief system is viewed by others as fantastic/ridiculous because of exigencies of conscience portrayed as specifically derived from Catholicism.

Many recent films have used fantastic imagery and narrative to critique the Catholic Church's spiritual and secular power or address the moral failures of its hierarchy. Victoria Surliuga's "The 'Fantastic' Roman Catholic Church in Italian Cinema" does this, discussing how Italian filmmakers use intersections of Catholicism and the fantastic to reflect their own religious beliefs or lack thereof as well as to question the "self-representation of the Church as fantastic," or fantastic-marvelous. In "The Satanic Saint in Maurice Pialat's *Sous le soleil de Satan*," Christa Jones argues that Pialat uses narratives of fantastic Catholicism — specifically those of demonic possession and the miracles of the saints — to critique the Church's inability to recognize true evil, especially in its own midst, a particularly interesting commentary in light of the recent sexual abuse scandals. David Annandale's focus extends beyond perceived failures of the Church as an organization to a critique of what he sees as monstrous in Catholic ritual, imagery and doctrine. In "Dark Imperative: Kant, Sade and Catholicism in Jess Franco's *Exorcism*," Annandale suggests that Franco's film of a serial killer priest inverts the spectacle of the Catholic Mass to critique the violent, possibly misogynistic and repressive impulses of the Catholic orthodoxy in films like *The Exorcist*. Shelley F. O'Brien returns to this theme in "Killer Priests: The Last Taboo?" while in "Mad Drunken

Exorcists: The Decline of the Hero Priest," Regina Hansen examines the ways in which current films like *Constantine, The Exorcism of Emily Rose* and *The X-Files: I Want to Believe* undermine the purported supernatural powers of the traditional priest/exorcist character, reveal that character's potential for monstrousness, and also, surprisingly, offer the potential for redemption. Finally, in "Otherness in *The Others*: Haunting the Catholic Other, Humanizing the Self," Anabel Altemir Giral and Ismael Ibáñez Rosales examine a film that uses the fantastic to portray elements of Catholic doctrine as ridiculous, but here with the purpose of reconciling the film's protagonist to Catholic spirituality in its best form. Giral and Rosales show filmmaker Alejandro Amenabar using the traditional tropes of the Gothic not to demonize Catholicism but to critique a too strict blind adherence to received dogma, and encourage an embrace of Catholic "sacramental imagination."

The connections between Catholicism and the filmic art form — their shared embrace of spectacle, together with film's potential as both vehicle for social criticism and conveyor of Todorov's "hesitation" between belief and skepticism — make Catholicism and fantastic film a rich area for continued study. The ongoing and constantly shifting history of attitudes toward Catholicism — its ritual, iconography, and dogma, its clergy and adherents — is played out in films of the fantastic as diverse as Amenabar's ghost story, Gilliam's comedic fantasies, the horrors of the "*Exorcist* universe" and the vampire mythos, and as the uncanny or marvelous element in realist films like *Gone Baby Gone*. The Catholic fantastic, rooted in the art and literature of the Middle Ages and transformed through the eras of the Gothic and Victorian Medievalism into the present day, is alive and well at the movies.

Works Cited

Freud, Sigmund. "The Uncanny." *Writings on Art and Literature*. Stanford, CA: Stanford University Press, 1997.
Griffin, Susan. *Anti-Catholicism in Nineteenth Century Fiction*. Cambridge, UK: Cambridge University Press, 2004.
Kane, Paul M. "Jews and Catholics Converge: *The Song of Bernadette* (1943)." *Catholics in the Movies*. Ed. Colleen McDannell. Oxford, UK: Oxford University Press, 2008, 83–105.
McDannell, Colleen. "Why the Movies? Why Religion?" *Catholics in the Movies*. Ed. Colleen McDannell. Oxford, UK: Oxford University Press, 2008, 3–31.
Nelson, Victoria. "Faux Catholic: A Gothic Subgenre from Monk Lewis to Dan Brown." *Boundary 2* 34:3 (Fall 2007): 87–107.
"Seamus Heaney: Interview with Charlie Rose." *Charlie Rose*. PBS. WGBH, Boston. 19 April 1996.
Todorov, Tzvetan. *The Fantastic: A Structural Approach to a Literary Genre*. Ithaca, NY: Cornell University Press, 1975; 1973.

Section One

Marvelous Catholicism

"When the Saints Go Marching In"
Saints, Money and the Global Marketplace in Danny Boyle's Millions

JOHN REGAN

> Fantasy is necessary. During childhood when children don't have much power but feel angst, fantasy gives some kind of salvation. When children face difficult and complicated problems, they will be beaten if they tackle them directly. You don't need a dubious phrase like "escape from reality." — Hayao Miyazaki

Many reviewers of Danny Boyles's *Millions* (2004) suggest that the film explores the conflict between old-world Catholicism and new world capitalism, between traditional morality and modern materialism.[1] According to this view, young Damian's encyclopedic knowledge of the saints and his fantastic engagements with them present an alternative, competing vision into the secular world of greed and materialism; consequently, in the words of one reviewer, Damian "discovers that his treasure is really in heaven" (Weldon) and the film espouses that money is the root of all evil.

However, such a reading overlooks the film's insistence that money can both corrupt and cure. In his quest to figure out the right thing to do with the money that literally falls out of the sky, Damian fully capitalizes on his opportunity to move beyond his own grief over the death of his mother and to lose himself in his good works. While he deeply ruminates about the true proper place of money in modern society, those around him are reduced to anxiously reacting to the impending shift from a national to a more global currency. Indeed, in an England where glitzy game show-style public service commercials herald the countdown to a New Year's day currency shift from pounds to euros, money is tossed from trains, pasted to walls, and chased after in a series of frantic scenes that underscore public anxiety over what's ahead in the new market world. Amid such a chaotic backdrop, Damian's fantastic interactions with the saints seem at times no more surreal than what's going on in the "real world" and, in fact, offer a calm, rational approach to how money should be handled. Thus through the fantastic appearances of Catholic saints such as Saint Clare, St. Francis, St. Nicholas, the Ugandan martyrs and St. Joseph, Damian develops a keener sense of the implications of the new market realities than those around him. Damian's awareness culminates in the film's final scene in which he decides that building wells in Ethiopia is the best way to use his remaining fortune, an act both saintly and sensible.

Set in contemporary Manchester, England, represented as "on the rise" with an upwardly mobile middle class and freshly built houses, Boyle's city is especially bright and inviting, perhaps a bit story-bookish for such a scrappy city but intentionally so — Boyle filmed *Millions* during the summertime to emphasize brightness; Manchester is colorful with sunny skies and deep green fields. Eight-year-old Damian (Alex Etel) and his ten-year-old brother Anthony (Lewis McGibbon) go to the "All Saints' School," which, despite its name, is decidedly secular, its auditorium resplendent with large colorful paintings of the contemporary icons David Beckham, Nelson Mandela, and J.K. Rowling. The events of the film take place in the days before Christmas, a holiday at once religious and commercial, near the end of one year and the beginning of the next, underscoring the sense of transition that permeates the film. Damian seems like a typical boy but events thrust upon him change his world dramatically — his mother dies from an undisclosed illness and his father is relocating the family to a new house. The film opens with the brothers biking through an under-construction subdivision and imagining that they live there — the boys lie in the grass as their daydream fantasy of a house being built unfolds before viewers with the use of computer animation and fast motion photography, and we soon learn that this will indeed become their real house.

As Damian's father packs up their belonging at their old house, he imagines that he hears his wife's laughing voice as he closes the door for the final time. Damian is on the stoop reading Joan Windham's *Six O'Clock Saints* (1934). This popular children's book plays a central role in the film. Windham (1904–1990), a British nurse, wrote a series of children's books about the saints over the course of four decades, and *Six O'Clock Saints* was her first and most frequently reprinted ("Windham"). The adjective "Six O'Clock" denotes the bedtime for children of the 1930s, and the appearance of the book suggests Damian's obsession with Catholic saints, foreshadows the fantastic appearance of the saints themselves, and hints that *Millions* is also a bedtime story for children. In the director's cut of the film, Boyle notes that the book was very popular in the 1950s but "you would never, ever, ever think of giving [it] to a kid" because of its "gore and suicide and madness." The depictions of the saints seem inappropriately graphic for a modern child, much like the tales of the Brothers Grimm. In an interview with Roger Ebert, *Millions* screenplay writer Frank Cotrell Boyce points out, "People think of saints as vaguely nice and virtuous but in fact they were often difficult, mad, driven by a different energy" (Ebert). Boyce adds that Martin Scorsese read *Six O'clock Saints* as a child and called it a "map of the imagination," one that pointed towards the restless energy that drives the characters in *Raging Bull* and *Mean Streets* (Ebert). The second reference to Windham's book in *Millions* is when it is shown glowing in the darkness of Damian's cardboard house down by the railway, its title visible, signifying the structure's status as a hermitage and visually alluding — albeit light-heartedly — to the scene in *Apocalypse Now* in which Sir George Fraser's *The Golden Bough* sits on Colonel Kurtz's nightstand.

Unlike a Scorsese or Coppola film, *Millions* is, after all, a family movie, so the blood, gore, and madness of the lives of the saints is sanitized and converted into comedy. For example, when Damian's teacher asks his class to give examples of people whom they consider heroes, while his classmates cite Manchester United footballers, Damian mentions that St. Agatha ripped out her own eyes, evoking a collective "Eeewwww!" from his classmates. Although Damian's brother advises him to avoid talking about saints so that he'll fit in better with his new classmates, Damian makes little effort to hide his obsession. The conversion of gory details from the lives of the saints into comedy continues later in the film when Damian meets the martyr saints of Uganda. One of the martyrs shakes his hand and Damian looks down at the mess left behind. The martyr apologizes, explaining that he was beheaded as he points to the large, somewhat fake-looking scar on his neck.

Indeed, comedy permeates the representation of St. Clare of Assisi, a twelfth century woman who was inspired by her friend St. Francis of Assisi to devote herself to a religious life. The first saint to appear to Damian in the film, Clare left her upper class family and started the religious order known as the Poor Clares. She embraced the Christian ideology known as "radical poverty" in which in "a loving relationship with Christ (or anyone else for that matter) the individual had to assume the material conditions of Christ, that is, the conditions of being poor and downtrodden" (Ritchey 834). While

Boyle has a bit of fun as St. Clare puffs away on a joint in homage to the fact that in 1958 Pope Paul VI named her the patron saint of television because of her professed ability to see visions from afar, her primary function is to ironically foreshadow a twist of fate — she who rejected material wealth heralds its sudden arrival to Damian. Immediately after St. Clare vanishes, an enormous duffel bag full of 230,000 British pounds crashes into his life, damaging his hermitage and forever changing his world. Damian believes the money was sent by God. If the bag of money crashing into the cardboard hermitage serves as, in the words of one reviewer, "a prophetic symbol of the power of mammon to destroy" (Weldon), the money also provides Damian with a focus beyond grieving for his mother and adjusting to a new home and school and on to the quest to figure out how best to use his new-found wealth.

Damian's first reaction to Clare's fantastic appearance in his cardboard house highlights his naivety and unquestioned faith: "Clare of Assisi! 1194–1253!" (*Millions*). As one reviewer aptly noted, Damian seems "like a schoolboy happy with knowing the correct answer" (Martin 1), indeed more excited that he can correctly identify her than that she has magically appeared. The sudden, fantastic appearance of an adult woman in a nun's habit in the boy's cardboard house surprises viewers and is the initial indication that the film moves beyond realism and into the fantastic.

Moreover, Damian's lack of hesitancy in accepting Clare establishes an important convention to the film — the gap between Damian's reaction and that of the viewing audience to the appearances of the saints. While he accepts the fantastic without reservation and asks St. Clare if she has come across his mother, whom he calls "St. Maureen," viewers are uncertain — are these saints real or are they the product of the boy's overactive imagination? In his study of the fantastic, Tzuetan Todorov identifies hesitation as the key feature of the genre: "Either total faith or total incredulity would lead us beyond the fantastic; it is hesitation which sustains its life" (36).

In her study of fantastic film and temporality, Bliss Cua Lim articulately summarizes Todorov's theory of the fantastic: "For Todorov, the fantastic is a drama of disbelief in which we never waver between two perspectives: either the world is charged with wondrous events that the laws of nature are inadequate to explain (the marvelous) or the impossible event is an illusion that scientific explanation can dispel (the uncanny)" (29–30). Lim adds that in Todorov's schema, "most texts are fantastic only for a certain duration of the reading, while the reader is still in the grips of uncertainty" (30). Yet *Millions* strives to maintain its fantastic stance throughout, an effort further complicated because the "real" people and "real" events often seem as fantastic as the appearance of the saints — the barrier between the real and the fantastic seems blurred. The glitzy commercials heralding the coming of the euro with venerable British actor Leslie Phillips and a blonde bombshell with bountiful cleavage create a scene more surreal than any of the saintly appearances; the pair are on a white stage set as if in the clouds, connoting the heaven awaiting those who embrace the shift to euros. These commercials are, after all, media inventions, but the events in Damian's life evem aside from the appearances of saints strain credulity—what, for example, are the chances that a bag of stolen money thrown from a train will land directly on a boy's cardboard house at the exact moment he is inside speaking to a saint, real or imagined?

While the representation of a spliff-smoking and spacey Saint Clare provides an irreverent element, Boyle opts to represent Saint Francis of Assisi (Enzo Cilenti) reverentially, resisting the temptation to satirize a target that seems especially ripe for caricature. As the *Oxford Dictionary of the Saints* points out, "The 20th century witnessed a wide-spread revival of interest in Francis, but also a tendency to see in him only those traits which appealed to individual writers (or film-makers). This resulted in caricatures of a sentimental nature-lover or a hippy 'drop-out' from society, which omit the real sternness of his character and neglect his all-pervasive love of God and identification with Christ's sufferings, which alone make sense of his life" (np). Indeed, in *Millions*, there is a seriousness and aloofness in its representation of St. Francis that separates him from the film's other saints. Unlike St. Clare, who sits unceremoniously on the floor of Damian's cardboard house, Francis is majestic. Viewers never see St. Francis in a close-up; unlike the other saints, he is always shot at a distance. On a bright, sunny day, Damian brings three boxes of birds that he purchased from a pet store to the top of a hill that offers a panoramic view of the city. Damian releases the birds and then in the distance St. Francis appears. To a soundtrack of swelling classical music, St. Francis stands like a magnificent statue overlooking the city below, a scene with the pomp, drama, and spectacle a viewer might expect from a cinematic representation of a beloved, legendary saint. Whereas Damian's interactions with the other saints are more involved, he quickly exchanges words with St. Francis, who watches the boy release the birds:

> "St Francis of Assisi! 1181–1226."
> "My first act as a saint."
> "What was your next one?"
> "Washing a leper."
> "A leper?"
> "You can just help the poor, Damian" [*Millions*].

Thus while Damian gains some direction from St. Francis and resolves to help the poor with his new-found wealth, he is, however, just as confused over who the poor are as he is over the definition of a leper. In his first effort at working out his epistemological quandary, he treats some street vendors to dinner at Pizza Hut, but he is disappointed when he discovers that they are not homeless people but instead commute from the suburbs into the city to do their odd jobs.

Damian's next target for his good works and charity establishes the film's theme of how the failures of the real people to practice what they preach complicate the boy's journey to "be good." In looking for saintly exemplars in the people around him, he is drawn to three Swedish Mormons who live in his housing estate. When a local police officer calls the homeowners together to discuss security during the Christmas season because new housing developments are especially tempting to burglars, one of the Mormons dismisses the policeman's dire warnings and paraphrases Jesus' words about earthly treasure: "If you store up your treasure on earth, it will be stolen. But if you give it away, it can't be stolen" (*Millions*), Damian is intrigued, and when the Mormon then identifies himself as a "Latter Day Saint," Damian exclaims, "Saints!" much to the consternation of his father, who shoos the boy off to the kitchen for cookies. Given the Mormons' altruistic sentiments and their spartan lifestyles — in a complex of big new houses theirs is sparsely furnished and doesn't even have a dishwasher — Damian concludes that they are poor, saintly souls who would know what is best to do with money.

To test out his theory, Damian resolves to give the Mormons some money to see what they do with it. He is aided by St. Nicholas of Myra (Harry Kirkham), who speaks in Latin (with English subtitles for the viewers). How the boy can converse with someone who speaks Latin is never explained, but in a fantastic film with saints coming and going, that's a minor breach of logic. St. Nicholas works with Damian in leaving money for the three Mormons — who in their blue suits, crisp white shirts, shiny complexions, and neatly trimmed blond hair come across squeaky clean and virginally pure — presumably saving them from poverty and enabling their good works. This scene parallels the legend of St. Nicholas.

The most commonly told story about Saint Nicholas involves a father, his three daughters, and a bag of gold. The father, it seems, was a poor man whose daughters were all of a marriageable age. Because the family was so poor, the father was unable to provide dowries for his daughters. Careers for women in the fourth century were, according to the legend, limited to marriage or prostitution. Rather than see these young women choose the latter course, Saint Nicholas hid outside the family's home one winter night and tossed a bag of gold through the open window, and, thus, the young women were able to marry and live happily ever after (Hermes 42).

But while in the legend St. Nicholas' charitable efforts were wholly successful in true fairy tale fashion, in *Millions* the effort fails, something the saint seems to anticipate. As Damian realizes that all of the money that he has brought will not fit in the door opening, St. Nicholas says, "Doesn't matter, the poor are always with us" (*Millions*). He alludes to Jesus' words, "For you will always have the poor with you, but you will not always have me" (Mark 14:7). While St. Nicholas's exact meaning here is puzzling — this passage is often cited by Christians who wish to caution against social activism — Nicholas's observation that Damian will have more opportunities in the future to help the poor implies that he will need those opportunities because the Mormons will not live up to his expectations. The Mormons are soon exposed as false saints when they use their newfound wealth to buy luxury items. When on the following day the three Mormons cruise by with large boxes of newly purchased electronic goods tied to their bicycles, Damian is crushed.

The arrival of the Ugandan martyrs provides Damian with a new direction for his charitable efforts. Between 1885 and 1887, twenty-two Ugandan males between the ages of 13 and 30 who refused to renounce their Christian faith were executed by Mwanga, the country's ruler who despised Christianity ("Lwanga"). In 1964 Pope Paul VI canonized the martyrs and proclaimed that they "herald the dawn of a new age," a time when the Catholic Church sought to expand its influence throughout the continent. If the canonization of the Ugandan martyrs signaled the Church's interest in expanding its work into broader geographical regions, the appearance of these martyrs in *Millions* serves to extend Damian's focus on charitable works beyond the local to the global, a focus he never relinquishes. When one of the martyrs tells him that building a well in Africa costs only one hundred pounds and would better many lives, Damian is delighted and relieved to have a less ambiguous blueprint in his quest to be good.

Moreover, it doesn't take Damian long to act upon his new imperative and the question of how a young boy can get his money to Africans in need of wells appears neatly resolved when a woman, Dorothy, arrives at his school to collect for the very same cause. Dorothy operates a moving trash bin by remote control and the bin moves around the cafeteria asking the students for pocket change. Damian puts a thousand pound roll in the talking trash bin, but Dorothy later discovers it, figures out that Damian put it there, and Damian's father is called into the headmaster's office. Damian cannot understand why she didn't just use the money as she said she would — what was the problem? Moreover, Damian's anxiety is compounded when Anthony explains that the money was stolen from a train, not delivered by divine intervention.

At this point enters the bad guy, a man dressed in stock villain black garb including a black knit cap described by Boyle as his "black halo" (Boyle). When he suddenly appears near the hermitage, the soundtrack shifts to ominous music and the sunny sky darkens. Damian mistakes him for a saint that the boy can't identify, looking like an earnest schoolboy who lets his teacher down because he didn't have the right answer.

Indeed, the recognition of the difference between fantasy and reality is reversed; while the audience instantly knows that this man is no saint and correctly assumes he is the train robber, Damian's hesitation and uncertainty towards the "real" man underscores that the boy may in fact be developing less confidence in "real" people. The man asks Damian if he has seen any money around and Damian says yes, he'll go back to his house to get it, but Anthony intervenes and returns to offer the man a glass jar full of coins and his brother a temporary reprieve.

The appearance of the next saint addresses Damian's dilemma of whether to return the money or continue to try to use it for good. Dorothy's unwillingness to get Damian's donation to those who need it compels him to take matters into his own hands; he retreats to his bedroom to stuff money into envelopes addressed to charitable organizations such as Oxfam and Christian Aid, but St. Peter appears. St. Peter seems dismissive of the boy's efforts at donating to charities. St. Peter suggests that while Damian should continue with his focus on good works, he is trying too hard to be charitable, a message that seems at odds with the radical poverty of St. Clare and St. Francis. St. Peter retells the famous New Testament story of the fishes and loaves with a new twist: a young boy led by example and did not take food that Jesus provided, leaving it for those who were more in need, and then the adults around him followed his example and the full plate was returned to Jesus. The real miracle, according to Saint Peter, was that the boy's unselfish examples inspired others to act likewise. St. Peter concludes, "You're trying too hard"; Damian replies, "I'm just trying to be good" (*Millions*).

Damian's meeting with St. Peter also underscores that the quest to find the best way to use the money has distracted him from his search for his mother, Saint Maureen. If anyone would have seen her, it would have been St. Peter, the keeper of the gates of heaven, but Damian does not ask him about her — Damian seems to have lost himself in the pursuit of doing good works, suggesting that a viable way to deal with grief is to lose oneself in helping others.

And as if meeting all of these saints has become exhausting for the young boy, while St. Peter talks, Damian gets ready for bed, matter-of-factly putting on his pajamas and brushing his teeth, his routine bedtime activities suggesting that to the boy, the fantastic has become common-place and a bit exhausting — Damian even falls asleep before St. Peter finishes his last words: "I'll have a word upstairs. See if I can get somebody more permanent on the case" (*Millions*).

Apparently that someone "more permanent" is Saint Joseph (Nasser Memarzia), the final Catholic saint to appear in the film. When St. Joseph pops up while Damian is rehearsing for his school's nativity play, Damian identifies him as "Joseph the Worker," emphasizing the saint's role as a humble laborer. Damian, who has been assigned the role of Joseph in the nativity play, quibbles with the director over his interpretation of the role; the director says Joseph was "tired," Damian says "excited," but after the director leaves, St. Joseph suggests, "focused" (*Millions*) as the most accurate. "Focused" stands out as a key word because throughout his dealings with the saints, that's what they've offered him — a focus beyond himself and his personal situation.

On the night of the nativity play, the robber appears backstage in the middle of the play and approaches Damian, but the boy is saved when the director comes looking for him. Sensing his reprieve from the bad guy is only temporary, Damian decides to flee — in playing his real-life part, he is tired, excited, and focused. Pulling the wooden nativity donkey that carries the big bag of money, he escapes into the Manchester night, a bright star like that of storybook Bethlehem beaming in the sky. In traditional nativity discourse, the donkey symbolizes humility, unceasing effort, and an unconditional willingness to serve — the very traits Damian exhibits throughout the film. He drags the wooden beast of burden through the dark streets and onto a city bus as he makes his way to his old house, a safe haven, and opens the door with the key St. Peter told him to keep safe. In Damian's absence, the nativity play continues; Joseph replaces Damian in the role of Joseph and speaks the boy's lines from behind a curtain. In a play about Jesus' miraculous birth, the first intervention of the fantastic into the real world discernible to characters other than Damian. Since the audience believes in the Christmas miracle, their faith is rewarded with a glimpse of the fantastic.

The plot then speeds up in a blinding swirl of events: Damian's father finds him in their old house, their new house is ransacked (presumably by the robber), and Damian and Anthony reveal to their father that they have the money. Damian's father scoffs at Damian's insistence that they give the money away to charity and he insists that the family keep it for themselves; the pound notes were just being sent away to be destroyed, he reasons, so why not keep them? Damian, however, assumes that Dorothy will agree with him that altruism is the best course of action but she again fails him and sides with his father, leaving him with the same pained expression as when he saw the Mormons return home with boxes of consumer electronics. In fact,

Dorothy takes charge of the family's mad dash to banks and exchange bureaus throughout the city to convert as many pounds as possible into euros before the deadline.

These frenzied actions culminate in an extraordinary Christmas Eve scene. The robber returns to claim the money and is captured by the police; Saint Joseph reappears to take back the wooden donkey, now beatified with a glowing halo on its head; and in the most jarring scene, when his father goes to answer the doorbell in the middle of the night, people seeking charitable donations are lined up single-file in a seemingly endless line that snakes down the street for as far as the viewer can see. As Boyle notes, "That's the way you see things as a kid and they don't appear to be rational or have an explanation but they do happen and you have to deal with the consequences of them." Damian gathers up a large stash of money and heads towards his hermitage.

That Damian's journey culminates in a meeting with his mother is no surprise to the viewer; in the logic of the film, the boy has proven his mettle and his faith is rewarded. He empties the pile of money on the railroad tracks, lights it on fire, and then leaps off the tracks to avoid on oncoming train. His mother then appears, face aglow as she sits beside the flames. For the first time, Damian acknowledges that what he sees may not be real: "I know you're a dream but I don't care" (*Millions*). As she explains to Damian that she is not a saint but is "in the running"; when he asks her what her miracle was, she answers, "You" (*Millions*). If Damian's good works have created the conditions by which his mother can miraculously appear, that his brother Anthony is not accorded similar contact with his mother seems a bit cruel. As Damian burns the money on the track, Anthony walks closer and watches them from a distance, allowed only a limited perception of his mother in that he appears to be able to see her but can't hear her. She tells Damian that Anthony has "a good heart but doesn't know where it is" (*Millions*), suggesting that Damian and his mother are united in an unwavering faith that the brother does not share. Before she vanishes, she urges Damian to remember that people are even more complicated than money and one needs to believe in their innate goodness. To Damian, this means moving beyond his past disappointments with the Mormons, Dorothy, and the other real people in his life and continue to keep believing in them, not just the saints.

Yet her words about Anthony's innate goodness and his inability to find his heart seem particularly prescient. As she anticipated, Damian's faith is soon vindicated when Anthony comes clean about the money he hid away for himself and gives it back to Damian. That Damian successfully changes his brother's attitude towards money and charitable works seems foreshadowed in the legend of St. Damian, a saint whose story is never mentioned in the film. St. Damian and his twin brother Cosmas were third-century doctors from Asia Minor who worked together to heal people but refused to take any money for their efforts (Meier). Always depicted together, they performed many extraordinary acts of healing and were nicknamed "the silverless" (Friedman 6). And Anthony shares, of course, the name of one of the most famous saints, St. Anthony of Padua, the patron saint of recovered objects who, like St. Francis of Assisi, devoted himself to charitable works ("Antony of Padua"). As the film winds down, with lost objects restored to rightful places and the brothers united in their focus on charitable works, wonders even greater than saintly apparitions are now possible. Damian's father and Dorothy follow the boys' lead and embrace similar changes of heart, joining them in the film's final fantastic scene as they blast off in a cardboard rocket to Africa and land to build wells, sing, smile, and splash with delighted Africans.

Notes

1. Quoted in Noriko T. Reider's "Spirited Away: Film of Fantastic and Evolving Japanese Fold Symbols." *Film Criticism* 29:3 (2005): 4–27.
2. Other reviews of *Millions* include David Denby's "Double Trouble," *The New Yorker* 81.5 (2005): 90–1; Ben Walters' "Millions," *Sight & Sound* 14.12 (2004): 56, 58; Lisa Schwarzbaum's "The Trainspotting Director Makes — Gasp! — a Family Film," *Entertainment Weekly* 811 (2005): 43; and Mark Kermode's "The Devil's Work," *New Statesman* 133 (2004): 45.
3. Boyce produced a book version of *Millions* based on his screenplay. His book won the 2004 Carnegie Medal, Britain's most prestigious award for children's books.

Works Cited

"Antony of Padua." *The Oxford Dictionary of Saints*. David Hugh Farmer. Oxford University Press, 2003. *Oxford Reference Online*. Web. 15 September 2010.
Boyle, Danny. Director's Commentary. *Millions*. 2004. DVD. Mission Pictures UK, 2005.
"Cosmas." *The Oxford Dictionary of Saints*. David Hugh Farmer. Oxford University Press, 2003. *Oxford Reference Online*. Web. 15 September 2010.
Cottrell Boyce, Frank. *Millions*. New York: HarperCollins, 2004.
Ebert, Roger. *Millions* Writer Wins 'Lottery.'" *Chicago Sun-Times*, 13 March 2005.
Evans, Robert A., and Alice F. Evans. "Uganda: Church of the Martyrs." *The Christian Century* 102 (1985): 726–7. Wilson Web. Web. 15 September 2010.
"Francis of Assisi." *The Oxford Dictionary of Saints*. David Hugh Farmer. Oxford University Press, 2003. *Oxford Reference Online*. Web. 15 September 2010.
Friedman, Steven Greg. *A History of Vascular Surgery*. Second Edition. Malden, MA: Blackwell Futura, 2005.
Gurney-Salter, Emma. "St. Clare of Assisi, 1194–1253." Contemporary Review 184 (1953): 94–7. Wilson Web. Web. 15 September 2010.

Hermes, Joan Garvey. "A Santa Claus to Believe In." *U.S. Catholic* 61 (1996): 42. EBSCO. Web. 15 September 2010.
Lim, Bliss Cua. *Translating Time: Cinema, the Fantastic, and Temporal Critique.* Durham, NC: Duke University Press, 2009.
"Lwanga, Charles." *The Oxford Dictionary of the Saints.* David Hugh Framer. Oxford University Press, 2003. *Oxford Reference Online.* Web. 15 September 2010.
Martin, James. "Of Many Things." *America* 192 no. 9 (14 March 2005).
Meier, Gabriel. "Sts. Cosmas and Damian." *The Catholic Encyclopedia.* Vol. 4. New York: Robert Appleton Company, 1908. 15 Sept. 2010
Millions [Motion Picture]. Dir. Danny Boyle. Perf. Alex Etel, Lewis McGibbon, James Nesbitt. 2004. DVD. Mission Pictures UK, 2005. Film.
Pope Paul IV. "The Glory of the Martyrs: A Sign of Rebirth." *Homily for the Canonization of the Ugandan Martrys.* http://www.catholicradiodramas.com/Saints_Works_P-S/paul_vi_Pope_homily_for_uganda_martyrs.htm. 15 September 2010.
Ritchey, Sara. *The Privilege of Poverty: Clare of Assisi, Agnes of Prague, and the Struggle for a Franciscan Rule for Women.* (Book Review). Vol. 76, 2007. Gale. Web. 15 September 2010.
Todorov, Tzvetan. *The Fantastic: A Structural Approach to a Literary Genre.* Ithaca, NY: Cornell University Press, 1975.
Weldon, Clodagh. "*Million* [Motion Picture Review]." *Journal of Religion and Film* 10.1 (2006). EBSCO. Web. 15 September 2010.
"Windham, Joan." *Contemporary Authors Online.* Thomas Gale, 2008. Web. 15 September 2010.1. Quoted in Noriko T. Reider's "Spirited Away: Film of Fantastic and Evolving Japanese Fold Symbols." *Film Criticism* 29:3 (2005): 4–27.

Blasphemy in the Name of Fantasy
The Films of Terry Gilliam in a Catholic Context

CHRISTOPHER MCKITTRICK

The films of American filmmaker Terry Gilliam all feature similar themes of fantasy and the effect delusions have on the dreamer. Though he no longer considers himself a religious person, Gilliam's religious upbringing influences how he views the relationship between reality and fantasy and the importance of moral values. Unusually, Gilliam's films reflect undeniably Catholic views of sin, redemption, and free will rather than those of his Protestant background. Furthermore, Gilliam's frequent use of symbolism and iconography — perhaps influenced by his early career as an illustrator and his days as designer and animator of Britain's Monty Python comedy group — utilizes Christian symbols, like angels, and specifically images of Catholicism, such as the clergy. Altogether, it is not surprising that Gilliam's use of Catholic themes and symbols render his films more entrenched with Catholic ideology than with the beliefs of any other form of Christianity.

Gilliam has frequently spoken about his religious upbringing in interviews throughout his career. Born in Minnesota, he was raised Protestant and was surrounded by strong anti–Catholic biases. Reflecting on this bias, Gilliam jokes that in Minnesota, "What you didn't do was go down the road that extra block and become a Catholic — one of those papists and slaves of Rome!" (Christie 6). Yet Gilliam earnestly recounts how instrumental his religious upbringing — specifically his immersion into the Bible — has been to his understanding of fantasy and the relationships between "good and evil, and responsibility, or sin or punishment" (Christie 8). Although on a basic level Gilliam saw Biblical stories as ultimate entertainment — "You can't beat those stories for scale and drama and passion" (Christie 5) — it is hard to imagine Gilliam's films without the struggle between good and evil that is at the heart of *Brazil*, and, even more distinctly, *Time Bandits* and *The Fisher King*. In this sense, Gilliam could not create his worlds of fantasy if he was not raised with the belief of the struggle between good and evil, which is central to both the Christian view of the world and the conflicts of Gilliam's films.

Despite his Protestant upbringing, Gilliam's films reflect an overtly Catholic view of sin. Part of this is rooted in the origins of the material Gilliam frequently uses — the roots of *Jabberwocky, Time Bandits, The Adventures of Baron Munchausen, The Fisher King,* and *The Brothers Grimm* are firmly entrenched in medieval European folklore that is dominated by outright Catholic themes. As discussed in Em McAven's "Sacramentality between Catholicism and the New Age in *The Lord of the Rings*," writers of fantasy fiction have distanced the genre from overt real world religious references since the mid nineteenth century, but the folklore Gilliam uses predates that, thus his work circumvents the New Age spirituality that the counterculture which embraced Monty Python also entrenched itself in. Another important connection between Gilliam's films and medieval Catholicism is his repeated emphasis on "quests." Gilliam takes this assessment even more specifically, once stating that:

> My wife Maggie says that I keep making the same film, except the costumes are different, and I'm beginning to think they *are* the same [...] there's society and there's the individual within it; there's the guy with the dream; there's the little man achieving something, and not ever quite getting what he wanted: he gets something — sometimes worse, sometimes better — but he seldom gets what he wanted; there's always a quest; there's this sense, as in *Brazil,* of paranoia; there's always greed, like the merchants in *Jabberwocky*; there's the love of craftsmanship; and there's always romance, though they're usually misdirected or unlikely romances [Christie 73–74].

Of course, the origins of the medieval Grail quests are rooted in the struggles between "good and evil, and responsibility, or sin or punishment" (in Gilliam's own words) found in Catholicism, much like the main themes of his films.

Gilliam particularly focuses on the struggle between good and evil in *Time Bandits*— after all, it is the only one of his films to feature God (called "The Supreme Being") as a character. Gilliam explains the impetus for including God as a character in *Time Bandits* came from his churchgoing youth:

> [Co-writer] Michael [Palin] and I had solid religious upbringings, so we grew up believing and thinking about God and religion and good and evil. I can't get those out of my system; they're a part of me. The normal approach in a kids'

film is to make the final character a wizard. But why not bring God into it? [...] The cosmic view appeals to me. I like to think I'm not alone, that there's a whole structure around us [Sterritt & Rhodes 18].

Though he only appears in the final minutes of the film, Gilliam's Supreme Being is a fascinating character. Gilliam's Supreme Being is orderly ("One thing I can't stand, it's a mess"), omniscient (when asked if he knew what was happening during the events of the film, he answers, "Well, of course. I am the Supreme Being. I'm not entirely dim"), and omnipotent (he is able to revive a dead Time Bandit), yet benevolent ("Well, I am the nice one"). All of these traits are equally associated with general Christian views of God. In line with this humorous, doddering exterior, the Supreme Being answers Kevin's question, "Why do we have to have evil?" with the inconclusive, yet telling, reply, "Ah ... I think it's something to do with free will." Despite the ambiguous nature of this reply, the Supreme Being suggests man has free will and therefore the choice of being good or evil. The dispute over whether or not man has free will was a central argument between the Catholic Church and Protestants during the Reformation.

The film's conception of free will is consistent with Catholic theologians' beliefs, including those of Augustine and Thomas Aquinas—that is, though God is omniscient and omnipotent, "human beings have free decision. Otherwise counsel and encouragement, commands and prohibitions, reward and punishment would all be pointless" (Aquinas 127). This belief in free will is irreconcilable with the initial (and in some denominations, current) Protestant belief in predestination, particularly as presented in the writings of Martin Luther and John Calvin, who both denied the concept of free will. This is inconsistent with Catholic thought—Prosper of Aquitaine, a disciple of Augustine, summed up the Catholic view as, "We must most sincerely believe and profess that God wills all men to be saved [...] That many [...] perish is the fault of those who perish" (Palladino 649), stating that those who fall under the sway of evil are responsible for their own actions—much like what the Supreme Being suggests in *Time Bandits*: evil must exist because of free will.

Another one of Luther's key arguments against the Catholic Church was his belief in the principle that salvation is justified by faith alone (*sola fide*), which the Catholic Church rejects. Justification by faith is still a cornerstone doctrine of many Protestant denominations. Yet this concept also cannot be reconciled with the path to redemption in Gilliam's films. For example, if *sola fide* was treated as valid in *The Fisher King*, Jack would find his redemption by accepting Christ, not from his good acts. Yet Jack appears to have no faith in God and thus cannot be justified or saved by such faith. His only references in the film to God are his arrogant sign-off ("Thank God I'm me") and when he questions Anne as to whether she believes in God. This makes the "Forgive me!" mantra from Jack's lost television series hypocritical—if Jack does not believe in God, who is supposed to forgive him? After all, Jack's idea of penance is to "pay the fine and go home"—which Jack actually attempts after he learns Parry's true identity by giving Parry money as a way to make up for his indirect role in the murder of Parry's wife. Interestingly, Jack's theory of "paying" for his sins is similar to the medieval abuses of selling indulgences that both Catholics and Protestants rejected during the Reformation. Both religions, like the film, deny that as a path to salvation.

The nature of evil is also explored in Gilliam's films. According to Reformation thought, evil exists because God plotted for its existence as part of a greater plan for humanity. Accordingly, since free will does not exist, neither good acts nor evils acts result from an individual's free choice, but rather from God's supreme will. Indeed, Calvin believed that "God chooses a certain portion of mankind to be saved; the others He positively and antecedently wills to condemn. God not only wills the damnation of the latter, but also directly wills moral evil or sin itself in the same way that He wills moral goodness" (Palladino 650). Of course, not only does that go against Evil's assertion in *Time Bandits* that the Supreme Being did not create him (following Catholic conceptions of the origin of evil), but Calvin's view implies (in contrast to the Catholic view) that man cannot choose to do good acts, because there is no free will. By that view, in *The Fisher King* Jack does not atone for his sins by completing Parry's quest for the "grail" in a selfless act because he had no free choice to do so, thus the act was not selfless or even a free decision. Though the "Little People" tell Parry that Jack will eventually take up Parry's cause—which might suggest that Jack is following a predetermined path—this argument appears invalid because Jack again achieves material success despite Parry's condition. Though Jack is comfortable with his rediscovered success, it is because of his conscience that he helps Parry, though it risks his reputation and career. Jack even insists to a comatose Parry "I control my own destiny ... not some floating, overweight fairies," and then shortly afterwards, "If I do this ... I want you to know it wouldn't be because I felt I had to ... or because I felt cursed or guilty or responsible [...] it's because I want to do this for you." Here, Jack is aware of his free will—indeed, in the Catholic view, as well as in the view of the film, Jack controls his own selfless act.

Curiously, before he goes on his Grail mission Jack first takes on the ultimate role of showing pity during the hospital scene. In the scene Jack cradles a homeless, homosexual cabaret singer in his arms as the singer recounts to

Jack his personal struggles. Jack and the singer are positioned similarly to Renaissance depictions of the Pietà. The Pietà is a traditional subject in religious art featuring the Virgin Mary cradling the body of the crucified Jesus, the most famous depiction being Michelangelo's sculpture in Saint Peter's Basilica. In Gilliam's Pietà, the singer — and those of his social class and sexual orientation — takes on the role of the sacrifice, while Jack peers down with sympathy, finally understanding that there are others in the world far more deserving of pity and compassion than himself. This is one of the acceptances that Jack must come to terms with in order to find redemption, yet Jack never appears to accept faith as one of them.

Gilliam is very clear about what he personally finds "evil," because often in his films he associates evil with the obsession with technology and money in modern society, both of which are (in his view) creations of man, not God. In *Time Bandits*, Evil sees the Supreme Being as foolish and unstable for not caring about technology, commenting that God ignores the microchip to instead waste his time creating parrots and slugs. Interestingly, Kevin's inattentive parents are also obsessed with their television and keeping up with their neighbor's latest technological acquisitions. They ignore Kevin and his more innocent, more fulfilling pursuit of knowledge. In fact, in the final scene of the film Kevin's parents are more concerned with saving their toaster and blender from their house fire than they are with the safety of their son, showing them to be corrupted by modern society. Though the Supreme Being destroys Evil in the film, this will not stop humanity — like Kevin's parents — from continuing to choose to do evil out of free will. According to the Catholic view, God did not create evil, but rather evil exists as a consequence to the gift of free will. As a matter of fact, in *Enchiridion*, Augustine argues that God "would never permit the existence of anything evil among His works," which shows that God did not create evil, yet "what is that which we call evil but the absence of good?" (Augustine 11). Accordingly, in *Time Bandits* Evil insists that *no one* created him and that he cannot be unmade despite his eventual defeat by the Supreme Being (though an overlooked piece of Evil's body kills Kevin's parents, showing that Evil is correct — evil is not unmade despite the Supreme Being's victory). In contrast, Calvin believed that an omnipotent God wills both good and evil acts to occur, yet this is incompatible with both the Catholic view and Gilliam's view of evil as demonstrated in *Time Bandits*.

Evil's obsession with technology and how it can be used to control the world is a telling comment on Gilliam's personal view of technology and modern society. In Gilliam's films, over-reliance on technology and rampant consumerism are representations of "evil" that not only cause the breakdown of

Kevin's family, but can, as seen in *Brazil*, destroy religion and society as a whole. Indeed, the main plot of *Brazil* focuses on the mistakes made by "perfected" technology and the methods used to cover-up mistakes that were not supposed to happen and thus denied to *ever* have happened in the first place. Meanwhile, though *Brazil* is set during the Christmas season, there appears to be very little religious observation left in the holiday — for instance, Lowry's mother rattles off about all the shopping she must do as she gives him a kitschy knick-knack as a gift, and she spends the holiday with her plastic surgeon instead of with her troubled son. There are only two references to Christ in regard to the season: first, a protester flouts a "Consumers for Christ" sign in a mall as a young girl asks the mall's Santa Claus for "my own credit card" for Christmas (similarly, in *The Imaginarium of Doctor Parnassus*, a Homebase home improvement store has a large "Only 364 shopping days until next Christmas!" sign), and the second is when Lowry sneaks past a group of police troopers practicing a painful rendition of *The First Nowell* in the basement of the Ministry of Information. Though the idea that an activist group of consumers would take a stand to promote Christ is a humorous one, these images of commercialization show this lack of respect for religion is one of the many things that make the world of *Brazil* so frightening. This contrasts with the images of a hybrid commercial and religious holiday presented in the fantastic world of Danny Boyle's *Millions*, as pointed out in John Regan's "When The Saints Go Marching In."

Similarly, Gilliam hints at the commercialization of religion as one of the precipitators of the downfall of society in his similarly dystopian film, *12 Monkeys*. In it, a deadly virus — reminiscent of the Black Plague — has forced humanity to live underground. One of the first significant images in the film occurs when James Cole ventures into a ruined city in search of clues to the origin of the virus. During his search he enters the remains of a department store which is decorated for the Christmas shopping season and a faint rendition of *Silent Night* can be heard over the store loudspeaker. However, because of time travel, Cole returns to the same shopping mall pre-plague. In the past, the store is selling a variety of tacky Hawaiian shirts as holiday gifts. Interestingly enough, Cole arrives to save the world during the Christmas season (with the same initials as Jesus Christ), yet even a savior cannot save society from our corrupt modern era of consumerism. Instead the Christmas story becomes the Apocalypse, highlighted by the inclusion of a quote from the King James Version of the Book of Revelation 15:7, "And one of the four beasts gave unto the seven angels seven golden vials full of the wrath of God, who liveth for ever and ever." This quote is first said by Dr. Railly during a lecture, and then it is repeated by an evangelical dressed as a knight during a street sermon. Though the King James Bible is not an edition of the Bible used by Catholics, Catholics do recognize the Book of Revelation as part of the biblical canon. Gilliam plays with this apocalyptic imagery by later showing Dr. Peters holding a tray of vials filled with a golden substance, perhaps components of the plague that he will use to murder millions later in the film. Peters gives his mad justification for unleashing the plague earlier in the film when he questions an uninterested Railly after her lecture. Taking into account the modern problems of human society, he asks her, "isn't it obvious that 'Chicken Little' represents the sane vision and that Homo Sapiens' motto 'Let's go shopping!' is the cry of the true lunatic?" We can only assume that Peters unleashed his plague as his response to mankind's abuses, highlighted by his anger against modern man's ignorance of major crises in favor of crass consumerism. Thus, it is appropriate to his thinking that he chooses to release the plague during the commercialized Christmas season.

Like *Time Bandits* and *Brazil*, evil is associated with modern society in *The Fisher King*. The world of shock jock Jack is full of greed, arrogance, and the use of technology to spread messages of hate. Jack is trapped in his own prison of sin—the lighting of the DJ booth in the opening scene makes it appear to be surrounded by vertical bars—although he's unaware of his imprisonment because of his egotism. Parry, on the other hand, rejects modern life for insanity to plunge himself into a monastic-like world of medieval chivalry and urban poverty, going so far as to give away the money that Jack gives him to "help" him because, as someone who is living outside of modern society, he has no use for money. It is not until Jack willingly becomes a "fool" by rejecting his place in modern society and puts on Parry's rags to save Parry that he is able to achieve salvation. This also goes against the Protestant rejection of free will—Jack has to choose to potentially sacrifice his rebuilt career and reputation and reject modern society to save Parry and to redeem himself, and Jack achieves his personal salvation through this selfless act.

Since Gilliam views man's development of technology as a means of modern corruption, this brings up the question of whether or not Gilliam advocates an almost monastic rejection of luxury and greed, like Parry does as a result of his insanity. Indeed, the negative power of greed rears its ugly head repeatedly in Gilliam's films—the merchants in *Jabberwocky*, Evil and the protagonists in *Time Bandits*, the high society of *Brazil*, shock jock Jack in *The Fisher King*, the French occupying forces in *The Brothers Grimm*, and thieving charity head Tony Shepherd in *The Imaginarium of Doctor Parnassus*. With the exception of the Time Bandits, all of these characters are evil.

Despite being raised in an anti–Catholic environment, Gilliam remarks that he felt comfortable with the iconography of Catholicism that the Protestant community he grew up in sternly rejected. Gilliam views this as part of his fascination with surrealism, stating that surrealism is "a moment when you take that leap and realize that nothing is just what it seems. I would have thought that religious studies would have understood this. Protestantism really took the fun out of it, throwing away all the graven images. That's why I feel so great walking into churches in Rome" (Christie 6). In particular, this symbolism would stick with Gilliam, as he admits "all the biblical imagery and symbolism is there as well; it accumulates and I find I'm constantly using it in different ways" (Christie 8). Surrealism and symbolism are two key concepts that are foundations of Gilliam's brand of fantasy that he has explored throughout his career as a filmmaker.

One of the dominant recurring Christian images in Gilliam's films is his use of angels. It is hard to view Sam Lowry's Icarus fantasy in *Brazil*—in which he is fully armored—without thinking of traditional depictions of the archangel Michael, and much as Catholics believe Michael is charged with battling against Satan and with rescuing the souls of the faithful, Lowry is "charged" to battle against the evils of his society and stand up for innocents like Archibald Buttle's family. Yet unlike Michael, Lowry is unable to accept such responsibility. Despite his fantasies, Lowry is no Michael. Instead Lowry's fantasy takes on the model of Icarus rather than the heroic Michael, paralleling Lowry's demise in the real world. Therefore, the angelic imagery in *Brazil* showcases idealism that is ultimately doomed to failure, like Lowry's own quest.

The Adventures of Baron Munchausen continues Gilliam's use of an angel as a harbinger of doom. Throughout the film, the elderly Munchausen is chased (and nearly killed) by a winged, skeletal figure, which the Baron identifies as his "death." In contrast to Michael, whom Catholics view as the "good" angel of death, this depiction of Death is consistent with various Christian depictions of the Grim Reaper, Death of the Four Horsemen of the Apocalypse and Santa Muerte, the "Saint Death" venerated by many Mexican Catholics. Furthermore, an angel is also a sign of doom in *12 Monkeys*. Here, an angel features prominently in the Christmas decoration in the aforementioned mall scenes. While Railly purchases a disguise for Cole in the store, the decorative angel is slowly being raised to its pedestal behind her. Though this might otherwise be seen as a good omen, Cole's mission is doomed to failure, since he has already seen the angel in the contaminated mall in his future. Gilliam even included an overt reference to angels in *Fear and Loathing in Las Vegas*. As Raoul Duke and Dr. Gonzo leave Beverly Hills for Las Vegas, Gilliam alludes to the story of God exiling Adam and Eve from the Garden of Eden by including an angel with a flaming sword standing outside the

Beverly Hills hotel. According to Gilliam, "The Beverly Hills crowd was [...] our Garden of Eden, even guarded by an angel with a flaming sword, from which they're expelled into the desert wilderness. Nobody understands most of this stuff, but that's what I'm doing: there's a structure there, with biblical overtones. You keep hoping that some people will spot things and make connections — I mean, how many angels with flaming swords are out there?" (Christie 252). As in his other films, this angel is also a warning — Duke and Gonzo are about to embark on a perilous journey, leaving serenity behind, never to return. Though many Christians of all denominations see angels as purely holy beings, Gilliam uses angels to sometimes provide a false sense of hope or a bad omen for his protagonists.

It is only in *The Fisher King* that Gilliam uses angels in their traditional role as a supportive force. However, unlike *Brazil* and *The Adventures of Baron Munchausen*, the angels, or, "Little People," are never seen on-screen and appear only in the mind of Parry, the mentally unstable and self-proclaimed knight-errant and "Janitor of God." Parry sees the "Little People" as providers of spiritual guidance on the way back to regaining his sanity, and describes them as "the cutest little fat people," not unlike typical depictions of cherubic *putti* from Renaissance art. Of course, Parry's "little people" could also be fairies (as Jack refers to them), but curiously enough in *The Adventures of Baron Munchausen* the goddess Venus is accompanied by two such "little fat people" angels holding a ribbon train for her. Renaissance paintings of Venus frequently featured putti in their iconography. In fact, putti are one of the few iconographic figures to appear in art of both pagan subjects (notably Venus and Cupid) and Catholic subjects (notably the Virgin Mary, as in Raphael's *Sistine Madonna*). In the same way, Gilliam's films deal with the relationship between the fantastic beasts of imagination and the real-life demons that haunt humanity's everyday life, including *The Fisher King* (Red Knight and greed and suffering), *The Brothers Grimm* (Mirror Queen and lying for personal gain), and *Tideland* (children's games and addiction and isolation). Gilliam's use of *putti* evokes the mixture of reality and fantasy that is evident in all of his films.

The Catholic clergy has often been a target for humor, and Monty Python is no exception. The group has numerous memorable sketches, like the recurring "Spanish Inquisition" sketch (which included Gilliam) from the *Flying Circus* television show and the "Last Supper" sketch from *Monty Python Live at the Hollywood Bowl*, which both portrayed Catholic authorities as having ineffectual influence — for instance, Python's Spanish Inquisition has humorously poor methods of torture (such as forcing someone to sit on a comfortable couch "until lunchtime"), and in the "Last Supper" sketch the

Pope has difficulty convincing Michelangelo not to include more than twelve apostles and one Christ figure in his latest painting. These portrayals carried over to the Python films, particularly *Monty Python and the Holy Grail.* The flagellant monks — who chant and hit themselves in the head with boards of wood — and the monks led by Brother Maynard who read the description of the Holy Hand Grenade from the fictitious Biblical "Book of Armaments" are shown to be devoted to their religious orders beyond the point of ridiculousness. In the final Python film, *Monty Python and the Meaning of Life*, nuns and priests dance and sing along to the song "Every Sperm is Sacred," an ode to the Catholic church's policies on birth control. The comedy in these various portrayals is mostly that of the absurd, yet in its absurdity it does not portray the clergy or Catholics as malicious or evil.

Following the humor established in the Python's work, Gilliam continued to mock the Catholic clergy in his own films. In his first solo film, *Jabberwocky*, Gilliam uses nuns in humorous ways. In her tower, the Princess is surrounded by a dozen nuns (called "The Blessed Sisters of Misery") who continuously bow to each other as they sew. Later, when reluctant hero Dennis inadvertently finds himself in the Princess' room while escaping the castle, the nuns mindlessly run about as they scream at the man who has invaded the chamber. However, after the Princess mistakes Dennis for her betrothed prince, she asks "Sister Jessica" to remove her habit so Dennis can escape dressed as a nun. Sister Jessica is clearly a man in disguise, which Dennis notices, though this is apparently unknown to everyone else. After Dennis escapes and begins to strip the habit off, a doomsday flagellant cult catches him and is unable to decide if he's the devil disguised as a nun or a nun disguised as the devil — either way, they decide to burn him at the stake. Even a brief scene between the shifty Squire and Dennis involves the Squire telling a wild tale about his battle with a group of "fighting nuns." Again, much of Gilliam's mocking of the nuns in *Jabberwocky* fits firmly in the farcical humor of Monty Python.

Yet Gilliam's *Jabberwocky* departs from the absurd clergy of his prior work with the Pythons in his portrayal of the Bishop as manipulatively evil. In fact, the Bishop receives the most negative portrayal in the film. Though the Jabberwock is terrorizing the countryside, the Bishop argues against eliminating the threat of the beast since it appears attendance at church has "tripled" and the coffers are fuller, despite the extreme poverty Gilliam shows the people of the city to be suffering (for example, one beggar has cut off his foot to help his panhandling, and at the end of the film Dennis sees that the beggar has cut off the other foot, no doubt to increase his earnings). This comments on the criticism that people are motivated to attend church mainly out of the fear of God's wrath, a concern that is just as relevant to modern religion as it was to medieval Catholicism. The Bishop shows his distaste for King Bruno's plan to slay the Jabberwock when, after a grand procession of luxury and music, he callously flicks only a drop of holy water to bless the champion knight and squire Dennis on their quest. Later, in a backroom meeting of the merchants who are profiting from the commoners taking refuge in the city because of the Jabberwock, the Bishop reveals that he has hired the villainous Black Knight to stop the champion knight from killing the Jabberwock. Again, this shows the Bishop to be more concerned with how the church can benefit from society's fear than with the welfare of his flock. In this way, Gilliam makes the Bishop — the representative of the church — the true "monster," since the mindless Jabberwock is only acting out its monstrous nature, while the Bishop institutes a way to manipulate the grave situation for his own gains.

Gilliam also shows clergy members shirking their true duties in *Brazil*. Though religion plays very little role in the Orwellian-influenced world of *Brazil*, Gilliam inserts a few references to religion into the film which show how the corruption of religion can render it impotent. In particular, a humorous, yet also troubling juxtaposition occurs early in the film with a group of nuns who appear to be on a tour of the Ministry of Information facility. The mob of people at the Ministry of Information seem to take no notice of the giggling nuns, a clear sign that there is little respect for religious figures in the world of the film (curiously, there is a similar group of ignored nuns walking through Grand Central Terminal in *The Fisher King*). The most alarming moment in the scene occurs when a nun stops to ask a police trooper about his rifle and, while handling it, points it directly at the trooper. Like the Bishop in *Jabberwocky*, this nun shows disregard for the sanctity of her position, though this seems fitting in the techno-dystopian world of *Brazil*. In a more humorous way, *The Imaginarium of Doctor Parnassus* features two nuns who look disgusted at the sight of the ragged Parnassus roaming the streets of London, only to later be charmed by Mr. Nick (i.e. Satan) as he hands them an apple, an obvious reference to the Fall of Man. Again, nuns are shown to shirk their duties (helping the downtrodden) to focus on sinful temptations. Gilliam also shows this abandonment in a more subtle way by naming the film's villain Tony Shepherd — which references his manipulative persuasive abilities, but also brings to mind priests, whom are often referred to as "shepherds" of their "flocks." With this, Gilliam again raises the question of whether priests are simply manipulators — like the Bishop in *Jabberwocky* — who are otherwise unconcerned with the welfare of their "sheep."

While it would be grossly inaccurate to label Terry Gilliam a "Catholic" filmmaker, Gilliam himself acknowledges the tremendous influence his religious upbringing has on the fantasy worlds that he creates. Though raised a Protestant, it is intriguing how Gilliam's personal views of sin, free will, and redemption relate more to Catholic beliefs than those instilled in him during his childhood. Indeed, though it is not surprising that a film as thematically "Catholic" as *The Fisher King* was chosen as one of the "ten best" films of 1991 by the United States Conference of Catholic Bishops, it is surprising that little has been written about the undeniably Catholic sensibilities reflected in the themes and imagery of Gilliam's films. Though Gilliam creates worlds of the fantastic, he never ignores the very human issues and questions that have always led man to look to faith for answers.

Works Cited

Aquinas, Thomas. *The Treatise on Human Nature: Summa Theologiae 1a 75–89*. Trans. Robert Pasnau. Indianapolis, IN: Hackett Publishing, 2002. Print.
Augustine. *Enchiridion on Faith, Hope, and Love*. Trans. Thomas Hibbs. Washington, DC: Regnery Publishing, 1996.
Brazil. Dir. Terry Gilliam. Perf. Jonathan Pryce, Robert DeNiro, Katherine Helmond. Embassy International Pictures, 1985. Film.
Christie, Ian, ed. *Gilliam on Gilliam*. New York: Faber and Faber, 1999. Print.
The Fisher King. Dir. Terry Gilliam. Perf. Robin Williams, Jeff Bridges, Amanda Plummer. Columbia Pictures International, 1991. Film.
The Imaginarium of Doctor Parnassus. Dir. Terry Gilliam. Perf. Andrew Garfield, Christopher Plummer, Richard Riddell. Infinity Features Entertainment, 2009. Film.
Palladino, A. G. "Predestination (In Catholic Theology)." *New Catholic Encyclopedia*. Vol. 11. 2nd ed. Detroit: Gale, 2003. 647–653. Print.
Sterritt, David, and Lucille Rhodes, eds. *Terry Gilliam Interviews*. Jackson: University of Mississippi Press, 2004. Print.
Time Bandits. Dir. Terry Gilliam. Perf. John Cleese, Sean Connery, Shelley Duvall. HandMade Films, 1981. Film.
Twelve Monkeys. Dir. Terry Gilliam. Perf. Bruce Willis, Madeleine Stowe, Brad Pitt. Universal Pictures, 1995. Film.

Sacramentality Between Catholicism and the New Age in *The Lord of the Rings*

EM MCAVAN

J.R.R. Tolkien was, as is well known, a Catholic from birth. Yet despite the best efforts of some writers, *The Lord of the Rings* remains a text that resists easy categorization as broadly Christian, let alone specifically Catholic. Canadian scholar Jes Battis argues that this is due to the fact that *Lord of the Rings* resists totalizing readings, creating "problematic and incomplete readings, for it occupies several literary modes — epic, romance, pastoral, and fantasy[1] — without firmly attaching itself to any of them" (909). As a result, current Tolkien studies, from literary and language studies, biography, religion to fantasy and science fiction studies, "do not maintain any sort of meaningful dialogue with each other" (910). Important theoretical work from Marxist, postcolonial, feminist and queer perspectives has been done on Tolkien, though these have frequently ignored the spiritual aspects of both the texts and their consumption. Other work has situated the text as a form of myth, relying on outmoded Jungian models of religion.[2]

Critical efforts to place *Lord of the Rings* as a Catholic text have been largely dependent on unconvincing biographical readings of Tolkien himself. This biographical approach often relies heavily on Tolkien's letters, which both explain his own approach to Christianity and Catholicism in particular, as well as providing privileged readings of his work. Indicative of this approach is Stratford Caldecott, who in *Secret Fire* reads Tolkien's letters, his academic essay "On Fairy Stories" and minor stories such as "Leaf by Niggle." The marshaling of what Michel Foucault called "the author function" as an explanatory tool is problematic, for arguably these texts (particularly the letters) have only been read by a tiny minority of Tolkien's audience and thus cannot be considered to provide the typical reading context for the *Lord of the Rings*' general reception.

Sacramentality and The Lord of the Rings *Novels*

The difficulty of finding a definitive religious reading of Tolkien's epic may have much to do with its position generically in the fantasy genre. Literary critic David Gooderham has argued that the fantasy fiction genre has since the 1860s lacked "explicit reference to [real-world] religious institutions, practices and beliefs [...] almost entirely" (156). He argues that the religious is overtly disavowed in the fantasy text, for the endeavor of "unreal" secondary world building is premised on its differentiation from our own. As Christopher McKittrick reminds us in this volume, director Terry Gilliam puts the idea humorously, saying, "The normal approach in a kids' [fantasy] film is to make the final character a wizard. But why not bring God into it? Why not stop fiddling around, and get right down to things?" Despite this generic "fiddling around," real-world religion is still however present in the fantasy text, albeit displaced from the literal into the metaphorical. Gooderham argues that fantasy functions as a metaphorical mode, so religion is "transpose[d] into the landscape, beings and activities of the secondary worlds of the fantasies" (156). We can therefore speak without paradox of the genre as being both spiritual and non-religious.

As Gooderham's argument suggests, religion in *The Lord of the Rings* is displaced into metaphorical subtext. Though it lacks overt Christian symbols, the influence of Norse myths is clearly evident in *The Lord of the Rings*, a legacy of Tolkien's research on Beowulf. Yet this usage of pagan myths is itself a turn towards the Christian. Ralph Woods rightly suggests that *The Lord of the Rings* is set in a "prebiblical period of history—a time where there were no Chosen People, no incarnation, no religion at all—from a viewpoint that is distinctly Christian" (209). Instead, the novels are infused with pagan melancholy that, like Beowulf, intuits the coming of the Biblical drama.

As a result of this implicit rather than explicit turn, we can see Christianity most clearly if we examine how Tolkien's world-building transmutes the religious into a deeply Catholic phenomenological outlook to the material world best described as *sacramental*. Sacramentality, as Vincent Miller points out, "is a broad sensibility within Catholicism manifested in doctrine, liturgy and popular culture" (189). Miller suggests that "sacramentality is an interesting example of a religious resource for countering consumer culture, because it challenges consumer culture not by critiquing consumption but by challenging the abstracting dynamisms of consumption itself" (189). Sacramentality resists the decontextualizing and flattening out principles of capitalist culture, challenging "the reduction of cultural objects to shallow postmodern signifiers by reinforcing their connections with other doctrines, symbols and practices" (Miller 194).

In Tolkien's novels, motifs like Galadriel's phial of light and the elvish lembas bread function as sacramentals, metonyms for the sacred embodied in the material. The phial of light is a crystal phial filled with water from Galadriel's fountain, which contains the light of a star. Galadriel gives the phial of light to Frodo Baggins "to light the dark places, when all the other lights go out" (367), a function which is itself suggestive. Light, of course, is the pre-eminent Christian metaphor — as Jesus says in John, "I am the light of the world. Whoever follows me will never walk in darkness, but will have the light of life" (John 8:12 NIV). If we continue this chapter further, in a confrontation with the Pharisees, he says that "you are from below; I am from above. You are of this world; I am not of this world" (8:23). The spatialization at work seems quite clear, "above" and "not of this world" are associated with the divine, and the "below" and "this world" with the profane. So, a star, which is indeed "above" and "not of this world" metaphorically has certain kinds of associations with the divine — and of course it is a star in Matthew 2:2 which announces Christ's birth to the Magi. So there is ample scriptural precedent for seeing Galadriel's phial as a sacramental, for it is a quite literal instance of the transcendental (the light of a star) combining with the immanence of materiality (the phial) to form a sacramental.

Lembas too is metaphorically resonant in a number of ways. Also given to the *Fellowship of the Ring* at Lothlórien, the bread has miraculous powers, staying fresh for months and requiring only a little to fill a stomach. One of the elves comments that "we call it *lembas* or waybread, and it is more strengthening than any food by Men" (360). Most heroic narratives tend to largely ignore food, but Tolkien instead creates a supernatural food. It is not the ecstatic food of ambrosia; rather, I think he has a more monotheistic referent in mind. One can firstly read the bread as being not merely a sacramental, but recalling a sacrament itself — the Holy Eucharist — for like the Eucharist, lembas bread sustains infinitely. However, given the implicit rather than explicit nature of religion in Tolkien's text, there is of course no mention of Jesus or the sacrament's redemptive promissory note ("For I tell you, I will not eat it again until it finds fulfillment in the kingdom of God" [Luke 22: 16] in Christian tradition. So the reading of lembas as Eucharist is necessarily incomplete. However, one could also read lembas as recalling manna, the sustaining cakes cooked and eaten by the Israelites in their trek through the desert in Exodus. Like manna, which tasted like wafers made with honey (Exodus 16:31), lembas is suggested to be sweet, "better than [...] honey-cakes" (360). In both readings therefore, what the lembas does literally (sustain the heroes through their trials) allows us to reflect metaphorically on the role of the divine in *spiritual* sustenance.

From Catholicism to the New Age

If it seems clear that *The Lord of the Rings* novels are fairly strongly Catholic in their approach to sacramentality, the *reception* of the novels has often been decontextualized from Tolkien's Catholicism. Although published in the early 1950s, Tolkien's trilogy was taken up by 1960s counter-culture, who saw in the texts a pastoral alternative to the military-industrial complex of the present. The counter-culture, however loosely defined, was in many ways influential in the popularization of certain New Age philosophies and practices. It was arguably the absence of an overtly Christian message that made the counter-culture embrace Tolkien far more strongly than the similarly pastoral C.S Lewis — and it is arguable that remains true today (though of course, the greater scope of the series probably helps a great deal too). Tolkien's enthusiasm for the pagan, too, endears him to a New Age that has often preferred to look for Celtic or Nordic spiritualities with which to oppose hegemonic Christianity. Displaced into the metaphorical Catholicism of the sacramental, the religiousness of the novels has largely been ignored by its millions of fans.

Peter Jackson's recent film adaptations further the process of decontextualization and abstraction significantly. The changes of the texts in Jackson's films — and indeed our reading of them — can be explained by registering the larger cultural shifts of late capitalist culture and the extraordinary growth of the gathering of movements called the New Age. The New Age is an loose conglomeration of beliefs and practices that encompass Western (especially American) embrace of Eastern practices like Buddhism, Taoism, yoga and meditation, the embrace of Celtic and other forms of pagan religions, use of crystals, belief in extra-terrestrials, appropriation of indigenous religions[3] and the spiritual pop-psychology of talk shows like Oprah Winfrey's. Slavoj Žižek goes so far as to call the New Age the hegemonic discourse of global postmodern capitalism (2001: 12).[4] While this overstates the case considerably — especially in a United States where the religious Right has increasingly made its political and cultural presence known — it is nevertheless true that the New Age has become a significant part of the Western spiritual landscape.

If this explains what the New Age consists of, the more salient question is what New Age beliefs and practices *do*. Sociologist Paul Heelas suggests that despite the heterogeneous elements, New Age movements largely have "the same (or similar) lingua franca to do with the human (and planetary) condition and how it can be transformed. This is the language of what shall henceforth be called 'self-spirituality'" (2). The first step in this self-spirituality is to discard the idea of "religion" altogether. Heelas argues that for New Age spiritual movements, the very term religion has become discarded. He says, "'Religion' is associated with the traditional; the dead; the misleading; the exclusivistic" (1996: 23). Rather than view their practices as religion, New Agers often use the term "spirituality" to more accurately capture what they consider to be more properly "lived" spiritual experiences. This shift in terminology is important, for it foregrounds the break that New Agers see themselves as having made with traditional organized religion, which they considered a set of beliefs and practices that are "not lived" in the same way. "Religion" is considered tied to institutions such as the Catholic and Anglican Churches, to be disconnected from if not totally opposed to real-life spiritual practice.

This removal of "religion" is most clearly exemplified by the New Age's removal of the transcendental God. This is not simply an atheist absence or denial of God's existence — instead, God is replaced in the New Age by the often nebulous idea of "spirit" or "energy." These ideas derive from Buddhism, Taoism and Hinduism but are largely disconnected from their traditions. The New Age appropriation of yoga or tantric sex, for instance, frequently refigures these practices as capitalist commodities, as more reliant on racialized exoticism than true mysticism. What replaces the authority of the church is the self, which becomes the only arbiter of truthfulness. "To experience the 'Self' itself is to experience 'God,' the 'Goddess,' the 'Source,' 'Christ consciousness,' the 'inner child,' the 'way of the heart' or, most simply and [...] most frequently, 'inner spirituality'" (Heelas 19).

The second important feature of the New Age is that it is often a consumerist movement. Lisa Aldred argues that "the majority of those who identify as New Age (or could be reasonably labeled as such by others) participate primarily through the purchase of texts and products targeted for the New Age market" (330). New Agers seek to escape the disenchanted world of late capitalism, but they do so through its very lifeblood — commodity purchase. Ironically, "as products of the very consumer culture they seek to escape [...]

New Agers pursue spiritual meaning and identification through acts of purchase" (329).

The combination of "self-spirituality" and consumerism becomes most clear when we consider the ways in which the New Age invokes a Weberian style "enchanted" world. The New Age looks for God in the material world, endowing the concrete with an indefinable "something more" of spirit. The New Age culls terms from disparate traditions — chi, prana, life force, spirit, energy — but they all remain similar in usage. This life force is held to be universal, flowing through everyone and everything. "Discovering the self" means getting in touch with this force, a collapsing of the boundaries between self and Other, reconciling nature and culture. Heelas points out that at its extreme, this belief tends to the narcissism that "nothing takes place outside of beyond themselves [that] has an autonomous existence" (25). This enchantment of course segues very easily into the materialistic, consumer imperatives of the New Age, which hold out the illusory promise that spiritual enlightenment is a commodity to be purchased (and for a reasonable price).

The New Age Tolkien

Although they attempt to be faithful to Tolkien's novels in style and spirit, Peter Jackson's more recent film adaptations of *The Lord of the Rings* nevertheless remove much of the Catholic spirit of the novels, extending this New Age reading even further. *The Lord of the Rings* adaptations borrow eclectically, incorporating both Christian and New Age symbols in a characteristically postmodern mishmash of Eastern and Western religious tropes signified through visual and musical references. Kristin Thompson, for instance, points out that "the widespread impact of martial-arts choreography from Japanese and Chinese films is reflected in [*The Two*] *Towers*" (49). She argues that Jackson's adaptations re-write Legolas as a kind of "action elf" (49) and even more improbably, Gandalf is refigured as a kung-fu monk. She says, "Gandalf the White's costumes and make-up appear to be derived [...] from those of the white-bearded monk (or white-eyebrowed *sifu*) figure in kung-fu films" (52). Gandalf, in Peter Jackson's films, becomes a kind of hybrid figure, referencing kung-fu monks and Merlinesque wizards alike. As a figure of wisdom and power, Gandalf becomes disconnected from any one tradition — a perfectly decontextualized New Age character. His wisdom and advice for Frodo and Bilbo, too, becomes part of his remaking as a New Age sage.

The music too is a melange of cultural references. Composer Howard Shore alternates between a foreboding Wagnerian brass score, Celtic pastoral themes, and a liturgical-referencing choral arrangement. While the brass score is largely there to build tension, the pagan elements of the narrative are reinforced by the Celtic themes — especially in their deployment in the Shire, which becomes a bucolic paradise. The Celtic and Norse influences are signalled too by the few vocal performances on the soundtracks — notably, the popular Irish New Age singer Enya sings the theme to *The Fellowship of the Ring*, and Icelandic singer Emiliana Torrini sings the haunting "Gollum's Song" in *The Two Towers*.

Visually, the films frequently make New Age style gestures to the transcendent, in the form of a transcendentally signified "spirit." We see this most clearly in the scenes featuring the Lady Galadriel. Dressed in long white flowing robes, Galadriel (played by Cate Blanchett) is introduced in *The Fellowship of the Ring* by an excess of light overwhelming the frame. The music is not Celtic here, rather it is a liturgy referencing choral signalling the transcendent — but of course, the New Age has long appropriated liturgical music (most especially in the form of mass-produced "Gregorian Chant" CDs). The largely CGI constructed scenes at Rivendell and the forest are shot in a hazy other-worldly light — a light which recalls not only countless Hollywood renderings of Heaven, but of New Age "near-death" experiences. This is explicitly referenced in Arwen's first appearance, where she portentously intones, "Frodo, I am Arwen. I've come to help you. Hear my voice, come back to the light." It is arguable that the rendering of the Elves in Jackson's films is supposed to be signalling the transcendent, literally transcending the human abilities of time (being incredibly long-lived) and capacity (for magic, telepathy, healing and so on). And of course, it is the Elves who leave Middle-Earth at the end of the story, moving on to what is suggested to be another plane of existence — but not, however, a Christian Heaven or Hell in Jackson's rendering, this is clearly a New Age style "other" place.

Another interesting cultural shift in the readings of the texts is in the notion of destiny. Destiny is a highly important idea in *The Lord of the Rings*, the destinies of Frodo as Ring-Bearer and Aragorn the Returned King seem to be writ large in the stars. But where Tolkien may have been gesturing towards the idea of divine Providence — that God has a plan for all people — arguably the New Age has reworked and disconnected the idea from a Christian framework.[5] Destiny in the New Age can appear as a form of pop-Buddhist "letting go" (Heelas 20) or of evidence for the existence of a transcendent "Spirit." One frequently notices the idea of destiny appear in the widely held sentimentalization of "guardian angels" or applied to "pre-destined" romantic relationships. While certain evangelical versions of Protestant Christianity have continued to use Providence as a means of reassuring its believers of the existence of a benevolent care-taker God, arguably the postmodern New Age is currently far more influential in popularizing the notion, such that the use of "destiny" in the *Lord of the Rings* films recalls the New Age before it recalls the Christian.

From Sacramentality to the New Age

So where does this leave *The Lord of the Rings* as a text — as a Catholic novel and a New Age series of films? It seems that it is neither, precisely. Complicating clear demarcations between the two is the undeniable fact that for contemporary readers the *Lord of the Rings* movies influence our reading of the book. Though the movies have generally been received as faithful adaptations, they feature a number of significant departures — most prominently in the love story between Aragorn and Arwen, a plot line lifted not from the books proper, but rather from Tolkien's copious footnotes. The movies make changes in other, less noticeable, ways too. Who could ignore the powerful rendering of Gollum in *The Two Towers* movie upon re-reading the book? Though Tolkien describes Gollum as a "thin little black fellow"[6] I think most readers would continue imagining him as Peter Jackson's pale white CGI-rendered character. Even though Tolkien himself is an avowed Catholic and is writing a work that is quite clearly not postmodern, it is arguable that current reception of Tolkien is in a decontextualized, detraditionalized fashion, and indeed that current reception of *The Lord of the Rings* is characterized by a slippage between the movies and the books. Clearly, and in characteristic postmodern fashion, the movie texts have rewritten the novels in their own image. Although as I have shown there are significant differences between books and movies, arguably in the way the two are received and consumed, those differences very often scarcely *matter*. Even texts written within established religious traditions can be used and reworked into de-institutional settings.[7] The fact that Tolkien largely eschews explicit reference to Catholicism made *The Lord of the Rings* quite easily appropriable into the "self-spirituality" of the New Age.

And so, in Jackson's films the sacramental has merged with a New Age–ized "god in all things." The hazy, other-worldly CGI rendering of sacramentals are indistinct enough to be easily assimilable to New Age conceptions of the transcendent as "spirit" that, unlike Tolkien's novels, ultimately discard the Godhead and instead place the sacred in the authentic corporeality of being. So while sacramentality is a distinctly Catholic practice, a similar sensibility may be found in New Age movements and New Age–ized discourses, which privilege bodily experience above all, situating the divine in the corporeal. This very much sees "God in all things," or at least the sacred, since the New Age frequently discards the Godhead for a language of Spirit. The sacred emerges in the "authentic" corporeality of being. In its environmentally friendly aspects (particularly Goddess worship or environmental movements), the New Age shows an attitude towards the corporeal and in particular to the natural that is close enough to the sacramental that Jackson's aestheticization can flow from one to the other. So we therefore see that the oft-opposed New Age and Christianity (exemplified in this instance by Catholicism) can be nevertheless entangled within one another. It is not unthinkable, for instance, to imagine subjects imbibing the New Age style "reverence for all living things" by watching Oprah during the week and then attending church services over the weekend.

The blurring between a Catholic sacramentality, a New Age respect for life, and a general postmodern turn towards the authenticity of the corporeal therefore demonstrates the difficulty of critically producing a "purely" Catholic text. Texts like *The Lord of the Rings* demonstrate how texts are constantly in dialogue with another, whether it be in the form of the palimpsest traces of older texts, or by being rewritten by newer texts. Rather than maintaining an either/or approach to Christian monism and New Age polytheism, one should look to the texts to see the constant tension between the two. *The Lord of the Rings* shows clearly how Catholic ideas like sacramentality can be modified by the aestheticizing qualities of the camera into a more decontextualized, consumer-friendly New Age package. For the sacramental carries with it the implicit dangers of consumerism — a sacramental aesthetic may be translated into consumerist object fetishism. And so, in its translation from page to screen, *The Lord of the Rings* has not solely become a New Age film, but one in which New Age meanings lie on top of earlier Catholic models — and indeed lying under those are the pagan myths Tolkien himself drew on. We have therefore come full circle in a sense. And this circularity becomes even clearer in the light of Miller's contention that "the Catholic 'sacramental imagination' may have provided a useful imaginative support for the emergence of consumer culture" (189). Though they appear to be in some ways opposed, the sacramentality of Tolkien's novels ultimately laid the foundations for the further commodified New Age abstraction of the Peter Jackson films.

Notes

1. Battis's usage of "fantasy" here next to the more venerable modes of pastoral, romance and epic is somewhat misleading, since arguably modern fantasy as it has emerged from the 19th century has drawn on those other modes. Indeed, their use in

Tolkien has undoubtedly led to their becoming constitutively generic characteristics of the modern fantasy genre.

2. See for instance, Elise McKenna's "To Sex up *The Lord of the Rings*" which is a study of the feminine in Peter Jackson's films.

3. This appropriation has been critiqued by Lisa Alfred, who argues that "New Agers romanticize an 'authentic' and 'traditional' Native American culture whose spirituality can save them from their own sense of malaise" (329). She argues that these appropriate New Age practices can obscure and even perpetuate the social oppression of Native Americans.

4. He says, "at the very moment when, at the level of the 'economic infrastructure,' 'European' technology and capitalism is triumphing world-wide, at the level of 'ideological superstructure,' the Judeo-Christian legacy is threatened in the European space itself by the onslaught of the New Age 'Asiatic' thought, which [...] is establishing itself as the hegemonic ideology of global capitalism" (12).

5. In the present volume, Christopher McKittrick points out that Providence is a peculiarly Protestant rather than Catholic Christian idea; however, Tolkien combines this with a more classically Catholic emphasis on free will—in particular, in the decisions of Frodo and Sméagol/Gollum.

6. Tolkien's rendering of race is dubious at best, the glorification of the blonde-haired and blue-eyed Elves, contrasted with the horror of the human-animal hybrid Orcs has meant that a number of far–Right neo–Nazi organizations have held up both books and movies as exemplary Aryan texts. Sue Kim in her article "Beyond Black and White: Race and Postmodernism in the *Lord of the Rings* Movies" gives Tolkien more leeway than the films, saying that "partly due to the novels' ability to explore symbolism, diplomacy and war, culture and history in greater depth and subtlety, the novels' black-and-white coding, while still strongly apparent, is more ambivalent than in the films." It's easy to see that Tolkien, writing in the 1940s and 50s in the dying days of Empire, has a text underpinned by a racist paternal epistemology, which given the historical context, most scholars have found understandable though not excusable. On the other hand, working 50 years later on the films, Peter Jackson should have known better.

7. See, for instance, the movie adaptation of Lewis's *The Lion, the Witch and the Wardrobe*, which was quite directly influenced by Jackson's trilogy. Downplaying overt religious moralizing in favor of suggestive symbols is just good commercial sense for capturing a mass-market post–Christian audience, although the movie also benefited from a post–*Passion of the Christ* tapping into an overtly religious pop-culture market.

Works Cited

Aldred, Lisa. "Plastic Shamans and Astroturf Sun Dances: New Age Commercialization of Native American Spirituality." *American Indian Quarterly* 24.3 (2000): 329–352.

Attebery, Brian. *Strategies of Fantasy*. Bloomington and Indianapolis: Indiana University Press, 1992.

Battis, Jes. "Gazing Upon Sauron: Hobbits, Elves, and the Queering of the Postcolonial Optic." *MFS Modern Fiction Studies* 50.4 (2004): 908–25.

Caldecott, Stratford. *Secret Fire: The Spiritual Vision of J.R.R. Tolkien*. London: Darton, Longman and Todd, 2003.

Foucault, Michel. "What Is an Author?" *Textual Strategies*. Ed. Josné Harrari. London: Methuen, 1980. 141–160.

Gooderham, David. "Fantasizing It as It Is: Religious Language in Philip Pullman's Trilogy, *His Dark Materials*." *Children's Literature* 31 (2003): 155–75.
Heelas, Paul. *The New Age Movement: The Celebration of the Self and the Sacralisation of Modernity.* Oxford: Blackwell, 1996.
Kim, Sue. "Beyond Black and White: Race and Postmodernism in the *Lord of the Rings* Films." *MFS Modern Fiction Studies* 40.4 (2004): 875–907.
Landa, Ishay. "Slaves of the Ring: Tolkien's Political Unconscious." *Historical Materialism* 10.4 (1998): 113–33.
The Lord of the Rings: Fellowship of the Ring. Dir. Peter Jackson. Perf. Elijah Wood, Viggo Mortenson, Sean Astin, Ian MacKellen, Sean Bean. 2001. DVD. New Line, 2002.
The Lord of the Rings: The Return of the King. Dir. Peter Jackson. Perf. Elijah Wood, Viggo Mortenson, Sean Astin, Ian MacKellen, Andy Sirkis, Miranda Otto. 2003. DVD. New Line, 2004.
The Lord of the Rings: The Two Towers. Dir. Peter Jackson. Perf. Elijah Wood, Viggo Mortenson, Sean Astin, Ian MacKellen, Andy Sirkis, Cate Blanchett. 2002. DVD. New Line, 2003.
McKenna, Elise. "To Sex Up *The Lord of the Rings*: Jackson's Feminine Approach in His 'Sub-creation.'" *How We Became Middle-earth: A Collection of Essays on* The Lord of the Rings. Ed. Adam Lam and Nataliya Oryshchuk. Zollikofen, Switzerland: Walking Tree, 2007.
Miller, Vincent. *Consuming Religion: Christian Faith and Practice in a Consumer Culture.* New York: Continuum, 2003.
Smol, Anna. "'Oh ... Oh ... Frodo!': Readings of Male Intimacy in *The Lord of the Rings*." *MFS Modern Fiction Studies* 50.4 (2004): 949–79.
Thompson, Kristin. "Fantasy, Franchises and Frodo Baggins: *The Lord of the Rings* and Modern Hollywood." *Velvet Light Trap* 52 (2003): 45–63.
Tolkien, J.R.R. *Leaf by Niggle.* London: Allen & Unwin, 1964.
Tolkien, J.R.R. *The Lord of the Rings.* London: HarperCollins, 2001.
Torre, Michael. "The Portrait of Evil in *The Lord of the Rings*: Reflections Personal, Literary, and Theological." *Logos: A Journal of Catholic Thought and Culture* 5.4 (2002): 65–74.
Woods, Ralph C. "Travelling the One Road: *The Lord of the Rings* as a 'Pre-Christian Classic.'" *The Christian Century* 110.6 (1993): 208–12.
Žižek, Slavoj. *On Belief.* London: Routledge, 2001.

"The Devil Made Me Do It"
Catholicism, Verisimilitude and the Reception of Horror Films
Rick Pieto

Introduction

In this essay I investigate how several participants[1] in an interview study on horror fandom discussed the relevance that Catholicism had on their experience of possession films. This finding is investigated using Tzvetan Todorov's notion of verisimilitude as developed in his book *Introduction to Poetics* (1981). Todorov views genres (in this case possession films) as having a relation not to reality but to an audience's construction of reality through discourses such as religion. Participants believed in the possibility of events or characters (including monsters) from horror films as being "real" in relation to their cultural, social or religious discourses. That is, what they believed to be true was constructed through various discursive formations such as religion, rather than any real experience with possessed humans, demons or satanic children.

Todorov on Verisimilitude

As Tzvetan Todorov (1981) describes it, genre traces a relation to two kinds of "verisimilitude"; the first relation deals with *generic* verisimilitude and what is probable to happen in a film because it is perceived to belong to a certain genre. A possession film, for example, in order to be believable the audience expects the film to follow generic rules and contain certain elements;

the possession of a person (usually a young girl), priests, crosses, demons and certainly exorcisms.

The other relation, for Todorov, deals with the genre and the audience's *social construction* of the "verisimilar":

> But there exists another verisimilitude, which has been taken even more frequently for a relation with reality. Aristotle, however, has already perceived that the verisimilar is not a relation between discourse and its referent (the relation of truth), but between discourse and *what readers believe is true* (emphasis added). The relation is here established between a work and a scattered discourse that in part belongs to each individual of a society but of which none may claim ownership; in other words to *public opinion*. The latter is of course not "reality" but a further discourse, independent of the work. Public opinion therefore functions as a rule of genre that relates to all genres [18–19].

This condition of *social* verisimilitude deals with the relation not between genre and reality, i.e., a referent or objective reality outside but between genre and the participant's involvement in "public opinion" or social discourses existing alongside the genre. When viewers of horror films believe the possibility of events or characters, including monsters, from horror films to be "real," it is in relation, not to any real experience with ghosts, demons or psycho killers but to the viewers' cultural, social or national discourses, that is to what they believed to be true as it is constructed through various social discourses such as the news or religion, i.e., the genre of public opinion. Todorov recognizes that public opinion "functions as a rule of genre that relates to all genres." For Todorov the verisimilitude of generic texts like horror films refers not to real life but to a public discourse that is not perceived as a genre but as reality thus giving it a certain force. It is important that we see Todorov's point that any question as to the "truth" of horror must be seen in the light of its fictional character and because of its fictional character any questions of truth or falsity are missing the point; unlike science, horror films or any fiction "cannot be subjected to the test of truth; it is neither true nor false, to raise this question has no meaning" (18). Todorov's insight on verisimilitude, and Steven Neale's reading of Todorov in his essay *Questions of Genre* (1995), clarified for me much of what my participants considered to be the relation between "verisimilitude" and horror films. I could not dismiss their claims as false since as Todorov asserts that is inappropriate and I could not count them as meaningless because their claims did have meaning. Taking Todorov's cue I contextualized their meanings not in relation to a referent or actual experience of possession but to their discourses of religion, which would fall under Todorov's term "public opinion," or discourse.

Furthermore my participants would agree with Aristotle's point regarding the relation of generic verisimilitude to an objective reality or lived experience.

Even though we see verisimilitude as having a claim on *believability* participants nevertheless made a fundamental distinction between the type of terror real life produces (e.g., actually being attacked or possessed) and the type of terror a horror film produces. In this excerpt Linda clearly recognizes the difference between the two types of terror:

> LINDA: The thing with horror films I'd rather get scared by them rather than having the sort of fear where there's an intruder in my house or like I'm getting attacked. Because it's a different sort of fear.
> INTERVIEWER: How is that different, that sort of fear?
> LINDA: It's more serious. It can traumatize you. Whereas with films, it's sort of false. Films are just something to play with, have fun with it.

Linda's statement relates to Isabel Pinedo's (1997) notion that the emotional reception of horror films is a "bounded experience of fear." "In terror, there is no insulation and no recreation because the re-creation of danger is complete, whereas in recreational terror, the violation and death of the body is experienced as partial. The experience of terror is bounded by the tension between proximity and distance, reality and illusion. In recreational terror, we fear the threat of physical danger, but the danger fails to materialize" (40). As Linda and Pinedo recognize there is an emotional distance in cinematic fear that allows one to "play" with it; there is no overwhelming trauma that would take away all pleasure from watching a film. Without the "insulation" that Linda and Pinedo note, real trauma would block any interpretive practice using discourses such as Catholicism or filmic genre and inhibit any real cinematic enjoyment. On several occasions participants described experiences with horror films that broke through this "boundedness," so to speak, and participants experienced so much displeasure they had to leave the theater or stop watching the tape or DVD.

Horror, Catholicism and Verisimilitude

Before we investigate the way in which Catholicism played into the reception of horror films it should be said there is a connection between Catholicism and fundamental elements within the genre of horror. For example there are shared similarities such as the crucifix and holy water in Catholicism and say vampire films. Film scholar Isabel Pinedo describes this connection between her background in Catholicism and her predilection for horror films:

> I was educated almost exclusively in Catholic schools. The visual and narrative imagery ... of Catholicism was a formative experience. I was fascinated by the narrative drama of Christ's torture and death, also known as The Passion ... a

stunning combination of bloody spectacle and excess-driven narrative. This dense thicket of imagery prepared me for my childhood introduction to televised horror — Twilight Zone, Outer Limits, Creature Feature, Night Gallery, Dark Shadows, and the television runs of Universal and Hammer films [1–2].

As Pinedo explains the mood, images and narratives of Catholicism resemble the generic attributes of horror films providing an easy transition from one to the other. On a similar note Karen, a twenty-five year old horror fan also raised as a Catholic who participated in the study, corroborated Pinedo's insight regarding Catholicism's parallel to horror, "So the whole idea of Catholicism is scary to a child anyway. I mean, you have this crucified guy, you have his torture and then you have all of this weird stuff. Why they teach children this stuff is beyond me. And it's a little scary." Like Pinedo, Karen discloses here the connection between her upbringing as a Catholic and her appreciation of horror. I am not saying there is a direct causal connection between being raised Catholic and becoming a horror fan however Pinedo and Karen both appreciate the manner in which Catholicism broadly overlaps with the genre of horror and furnishes an "introduction" to the "torture" and "weird stuff" contained in the horror genre thus facilitating fan linkages between the two discourses vital to the emergence of verisimilitude.

Several participants discussed the relevance that Catholicism had for their reception of horror subgenres such as possession or satanic films and for specific films such as *The Exorcist* (1973), *Stigmata* (1999), *Lost Souls* (2000) and *The Omen* (1976). One such participant Linda, an 18-year-old, self-described horror fan, directly described her viewing of a possession film like *The Exorcist* and the significance it held for her because of her experience as a Catholic:

> LINDA: See with the whole priest thing there was nothing else that I saw on television with a priest involved and it just blew me away. It was familiar to me, like that sight of the priest. It was so familiar to me. And just to see him in that sort of setting... The role of the priest really made it believable. If you just had a regular person do that it would have been different but the fact that they included the church and just that whole symbol with the priest.

In this excerpt we witness how Linda's reception of a possession film like *The Exorcist* is powerfully influenced by the discursive practices of Catholicism; as Linda states, where else would she come across such images and objects? For Linda the discourse of Catholicism with its rituals and figures not only frames her interpretation of films like *The Exorcist* but also makes them especially frightening. Although priests constitute real experiences for Linda they are nevertheless discursive constructs of Catholicism; for Linda the figure of the priest performing an exorcism in *The Exorcist* did not relate to any direct experience she might have had but related to her knowledge that priests in the Catholic Church perform such rituals. In this sense, the figure of the priest operated discursively in relation to her reception of *The Exorcist*. As Todorov's concept of verisimilitude demonstrates, this mingling of discourses is a matter of belief, a matter of an individual's construction of believability out of the referencing of discourses. As Linda realizes, the meaning and the emotional responses invoked by the film's priests and other iconography would be quite different if she were not raised as a Catholic and if that were not part of her belief system. Thus, for Linda, Catholicism as a discourse provided a powerful context from which to interpret possession films.

Karen had a similar experience to Linda's in terms of the connection between her experiences of Catholicism and horror films, particularly *The Exorcist* and *Lost Souls*:

> KAREN: Having been raised Catholic, and I guess this would even get into more religious horror films — stuff like *Lost Souls* ... which I thought was a different version of *The Exorcist*. I know when I was a kid I was always scared that the crucifix, the cross, that Jesus' head would turn and look at me. In *Lost Souls*, that actually happened and I really freaked out in the movie theater. I really almost left because it was so ... it was like childhood coming to life. As a Catholic you're taught that this stuff actually happened. So it wasn't just a movie. It was possible reality. You know, crucifixes bleeding was something that the Church had documented as fact. So I was always on the lookout. I was like, it could happen at any time. So seeing these movies, it wasn't just fiction for me.

Like Linda, Karen regarded the discourses of Catholicism as lending an element of verisimilitude to the narratives and images of certain horror films. The element of belief in these supernatural narratives, something Catholics may strongly believe in, increases the verisimilitude of horror films for Catholic fans. As Karen describes it, for Catholics the teachings of the Church are a matter of faith and this faith increases their believability and credibility: this supplies Karen with a framework through which she can see the fictions of horror films such as *Lost Souls* or *The Exorcist* as a "possible reality." However her reaction to the image of the crucifix in *Lost Souls* seemed to play, not only on her religious faith but also on a highly charged personal fantasy associated with the iconography of Catholicism; what is remarkable is the commonality between the director's vision of what would be frightening about a crucifix and Karen's fantasy.

Karen seems to suggest here, and Linda would agree, Catholicism's similarity with the horror genre consists in the act of conveying fear-inspiring narratives and images. As Ron Tamborini and James Weaver (1996) point out in their essay *Frightening Entertainment: A Historical Perspective of Fictional*

Horror (1987) the tellers of scary tales exercise authority over the audience through a specific type of dynamic:

> The emerging power relationship is this: Those who are not perturbed by fears and who manage to evoke fears in others attain a degree of control over these others. They do so by their show of fearlessness, presumably because it projects superior ability to cope with fear-inducing conditions. Even if others' fear is not manipulated by the fearless, the show of fearlessness has this consequence. The fearless seem to have the answers, at least as far as dealing with the threatening happenings is concerned. The fearful, in contrast, are lacking the answers and should seek protection from those in the know. Stated more drastically, the fearless, by projecting the ability to cope and protect, define themselves as leaders, whereas the fearful, by turning to the fearless for help and comfort, place themselves in the role of followers [9].

In this sense Catholicism attempts to regulate the moral and spiritual behavior of individuals by frightening them. Although Catholicism consists of many beautiful narratives, images and rituals, it also employs a rich store of frightening stories and representations that tell of punishment, damnation and loss. The ownership and control of these horrifying stories and images by the Catholic Church grants it a certain power over church followers. Similarly the horror genre as a social and ideological institution seeks to control audiences with all types of ideological and moral prohibitions while subjugating them to frightening stories. A good example of this would be the moral and ideological lessons in the slasher film concerning teenage sexuality. It has been noted that the monster in slasher films seeks out sexually active teens for victimization; this can easily be construed as a form of punishment for transgressing social and moral interdictions regarding sexuality similar to what the Catholicism says about teen sexuality. The teen audience is frightened into conforming to social and religious mores. Taking this notion of control one step further, the Catholic Church and horror fan culture could be seen as regimes that attempt to control and maintain the respective discursive practices of their members, i.e., to manage the way in which they view and interpret the world and their own experiences. However this attempt at controlling others through the telling of scary stories in no way exhausts or completely restricts the range of interpretations and actions that its members (Catholics or horror fans) perform.

The power of Catholicism as a discourse and an influence on the reception of horror films can be better understood by Ashley's interpretation of *The Exorcist*. Ashley who described her upbringing as non-religious and had no belief or investment in Catholicism failed to see the power or intensity of *The Exorcist*:

ASHLEY: I think part of it was that I'm not religious and I don't believe in it. I didn't grow up with religion and I don't associate myself with any sort of religion and that makes it completely irrelevant to me. I can't relate to it. It just seems so silly that people can get so wrapped up in something like that. I didn't even get a good scare out of it. I don't believe in being taken over by a spirit or any evil taking over your body because I don't believe in any sort of religious affiliation.
INTERVIEW: So it doesn't relate to you?
ASHLEY: It's sort of fantastical to me. I think if you believe in that idea and then something has happened like that, and you're told about it through religion when you're growing up, I can see how you could be scared by it. I mean the priests didn't really faze me. The ritual didn't bother me. It was just sort of ridiculous and gross and disgusting. I'm not looking at it within a religious context but from the mere entertainment fact. I think that movie only really worked on people who believe in it and people who are, who have some sort of religious background.

Ashley explicitly sees the affinity of Catholicism and possession films like *The Exorcist*. As she states, the image of the priests, the exorcism ritual, the theme of Satan, all the elements that fascinated and frightened Linda and Karen (both raised as Catholics), had little impact on Ashley. Ashley consciously recognizes the role religion plays in her reception of *The Exorcist* and the film's inability to frighten her and merely affect as a "mere entertainment fact." Here with the mention of Ashley's lack of religious involvement and the influence that lack of involvement has on her experience of *The Exorcist* (and the fact that she introduces the word "relevant"), it is possible to see how my use of Todorov's notion of verisimilitude easily approaches the notion of "relevancy" particularly in the way the notion engages with issues of identity. Todorov's idea of verisimilitude as an intersecting of discourses of believability within a reader's interpretation of texts carries over into the notion of relevancy; the manner in which the cultural identities of horror fans intersect with the horror text to produce meaning. The notion of relevancy as used by Fiske (1988) relates to how "a viewer makes meanings and pleasures from television that are relevant to his or her social allegiances at the moment of viewing; the criteria for relevance precede the viewing moment" (247). Ashley's encounter with *The Exorcist* and other possession and religious subgenres of horror, was greatly influenced by her lack of "social allegiance" to Catholicism; the meaning she assigned to *The Exorcist* was produced out of her lack of religious affiliation and this interpretive act rendered any emotional involvement with the film nearly impossible. Furthermore Catholicism as a cultural identity indicates for horror audiences the significance of identity formations *other than age*. Thus we could not attribute to *The Exorcist*, and by extension the horror genre itself, any stable or essential meaning that would move from one audience to another across a range of cultural discourses and identities. We see here with our discussion of Catholicism and *The Exorcist* how fans' interpretations occur at the intersection of cultural identities and particular films. This notion of relevancy would also explain how horror fans could have very different, even contradictory readings of the same film. Although Ashley could appreciate the film as a horror fan, and here her cultural identity and competencies overlap with Linda's and Karen's without a cultural knowledge and commitment similar to Linda's and Karen's, Marsha was distanced from any pleasure or sustained emotional response to *The Exorcist*.

News and Horror: Secular Verisimilitude

It is important that we not think of the participants mentioned above as deluded in their religious belief and therefore more gullible to fantasy. It was not only a religious discourse such as Catholicism that framed the reception of horror films. A secular genre such as the news operated in a similar manner.

Audrey, a 21-year-old horror fan at the time of the interviews, goes on to explicitly mention the relation between horror films and television news and the problems this relation presents:

> AUDREY: Yeah. Like you look at today's news and you think your average human being are doing all these horrible things. That's scarier to me than a demon... But with that the blur between reality and fiction is complex; especially when you hear about all this genocide and murder and experimentation, the Nazis and Milosovich.
> INTERVIEWER: So how do you distinguish between horror films and the news?
> AUDREY: You don't. [LAUGHS] No... That's why I particularly find that scarier, because it's harder to distinguish between our world and the world that Hollywood creates. That's what scares me. These fantasy films, they're not going to really happen.

Here Audrey draws into the interview the names of serial killers and genocidal mass murderers like Adolph Hitler and Slobodan Milosovich from the genre of news. Here the discourse of news can be viewed as a form of horror as it reports on the disorder connected with the deranged psyches of individuals both private and public and not from demons, vampires or zombies. The supernatural, so prevalent in Linda and Karen's interviews, is easily dismissed by Audrey because the threat and chaos represented by supernatural monsters pales in relation to real horrors. Nevertheless it must be reiterated that Audrey's appeal to the news is still within the realm of a specific genre, as Todorov would point out, that of the news and not actual events or people

Audrey has experienced. It is based on Audrey's involvement in the structures of belief, or to use Todorov's phrase, public opinion and the realism of news as a document of reality and therefore believable. The "realistic" genres of news and documentaries with their perceived basis in fact were a powerful discourse for these participants, which they used to frame and interpret the meaning of horror films. These interpretations (and fears) are not tied up in the suspension of disbelief as is customarily associated with supernatural monsters but in the continuation of belief from the non-fiction genres of news and documentary into the fictional genre of horror.

Verisimilitude as understood by Todorov also came into play with the way participants interpreted certain types of monsters; for my participants the "psychological" or "psychopathic" monsters were often more terrifying because of their likelihood of being more probable and therefore more real unlike supernatural monsters that were thought of as impossible and hence unreal and therefore easily dismissed.

For example Audrey declared how Norman Bates and Hannibal Lecter were more terrifying than Freddy Krueger because of Norman's and Hannibal's human attributes:

> AUDREY: Hannibal Lecter is a man. He's flesh and blood. He can be stopped by a bullet. And he has this appearance of normalness ... and intelligence. And he's definitely an academic. And like definitely he's well-bred, high society. He is not the caricature of a serial killer. He is your uncle or your neighbor, yet he can do these horrifying things. And the actions of men I find are scarier because they are more realistic. Like this could actually happen. Then with Freddie Krueger, I'm not really scared that Freddy's going to come after me. I don't have any fear of that. Do I have a fear that a man in a business suit can pull out a knife and cut me up into little pieces? Yeah, that's more probable to me than Freddie. Because it was scarier to me to know that it could be my nice, white Anglo-Saxon neighbor, who can be like this terrifying human being or monster. You don't have to define it as Freddie Krueger versus Norman Bates. Like they're both monsters. Just one has the physical outward monster appearance. Where Norman Bates is all inner.

Here Audrey mirrors many of the participants' feelings concerning the fear of more human monsters, monsters, as Audrey says "not in a physical sense. You have a perfectly normal looking man or woman who is a monster psychologically and takes their monstrous rage out on a person." These types of monsters were more frightening because they were more "realistic," hence more believable, than a supernatural monster like Freddy Krueger. What makes this type of monster even more terrifying, for Audrey, is its unseen quality, the fact that their normal exterior provides invisibility; Audrey combines the realism of psychopathic monsters with their ability to blend in, to be the "white Anglo-Saxon neighbor." This lack of an exterior appearance of monstrousness exemplified by monsters such as Norman Bates, Francis Dolarhyde or Wild Bill, as opposed to the visible monstrosity of Freddy Kreuger, presents the paranoid possibility that anyone now can be a monster underneath their seemingly normal exterior. With the introduction of Norman Bates, as Audrey points out, Hitchcock gave audiences a different kind of monster, different in several ways: a monster that was not exotic or supernatural but a monster that concealed his monstrousness beneath a veneer of normality.

It could be mentioned here that Norman Bates is not external to American life but is part of the regular patterns and behaviors that typify it. With *Psycho* (1960) the events of horror and the existence of monsters is now a product of the American way of life. Compare Norman to the monsters of the classic horror films (e.g. Dracula), who diverge from us, not only in their "abnormality," in their exoticness, but also in their difference from the prescribed patterns of American life. We recognize these monsters not only for their perversity and malformation, but also for not being from around here. With their foreign accents and connections to faraway lands, the classic horror film monsters are really outsiders. The narratives of these classic horror films frequently end with the vanquishing of the exotic monster and the ideological strengthening of the borders of normality within our nation and our psyches. As Audrey recognizes, normal life is no longer disrupted by a force external to it; according to Hitchcock and other horror directors, horror comes from within the bounds of normality itself.

Here Audrey echoes David Tudor's (1989) historical distinction between "secure and paranoid" periods in horror films. Tudor saw the sixties and *Psycho* as inaugurating this change, as a watershed period in the history of horror films. Tudor specifically identifies an overall trend where horror films move from expressing a general "security" to a more "paranoid" sensibility. For Tudor the secure world of the pre-sixties horror film where monsters were vanquished, official authority legitimated and the threatened social order reestablished was left for a post-sixties paranoid world where monsters were seldom conquered, people were left on their own, and disruption was unending.

Conclusion

It would seem from this discussion on verisimilitude that watching horror films and being frightened by them has much to do with experiences of belief both in the cinematic sense of "suspension of disbelief" and in the religious connotation of religious belief. The notion of belief is often cited in reference to the viewing of fictional films and the occurrence in the audience of a "suspension of disbelief," a psychological state within the audience that (supposedly) explains their reacting to known fictions *as if* the fictions were real. However this notion of the belief in fictions resting on a suspension of disbelief does not fully explain what my participants seemed to be saying. Despite the realization that horror films were emotional simulations different from real traumas there was among some of the participants a belief in certain aspects of certain kinds of horror. With participants like Linda and Audrey there was more of, as Crane describes it, a "manufacture of particular kinds of belief" (1994, 47). For horror fans it is not so much a matter of disavowing their sense of reality as much as it is activating different discourses of belief in behalf of a horror film's reality that has as much plausibility as reports of serial killers and demonic possession. The horror film does not exist isolated from reality so that fans are continually struggling against a compelling sense of unreality but rather the horror genre as a discourse exists along side, even interwoven, into different discursive realities. It takes little effort for horror fans to "manufacture" belief in the reality of certain subgenres of horror when the factual discourse of news and the genuine discourse of religious belief support and reflect terrifying stories of serial killers, priests and demons.

This similarity, as illustrated by Karen and Linda, between horror fandom and membership in the Catholic Church seem to be, one some level, based on a "nomadic wandering" through discursive communities in which the participants "poach" and overlay similar iconographies, narratives and emotions from one discursive community to the other. The striking interconnectedness between religion and horror with these participants reveals a compelling condition of modern horror films in general; the genre of horror, rather than being a disreputable, marginalized genre sectioned off to a limited area of culture, is a powerful popular discourse that reaches out and intersects with all manner of popular cultural discourses such as the religion and news.

The findings in this research can be compared to other reflections on generic and social verisimilitude such as statements by Steven Neale in his essay *Questions of Genre*. Here Neale discusses the relation of generic and social verisimilitude:

> Fifth, and finally, it is often the generically verisimilitudinous ingredients of a film, those elements that are often least compatible with regimes of cultural verisimilitude — singing and dancing in the musical, the appearance of the monster in the horror film — that constitute its pleasure and thus attract audiences to the film in the first place [162].

What Neale is saying here is that the pleasure of fantastic genres derives from their transgression of cultural verisimilitude and although I would agree with Neale's point, his statement fails to recognize how my participants were connecting generic and cultural discourses in their construction of verisimilitude and how they gained pleasures from the construction of cultural verisimilitude in the possession film. It was not the incompatibility of the possession film with cultural verisimilitude but its compatibility with the reality of religious discourse. For Linda and Karen what constituted verisimilitude and pleasure was not an incompatibility with unrealistic cultural discourses or verisimilitude but the relevance of Catholicism as a believable (and in this sense realistic) discourse.

From the viewpoint of methodology this discrepancy between my participants conception of verisimilitude and Neale's concept illustrates the advantages of qualitative research and how it brings to light experiences and examples not always envisioned in purely theoretical formulations.

Notes

1. The data this paper is based on was taken from a larger study where extended open-ended interviews were utilized with six participants. I collected roughly six hours of interviews with each participant over a period of about two months from January to February of 2003. I worked from a standard list of questions but always allowed for the participants to introduce new topics and lines of inquiry into the interviews. My participants were all self-identified horror fans and a preliminary interview was conducted to ascertain the level of interest in the horror genre. So, for example, all of the participants on a short survey marked horror films as their favorite genre. Their involvement in the horror genre played out in the actual interviews through their extensive insider knowledge of horror films and television, their viewing practices and other fan behaviors. All participants were drawn from the college student population of New York City and ranged in ages from 18 to 25. There were two males and four females. Five were Caucasian and one female participant identified herself as Haitian-American. All identified themselves as middle class. The participant's names have been changed to maintain confidentiality.

The participants in this paper are:

Ashley (female) at the time of the interviews was eighteen years old and a first-year college student in a large private university located in a large northeastern city. She was white and considered her family to be middle class and her parents were married. She designated her religious preference as "none."

Karen (female) at the time of the interviews was twenty-five years old and a junior in a private university in a large northeastern city. She designated her race as white. Her family's current marital status was married and she considered herself to be middle class. Under religion she listed "other" and specified "pagan" although she was raised Catholic.

Linda (female) was eighteen years old. She was a first-year college student at a large private university located in a large northeastern city. She was the only participant of color and designated her race/ethnicity as Haitian-American. She identified her family as middle class and the marital status of her parents as married. Her religious preference was Catholic and she indicated in the interviews that she was still active in the Catholic Church.

Audrey (female) was twenty-one years old at the time of the interviews. She was a senior in a large private university located in a large northeastern city. She described herself as white. Her family is middle class and the marital status of her mother is single. Under religious preference Audrey stated that she was raised Catholic and is currently undecided.

Works Cited

Crane, Jonathan. *Terror and Everyday Life: Singular Moments in the History of the Horror Film*. Thousand Oaks, CA: Sage Publications, 1993.

The Exorcist. Dir. William Friedkin. Perf. Linda Blair, Ellen Burstyn, Max von Sydow, Jason Miller. Warner Bros, 1973. Film.

Fiske, John. "Critical Response: Meaningful Moments." *Critical Studies in Mass Communication* 5 (1988): 246–251.

Halloween. Dir. John Carpenter. Perf. Jamie Lee Curtis, Donald Pleasance, Tony Moran. Trancas International Films, 1978. Film.

Lost Souls. Dir. Janusz Kaminski. Perf. Winona Ryder, Ben Chaplin, Sarah Wynter. Castle Rock Entertainment, 2000. Film.

Neale, Steven. "Questions of Genre." *Film Genre Reader II*. Ed. Barry Keith Grant. 2nd ed. Austin: University of Texas Press, 1995. 159–183.

The Omen. Dir. Richard Donner. Perf. Gregory Peck, Lee Remick, David Warner. Twentieth Century–Fox, 1976. Film.

Pinedo, Isabel. *Recreational Terror: Women and the Pleasures of Horror Film Viewing*. Albany, NY: State University of New York Press, 1997.

Psycho. Dir. Alfred Hitchcock. Perf. Janet Leigh, Anthony Perkins, Martin Balsam. Shamley Productions, 1960. Film.

Stigmata. Dir. Rupert Wainwright. Perf. Patricia Arquette, Gabriel Byrne, Jonathan Pryce. Metro Goldwyn Mayer, 1999. Film.

Tamborini, Ron, and James B. Weaver. "Frightening Entertainment: A Historical Perspective of Fictional Horror." Eds. J. B. Weaver and R. Tamborini. *Horror Films: Current Research on Audience Preferences and Reactions*. Mahwah, NJ: Lawrence Erlbaum, 1996. 15–32.

Todorov, Tzvetan. *Introduction to Poetics*. Minneapolis: University of Minnesota Press, 1981.

Tudor, Andrew. *Monsters and Mad Scientists: A Cultural History of the Horror Movie*. Oxford, UK: Basil Blackwell, 1989.

"The Power of Christ Compels You"
Moral Spectacle and The Exorcist *Universe*

ALEXANDRA HELLER-NICHOLAS

On November 15, 1972 — shortly before the ten-year anniversary of his papacy — Pope Paul VI delivered a speech called "Confronting the Devil's Power," where he warned of the tangible reality of the Devil in the contemporary world. For Vittorio Messori, the shockwaves this speech triggered outside the Church demonstrated that "no other topic unleashes such a storm of indignation among the mass-media of secularized society as that of the 'devil.'"[1] The reasons for this storm appear self-explanatory: this General Address was feared to confirm secular suspicions that the Catholic Church was entrenched in archaic folklore, rather than offering a dynamic spirituality suited to the demands of the twentieth century. Despite the more progressive aspects of his papacy — such as his anti–Vietnam War speech to the United Nations in 1965, the modernization of various aspects of the church through Vatican II, and a dedication to internationalizing the Church that garnered him the title "The Pilgrim Pope" — Paul VI's talk of the Devil was feared to present a pontiff giddy on superstition, rather than one in touch with the pressures of contemporary life. The Vatican's website claims Paul VI suffered from "unaccountably poor press,"[2] and this may be one of the reasons: that his official biography does not mention any of his famous declarations regarding the Devil suggests there may remain some discomfort regarding this particular issue.

The relation of this speech to William Friedkin's blockbuster *The Exorcist*

(1973) has not been overlooked. Mark Kermode, David Bartholomew, and Howard Newman all acknowledge its importance, and both Kermode and Bartholomew quote this same excerpt:

> Evil is not merely a lack of something, but an effective agent, a living spiritual being, perverted and perverting. A terrible reality... So we know that this dark and disturbing spirit really exists and that he still acts with treacherous cunning; he is the secret enemy that sows errors and misfortunes in human history. The question of the Devil, and the influence he can exert on individual persons as well as communities ... is a very important chapter of Catholic doctrine which is given little attention today, though it should be studied again.[3]

Paul VI's declarations concerning the Devil pertain to "the mystery of evil": if, as he states, "the Christian vision of the universe and of life is ... triumphantly optimistic," then

> Are the defects in the world of no account? What of the things that don't work properly in our lives? What of suffering and death, wickedness, cruelty and sin ... what of evil? Don't we see how much evil there is in the world — especially moral evil, which goes against man and against God at one and the same time, although in different ways? Isn't this a sad spectacle, an unexplainable mystery?[4]

But, he continues, the Devil is much more than merely a "sad spectacle": so great was the need for an investigation into this terrain that he added it "is a very important chapter of Catholic doctrine which should be studied again... Some think a sufficient compensation can be found in psychoanalytic and psychiatric studies or in spiritualistic experiences, which are unfortunately so widespread in some countries today."[5]

The phrase "sad spectacle" provides a conceptual launch pad into this chapter's analysis of what will be referred to as *The Exorcist* universe. Rather than viewing the films that construct *The Exorcist* franchise through the polarized assumptions of official/unofficial or original/copy, it is fruitful to reconfigure critical perception to encompass a holistic textual "universe," where the nuance and variations amongst the shared tropes, themes and iconography are evaluated outside of the orthodox parameters of taste. In practical terms, this exposes filmic artifacts that have traditionally fallen outside the critical scope of so-called "legitimate" scholarship to critical consideration. Exploitation "rip-offs" of *The Exorcist*— such as *Şeytan* (Metin Erksan, 1974) and *Un urlo nelle tenebre (Exorcist III: Cries and Shadows*, Elo Pannacciò, 1975) — rarely appear amongst the many treatments of *The Exorcist* phenomenon that exist, so the significance of how they merge and deviate from Friedkin's film have gone largely unremarked. This chapter strips away the highbrow/lowbrow distinctions that have traditionally quarantined the "trashier" additions to *The Exorcist* universe in order to examine moral spectacle.

Moral spectacle manifests at the intersection of history, sensation and a text's conscious or unconscious moral message. The phenomenon of the spectacle has a privileged position in Roman Catholic faith, as it hinges upon a belief in the unseeable: this is evident in the often grand spectacle of the Mass itself, or as it pertains to Paul's first epistle to the Corinthians; "For I think that God hath set forth us apostles last, as it were appointed to death: for we are made a spectacle unto the world, and to angels, and to men" (4:9). It is through a profoundly *moral* spectacle (but one that depends also upon history and sensation) that *The Exorcist* universe attempts to make tangible that which is associated with a spiritual realm. Just as Paul VI's speech encourages a concrete investigation into the material reality of the Devil in the modern world, the moral spectacle active within *The Exorcist* universe — in all the hyperactive and visceral theatricality that appears in both high and lowbrow manifestations of the trope — is presented as not merely "sad," but as intense and often contradictory.

Spectacle has its own history as a secular phenomenon, and as such the moral spectacle of Roman Catholicism in *The Exorcist* universe can be seen to function in two parallel yet overlapping ways. Many rituals of Roman Catholic faith such as the Eucharist and confession, can be understood as spectacular ethical gestures, the performances of which in part defines the practice of "being" Catholic. But at the same time, Roman Catholic rituals (in exorcism films, at least) are strong ethical signs in the broader non–Catholic cultural imagination that symbolize a less theological and more melodramatic notion of "good" (one defined by its direct opposition to "evil"). Roman Catholicism cannot claim sole ownership of this binary, and the dynamism of *The Exorcist* trope lies in the simultaneous ability of its representation of "evil" to function as a powerful moral signifier in both Christian (religious) *and* secular (melodramatic) contexts. At stake in both manifestations of Roman Catholicism as moral spectacle across these films is the very mechanics of religious ritual itself: it is an ethical apparatus that propels narrative, thematic and even stylistic components. This, more than any other feature, is what has rendered *The Exorcist* trope so enduring, permitting its expansion to cultural contexts beyond Christianity.

The Exorcist *Universe: History, Sensation, and the "Moral Occult"*

The films that construct *The Exorcist* universe range in scope from the mainstream to the paracinematic, the explicit to the poetic, and from the older to the contemporary. But as demonstrated in the unauthorized exploitation titles in particular, *The Exorcist's* apparent dualisms are rich in complexity. Based upon the 1971 novel of the same name by Catholic author William Peter Blatty, the success of the original blockbuster spawned a range of sequels and prequels that construct a complex and at times contradictory universe. These films include *The Exorcist II: The Heretic* (John Boorman, 1977), *The Exorcist III* (William Peter Blatty, 1990), *The Ninth Configuration* (William Peter Blatty, 1978), *Exorcist: The Beginning* (Renny Harlin, 2004) and *Dominion: Prequel to the Exorcist* (Paul Schrader, 2005). Of lesser repute are the unauthorized low-budget imitators that sought to profit on Friedkin's success, such as the exploitation films *Abby* (William Girdler, 1974), *Cathy's Curse* (Eddy Matalon, 1977), *Un urlo nelle tenebre* (*Exorcist III: Cries and Shadows*, Elo Pannacciò, 1975), *Exorcismo* (Juan Bosch, 1975), *L'Ossessa* (*The Sexorcist, The Eerie Midnight Horror Show*, Mario Gariazzo, 1974), *Magdalena: Possessed by the Devil* (Walter Boos, 1974), *L'Anticristo* (*The Tempter*, Alberto De Martino, 1974), *Chi Sei?* (*Beyond the Door*, Ovido G. Assonitis, 1974), and *Şeytan* (Metin Erksan, 1974).

Although *The Exorcist* was one of the most defining Hollywood blockbusters of the 1970s, its origins were personal. Jesuit-educated Blatty found in the story of the real-life exorcism of a 14-year-old boy from Maryland in 1949 the validation of his own Catholic faith after his mother's death.[6] Regardless of whether this early event was a genuine supernatural phenomenon or something with a more scientific explanation, its impact on Blatty was substantial. Although the novel had originally been intended as a factual account of the Maryland exorcism, Blatty turned his project towards fiction when the boy's family refused to assist with his project.[7] But these documentary origins impacted both Blatty and Friedkin tonally, and much attention has been lavished upon Friedkin's vigilante-style directorial techniques that included assaulting actors to garner authentic reactions. These histrionics were not restricted to the film's production, and rumors circulated that some screenings provoked fits of vomiting, fainting, and crying, and even suicides, murders and miscarriages.[8] Evangelist Dr Billy Graham publicly declared this was because "evil was embedded in the celluloid of the film itself,"[9] but such controversy merely inflamed public interest even further. Friedkin recognized this, and actively encouraged rumors about an *Exorcist* "curse." The death of family of key cast members, injuries, fires, and "mystery" illnesses were all strongly rumored to be the result of supernatural intervention in the film's production.[10]

For critics like Colleen McDannell, it is impossible to view *The Exorcist* as anything but a Roman Catholic movie, and both she[11] and Andrew Sarris[12] identify it as specifically Jesuit in both content and themes. But this is certainly not the only path of critical investigation that has been pursued. For others, much of the film's impact is claimed to lie in its poignant encapsulation of its zeitgeist, claiming it captured the volatile and paranoid socio-political state of the United States in a nation dominated with news of Charles Manson, Altamont, the Vietnam War and Watergate.[13] For Kendall R. Philips, the tensions within *The Exorcist* also reflected more intimate concerns of those living in a decade which saw a radical shift in family life: the increase of divorce paralleled a drop in birth rates, and the post-hippie generation carried into their adult lives a deep mistrust of traditional values.[14] The paradox and power of *The Exorcist* from this historical perspective is its utilization of confusion to create hope. That this hope was coded as Roman Catholic yet still held secular appeal is one of the primary areas of interest in this chapter.

The tension between opposing forces typifies many critical approaches to *The Exorcist*. Bob McCabe pegs the film's success on its contrast of "the real and the unfathomable,"[15] while for Andrew Sarris, there are a range of significant binaries that include the rational and irrational, modernism and medievalism, and science and religion.[16] Mark Kermode suggests *The Exorcist* includes significant tensions between the modern with the archaic, the regressive and the progressive and the "divine and the apparent."[17] Good and evil also provoke popular interpretations, and these translate into the film's stylistic contrasts of dark/light, black/white and noise/silence. Fittingly, film reviews were themselves often polarized. What Vincent Canby rejected as "a chunk of elegant occultist claptrap,"[18] Stanley Kauffman celebrated as a genre *tour de force*.[19] It was not only critics who held opposing views: while the film was both praised and criticized by Christian groups in the United States, the Tunisian government banned it for being biased towards Christianity.[20] Even the numerous sequels and prequels suggest similar oppositions: there are two competing versions of the original film itself, Friedkin's 1973 version and a version released in 2000 as *The Exorcist: The Version You've Never Seen*. There are two sequels, John Boorman's critically lambasted *The Exorcist II: Heretic*, and Blatty's own directorial addition to the series, *Exorcist III* (based on his novel *Legion*).[21] Even recently, there were competing prequels: Paul Schraeder's *Dominion: Prequel to the Exorcist* and Renny Harland's *Exorcist: The Beginning*.[22]

The global success of *The Exorcist* demonstrates that its drama of polarized good and evil appealed to Christians as well as non–Christians. The binaries that construct the moral framework of good versus evil as mentioned in Paul VI's famous speech (understood as God versus the Devil) are compatible with the same ethical framework as melodrama. Peter Brooks writes in his seminal book *The Melodramatic Imagination: Balzac, Henry James, and the Mode of Excess* (1976) of its eponymous vision of a world "subsumed by an underlying Manichaeism ... putting us in contact with the conflict of good and evil played out under the surface of things."[23] Melodrama's dependence upon easily identifiable characterizations is defined along a clear moral trajectory between good and evil. This is symptomatic of its semiotic nature, and Brooks' notion of a symbolic melodramatic "language" finds a distinct symbolic parallel in *The Exorcist*'s possessions and exorcisms: "melodramatic good and evil are highly personalized: they are assigned to, they inhabit persons who indeed have no psychological complexity but are strongly characterized."[24] Like the exorcism, "the ritual of melodrama involves the confrontation of clearly defined antagonists and the expulsion of one of them."[25]

Central to Brooks' work is the notion of the moral occult, "the hidden yet operative domain of values that the drama ... attempts to make present within the ordinary."[26] The moral occult is the central feature of melodrama, as it "strives to find, to articulate, to demonstrate, to 'prove' the existence of a moral universe which, though put into question, masked by villainy and perversions of judgment, does exist and can be made to assert its presence and its categorical force among men."[27] Melodrama's dramatic play of moral signs is therefore a dual strategy of occlusion and revelation, its defining excesses constructing a spectacular narrative Trojan horse with ethical content hidden within. That melodrama appears to replicate Christian ethical structures on a secular level is no coincidence: for Brooks, the French Revolution established a vital shift for the popular ethical consciousness, whose faith in God and the King had been so brutally shaken by the brutal political realities of the time. Melodrama thus "comes into being in a world where the traditional imperatives of truth and ethics have been violently thrown into question, yet where the promulgation of truth and ethics, their instauration as a way of life, is of immediate, daily, political concern."[28] Propelled by the violent force of the Revolution, ethics were suddenly in the domain of the secular, rather than its traditional sphere of the royal and religious. It is in this context that melodrama flourished, with Brooks suggesting "we may legitimately claim that melodrama becomes the principal mode for uncovering, demonstrating, and making operative the essential moral universe in a post-sacred era."[29]

In this sense, melodrama can be considered less a genre than a tendency of contemporary storytelling. Christine Gledhill suggests that melodrama is a "genre-producing machine,"[30] "an organizing modality of the genre system (that) works at Western culture's most sensitive cultural and aesthetic boundaries, embodying class, gender, and ethnicity in a process of imaginary identification, differentiation, contact, and opposition."[31] Consequently, horror films like *The Exorcist* may be understood in relation to melodrama even if they are not "melodramas" *per se*.[32] Both Tom Gunning and Adam Lowenstein refer to horror directly in their discussions of the moral occult. Gunning's essay "The Horror of Opacity: The Melodrama of Sensation in the Plays of Andre de Lorde" (1994) argues that the historical specificity of Brooks' analysis does not take into account the significance of later technological advancements (both on stage, and later in the cinema) that he claims "bring other aspects of the melodramatic tradition to the foreground."[33] These technological aspects, he argues, give rise to a second, equally important feature of melodrama: sensation or thrill. This experience is a direct result of horror's spectacular excess, and is therefore as much a feature of melodrama as the moral occult itself, from the Grand-Guignol theatre to horror films of the 1970s and 1980s.[34]

History is also of concern to Adam Lowenstein in *Shocking Representation: Historical Trauma, National Cinema, and the Modern Horror Film* (2005). He considers history as vital to melodramatic constructs as sensation and the moral occult themselves. Responding to both Brooks and Gunning, Lowenstein contends that any moral or physical aspects are inseparable from a given texts historical context. For Lowenstein, "the horror of this spectacle, rather than being a dramatic dead end terminating only in sensation, returns personal and political audience affect to a traumatic public event — the kind of event subjected to widespread exposure that threatens to overwhelm any meaningful response."[35] He therefore identifies horror as a "return to history through the gut."[36] With its excessive depictions of neon green vomit, spider-walking and head-spinning, moral spectacle in *The Exorcist* is not only a return to history through the gut, but also to the intersection of Roman Catholicism and melodrama. In the broader *Exorcist* universe, the language of melodrama allows moral spectacle to function beyond a purely theological context, even when that spectacle is constructed explicitly through Roman Catholic iconography. This moral spectacle occurs at the very moment of horrific avowal, where that which has been equally feared, dreaded, promised and eagerly awaited manifests on screen. As shall now be explored further, it is sometimes the least reputable or credible exploitation "knock-offs" that expose the complexity of moral spectacle in *The Exorcist* universe.

Beyond East and West

Many exploitation filmmakers, exhibitors and distributors were more than willing to profit on the success of *The Exorcist*. In some instances, this intent was made clear through the titles (or re-titles) of films alone, such as in *Exorcismo*, *The Sexorcist* and *Exorcist III: Cries and Shadows*. But to quarantine these films *en masse* from the so-called mainstream *Exorcist* sequels and prequels is not easy, complicated by the fact that at the time of the film's release, there were critics who claimed Friedkin's 1973 film was *itself* an exploitation film.[37] The exploitation films inspired by *The Exorcist*, however, escape this valorization, and instead demonstrate a clear instance of what Matt Hills has called "para-paracinema."[38] Jeffrey Sconce coined the term "paracinema" in his seminal essay "Trashing the Academy: Taste, Excess, and an Emerging Politics of Cinematic Style" (1995)[39] to refer the site of cinematic interest to an exploitation and cult film audience whom consider themselves as opposed to mainstream film tastes. But for Hills, rather than a binary division, paracinema itself can be broken down further between valorized cult and exploitation films, and those that have been ignored both critically and by paracinematic audiences. His examples include the multiple proliferations of sequels that haunt the slasher subgenre — so while the first in this notoriously sequel-happy subgenre are often celebrated, the seemingly infinite sequels have not been allocated the same value. What may at first appear to be a clear binary opposition between authorized/unauthorized collapses when looking at *The Exorcist*'s progeny from this perspective. Consequently, such tenuous boundaries can be (at least temporarily) removed to establish fresh insight into *The Exorcist* universe, and the function of moral spectacle within it.

Şeytan vividly demonstrates the strength of this approach. One of the most ideologically explosive criticisms rallied against *The Exorcist* centers on its characterization of the demon as Middle Eastern. For Tim Jon Semmerling, the demon typifies his delineation of the 'evil' Arab figure,[40] while the film itself is an "Orientalist-imagined struggle between an Eastern bogeyman (the Arab demon) and the Western hero (the exorcist), turned upside down."[41] Semmerling paints an evocative picture of the events that constructed the Western (American) vision of this region at the time of the film's release: the joint Syrian and Egyptian surprise attack on Israel, Palestinian terrorism in Europe, oil embargos against the west and a public demand by Libya for "pan–Arabism": "The American public had been primed to believe that the Arabs were rising up from their 'dusty and dingy' capitals, infiltrating the security of American lives, and demanding to be treated with 'deadly seriousness.'"[42]

The Exorcist was not released in Turkey until 1982, and continuing a growing trend in that country to produce cheap, unauthorized imitations of international blockbusters to profit locally on the global hype, producer Hulki

Saner employed award-winning director Metin Erksan for his remake of *The Exorcist*. Although Erksan had won a Golden Bear at the Berlin Film Festival in 1964 for *Susuz yaz*, few would warrant *Şeytan* as deserving similar recognition. But it is precisely the film's low production values that have made it a source of interest for cult audiences internationally as a "so-bad-it's-good" trash artifact. Regardless of its artistic merits, *Şeytan* typifies what Laurence Raw defines as one of the driving concerns of Turkish national cinema: "Since its inception, the Turkish film industry has focused on the struggles — whether social, personal or political — experienced by people caught between two cultures, European and Islamic."[43] On one hand, while Turkey has spent more than fifty years attempting to join the European Union, it is impeded by its status as "Islamic Other." At the same time, the Turkish Republic "has been reluctant to consider itself a part of the Middle East, even though it shares its religion with neighbouring countries such as Iraq and Egypt."[44]

In his excellent treatment of *Şeytan*, Ian Robert Smith captures Turkey's unique position in relation to the East-meets-West foundations of *The Exorcist*: "Turkey is *both* Muslim and secular, a country that is *both* European and Asian."[45] So while much critical discourse surrounding *The Exorcist* focuses on binary oppositions, *Şeytan* is culturally positioned to show just how tenuous these distinctions are. Özkaracalar's observation that "the plot of *The Exorcist* actually fits very well and makes perfect sense in a Turkish setting"[46] cannot be underappreciated, and in many senses the film appears to mimic Blatty's original book more closely in its determination to make the line between priest and professional far less distinct. Father Karras is replaced by a secular psychologist, Tugrul, who has written a book called "Şeytan": as the Turkish word for "Satan" it is no coincidence that this is the same name as a volume that Karras refers to in Blatty's book that is eradicated completely from Friedkin's adaptation. And as Ian Robert Smith points out, that *Şeytan* finishes with the possessed girl visiting a mosque is less ambiguous in terms of Blatty's original spiritual message than Friedkin's adaptation.

There is no denying that *Şeytan*'s reduction of Friedkin's carefully constructed vignettes to ones replicated with less care, money and consideration for narrative logic are pleasurable on an ironic level. But — perhaps inadvertently — its deviations allow great insight into the cultural assumptions built into Friedkin's film. In the film's notorious "crucifix masturbation" sequence, Gul (the Regan MacNeil character, played by Canan Perver) uses a paper knife with the head of the demon Jinn instead of a cross. This is a crucial deviation from the Blatty/Friedkin universe: as Semmerling rightly points out, the scene with Regan is not "masturbation" at all, as it is the demon Pazuzu who forces her to do it, thus characterizing the attack as a sexual assault rather than masturbation as such.[47] By raping her "with" Jesus, the demon shows its dominance over both Christian symbolism and Regan's body. But if the demon attacks her with a symbol *of itself* as he does in *Şeytan*, the symbolic nature of the assault changes fundamentally: it is less an attack on Christian iconography, and more explicitly one aimed with the sole intent of violating the young girl's body by the demon. The scene therefore becomes solely about control over Gul's body. So while Merrin in *The Exorcist* hurries to explain to Karras that the reason the demon chose to possess Regan was to get at them, in *Şeytan*, the torture of Gul suggests that she alone is the demon's intended victim. However, despite the crucial theological change in this symbol and the meanings inherent in that exchange, the intended visceral response is effectively the same. This suggests that it is more the action itself that is the issue (the demon's sexual violation of the young girl), rather than the power granted to any particular symbol. The rape of the girl is what is shocking: the symbolism utilized in this attack is second to the intensity of the act itself.

The so-called "Turkish Exorcist" may not revolutionize understanding of the better-known original, but it is uniquely positioned to expose the mechanics behind culturally specific assumptions that American and British critics in particular have held as fundamental to their analysis of Friedkin's film. If *Şeytan* is contextually marked at one end of the spectrum by Turkey's particular blend of supposedly "Eastern" and "Western" cultural and theological signs, then the Italian exploitation film *Un urlo nelle tenebre* and its references to the Vatican may be claimed to be far closer to the original book's roots in Roman Catholicism. It is in their extremes that these two films unite to illustrate just how concretely moral spectacle across *The Exorcist* universe manifests.

Trashing the Vatican

Like *Şeytan*, *Un urlo nelle tenebre* was another *Exorcist* clone clearly willing to exploit Friedkin's success. *Un urlo nelle tenebre* was released under a variety of names with little to do with its literal translation of "A Roar in the Darkness": *Naked Exorcism, The Return of the Exorcist,* and *The Exorcist III: Cries and Shadows*. *Un urlo nelle tenebre* lacks the notoriety of fellow Italian *Exorcist* rip-offs *L'Anticristo* and *Chi Sei?*, and with its combination of horror and nunsploitation, of the three it is arguably the least coherent narratively. As Tamao Nakahara explains, Italian films dealing with such exploitative and explicit religious content at this period were in part a result of the cultural changes that resulted from Vatican II, in which Pope Paul VI had played such a central role. A focus on "freedom of expression had an effect on films that toyed with religious subject matter. Although scandalous films continued to be heavily censored or confiscated in Italy, filmmakers and writers could criticize the censors more openly during the 1960s. By the 1970s, although government censorship was still in place, the church could rarely muster the influence to interfere with film releases."[48]

In this context, it is perhaps unsurprising that Italian *Exorcist* films such as *L'Anticristo* and *Un urlo nelle tenebre* were so eager to incorporate contemporary issues within the Church much more explicitly than their foreign counterparts. The plot of *Un urlo nelle tenebre* is straightforward enough: teenager Piero (Jean-Claude Verne) photographs a strange woman (Mimma Monticelli) who, through a cursed amulet, causes him to become possessed. It is up to his nun sister Elina (Patricia Gori) and an exorcist (Richard Conte) to save the boy's soul. Combining orgiastic black masses with scenes of the possessed boy's destruction, *Un urlo nelle tenebre* could be classified as unremarkable if it were not for its opening sequence.

The film begins simply with the sound of a crowd: there is no music, giving it a deliberately documentary-like tone. People are shot in medium close up with a shallow depth of field to create a busy blur of activity, while also establishing a sense of intimacy and immediacy. A crowd gathers, and their attention is turned in one direction. There is the sound of chatter as the crowd grows, and this group consists of a broad demographic: black people and white people, the elderly, families, single men and women, children, soldiers, adolescents, nuns, and even businessmen. Some look at the camera, but most do not as it wanders (via hand held camera) through the crowd. Enough of the location is shown to be able to identify the fountain in St. Peter's Square in the Vatican. There is a male voiceover, but the speaker is never shown. He says:

> Beloved brothers, it is with a heavy heart that we address our ways today. In these sad tormented times tempests of horror and violence seem to be breaking over the world. The deadly breath ... [breaches] the very foundations of our faith, vanishing from your hearts the sweetness ... extinguishing in us the pure flame of love. But do not fall prey to doubts and in servitude, hold fast. The devil ... will never break the citadel of the church. Blinded by pride, some would try to convince us that the devil does not exist, that he is nothing but an abstract idea. Such ideas are folly. Brothers, today more than ever Satan is present and active in the world [*Un urlo nelle tenebre*].

As the speech continues, footage of the possessed Piero tied to his bed (one that replicates very closely that of Regan MacNeill) is intercut with shots of the listening crowd.

Associations between this opening speech in Saint Peter's Square and Paul VI's famous General Audience are clear. The deliberateness of the filmmakers to create a sense of verisimilitude in these opening moments is also apparent: the absence of non-diegetic music, but more crucially is the decision to not show who is delivering the speech. Without seeing an actor, but being able to readily identify parallels between Paul VI and the speech within the film, there is a conscious suggestion that the issue in question (that the Devil is real) is one that is both a contemporary issue within the Church at this period, and that the story of Piero that follows is therefore responding to this issue. There can be little debate that the film is eager to exploit the topicality of Paul VI's speech and the international success of *The Exorcist*. At the same time, rather than Friedkin's deliberate attempt to separate himself from the very real theological issues in Blatty's novel, *Un urlo nelle tenebre* is far more comfortable in its refusal to see exploitation and theology as mutually exclusive. *Un urlo nelle tenebre*'s explicit reference to Paul VI's controversial speech again demonstrates how exploitation films can expose the centrality of moral spectacle across *The Exorcist* universe. While the trash remakes may offer different pleasures than its more reputable counterparts, films such as *Un urlo nelle tenebre* and *Şeytan* offer significant sources of insight into how crucial aspects of sensation, history and morality combine to create moral spectacle through the lens of religion.

It is through moral spectacle that the films that construct *The Exorcist* universe present evil as a tangible, visible and visceral phenomenon. Despite its perverse nuns and its orgiastic black masses, *Un urlo nelle tenebre*'s attempts to turn papal preaching into some kind of (albeit crude) material practice. The significant inclusion of the non–Catholic *Şeytan* to *The Exorcist* universe demonstrates how moral spectacle can even transcend the specificity of Roman Catholicism, and thus expose its moral apparatus as one that fulfils a secular, melodramatic logic as much as it tells a purely Roman Catholic story. The moral spectacle of Roman Catholicism in *The Exorcist* universe may merely appear to exploit Roman Catholicism for nothing but commercial reasons. But in the spirit of Blatty's original project, it may also be possible to glean something more sophisticated — both ethically and critically — from even these trashiest of films, "by honor and dishonor, by evil report and good report: as deceivers, and yet true" (2 Corinthians 6:8).

Notes

1. Joseph Cardinal (Pope Benedict XVI) Ratzinger with Vittorio Messori, *The Ratzinger Report: An Exclusive Interview on the State of the Church* (San Francisco: Ignatius Press, 1985), 135.

2. See: "Pope Paul VI 1963–1978 Official Biography," Vatican website, 20 December 2009, http://www.vatican.va/holy_father/paul_vi/biography/documents/hf_p-vi_bio_16071997_biography_en.html.
3. David Bartholomew. "*The Exorcist*: The Book, The Movie, The Phenomenon." *Cinefantastique* 3:4 (Autumn 1974), 163; Mark Kermode. *The Exorcist*, Revised 2nd Edition (London: BFI, 2003), 8.
4. "Confronting the Devil's Power," Address of Pope Paul VI to a General Audience, November 15, 1972, *Papal Encyclicals Online*, accessed 20 December 2009, <http://www.papalencyclicals.net/Paul06/p6devil.htm>.
5. Ibid.
6. Les Keyser, and Barbara Keyser. *Hollywood and the Catholic Church: The Image of Roman Catholicism in American Movies* (Chicago: Loyola University Press, 1984), 197.
7. Bob McCabe. *The Exorcist: Out of the Shadows* (London: Omnibus Press, 1999), 20.
8. McDannell, 202.
9. Ibid.
10. McCabe, 148.
11. The centrality of Jesuit faith is crucial to McDannell's analysis, and it is of note to this analysis that from a Catholic perspective she argues that *The Exorcist* is not "an expression ... of Catholic dualism but rather ... a complicated Jesuit spirituality" (208). Much of her attention is focused on the importance of a secular as well as theological education to the Jesuits. Father Karras' status as a "hyphenated priest" (209) is not unique to *The Exorcist*, but rather the product of a Jesuit education that aimed to produce precisely this model of priest-professional (209). There is little doubt, however, that the distinction between secular/science and religion/faith is far less opaque in Blatty's original novel, where the status of both Karras and Merrin as "priest-professionals" are not only more explicitly established, they also provide crucial aspects to the narrative that are absent in the film version.
12. McDannell, 198–9.
13. Kermode, 8; Kendall R. Phillips. *Projected Fears: Horror Films and American Culture* (Westport, CT: Praeger Publishers, 2005), 108.
14. Phillips, 109.
15. McCabe, 26.
16. Sarris, 155.
17. Kermode, 24, 10.
18. Vincent Canby. "Blatty's *The Exorcist* Comes to the Screen," originally published in the *New York Times*, 1973, reprinted in Peter Travers and Stephanie Reiff, *The Story Behind* The Exorcist (New York: Signet Books, 1974), 150.
19. Stanley Kauffman. Review: *The Exorcist*, originally published in *The New Republic*, 1974, reprinted in Peter Travers and Stephanie Reiff, *The Story Behind* The Exorcist (Signet Books, New York, 1974), 152.
20. Kermode, 86–7.
21. All based on novels he has written, *The Exorcist*, *The Ninth Configuration* (also known by the title *Twinkle, Twinkle Killer Kane*), and *The Exorcist III* construct what has unofficially been tagged as Blatty's "faith" trilogy (McCabe, 170). Blatty also directed the latter two titles.
22. The long-awaited *Exorcist* prequel was initially to be directed by John Frankenheimer, but he was replaced by Paul Schraeder when Frankenheimer became terminally ill. Schraeder was, however, dumped from post-production of *Exorcist:*

The Beginning by Morgan Creek Entertainment (Kermode, "Exorcise Cycle" 10). Renny Harlin was brought into the project, and the film finally released as *Exorcist: The Beginning* in 2004 was his version. But this did not mark the end of Schraeder's involvement in *The Exorcist* universe. He re-edited his original material together and released an alternative prequel as *Dominion: Prequel to The Exorcist*.

23. Peter Brooks. *The Melodramatic Imagination: Balzac, Henry James and the Mode of Excess* (New Haven: Yale University Press, 1995), 4.

24. Brooks, 16.

25. Brooks, 17.

26. Brooks, viii.

27. Brooks, 20.

28. Brooks, 15.

29. Ibid.

30. Christine Gledhill. "Rethinking Genre," *Reinventing Film Studies*, eds. Christine Gledhill and Linda Williams (London: Arnold, 2000), 227.

31. Gledhill, 239.

32. The horror film's reputation as a potential site for subversion in part may stem from its unique ability to establish assumptions about a melodramatic universe with the precise intention of collapsing them. Films like Brian De Palma's *Carrie* (1976) and Wes Craven's *Last House on the Left* (1972) are examples of horror films that establish what appears to be a clear Manichean universe, only to have their shocking conclusions shatter the very foundations upon which it appeared to initially be based.

33. Tom Gunning. "The Horror of Opacity: The Melodrama of Sensation in the Plays of Andre de Lorde," *Melodrama: Stage, Picture, Screen*, ed. J. Cook, J. Bratton and C. Gledhill (London: British Film Institute, 1994), 51.

34. Gunning, 60.

35. Adam Lowenstein. *Shocking Representation: Historical Trauma, National Cinema and the Modern Horror Film* (New York: Columbia University Press, 2005), 47.

36. Lowenstein, 48.

37. Jon Landau describes it as "nothing more than a religious porn film" (see: "The Devil in Mr. Friedkin," originally published in *Rolling Stone Magazine*, 1974, reprinted in Peter Travers and Stephanie Reiff, *The Story Behind* The Exorcist [New York: Signet Books, 1974], 160).

38. Matt Hills. "Para-Paracinema: The *Friday the 13th* Series as Other to Trash and Legitimate Film Cultures," in *Sleaze Artists: Cinema at the Margins of Taste, Style and Politics*, ed. Jeffrey Sconce (Durham: Duke University Press, 2007), 219–239.

39. Jeffrey Sconce. "Trashing the Academy: Taste, Excess, and an Emerging Politics of Cinematic Style," *Screen* 36.4 (1995): 371–91.

40. Tim Jon Semmerling. *"Evil" Arabs in American Popular Film: Orientalist Fear* (Austin: Texas University Press, 2006), 30.

41. Semmerling, 31.

42. Semmerling, 58.

43. Laurence Raw. Review: Gönül Dönmez-Colin, *Turkish Cinema: Identity, Distance and Belonging*; Rekin Teksoy, *Turkish Cinema*. *Screen* 50.3 (Autumn 2009): 362.

44. Raw, 362.

45. Ian Robert Smith, "The Exorcist in Istanbul: Processes of Transcultural Appropriation Within Turkish Popular Cinema," *Portal Journal of Multidiciplinary International Studies* 5.1 (January 2008). 1 July 2010 <http://epress.lib.uts.edu.au/ojs/index.php/portal/article/view/489/584>.

46. Kaya Özkaracalar. "Between Appropriation and Innovation: Turkish Horror Cinema." *Fear Without Frontiers: Horror Cinema Across the Globe* (Gottalming: FAB Press, 2003), 214.

47. "If we accept the rape thesis, then we should reconsider what is commonly referred to as the 'crucifix masturbation' scene. This notable scene may be masturbation of the demon, but it is also a shocking rape of a little girl with a holy object doubling as a dildo" (Semmerling, 50).

48. Nakahara is careful to add that the burst of religious-themed exploitation films in this period can hardly be considered solely as a response to theological issues: economic factors within the Italian film industry, he suggests, were even more critical (Tamao, 125–6).

Works Cited

Bartholomew, David. "*The Exorcist*: The Book, The Movie, The Phenomenon." *Cinefantastique* 3:4 (Autumn 1974): 8–21.
Blatty, William Peter. *The Exorcist*. London: Corgi Books, 1974.
Brooks, Peter. *The Melodramatic Imagination: Balzac, Henry James and the Mode of Excess.* New Haven: Yale University Press, 1995.
Canby, Vincent. "Blatty's *The Exorcist* Comes to the Screen." Originally published in the *New York Times*, 1973. Reprinted in Peter Travers and Stephanie Reiff. *The Story Behind* The Exorcist. New York: Signet Books, 1974.
"Confronting the Devil's Power." Address of Pope Paul VI to a General Audience. 15 November 1972. *Papal Encyclicals Online.* 20 December 2009. <http://www.papalencyclicals.net/Paul06/p6devil.htm>.
The Exorcist. Dir. William Friedkin. Perf. Ellen Burstyn, Linda Blair, Max von Sydow, Jason Miller. 1973. Warner Bros., 1998. Film.
Gledhill, Christine. "Rethinking Genre." *Reinventing Film Studies.* Eds. Christine Gledhill and Linda Williams. London: Arnold, 2000.
Gunning, Tom. "The Horror of Opacity: The Melodrama of Sensation in the Plays of Andre de Lorde." *Melodrama: Stage, Picture, Screen.* Ed. J. Cook, J. Bratton and C. Gledhill. London: British Film Institute, 1994. 50–61.
Hills, Matt. "Para-Paracinema: The *Friday the 13th* Series as Other to Trash and Legitimate Film Cultures." *Sleaze Artists: Cinema at the Margins of Taste, Style and Politics.* Ed. Jeffrey Sconce. Durham: Duke University Press, 2007. 219–239.
Kauffman, Stanley. Review: *The Exorcist.* Originally published in *The New Republic*, 1974. Reprinted in Peter Travers and Stephanie Reiff, *The Story Behind* The Exorcist. Signet Books, New York, 1974.
Kermode, Mark. "Exorcise Cycle." *Sight and Sound* 5 (October 2003): 10.
_____. *The Exorcist.* Revised 2nd Edition. London: BFI, 2003.
Keyser, Les, and Barbara Keyser. *Hollywood and the Catholic Church: The Image of Roman Catholicism in American Movies.* Chicago: Loyola University Press, 1984.
Landau, Jon. "The Devil in Mr. Friedkin." Originally published in *Rolling Stone Magazine*, 1974. Reprinted in Peter Travers and Stephanie Reiff, *The Story Behind The Exorcist.* New York: Signet Books, 1974.
Lowenstein, Adam. *Shocking Representation: Historical Trauma, National Cinema and the Modern Horror Film.* New York: Columbia University Press, 2005.
McCabe, Bob. The Exorcist: *Out of The Shadows.* London: Omnibus Press, 1999.
McDannell, Colleen. *Catholics in the Movies.* Ed. Colleen McDannell. New York: Oxford University Press, 2008.

Özkaracalar, Kaya. "Between Appropriation and Innovation: Turkish Horror Cinema." *Fear Without Frontiers: Horror Cinema Across the Globe*. Gottalming: FAB Press, 2003. 204–217.
Phillips, Kendall R. *Projected Fears: Horror Films and American Culture*. Westport, CT: Praeger, 2005.
"Pope Paul VI 1963–1978 Official Biography." Vatican website. 20 December 2009. <http://www.vatican.va/holy_father/paul_vi/biography/documents/hf_p-vi_bio_16071997_biography_en.html>
Ratzinger, Joseph Cardinal (Pope Benedict XVI), with Vittorio Messori. *The Ratzinger Report: An Exclusive Interview on the State of the Church*. San Francisco: Ignatius Press, 1985.
Raw, Laurence. Review: Gönül Dönmez-Colin, *Turkish Cinema: Identity, Distance and Belonging*; Rekin Teksoy, *Turkish Cinema. Screen* 50.3 (Autumn 2009): 361–364.
Sarris, Andrew. "Out, Out, Damned Demon!" Originally published in *The Village Voice*, 1974. Reprinted in Peter Travers and Stephanie Reiff. *The Story Behind The Exorcist*. New York: Signet Books, 1974.
Sconce, Jeffrey. "Trashing the Academy: Taste, Excess, and an Emerging Politics of Cinematic Style." *Screen* 36.4 (1995): 371–91.
Semmerling, Tim Jon. *"Evil" Arabs in American Popular Film: Orientalist Fear*. Austin: Texas University Press, 2006.
Şeytan. Dir. Metin Erksan. Perf. Canan Perver, Cihan Unal, Meral Taygun. Saner Film, 1974. Film.
Smith, Ian Robert. "The Exorcist in Istanbul: Processes of Transcultural Appropriation Within Turkish Popular Cinema." *Portal Journal of Multidisciplinary International Studies* 5.1 (January 2008). 1 July 2010 http://epress.lib.uts.edu.au/ojs/index.php/portal/article/view/489/584.
Tamao, Nakahara. "Barred Nuns: Italian Nunsploitation Films." *Alternative Europe: Eurotrash and Exploitation Cinema Since 1945*. Eds. Ernest Mathijs and Xavier Mendik. London: Wallflower Press, 2004. 124–133.
Un urlo nelle tenebre. Dir. Elo Pannacciò. Perf. Richard Conte, Francois Prevost, Patrizia Gori. Colosseum International, 1975. Film.
Vaughn, Stephen. *Freedom and Entertainment: Ratings the Movies in an Age of New Media*. New York: Cambridge University Press, 2006.

Our Lady of Fátima and Marian Myth in Portuguese Cinema

PAULO CUNHA *and* DANIEL RIBAS

The Marian myth and Our Lady of Fátima are part of a long tradition in Portuguese society. They form a collective unconscious that belongs to Portuguese culture from the intense fights of the First Portuguese Republic, through the New State dictatorship until the Democratic regime instated 25 April 1974. As a consequence, Portuguese cinema also portrays, throughout its history, the apparitions of the Virgin Mary, known in Portugal since the late 1920s as Our Lady of Fátima. It is the purpose of our study to analyze how the apparitions and Our Lady of Fátima appear in Portuguese national cinema and the way it portrays the Marian myth. It is our objective to analyze the changes occurring within the nation's political and sociological systems and their connection to the Fatima-themed movies produced. It is obvious that the different political structures used cinema as a medium to ideologically influence audiences. For the purpose of this study we decided to analyze only the fictional feature films produced in Portugal. The myth has proven to be a much-worked theme.

Like some other popular religious events occurring in the 19th century, the so-called "apparitions" or "Fátima miracles" occurred in a small rural community. Between May and October of 1917, the Virgin Mary appeared to three young shepherds and transmitted to them a number of personal, national and international messages (Neto 142). Since the implementation of the Republican regime in Portugal, on 5 October 1910, social relations between the Catholic Church and the Portuguese state were not peaceful. Republican anti-clerical idealism, known publicly since the late 19th century, intended to diminish, in a radical way, the influence of the Catholic Church in Portuguese society. The expected Catholic reaction to this fact initiated a true religious war all over the country, causing a strong confrontation with the republicans, who were intending to transform Portuguese social reality based on the elitist project of the so called free thinkers (Neto 129). At the beginning of the "Fátima miracles" process, the ecclesiastical powers felt threatened by the Marian manifestations, prohibiting all members of the clergy from participating in popular gatherings in Fátima (Mónica 21). This would soon change, however. Europe was in a clear crisis of values due to the devastating effects of World War I (1914–18) and the country was decimated by the so-called "Spanish flu" epidemic. The Fátima gatherings came to be cleverly exploited by the Catholic Church, which managed to "extract from these facts some interpretations and consequences that had a great deal of influence over the masses and contributed to a refreshment of faith" (Monica 21). In an organized way, these Fátima gatherings became associated with a "religious rebirth" promoted by a new generation of intellectuals, disappointed with the political and social instability of the republican regime. This religious revival, supported by associations such as the "Catholic Union" (1913) or "Portuguese Catholic Center" (1917), helped in an objective way to regain some of the privileges of the Catholic Church in Portuguese society (Neto 143).

From December 1917 on, after the military coup commanded by the conservative dictator Sidónio Pais, the new regime — New Republic (1917–1918) — made some efforts to reinforce diplomatic relations with the Vatican and actually promoted the religious pacification of Portuguese society. The progressive installation of a peaceful environment between those most disappointed with the republican regime began with the new law referring to the separation between the state and the Church (despite maintaining the laicization of the state) as well as the participation of Sidónio Pais in religious ceremonies, the first such participation by a Portuguese president since the implantation of the Republic (Malheiro Silva qtd. in Neto 145).

It was in the 1920s that top hierarchic representatives of the Catholic Church began to organize, observe and control the Marian cult in Fátima:

> Fátima propaganda, organized by priest [Manuel Nunes] Formigão (1883–1958) in the *Voice of Fátima* helps to understand the purpose of the new cult in the reorganization of Catholicism in Portugal. [...] Formigão made a big case for the fact that Fátima is "precisely in the geographical centre of the country." This geographical position made it the "national sanctuary" [Ramos 488].

Aside from its strategic geography, Fátima's location also had a historically peculiar position:

> Fátima was located in the old feudal lands of Nun'Álvares, count of Ourém, the winner of Aljubarrota's batlle.[1] Fátima's cult came together with Nuno Álvares',

whose cult had been recognized by the Ritual Congregation in 1918. In 1920, the government of the Republic itself instituted the patriotic party on the 14th of August, Aljubarrota's day, giving more value to Nun'Álvares. Formigão even invented a sacred triangle, with Fátima, Aljubarrota and the battle, setting together the Virgin, the supreme commander (Nun'Álvares) and the war effort of the Republic [...] In 1928 [...] the army and the Church united in jointed commemorations of religion and homeland [Ramos 4493].

On 26 June 1927, five years after the legal acceptance of Fátima, Leiria's bishop presided, for the first time, over an official ceremony in Cova da Iria, after the blessings of the Way of the Cross. In the following year, the construction of the basilica would begin.

It was in this particular context that the first cinematographic project related to the phenomenon of Fátima came up. In 1927, Rino Lupo, an Italian cineaste who had lived in Portugal for a decade (1921–1931), decided to create the first fictional production inspired by the apparitions: *Fátima Milagrosa/ Miraculous Fátima*. Lupo's drama, from 1928, is preceded by a prologue that describes the events of 1917 and the evolution of Fátima's cult. During the first ten minutes, we can see the staging of the apparitions with real images of the Marian cult in Fátima, which are presented as a kind of journal of actualities, and include documentary images of the official ceremonies and pilgrimages in 1927.[2]

The story, as we can define it, starts after this prologue, at Minho, one of the most Catholic regions of Portugal. The Count of Unhais has just died, leaving his wife and daughter, Maria Helena, in serious financial trouble. Despite the servants' loyalty — in particular the family of Aninhas, a young quadriplegic believer in the Virgin Mary — the two broken aristocrats see themselves forced to leave for Lisbon, surviving under serious difficulties. Hiding her identity, young Maria Helena manages to get a job in the Count of Salgueiros' palace. There, she meets his son Anthero, a bohemian and lady's man, with whom she falls in love, though never giving herself up to sexual temptation. Influenced by Aninhas, Maria Helena and her mother decide to make a pilgrimage to Fátima, a pilgrimage that will change their lives. On their way there, the broken aristocrats visit the Batalha monastery, where they venerate Nun'Álvares Pereira and the Portuguese killed in World War I. In Fátima, during the celebration of the mess, two miracles occur: Aninhas recovers from her paralysis and Anthero gives up his bohemian life and proposes to Maria Helena. Back in Minho Palace, they are all happy: Maria Helena and Anthero have their first son, the Countess of Unhais marries the Count of Salgueiros, and Aninhas and her family become the aristocrats' servants again.

Miraculous Fátima is, essentially, a movie of "corrections," both morally and socially: the "miracle" of Aninhas' recovery corrects the inability of medicine and science to regain happiness for the young believer; the transformation of Anthero into a family man corrects his life of social and moral deviance; the marriage between Anthero and Maria Helena corrects the injustice that led the aristocrats to give up their social status and hide their real identity. In reality, the film focuses on a much greater "conversion": the conversion of a decadent country, corrupted by the laicist ideals of the first Portuguese Republic, to the moral and social virtues of the Catholic faith, values that were spread by the Dictatorship installed by the military movement of 28 May 1926. In keeping with its politics, the film has a normative ending, in which social classes maintain their natural division. This type of ending will become essential to many movies associated with the dictatorial regime.

Miraculous Fatima uses documentary images of the Marian cult in Fátima, but the film is also an historical document in itself, because it shows the real social and cultural environment of the time, the ideological changes that legitimated Fatima's "happenings" for the politicians in power. The pilgrimage of the characters through the Batalha monastery — where, according to the film's subtitles, the "humble heroes of Portugal rest in their eternal sleep, in the Epic cathedral of our nation country" — reinforces that alliance between political and religious power during that era. The film also features some techniques that insured its popular success. *Miraculous Fátima* was one of the first Portuguese films to include special visual effects, including the technique of *overlapping* created by Georges Méliès. In the context of the movie, this technique lends credibility to the narrative, especially in the sequences of "sightings" of the Virgin Mary and the famous "miracle of the sun."

The gatherings of believers in Fátima contributed to the ideological institutionalization of the Estado Novo/New State. In May 1942, the 25th anniversary of the apparitions, occurred one of the largest pilgrimages of all. On the following October 31, Pope Pius XII, speaking in Portuguese on the radio, consecrated the whole world to the Immaculate Heart of Mary. Purportedly by request of the Virgin Mary herself, he made special mention of the communist Soviet Union. These circumstances were significant to the producer João César de Sá, who decided to produce a project on the Marian theme, and invited the experienced director Jorge Brum do Canto to direct it. The action of *Fátima, Terra de Fé/Fátima, Land of Faith* (1943) is focused on the character of Doutor António da Silveira, a surgeon and rational university teacher, a non-believer who goes through a family crisis because he doesn't want to accept that his child be baptized in the Catholic religion.

The rationalism and atheism of this main character are put at stake by the Catholic devotion of his family and by the death of a patient for whom he nurtured a special tenderness. The accident in which his son is involved, putting his life at risk, will be a determining factor in Silveira's conversion. Concluding that his son is severely injured and convinced that medicine can't help him, *Silveira* takes his child to Fátima. In the sanctuary, when sick people are receiving their blessings, the child suddenly awakens, leading to the conversion of his father and to the reunification of his whole family. Inspired by the work of the Catholic writer Mello e Alvim, who also wrote the screenplay of the film, *Fátima, Land of Faith* is called by the historian Álvaro Garrido a "mystic melodrama (...) assuming an ideological sense, even though we cannot say without any doubt that it is a perfect example of what is called the regime cinema. Anyway, *Fátima, Land of Faith* states certain basic aspects of salazarist catholic cinema. It sure did please the National leaders and those responsible for the official propaganda settings" (280). There is no doubt that this piece of cinema "underlined the nationalist and religious ideology, claiming the untouchable trilogy of Salazar's educational 'God, Fatherland and Family'" (Garrido 281). In conclusion, in a regime that "worshiped the Virgin of Fátima as patron of this nation and savior of the country, the Marian cult and the need to justify its ideological diffusion found in the Brum do Canto's movie a privileged way to do it" (Garrido 281).

Indifferent to these institutional issues, the cult of Our Lady of Fátima had a significant growth in the Portuguese population, and the Estado Novo did not minimize this popular support. According to statements in the Catholic press, the participants in the celebration of apparitions had grown to three hundred thousand pilgrims at the end of the first decade of pilgrimages (Torgal 111). Internationally speaking, Fátima's status had an auspicious growth in the contexts of Spanish Civil War (1936–39), Second World War and the Cold War. In 1951, about a decade after Pope Pius XII's consecration, the auxiliary bishop of Boston, Fulton Sheen, declared, "The Red Square in Moscow had its answer in the White Square in Fátima" (Mónica 21). Four years later, Cardinal Cerejeira said that Fátima was "a lighthouse of hope against the atheist communism that threatened to conquer the world and destroy the Church" (Mónica 21). He also maintained that if Lourdes was the answer of the Virgin to the rationalism of the 1800s, Fátima would be the answer of the 20th century to Communist atheism (Mónica 21).

In the first years of the 1950s, certainly influenced by the media coverage which implied that Fátima's Marian cult was consolidating internationally, there were two foreign movies that would help to internationally popularize the events of 1917: *La Señora de Fátima* (1951) by Rafael Gil and *The Miracle of Our Lady of Fátima* (1952) by John Brahm. The first movie is a Spanish production, with the cooperation of a Portuguese producer (Aníbal Contreras) and can be thought of as an historical movie, a very popular genre in 1950s Portuguese and Spanish cinema. The second was a North American production of Warner Bros. Pictures that reflected pretty well its opinion on the ideological context of the Cold War. Before focusing on the dramatic story centered in the apparitions of 1917, the movie has a brief prologue about the environment of religious persecution happening in Portugal since the implementation of the republican regime and there are clear references to the geopolitical scenery of post Second World War.

Both movies start with a political and social introduction, transmitting the official version of the facts: the first apparition, the lack of belief of the people, the political persecution of the administrator, the hesitation of the local Church and the so called miracle of the sun. At the same time that the official story is told, the movies also include dramatic fictional elements that do not belong to the official versions. Finally, in the last minutes of both films, there are real images of Fátima's sanctuary, images that were shot during the celebrations of fall 1951. By including these "truthful" images the filmmakers intend to reinforce credibility and verisimilitude in the story as presented. In general, the movies accomplish their missionary intention towards the audience. Premiered worldwide in August 1952 (in the United States' theatres), the movie from John Brahm would be commercially exhibited in several countries of Western Europe. *Señora de Fátima* had, possibly, a more modest distribution, one focused on the Latin American market. In Portugal, both films were received with strong enthusiasm by the press and by ecclesiastic authorities. The critical assessments of the *Cinematographic Bulletin of the Film Bureau of Cinema and Radio*[3] are examples of the Catholic Portuguese authorities' positive reception to these two works: the movie by Rafael Gil is "recommend to all" and John Brahm's film was considered a "show that we recommend to all families and that propagates afar the message of Fátima" (n.p.).

At the ending of Second World War, political and social events would, gradually, separate Salazar's regime from his Catholic supporters. After 1945, the world changed and Catholicism changed too, at least in what concerned the development of a "new social and political democratic consciousness," one that reinforced the "growth of generational differences inside the Church, that were getting larger not only from within but also in the Church's relations with the State" (Cruz 191–192). According to the official, National Statistics Institute, drawing on available data from the General Census of the Portuguese Population for the twentieth century, Portugal is a country homogeneously

Catholic: "Catholics have always been the majority population, although their number has been regularly decreasing, a level higher than 99 percent in the census of the last year of the 19th century to just over 77 percent in the last census of the 20th century." There are no data available for all the decades, but looking at a few of the data for the years available for the duration of the New State we see, in 1940, the number of Portuguese Catholics stood at 93 percent of the population, rising successively to 97 percent in the censuses of 1950 and to 98 percent in the censuses of 1960 (Valério 725–730). In May 1967, during the celebrations of the 50th anniversary of the apparitions, Paul VI would become the first pope to visit Fátima's sanctuary. The popular enthusiasm was already huge, but the major coverage of this visit by the national and international media would give even more relevance to the event. Not even the uncomfortable diplomatic problem between Salazar and the Vatican due to the visit of Paul VI to India in 1964[4] could diminish the national and international importance of the event.

The events of Fátima were very little inspiration to Portuguese fictional cinema during the Estado Novo. Between 1933 and 1974, only *Fátima, Land of Faith!* presented direct references to Our Lady Fátima. In documentary, the story was no different. Between 1933 and 1974, we can find only ten short documentary films: *Fátima* (1946); *Nossa Senhora de Fátima em Madrid [Our Lady of Fátima in Madrid]* (1948); *Fátima e o Ano Santo [Fátima and the Good Year]* (1951); *Fátima — Encerramento do Ano Santo [Fátima — The Ending of the Good Year]* (1951); *The Road to Fátima* (1954); *Fátima — Altar do mundo [Fátima — Altar of the World]* (1956); *Fátima das criancinhas [Little Children Fátima]* or *Peregrinação internacional das crianças a Fátima [International Pilgrimage of Children to Fátima]* (1967); *Fátima — Esperança do mundo [Fátima — Hope of the World]* (1967); *O Papa em Fátima [The Pope in Fátima]* (1967); *Fátima no Médio Oriente [Fátima in the Middle East]* (1968); and *Fátima Ultreia Jubilar* (1968).

An analysis of these facts leads to the conclusion that, during Salazar's dictatorship, two main moments, focused by the media, gave Fátima's sanctuary international visibility: the consecration of Pope Pius XII in 1951 and the visit of Paul VI in 1967. In the new political framework after the Second World War, Salazar's regime brought several ways to approach the Western bloc in confrontation of the Cold War. The growing international popularity of Marian devotion at Fátima enhanced, therefore, the international public image of the Portuguese and objectively contributed to this trend of international integration developed by Portuguese diplomacy since the mid–1940s. Simultaneously, the process of internationalization of Marian devotion at Fátima benefited greatly the Portuguese emigrant communities scattered across five continents, and led to the establishment in several countries of institutes of consecrated life, fraternities, associations and movements affiliated to the Marian cult of Fátima.

On 25 of April 1974, a democratic revolution known as the "Carnation Revolution" marked the break from the "New State" dictatorship. Intense debate over different ideas for the future of Portugal marked this period, one side led by the Socialist Party and the other led by the Communist Party. The country was, at that time, very in debt to left wing ideas, in strong contrast to the fascist trilogy of "God, Fatherland and Family." In this climate, Manoel de Oliveira directed an existential project that went against the spirit of the time: *Benilde Ou a Virgem-Mãe [Benilde or the Virgin Mother]* (1974), based on the play with the same title (1947) by José Régio. The narrative takes place in an upper class home at Alentejo, in the social context of a bourgeois family. It is there that Benilde, a young woman living with her father, appears mysteriously pregnant. The girl claims that the pregnancy was a divine wish and all the other characters watch, incredulous to her apparent delusion. Oliveira interrogates, through several characters (Benilde's father, the priest or the doctor), the contradictions between faith and rational thinking. All the film elements seem, in that manner, to symbolically convey the contradictory meanings of the film (also present in the original play). In the words of Ronald Balczuweit: "[The plot of the play] is an enigma, a 'miracle' (as Benilde says), or a sin. The doctor calls it a fact; the aunt considers it to be a lapse. In fact, it is all this at the same time: Benilde is pregnant but denies that she has ever been with a man." The narrative confirms, therefore, that Oliveira "is not interested in offering an answer by solving the enigma or by affirming the miracle" (Balczuweit 114).

In this sense, Oliveira's film takes on the discourse of Régio's play, giving an important role to the dialogues, which are almost omnipresent throughout the narrative. This is also why *Benilde or the Virgin Mother* is a film that questions cinema as an autonomous art form, separate from theatre (in this films well known initial sequence, Oliveira films the reverse part of the sets, revealing the technical apparatus).

During these teeming years, controversial filmmaker, António de Macedo, directed two films that would openly criticize the miracle of Our Lady of Fátima. They are *Fátima Story* (1975)[5] and *As Horas de Maria [Maria's Hours]* (1976). Macedo was, since his debut with *Domingo à Tarde [Sunday Afternoon]* (1966), a director at the margins, making a parallel career with the directors of the New Cinema movement. With *Maria's Hours*, Macedo tells a story that serves as a metaphor for the human dilemmas of existence, and also critiques, subtly, the ritual of penitence and adoration of Our Lady of

Fátima. The narrative begins with a strange story told by a nun to a doctor and head of a mental hospital. The nun wants to admit her niece, whom she believes to be mentally ill. In fact the niece, Maria, is blind and very devoted to Our Lady of Fátima. The film takes place in a degraded and very old hospital where Maria is an inmate. The whole narrative deals with long conversations between the doctor and Maria, sometimes in the presence of her aunt. In these dialogues, there is a kind of rationalization by the doctor, who tries to understand Maria's devotion. At the same time, trying to persuade her against her faith, he tells the alternative stories found in the apocryphal gospels, in which the figure of Jesus is very different from the Biblical gospels. In these sessions, the doctor will later discover some hidden facts about Maria's past life, especially pertaining to her relationship with her mother: extra-marital relations and the subsequent death of Maria's father, who committed suicide (it is told that he had said, at the dinner table, "I prefer death over shame").

In this sense, *Maria's Hours* is a serious critique of a kind of blind devotion to Fátima, in the form of a mentally ill young (and possibly virginal) woman, who is also physically blind, in an obvious statement on her faith. To acknowledge that madness, Macedo shows documentary footage taken in Fátima revealing poor people in acts of penance.[6] This footage is shown continually throughout the film between the conversations of Maria and the doctor. Moreover, heard from time to time is the background sound of mourning devotees, recorded live at Fátima. In this sense, it seems that Macedo is giving, with the footage and the soundtrack, the inner point of view of Maria. She incarnates that physical and mental disorder presented also by the people in Fátima. In fact, the film has two secrets, the one that Maria carries (revealed late in the film), and the overall secret of Fátima, which is condensed in the faith of those people. The dialectical conversations between Maria and the doctor attempt to illuminate those secrets, trying to understand that particular human behavior. It is as if Macedo is the doctor aiming to diagnose the disease of faith.

Maria's Hours is the statement of the doctor, who is an alter ego for Macedo and his visions on faith and the cult of Fátima. The film, although produced in 1976, premiered only in 1979 with public controversy:

> Violent sermons against the film by bishops; several parishes all over the country sent a petition demanding the prohibition of the film (claimed as a blasphemy); aggression toward spectators in the première; bomb threats; vandalism at the theatre's façade; and the case goes to the National Parliament, where some deputies demand censorship for the films financed by the Portuguese Institute of Cinema" [Matos-Cruz 76–77].

Moreover, the national authority for the classification of the movies, Film Bureau for Cinema and Radio,[7] later stated, "A lot of pressures came to us from diverse sensibilities, asking for a campaign towards the prohibition of the film's exhibition."

In 1982, Pope John Paul II visited Fátima in the aftermath of the assassination attempt at St. Peter's Square on 13 May 1981. He later stated that the miracle of his survival was to be credited to Our Lady of Fátima. These events led to the affirmation of Our Lady of Fátima in the international Catholic consciousness and to the increase of the national devotion. With this Pope's visit, were produced two films of medium length: *Fátima Viva [Fátima Alive]* (1982) and *Fátima—A esperança veste-se de branco [Fátima—Hope Is Dressed in White]* (1983), both directed by João Mendes in a production of Telecinemoro. In the final year of the decade and in the nineties, were also produced three other films: *Fátima—O Milage [Fátima—The Miracle]* (1989), by Alberto Gonçalves; *Aparição [Apparitions at Fátima]* (1992), by Daniel Costelle; and *Fátima* (1995), by Ruy Ferrão. These films serve as guides to newcomers to Fátima and its history and, therefore, are mainly to be credited as Catholic productions.

In the nineties, Our Lady of Fátima was used in Raul Ruiz's film, *Dark at Noon* (1992). The narrative is a typical Ruiz surrealism, mixing several stories in an intricate puzzle of characters. Nevertheless, there is a central character, Docteur Felicien, who is a miracle consultant for the Church. He comes to Portugal, to a very odd location where all the people behave strangely, even the rich family that seems to control the place. It is in that location that the Virgin Mary appears several times in a way that resembles the apparitions of Our Lady of Fátima. Even though the plot is difficult to understand linearly, we can see that Ruiz is making fun of the events of Fátima. At the end of the decade came the production of *Fátima* (1997), directed by the Italian Fabrizio Costa. The film was not successful, even with a Portuguese cast of renowned actors: Joaquim de Almeida, Catarina Furtado and Diogo Infante, all of them with credits in Portuguese television and cinema. Intended for theatres, the film premiered in Portugal directly to video. The narrative seems almost a docudrama and hews very closely to the events of the apparitions, portraying also the political and social context of Portugal in the later years of the 1910s decade. In this sense, the film tries to elucidate the clash between the political republican regime and the Catholic Church. The regime was trying to create a secular society, breaking the ancient strong bonds with the Catholic authority. That was part, also, of the history of the apparitions, especially with the arrest—as shown in the movie—of the three children on 13 August 1917. In this context, the film creates a secondary plot with a love story between Margarida, a Fado singer, and Dário, the son of a prominent figure in the republican state. This figure, seeing his power in question, forces the exit of

Margarida from the big city. She goes to her fathers' house in Fátima. The film also introduces the character of Avelino, a journalist for *O Século*, the biggest newspaper at the time. Later on, Avelino and Dário go to Fátima (the first covering the story of the apparitions, the second following his love), and demonstrate how the city and its bourgeoisie will come to believe in the miracle. In fact, the story of Avelino is a true story: a reporter from *O Século* began by joking about the apparitions, but later witnessed the miracle and wrote about it.

Fátima tries to function as a fresco of those years and also aims to address international audiences, managing to teach history and the Portuguese traditions: the Fado (a national sad song played in Lisbon bars) is all over the film score, as are some country customs (for example, a female reunion, at night, in which they separate the corn from its leaves, singing popular songs). The production resembles a top television series, with extra care for the geography of Fátima. In the later part of the film, *Fátima* also tries to make a statement about the meaning of the apparitions: in an editing room we see a contemporary director mixing the final cut of the film with some other images from 20th century history.

Finally, in the first decade of the 21st century, two Portuguese movies use Fatima as a subject: the documentary *Em Fátima Rezei por Ti [In Fátima I Prayed for You]* (2000), by Gonçalo C. Luz; and the fiction film *O Milagre Segundo Salomé [The Miracle According to Salome]* (2004), by Mário Barroso, based on the book with the same title by José Rodrigues Miguéis. The book, released in 1975, was already very critical of the miracle, presenting in its narrative an alternative version: Here, it is a prostitute who goes to her home village, close to Fátima, and appears as the vision that the three children have. Meanwhile, the book presents the social context: the conflicts inside the political regime and the relations towards the Church. The film also portrays, in an impeccable manner, those years: wardrobe, location and props create a very good period film, unique of its kind in Portuguese cinema. The film also is the debut project in the long career of the director of photography Mário Barroso. The film tells the story of Salomé, a young prostitute who is taken from the brothel by Sertório Cerqueira, a rich and prominent man. She falls in love with Gabriel, a young and enthusiastic republican, who writes political articles about issues of faith and the Republic. Salomé tries to run away from this love, escaping to her home village, near Fátima. It is there that the crucial scene takes place: on the path to her village, she stops to see the wonders of the landscape. In that moment, three children see her. The camera portrays this moment as the possible vision of Our Lady of Fátima in the eyes of the three young shepherds: they see the beauty *Salomé* on a hill as the sun dazzles them. The film evolves towards a tragic ending, in which Gabriel and Salomé are killed by a soldier in a mixture of jealousy and political conflict.

As a context for this narrative, the film shows us that the Fátima miracles were, at the time, major events for the political and religious authorities. There is in a secondary plot, several meetings between Sertório Cerqueira and Mota Santos, about a conspiracy regarding the "General." Almost at the end of the film, there is also a crucial scene: we see a meeting, with Mota Santos, Sertório Cerqueira, a priest and some other people, in which they present the model for the sanctuary to be built at Fátima. Mota Santos will later say, in this scene, that this represents the secularization of the miracle of Fátima.

Finally, there were also two international productions in this last decade that can be seen as docudramas: *The 13th Day* (2009) by Ian & Dominic Higgins, and *The Call of Fátima* (2005). The first one tries to dramatize the story of the apparitions as told by the Catholic canon, and the second mixes the historical story with documentary footage of the sanctuary and the voice of a narrator. As we can see, there was a shift in the production of films that thematize Our Lady of Fatima since the revolution of 1974. This shift was only possible in a new democratic and free society, where the republican regime has tried to build a new secular culture. In the seventies, a film such as *Maria's Hours* was claimed to be a blasphemy, but in 2004, *The Miracle According to Salomé*'s strong questioning of the myth did not create controversy. Still, it is worth noting that these are the only two fiction films that deal critically, since the late 1920s, with Our Lady of Fátima.

It was at the outset of the 21st century that Francisco and Jacinta Marto — the two brothers that witnessed, with Lúcia, the apparitions — were beatified by Pope John Paul II, in his third visit to Fátima, on 13 May 2000. Curiously, confirming the growing importance of Our Lady of Fátima in international Catholicism, Pope Benedict XVI visited the Sanctuary of Fátima in May 2010 to celebrate the apparitions.

Notes

1. Aljubarrota's Battle is one of the most important moments in Portuguese national history because it definitively consolidated Portugal's independence, until then, still forming itself. This battle happened on 14 of August 1385 and the Portuguese army led by Nun'Álvares Pereira and João Mestre de Avis (future King João I of Portugal), came from this battle victorious. On the spot of the confrontation, King João I had the monastery of Santa Maria da Vitória built — it came to be known as Mosteiro da Batalha — in order to commemorate the victory at Aljubarrota.

2. In 1928 and 1929 two movies would be shot in Fátima under the theme of the pilgrimages and the Marian cult: *Pilgrimage to Fátima* (1928, a Raul Lopes Freire production) and *Pilgrimage to Fátima* (1929 Brazilian newspaper *Revista Mundial*,

Agesilau de Araújo production in Brazil). In 1931, another movie was shot: *Fátima* (1931, Lisboa Filme production). These movies, whose negatives were lost, are classified as newsreel and had the purpose of spreading through the country and abroad the Marian Cult in Fátima.

3. The Film Bureau of Cinema and Radio is a Catholic agency, whose mission is to assess the moral and aesthetic value of film in the Portuguese market.

4. In December 1964 Paul VI's visit to India the colonial political Portuguese position. Salazar felt himself offended by the fact that the Pope visited a country that, in December 1961, had invaded and occupied in a hostile way the territories under Portuguese administration in Goa, Damão e Diu. In his visit, Paulo VI did not condemn the takeover and also refused to comment on the importance of Portuguese missionaries in the evangelization of India.

5. Although there is a copy of *Fátima Story* in ANIM — Arquivo Nacional das Imagens em Movimento/National Archive of the Moving Images — it is impossible to see the film because its negative is very degraded and is waiting for a restoration.

6. It is normal, at Fátima, to see poor people paying promises to Our Lady of Fátima for requests they made to her. These penances are usually in form of long walks to Fátima and walks on knees in the Sanctuary. There are also a lot of different forms of candles.

7. See footnote 3.

Bibliography

Balczuweit, Ronald. "The Cinema as Scene of Language: An Analysis of Manoel de Oliveira's Adaptation Strategies." *Dekalog: On Manoel de Oliveira*. Ed. Carolin Overhoff Ferreira. London: Wallflower, 2008. 110–121.

Benilde Ou a Virgem-Mãe [Benilde or the Virgin Mother]. Dir. Manoel de Oliveira. Perf. Maria Amelia Matta, Jorge Rolla, Varela Silva. Centro Portugues de Cinema, 1975. Film.

The Call of Fátima. Nar. Fr. Michael Maher. Euro France Group, 2005. Documentary.

Costa, João Bénard. *Histórias do Cinema*. Lisbon: Imprensa Nacional Casa da Moeda, 1991.

Cruz, Manuel Braga da. *O Estado Novo e a Igreja Católica*. Lisbon: Editorial Bizâncio, 1999.

Fátima. Dir. Fabrizio Costa. Perf. Joaquim de Almeida, Catarina Furtado, Diogo Infante. Animatógrafo, 1997. TV.

Fátima Milagrosa [Miraculous Fatima]. Dir. Rino Lupo. Perf. Rafael Alves, Beatriz Costa, Maria Júdice da Costa. Lupo Film, 1928. Film.

Fátima Story. Dir. Antonio de Macedo. 1975. Film.

Fátima: Terra de Fe [Fátima: Land of Faith]. Dir. Jorge Brum do Canto. Perf. Barreto Poeira, Graça Maria, Oliveira Martins. Filmes Portugueses César de Sa, 1943. Film.

Garrido, Álvaro. "Fátima, terra de fé! e Capas negras e os seus contextos." *O Cinema sob o olhar de Salazar...* Ed. Luís Reis Torgal. Lisbon: Círculo de Leitores, 2000. 274–303.

As Horas de Maria [Maria's Hours]. Dir. Antonio Macedo. Perf. Cecilia Gumaraes, Eugenia Bettencourt, Joao D'Avila. Cinequanon, 1979. Film.

Matos-Cruz, José de. *António de Macedo. Viragem de uma época*. Lisbon: Sociedade Portuguesa de Autores and Publicações Dom Quixote, 2001.

94   Section One. Marvelous Catholicism

O Milagre Segundo Salomé [The Miracle According to Salome]. Dir. Mario Barroso. Perf. Nicolau Breyner, Ana Bandeira, Ricardo Pereira. Gemini Films, 2004. Film.
The Miracle of Our Lady of Fátima. Dir. John Brahm. Perf. Gilbert Roland, Angela Clarke, Frank Silvera. Warner Bros, 1951. Film.
Mónica, Maria Filomena. "Fátima." *Dicionário de História de Portugal.* Oporto: Figueirinhas, 1999. Vol. 8. 21–22.
Neto, Vitor. "A questão religiosa: Estado, Igreja e conflitualidade." *História da Primeira República Portuguesa.* Lisboa: Tinta-da-China, 2009. 129–148.
L'Oueil qui Ment [Dark at Noon]. Dir. Raul Ruiz. Perf. John Hurt, Didier Bourdon, Lorraine Evanoff. Animatógrafo, 1992. Film.
Ramos, Rui. *A Segunda Fundação 1890–1926.* Lisbon: Editorial Estampa, 2001.
La Senora de Fátima. Dir. Rafael Gil. Perf. Inês Orsini, Fernando Rey, Tito Junco. Aspa Films, 1951. Film.
Torgal, Luís Filipe. *As "aparições de Fátima." Imagens e representações.* Lisbon: Temas e Debates, 2002.
The 13th Day. Dir. Dominic Higgins and Ian Higgins. Perf. Filipa Fernandes, Jane Lesley, Michael D'Cruze. 13th Day Films, 2009. DVD.
Valério, Nuno (coord.). *Estatísticas Históricas Portuguesas.* Lisboa: Instituto Nacional de Estatística, 2001.

SECTION TWO

Uncanny Catholicism

Music That Sucks and Bloody Liturgy
Catholicism in Vampire Movies

Isabella van Elferen

Peasants walking two-and-two came behind, they were singing a funeral hymn. [Carmilla] said brusquely, "Don't you perceive how discordant that is?" [...]. Her face underwent a change that alarmed and even terrified me for a moment. It darkened, and became horribly livid; her teeth and hands were clenched, and she frowned and compressed her lips [...]. At length a low convulsive cry of suffering broke from her, and gradually the hysteria subsided. "There! That comes of strangling people with hymns!" [LeFanu 85–86].

Sheridan LeFanu's *Carmilla* (1872) is but one example of the close connection between vampires and Catholicism. Early modern vampire lore, Victorian vampire novels and twentieth-century vampire cinema alike represent the vampire as the religious Other to Christianity whose sinful soul can be redeemed only through the workings of Catholic rituals. Catholicism acquires an uncanny, Gothic dimension in vampire fiction, as its supernatural dimensions are aligned closely with vampiric ghostliness and transgression. Music plays an interesting role in the vampire's Gothicized Catholicism: it is the singing of a funeral hymn that makes Carmilla grow almost beastly as its "discordant" tones touch the innermost core of her vampiric being. Only recently vampire fiction seems to have shaken off its Catholic heritage; while Suzy McKee Charnas' novel *The Vampire Tapestry* (1980) and Joel Schumacher's film *The Lost Boys* (1986) demonstrated that non-religious cultural forces like consumerism and Darwinism create their own vampires and monsters, more recent works such as *Buffy the Vampire Slayer* (1997–2003) on television and Stephenie Meyer's *Twilight* series (2005–2008) in book and film develop the notion that the vampire is no longer Other, but a boy (or girl) next door that could have been us (cf. Zanger). While sound and music figure prominently in vampire literature, the advent of sound film in the early 20th century made it possible to not only see but also to hear vampires. After an exploration of the historical and religious connections between Catholicism and vampirism this article investigates the role of music in vampire films, arguing that its liturgical potential induces a transgression into the borderlands of Gothicized Catholicism.

The Gothic Antichrist

Although vampire stories have existed at least since the early Middle Ages, vampire fiction only really began to blossom with the rise of the Gothic novel and, later, Gothic cinema. The Gothic genre emphatically picked up on the connections between vampires and Catholicism; the mutual antitheses and attractions between the two have been elaborately represented from *Carmilla* to the various cinematic adaptations of Bram Stoker's *Dracula*. One background to the lasting Gothic attention for the vampire–Catholicism theme can be found in the complex historical relationship that Gothic itself has with Roman Catholicism. Gothic literature originated in the 18th century as a reflection on (and criticism of) cultural tensions between rationality and irrationality in Enlightenment society. Stronger even than the sentimentalism of that age, the Gothic novel sought to unravel "what the Enlightenment left unexplained, [...] to reconstruct the divine mysteries that reason had begun to dismantle, to recuperate pasts and histories that offered a permanence and unity in excess of the limits of rational and moral order" (Botting, 23). Gothic — in 18th-century ghost stories as well as 19th- and 20th-century cinema and music — signifies the transgression of such limits, a crossing of borders in order to engage in the ongoing dialectic between seemingly opposed cultural forces. Gothic disentangles the societal conventions that establish such oppositions and explores the ir/rational and super/natural borderlands where opposites converge: it places its audience in the twilight zones where the past lives in the present, phantasm is part of reality, where death and life concur and evil resides in good. Catholicism was considered primitive and superstitious compared to Protestant and Enlightenment rationality, and such diverse themes as transubstantiation, resurrection, rituality, and convents were incorporated in early Gothic novels in terms of ghostliness, haunting, and excess (Sage, Chapter 2). Works such as Ann Radcliffe's *The Mysteries of Udolpho* (1794), Matthew Lewis's *The Monk* (1796), and Charles Maturin's *Melmoth the Wanderer* (1820) can arguably be read as post–Enlightenment reactions to the irrational, transcendent aspects of Catholic theology and devotional practices. This Gothicizing of Catholic themes also led to a reviving of old ideas pertaining to the vampirical nature of the Catholic Eucharist, and an increase in vampire fiction.

Bram Stoker's *Dracula* can in many ways be described as a nineteenth-century epitome of Gothicized Catholicism. Stoker represents Count Dracula as an Antichrist who unifies the human and the monstrous superhuman and thus reverses Christ's anthropology. More importantly, he reverses Christian eschatology, replacing Christ's sacrificial blood-giving with predatory blood-drinking and the resurrection into eternal life with condemnation to eternal un-death. Christ symbolizes the highest good and gives life, Dracula is the embodiment of evil and takes it; and in both cases blood is the medium. The mise-en-scene of the novel is supremely suitable to house this Gothic plot, with Transylvania as the gloomy twilight zone between Orthodox and Catholic religion as well as between Christianity and Islam, and the crossing over the Borga Pass offering "uncanny views" (intertitle in Murnau's *Nosferatu*) into the darkly mysterious world of the "other side." The vampire's unpredictable, irrational world is consistently contrasted with the rational framework of "our scientific, matter-of-fact nineteenth century" (210), from which the novel originated. And even though Jonathan Harker's changing attitude towards the crucifix given to him by a peasant woman could be regarded as a victory of Catholic rituality over the Protestant word,[1] it still is depicted as an eerie relic, a half sinister, half sacramental object with occult powers.

Just like Catholic superstition, the uncanny figure of the vampire simultaneously repelled readers and appealed to them. Vampirism offers eternal life, but killing and drinking "the hellish life-drink of blood" (intertitle in Murnau's *Nosferatu*) is required in order to maintain it. Vampires, moreover, claim the power over life and death, a power that according to Christian theology should be God's only. This hubris leads to a Gothic fall from grace, an excommunication from paradise. For this reason, excommunication prior to death was believed to increase the risk for vampirism after death in early vampire lore. The 18th-century French Jesuit Dom Calmet gives an elaborate account of the alleged circumstances surrounding excommunication and vampirism, a folkloric belief that reappears in the works of the converted Catholic priest Montague Summers around 1900 (Calmet 87–94; Summers 84ff.). The theory is that excommunicated or sinful people who died without contrition can be raised from the grave by the Devil, but as his powers do not suffice to raise the dead to life, undeath ensues (Summers 182; cf. Calmet 186–187). By creating vampires Satan thus inverses both the biblical Creation and the Fall, which are the circumstances from which he himself was born. This act of negative replication is represented in vampire fiction as a doubled Gothic reversal (think, for instance, of Anne Rice's elaborate description of it in *Interview with the Vampire* [23–24] and Neil Jordan's cinematic rendering of that scene). It is the Devil's alleged objective in this subversive act to entice his victims into sinful hedonism and thereby to sow doubt regarding God's powers (Summers 200ff.); and so the vampire's status as an uncannily seductive Antichrist is inherent to its very genesis. The struggle between the supernatural powers of vampirehood and those of the Catholic Church becomes apparent in *Interview with the Vampire*. Louis enters a cathedral and experiences how the sacraments that once were holy to him have now lost their meaning:

> God did not live in this church; the statues gave an image to nothingness. *I* was the supernatural in this cathedral. I was the only supermortal thing that stood conscious under this roof! Loneliness. Loneliness to the point of madness. The cathedral crumbled in my vision; the saints listed and fell. Rats ate the Holy Eucharist and nested on the sills [158–159].

The sacraments whose workings Louis laments are considered to be the physical representation of God's grace in the Catholic Church, and the excommunicated vampire no longer has access to them (Summers 86). In Francis Ford Coppola's *Bram Stoker's Dracula* (1992) the vampire is even further removed from divine grace as Vlad Tepes is shown denouncing God and excommunicating himself at the beginning of the film. The price vampires pay for eternal life is the doom of their souls: drinking blood means the exclusion from sacramental grace.

Here, too, Gothic descriptions of Catholic ritualism and vampiric blasphemy show a deep connection, a mutual dependency almost, as the only appropriate protection from vampirism is to apply the same sacraments and rituals which vampires lack access to. The examples are well known. Almost every vampire book or film mentions crucifixes and crossing oneself, Holy Water, communion wafers, and priestly prayer; to these specifically vampiric rituals such as the stake through the heart are added. In order to undo the vampire's supernatural power, then, another supernatural force is required — white magic is needed to disable black magic. Rituals and sacraments can be defined as transcendent passageways between the human and divine, but also between the light and the dark: if this passageway is entered without the proper — in this case Catholic — guidance, occult — in this case vampiric — forces can exert their powers and grasp the ignorant subject. In Orthodox Catholicism, for instance, dying is seen as the passing over to an unworldly realm and the rituals surrounding death and burial are therefore rites of passage; it is very dangerous to interfere with these without proper spiritual guidance as the transcendent state of the deceased can be abused by the undead (McClelland 55–56). The only way to undo the effects of occult ritual is countering it by way of church rituals performed in the evocation of divine grace. Van Helsing sets out to save Lucy's and Mina's undead souls, employing ritual powers in order to erase Dracula's blasphemic transgression of the "borders between God and man" (259). Even the desecration of a grave is deemed a "pious sacrilege" (LaFanu 108) when it takes the shape of a Catholic ritual: it is a transgression that undoes another transgression, using divine supernatural powers to counter evil ones. Interestingly, therefore, the very aspects of Catholicism that are described as superstitious, irrational and transcendent in Gothic vampire fiction also offer a weapon against occult irrationality and transgression. The Gothicized Catholicism of vampire fiction, intangible and uncontrollable as its rituality is in comparison to the Protestant *sola scriptura*, constantly explores the boundaries between light and dark, sense and reason, life, death and undeath.

One consequence of the prominence of Catholic ritual over the Protestant word in vampire fiction is an ongoing scholarly debate over the religious inclinations of diverse characters and authors — especially professor Van Helsing and Bram Stoker in *Dracula*. In view of the fact that Catholicism is both depicted as superstition and as a remedy against other, non–Christian superstitions, it seems to be impossible to come to an unambivalent answer to such questions. Rather than trying to gauge the specifically Catholic or Protestant tendencies in various individual works, I should like to investigate the theological ambivalence inherent to vampire fiction. While the rituality described above clearly refers to Catholicism, for instance, both the vampire's blasphemy of claiming power over life and death and the literary figure of the Antichrist could equally indicate Protestantism. The vampiric inversion of the communion as well as the vampire's blood baptism even show a more complex theological background to the genre, and so they need to be studied in more detail.

Vampires are often said to subvert the Catholic Eucharist, but the drinking of blood itself is a simple result of the Christ/Antichrist reversal, and points to Christian religions in general. The regular occurrence of the Old Testament verse "The blood is the life" (Dt. 12:23, cf. Lv. 17:11–14) in Stoker's *Dracula* is similarly general, referring to the basis of Christian communion theology. An often-quoted passage in Dracula scholarship is the Count's cowering back upon seeing the communion wafer (247), which is thought to be a reference to Catholic transubstantiation; but again it is both in Catholic and in Protestant doctrines that the wafer represents the actual body of Christ. Whereas transubstantiation can only take place through a priest's liturgical consecration of the wafer, Protestant communion is operative through *Real-*

präsenz, the a priori real presence of the body and blood of Christ in communion wafer and wine. The *Realpräsenz* doctrine was installed in the 1530 Augsburg Confession as the first dogmatic Protestant abolishment of "supernatural" practices in Catholicism: a human should not have the power to change bread and wine into Christ's body and blood, and instead these should be believed to be already present in their earthly forms. The communion wafer passage could therefore easily allude to *Realpräsenz*, and the fact that Renfield believes himself to be in the "Real Presence" (Stoker 98) of his messianic and capitalized "master" (which turns his time in the lunatic asylum into an Advent period) points in the same, Protestant direction. The actual vampiric blood giving and blood drinking, however, clearly operates under a Catholic, transubstantiative principle: the transformation induced by the vampire's bite happens through an instantaneous supernatural power, not because of an a priori presence in the victim's blood. The close alignment of Protestant and Catholic communion theologies in vampire fiction is best demonstrated by the notorious scene from Stoker's book (246–248) in which Dracula lets Mina drink from a wound in his side. In Coppola's cinematic representation of the scene Dracula's posture, standing on his knees with his arms wide spread as Mina drinks from his side, is an obvious reference to Christ's crucifixion — with his kneeling emphasizing the sacrificial nature of both bloodlettings — which in its emphatically sensual presence is reminiscent of Catholic iconography. But Protestantism has a long tradition with this type of imagery also, as becomes clear from the following communion poem by poet-theologian Erdmann Neumeister from 1722 (1171; cf. Van Elferen, 2008, Chapter 5):

> So I come then, my heart's delight,
> To that pleasant hour.
> I lay my head on Your breast,
> I suck on Your wounds.
> Graciously gave me food and drink,
> And kiss me, dearest Jesus,
> With the kiss of Your mouth.

Coppola shapes the scene as a mock Eucharist: Dracula invites Mina to the communion with the quasi-liturgical words "drink and join me in eternal life," to which she responds equally solemnly, "take me away from this death." Even this vampiric liturgy could indicate Protestant as well as Catholic religiosity, as a believer's death wish out of love for Jesus is a generic characteristic of sentimental Christian poetry — the following lines could express Mina's desire but are taken from a Protestant prayer book: "If I abide in you / Then death is life to me; my decay is my beautification" (Greiffenberg 560). Again it is only in the effect of drinking that the scene veers towards Catholicism rather than Protestantism, as Mina's unholy communion is clearly transubstantiative and Dracula's blood turns her into a vampire. Rather than indicating the unambivalently Catholic background of either Stoker or Coppola, I would argue that the ways in which these authors represent the vampirical inversion of the communion demonstrates that the Gothicized Catholicism of vampire fiction tests the boundaries between superstition and reason.

Theologically even more interesting are the "baptism in blood" scenes in Stoker (280) and Coppola. The Catholic church regards the sacrament of baptism as a specific form of transubstantiation: the water represents God's grace which washes original sin away through Christ's sacrificial death and resurrection. Catholic liturgy accordingly describes baptism as a "mystery" and a "wonder" and includes an exorcism of evil before the administration of the sacrament. After an invocation of the saints the celebrant prays:

> Almighty and ever-living God, you sent your only Son into the world to cast out the power of Satan, spirit of evil, to rescue man from the kingdom of darkness, and bring him into the splendor of your kingdom of light. We pray for this child: set him/her free from original sin, make him/her a temple of your glory, and send your Holy Spirit to do well with him/her.

Parents and godparents are then asked to confirm a five-fold rejection of sin, evil and "Satan, father of sin and prince of darkness." After this lengthy denouncement, baptism is administered in Holy Water and oil, and the child is clothed in a white baptism garment that symbolizes her entry into the Catholic Church.

Protestant theology regards baptism to be a reminder of both the Covenant and the Passion. The water in Baptism serves as a double washing away of sins: the believer is baptized through the biblical Flood and, more importantly in this context, through Christ's blood spent in the Passion, which was regarded a cleansing bath (Van Elferen, 2005). Anglican liturgy does not involve an explicit exorcism or rejection of evil, but does include a signing with the cross and the wish that baptism delivers one from "the powers of darkness." The Gothic overtones in both the Catholic and the Protestant baptism rituals are no coincidence: vampire fiction inverses them in word and deed—and crosses the borders of denomination.

If the Catholic and Anglican liturgies are compared to Coppola's screening of Lucy Westenra's ravishment and vampiric baptism it becomes clear that both religions can be traced in the scene. The Protestant doctrine of baptism as a reminder of the Covenant is abundantly present in the shape of a literal flooding of the room in blood; the blood splatter (an almost blasphemous reference to B-horror) is even parted in the middle, like a veritable Red Sea.

Lucy's immediate conversion to vampirism, however, indicates Catholic religiosity. Count Dracula appears at her window, ridiculing the magical powers of liturgy, annihilating the exorcism in the baptism ceremony and instead solemnly announcing his own magic, his own powers, and the baptism of blood: "Your impotent men with their foolish spells cannot protect you from my power. I condemn you to living death, to eternal hunger for living blood." Lucy's baptism is interspersed with crosscuttings to Jonathan and Mina Harker's wedding ceremony in Romania. Here yet another denomination enters Coppola's religious melting pot as the crowning of bride and groom indicates an Orthodox wedding ceremony. Coppola's curious choice to let this ceremony be accompanied by the "Dies irae" ("Day of wrath, day of mourning") from the Catholic funeral mass enhances the Gothic doublings between the two scenes. Lucy receives the baptism in blood which definitively binds her to the vampire while Mina is bound to Jonathan through the sacrament of marriage; while Dracula's unholy ritual floods Lucy in sin, the Orthodox Catholic wedding liturgy should save Mina from sin as it proclaims marriage as "the one blessing that was not forfeited by original sin or washed away in the flood." At the climax of the scene Jonathan and Mina's kiss of love is intercut by Dracula and Lucy's kiss of death, which after a fade to black is immediately followed by a shot of the undead Lucy in her coffin, her white dress functioning simultaneously as baptism garment and bridal gown.

The pervasive ambivalence in this scene is characteristic for Gothic vampire fiction: the vampire simultaneously invokes fear and desire, the transcendent potential of rituality can exert its powers both in favor of and against him, and through them the twilight zones in between and beyond Catholicism, Protestantism and even Orthodoxy can be opened — even if these prove an uncanny ride. Alison Milbank has pointed out *Dracula*'s syncretic "union of Protestant word and Catholic sacrament," a synthesis that reflects religious battle (21). Dracula — and many vampires after him — poignantly demonstrates the struggle between two religious systems and their shortcomings: the old irrational versus the new sensually deprived Christian Church. If vampires are generally perceived to have a closer relationship to Catholicism, that is only through those supernatural, intangible, non-verbal aspects of Catholicism that have been Gothicized since the 18th-century Gothic novel. It is not the blood drinking that relates vampires to Catholicism, nor is it the vampire's blasphemous power over life and death, nor its excommunication from God's grace in the sacraments, nor even its subsequent eschewing of crucifixes and churches, for all of these factors could point to Protestant as well as Catholic theology. The only real connection between vampires and Catholicism can be found in the black or white magic of un/holy ritual. The "holy circle" that Van Helsing makes out of crumbled communion wafer to protect Mina Harker from Dracula's powers and which is clearly a reference to the magic circle of witchcraft is an indicator of the link between the two forms of transcendence.

During the 20th century the theological specificities of vampire representation have gradually become even more blurry, resulting ultimately in the "boy-next-door vampire" depicted in *Twilight*. Apart from the odd crucifix very little religiosity can still be found in vampire books and films. In post–Stoker, post–Coppola cinema, Catholicism and Protestantism are often thrown into one big supernatural, potentially vampiric pile. Yet the supernatural aspects of vampire movies are often ascribed to Catholicism rather than Protestantism, for precisely the same reasons that 18th-century authors Gothicized that religion: because it entails rituality and therefore an uncontrollable transgressive potential. Victoria Nelson employs the phrase "faux Catholicism" for the "fantasy pop religion" that appears in vampire films among others and that has much less to do with theology than with "its perceived magical talismans" (88). I do not think that there is much difference between this contemporary Gothicizing of popular imaginations regarding Catholicism and those in the 18th century: both revolve around the same aspects of Catholic religion, and both give a typically Gothic view of what might happen when the transcendent gateway of its rituality is left open. And even if the religious backbone of vampire fiction has become somewhat obscured in the process of secularization, moreover, its traces are still audibly present in cinematic representations of vampires. Vampire movie soundtracks, it will be argued in the remainder of this article, provide even seemingly secularized bloodsucker films with the Gothicized Catholicism from which the genre originated.

Phantom Sounds, Vampire Soundtracks

Sound and music play a strong role in vampire literature, as becomes clear in the quotation from *Carmilla* at the beginning of this article. Considering that literature is a silent medium, this genre of fiction devotes a remarkably large amount of space to the textual description of sound. The vampire's ephemeral, disembodied presence is often announced by disturbing sounds that have exactly the same spectral quality as the creatures whose approach they herald, as two famous examples illustrate:

There seemed a strange stillness over everything; but as I listened I heard, as if from down below in the valley, the howling of many wolves. The count's eyes gleamed, and he said: "Listen to them — the children of the night. What music they make!" [Stoker 24].

And then this next thing, this next thing was ... sound. A dull roar at first and then a pounding like the pounding of the drum, growing louder and louder, as if some enormous creature were coming up on one slowly through a dark and alien forest, pounding as he came, a huge drum. And then there came the pounding of another drum, as if another giant were coming yards behind him, and each giant, intent on his own drum, gave no notice to the rhythm of the other. The sound grew louder and louder until it seemed to fill not just my hearing but all my senses, to be throbbing in my lips and fingers, in the flesh of my temples, in my veins [Rice 23].

Literary descriptions of vampire sound share a number of characteristics. Firstly, vampire sound is emphatically disembodied. Just like the vampire itself, the sounds it brings forth are echoes of an impossible reality. Secondly, vampire sound forms a spatial as well as temporal displacement of the presence of the vampire. Because it is often an echo it possesses a certain past-ness; but as an announcement of the vampire's arrival it also is a premonition of the future. Vampire sound, therefore, is transgressive in nature, representing supernatural shifts in embodiment, time and space. It can cross borders and drag the listener with it in its transgressive movements. Lastly, these sounds are described as an eerie sort of music — and so the relationship between vampire sound and vampire music needs studying.

The characteristics of vampire sound described in Gothic novels were taken over by early film, translating the virtual sound in literature into actual sound as well as music accompanying the visual. In early film two different types of composed soundtracks can be distinguished. In the silent movie era the visual track could be accompanied by a separate musical track that gave the audience narrative clues with regards to what was happening on screen; in the early sound movie, dialogue and diegetic noise were audible while music was often only added for opening credits or changes of scenery. The fact that both types of composed film soundtrack required recording technology is important in relation to the disembodied and dislocated characteristics of vampire sound. Just like vampire sound, recorded sound is physically, temporarily and spatially dislodged: recording and replaying sound means disconnecting "live" sound from its origin, thereby making it un-live while it is also un-dead. Recorded voices are phantom voices that, like phantom pain, are the ghostly, haunting remainders of their former physical self; for this reason early recording technology was received with as much fear as enthusiasm (cf. Sterne, Chapter 6).[2] This uncanny aspect of media is often employed in Gothic literature and cinema as a representation of the spectral, and it is especially effective in vampire fiction. The resemblance between the undead state of the vampire and the medial phantom voices has almost become commonplace. Vampire stories are often presented as epistolary novels (Stoker's *Dracula*) or orally transmitted frame stories (Rice's *Interview*) providing the reader with a mediated, second-hand story, which results in an even more hazy representation of the vampire and its transgressive whereabouts. Many vampire films take special effort to transmit the hypermediacy of the genre into their cinematic language as if to rub in the ghostly unreliability of mediation (Murnau's *Nosferatu*, Coppola's *Dracula*, Merhige's *Shadow of the Vampire*).

Rebecca Coyle argues with regards to the soundtrack to *The Blair Witch Project*, a film that obviously builds on the uncanny dimension of mediation, that sound in this film functions as a foreboding, a suggestion of unseen and undefined but imminent horror. Precisely because of their offscreen, spectral character, the *Blair Witch* sighs, shrieks and forest sounds force the viewer to imagine the source of that horror — which may even lie within ourselves (224). This of course brings in the Freudian uncanny that is essential for vampires and their representation: because phantom sound gives invisible, lurking presences a voice it is actively involved in the return of the repressed. Sound's relation to the unseen-uncanny can be described in terms of what David Wills has termed "dorsality," that which is behind our back, in the darkness, sinister, which can't be seen unless we turn around: that which forces us to reconfigure our cognition of ourselves in relation to both the temporality and the otherness of the world around us. The dorsal is not perceivable through sight but comes to us through other senses: "sometimes through [...] smell, [...] but more likely through hearing, announcing itself in a whisper or a shout, in a rumble or a murmur" (12). Phantom sound can express the dorsal, uncannily tangible dimension that is shared by Gothicized Catholicism and vampirism. And this is exactly the function it has in vampire films. Just like in the literary examples, the presence of a vampire can often be perceived in vampire cinema through supernatural sounds. Murnau's *Nosferatu* (1922) starts with the following intertitle "Nosferatu — does this word not sound like the midnight call of a death-bird?" The literary sound of the vampire is here brought onto the silent (!) film screen as an uncanny echo, a dorsal sound. Bela Lugosi's *Dracula* (1931) is accompanied by many a squeak, a thunder, and a howl with similar functions.

When cinematic vampire sound turns into vampire music its spectral relation to corporeality, time and space is further intensified through music's nearly infinite associativity: much more than single sounds, music can arouse an endless and incredibly immersive chain of connotations. Don Ihde has theorized this quality of sound and music as "auditory imagination," the fact that one always hears more than one hears:

> There is, in auditory imagination, the possibility of a synthesis of imagined and perceived sound [...]. But in this case the auditory "hallucination" is not a matter of hearing one thing as something else but a matter of doubled sound, a synthesized harmonic echo [132–133].

The echoes generated by auditory imagination are inherently spectral as hearing music, whether attentively or inattentively, always stirs unconscious feelings or memories. Kevin Donnelly has argued that musical connotations acquire a ghostly dimension in movie soundtracks, serving as a "repository of reminders, half-memories and outbursts of emotion and the illogical[,] these 'ghosts' and 'memories' that can haunt a film" (21). The connotations of non-diegetic film music, as a dorsal commentary to the visual, can turn a seemingly neutral scene into a locus of imminent danger: with the right soundtrack, an innocent basement staircase turns into a descent into certain doom (and if it gets too scary you just hit the mute button on the remote). Movie music can make the known world seem to have unknown qualities, it can make the viewer look over her shoulder to check what is behind her; it can add a layer of Freudian uncanniness to film footage because it is able to awaken repressed anxieties in the viewer. The converging lines of auditory imagination, spectrality and disembodiment in phantom sound, moreover, create an uncanny musical virtuality that is uniquely suitable for the expression of Gothic themes.

Film composers have employed the Gothicizing potential of recorded music from early cinema on. The title of the first cinematic adaptation of *Dracula*, Friedrich Murnau's *Nosferatu: A Symphony of Horror*, is telling in this respect. In silent movies, music is the only auditory medium that can influence the viewer's perception of the visual, and the "Fantastisch-Romantische Suite" that Hans Erdmann composed for *Nosferatu* does so very effectively: from the beginning it is almost possible to listen to the film without looking. Such non-diegetic music shares important characteristics of the phantom sound of vampires, as it is "a disembodied voice, coming through from the 'other side,' seemingly emanating from nowhere" (Donnelly 19).

The leitmotif, as a specific form of non-diegetic film music, serves as an indicator of vampires' specific characteristics. Vampire leitmotifs tend to center around three general themes: ghostliness, otherness, and danger. While non-diegetic vampire music is built on the principle of phantom sound, more explicitly spectral sounds are often used in specific leitmotifs to express the vampire's ghostly nature. The brides of Dracula in Coppola's film are given hoarse voices that sound strangely distorted, as if they come from fading tape recorders. The conflation of seductive whispers with the phantom sound of studio distortion precisely matches the simultaneously erotic and undead nature of these creatures. The vampire's otherness is expressed in various ways. *Nosferatu* and its 2000 remake *Shadow of the Vampire* (soundtrack Dan Jones) musically characterize the vampire through Eastern Europe-orientalism, with solo clarinets or violins playing melancholy syncopated melodies over a bass drone in open fifths. Vampiric otherness is consistently treated as threatening and dangerous in the Hammer Dracula films, whose rather repetitive set of vampire leitmotifs have grown into "a musical reference bank for future horror-film composers" (Hannan 71). The vampire's otherness develops into plain monstrosity in the leitmotif that Wojciech Kilar composed for Coppola's *Dracula*, in which a repeated second interval serves as a musical reminder of the *Jaws* monster. These leitmotifs provide a more effective and adequate means of expression than, for instance, diagonal camera angles or stop-frame camera movement, as they even indicate vampiric presence when it is not (yet) visible onscreen. The vampire leitmotif, in this way, functions as a dorsal echo that precisely fits the disembodied, dislocated and temporally dislodged subject matter it represents.

The vampire's relation to the Catholic supernatural, too, is musically expressed in film. As in vampire mythology and literature, the most distinctive musical aspect of the vampire's Gothicized Catholicism is its rituality. The occult rituals of the vampire are accompanied by liturgical music, Gothic music specifically tuned to the spectrality and auditory imagination surrounding the transgressions between life and (un-)death, reason and superstition, and Protestantism, Catholicism and secularism.

Gothic Catholicism and Bloody Liturgy

Besides giving a voice to the phantoms that populate Gothic ghost stories, film music is also able to create an aural manifestation of the uncanny twilight zones that these spectres roam. Through the effects of auditory imagination, sounding music creates a virtual time and space outside the here and now that is defined only by musical laws of tempo and rhythm, melody and harmony. This musical universe is far from static: it constantly moves and changes, and along with it so do the listener's connotations, her reminiscences and premonitions. Musical experience is a constant decontextualization, a constant fading of one reality into another. The same goes for movie soundtracks, whose virtual reality exists parallel to the visual narrative; in the case of vampire film music, the disembodied and spectral qualities of phantom sound can make the uncanny, undead virtuality of vampires overlay the seemingly safe actuality of humans. As musical virtuality is as changeable as musical connotations are, these soundtracks allow the human and vampiric, the light and dark, the good and evil to fade into one another almost without a break. This music does exactly what Gothic literature has done since the 18th century: it Gothicizes familiar truths and realities. And it does so very effectively, since film music's Gothicizing ways are dorsal, unpredictable and invisible, so that even the inattentive listener in the cinema is inevitably taken along on the musical journey over the borders of reason and into the twilight zone of the Gothic ghost story. Vampire soundtracks, in short, not only express but also induce the transgression from reason and Protestantism to irrationality and Gothicized Catholicism.

The transgressive function of vampire music can be described as a particularly specific kind of film musical "suture," the binding together of seemingly unrelated parts of the film diegesis through continuous music (Gorbman 63–68). Using exactly those characteristics of non-diegetic music that Donnelly has described as spectral, music can make the attractive, seductive side of vampires flow gradually into their evil, blasphemous side, and the other way around. In Tony Scott's *The Hunger* (1979), for instance, rock music makes way for Gregorio Allegri's poignant *Miserere* as the vampire Miriam Blaylock lays her dying victim-husband John to rest with her other past loves. The serene music with its angelic connotations gives John's death a sacred dimension, undoing the vampiric hubris of undeath and thus restoring "the borders between God and man." Van Helsing needs a ritual to do what music can do all of its own: it moves narrative and spectator/listener from vampiric to human realms. Scott's choice for such evidently Catholic music is no coincidence — this is liturgical music, music that is an intrinsic part of Catholic ritual. Just like exorcism rituals and vampiric mock rituals, liturgical music is able to open up the passageway between life and death, good and evil, sacred and satanic. Because of the joined forces of auditory imagination, spectrality and phantom sound in vampire soundtracks this Gothic liturgy is even more effective than textual or visual rituality.

Liturgical music in vampire films indeed operates at the very core of Gothicized Catholicism. The Lucy and Dracula vs. Mina and Jonathan scenes from Coppola's *Dracula* illustrate the point. While the simultaneity of the two scenes can visually only be hinted at by the shot-after-shot crosscuttings, the *Jaws*-like Dracula leitmotif is musically simultaneous to the "Dies irae" of the Orthodox wedding, and both are part of a grand orchestral buildup towards the kiss of love/kiss of death climax at the end of the scene. It is only in the virtual reality of the musical soundtrack that the transgressions take place. The vectors of musical connotations induce the passages from life to undeath and from blasphemous threat to sacramental protection. While film scenario and cinematic screening introduce the various Protestant, Catholic and Orthodox components of this scene, its soundtrack amalgamates them into the religious borderland of vampiric ritual. This music functions as the liturgy of Gothicized Catholicism.

Like books and films, vampire movie soundtracks have become decreasingly religious in recent years, and pop and rock music characterize the boy-next-door-vampire. Whenever reference is made to the vampire's religious or ritual background, however, it is always with musical accompaniment. Sometimes this is specifically Catholic music like the "Miserere" or the "Dies irae," but often vampire films employ a musical form of faux Catholicism. The opening credits to Neil Jordan's cinematic adaptation of *Interview with the Vampire: The Vampire Chronicles* (1994) are scored by Elliot Goldenthal in ethereal, textless motifs sung by female voices which are clearly meant as a reminder of Catholic church music. The vocal rather than instrumental scoring indicates the human agency in this transgression to the divine, or the vampiric. Very similar music is used in the opening scene to Coppola's *Dracula*. After Vlad Tepes excommunicates himself in his chapel he kicks over the baptismal font, spilling its water over the floor; its instantly turning blood red establishes the vampiric inversion of the Catholic sacrament of baptism. Dracula goes on to stab the cross, which starts to bleed, and with his drinking of it and renouncing the Eucharist and God the vampiric Antichrist is born. The scene is scored with wordless vocal motifs rising up in repeated sequences accompanied by thumping beats in percussion and brass. The musical lines climax in a big dissonant chord and drum as the film title appears on the screen: here is Dracula. At the end of the film, when Dracula dies and the vampire Mina is born, the same wordless vocal lines return. This is faux Catholic music, whose connotations are Gothicized reminders of the close connections between white and black magic, vampiric and Catholic rituality. While Protestant liturgical music has a mediating function between God and man, Catholic liturgy, just like Catholic ritual, is able to transcend those borders. As it was exactly such transcendent characteristics that Catholicism was first Gothicized for in the 18th century, the liturgical music in vampire soundtracks has exactly the same function as the "discordant" funeral hymns in *Carmilla* and earlier Gothic vampire novels: it challenges the boundaries between scientific reason and supernatural irrationality.

Vampire movie soundtracks, in conclusion, are able to do more than just give very precise musical representations of the stories they are composed for. The disembodied quality of phantom sound matches the ephemeral nature of the vampire, and the ghosts and hauntings inherent to the listening experience indicate the vampire's spectral presence. More importantly, music invokes the Gothicized Catholicism that is at the basis of the vampire genre, and it can actively set in motion the most distinctive aspect of that borderland of undeath, transcendence and inverted ritual.

Only music that sucks can accompany bloody liturgy.

Notes

1. The term "Protestant" in this article refers to shared characteristics of various Protestant theologies; with regards to liturgy the article focuses specifically on Anglicanism as the frame of reference for the mostly English non–Catholic vampire fiction discussed here.

2. Sterne (298) quotes an article from the *Scientific American* stating that "speech has become, as it were, immortal" ("A Wonderful Invention — Speech Capable of Indefinite Repetition from Automatic Records," 17 November 1877, 304).

Works Cited

Botting, Fred. *Gothic*. London: Routledge, 1996.
Bram Stoker's Dracula. Dir. Francis Ford Coppola. Perf. Gary Oldman, Winona Ryder, Anthony Hopkins. Columbia Pictures Corporation, 1992. Film.
Calmet, Dom Antoine Augustine. *Treatise on Vampires & Revenants. The Phantom World. Dissertation on those Persons who Return to Earth Bodily, the Excommunicated, the Oupires or Vampires, Vroucolacas, &c.* (1746). Transl. Henry Christmas. Ed. Clive Leatherdale. Brighton: Desert Island Books, 1993.
Coyle, Rebecca. "Spooked by Sound: The Blair Witch Project." *Terror Tracks: Music, Sound and Horror Cinema*. Ed. Philip Hayward. London: Equinox, 2009. 213–228.
Donnelly, Kevin. *The Spectre of Sound: Music in Film and Television*. London: British Film Institute, 2005.
Gorbman, Claudia. *Unheard Melodies: Narrative Film Music*. Bloomington: Indiana University Press, 1987.
Halfyard, Janet K. "Music of the Night: Scoring the Vampire in Contemporary Film." *Terror Tracks: Music, Sound and Horror Cinema*. Ed. Philip Hayward. London: Equinox, 2009. 171–185.
Hannan, Michael. "Sound and Music in Hammer's Vampire Films." *Terror Tracks: Music, Sound and Horror Cinema*. Ed. Philip Hayward. London: Equinox, 2009. 60–74.
Ihde, Don. *Listening and Voice: Phenomenologies of Sound*. Albany: State University of New York Press, 2007.
LeFanu, Sheridan. "Carmilla" (1871). *Children of the Night: Classic Vampire Stories*. Ed. David Stuart Davies. Ware, Hertfordshire: Wordsworth, 2007. 65–130.
Malleus Maleficarum: The Notorious Handbook once used to condemn and punish "witches." Translated by the Rev. Montague Summers. Ed. H. Kramer and J. Sprenger. San Diego: The Book Tree, 2000.
McClelland, Bruce. *Slayers and Their Vampires: A Cultural History of Killing the Dead*. Ann Arbor: University of Michigan Press, 2006.

Milbank, Alison. "Powers Old and New: Stoker's Alliances with Anglo-Irish Gothic." *Bram Stoker: History, Psychoanalysis and the Gothic*. Ed. William Hughes and Andrew Smith. Houndmills, Basingstoke: Macmillan, 1998. 12–28.
Nelson, Victoria. "Faux Catholic: A Gothic Subgenre from Monk Lewis to Dan Brown." *boundary 2* 34/3 (2007). 87–107.
Neumeister, Erdmann. *Tisch des Herrn*. Hamburg: Kißner, 1722.
Nosferatu. Dir. Friedrich Wilhelm Murnau. Perf. Max Screck. Jofa-Atelier Berlin-Johannisthal, 1922. Film.
Rice, Anne. *Interview with the Vampire*. London: Time Warner Books, 2006.
Sage, Victor. *Horror Fiction in the Protestant Tradition*. New York: St. Martin's Press, 1988.
Shadow of the Vampire. Dir. E. Elias Merhige. Perf. John Malkovich, Willem Dafoe, Udo Kier. Saturn, 2000. Film.
Sterne, Jonathan. *The Audible Past: Cultural Origins of Sound Reproduction*. Durham: Duke University Press, 2006.
Stoker, Bram. *Dracula*. New York: Norton, 1997.
Summers, Montague. *The Vampire* (1928). London: Studio Editions, 1995.
Van Elferen, Isabella. "Let Tears of Blood Run Down Your Cheeks: Floods of Blood, Tears and Love in German Baroque Devotional Literature and Music." *Blood in History and Blood Histories*. Ed. Mariacarla Gadebusch Bondio. Florence: Sismel, 2005. 193–214.
_____. *Mystical Love in the German Baroque: Theology, Poetry, Music*. Lanham, MD: Scarecrow, 2008.
Von Greiffenberg, Catherina Regina. *Des Allerheiligst= und Allerheilsamsten Leidens und Sterbens Jesu Christi*. Nuremberg: Hofman, 1672.
Wills, David. *Dorsality: Thinking Back through Technology and Politics*. Minneapolis: University of Minnesota Press, 2008.
Zanger, Jules. "Metaphor into Metonymy: The Vampire Next Door." *Blood Read: The Vampire as Metaphor in Contemporary Culture*. Ed. Joan Gordon and Veronica Hollinger. Philadelphia: University of Pennsylvania Press, 1997. 17–26.

"The Blood Is the Life"
Roman Catholic Imagery in American Vampire Films of the 1930s

ANN KORDAS

"The blood is the life, Mr. Renfield," Count Dracula informs the hapless Englishman who has traveled to Transylvania as his agent only to find himself a prisoner of the vampire Count. This line, taken from the Old Testament, which appears in Tod Browning's 1931 film *Dracula*, starring Bela Lugosi, contains the essence of what it means to be a vampire. It also contains the essence of what it means to be a Roman Catholic. The conflation of the two, vampire and Catholic, was not accidental. For centuries, European peasants had perceived the vampire (if perhaps only subconsciously) as essentially Roman Catholic in its characteristics and attributes, and Bram Stoker's 1897 novel *Dracula* recreated this "Catholic" vampire and made it familiar to the educated classes of Europe and the United States. In the United States at this time, just as motion picture technology was developing, Americans were also experiencing the rebirth of a virulent fear and hatred of Roman Catholics. It is thus not surprising that Roman Catholic characters, imagery, and motifs would be incorporated into early American horror films as elements intended to provoke fear. Even less surprising is that the first true American horror film would star a vampire, the most "Catholic" of all monsters.[1]

By the time that the movie *Dracula* was produced, distrust of Roman Catholicism had been a significant feature of American life for years. The Catholic Church and its adherents had struck fear into the hearts of Protestant Americans since the very founding of the country. Most colonies offered no protection for Roman Catholics even when they extended religious protection to the members of a wide variety of other religious groups. Protestant politicians, businessmen, writers, and ministers emphasized the supposedly strange, exotic, and undemocratic features of Catholic belief and practice. Catholics, these writers informed Protestant Americans, were not allowed to choose their priests or their bishops. Independent religious thought was not encouraged. Confessing one's sins to a priest and requesting forgiveness was depicted as a craven, subservient act, and Catholics were regarded as minions of an authoritarian Pope who were willing to follow his every order, even if it meant killing their Protestant neighbors — which many anti–Catholic "authorities" insisted was part of the Pope's plan for the United States. Finally, the exotic dress, celibacy, and segregation from the rest of society required of monks and nuns troubled many Protestant Americans who saw in such practices something "secretive" and "unnatural."

Fear of Roman Catholics in the United States increased greatly in the 1830s and 1840s when the first large numbers of Catholic immigrants, mostly from Ireland, reached the shores of the United States in what many native-born, Protestant Americans perceived as nothing less than an invasion. (A cartoon of the time depicts a swarm of bloodthirsty crocodiles wearing bishops' miters invading Washington, DC, via the Potomac.) At this time, American printing presses turned out a variety of both reprints of British works and original books and pamphlets that decried the practices of Roman Catholicism. Many of these works focused especially on the plight of women who entered convents. Such books were often the works of Protestant women who claimed that they had been held against their will in convents and subjected to unspeakable horrors by nuns and priests. In 1835, for example, Rebecca Reed, a young Catholic convert who had attended an Ursuline convent school for young women in Charlestown, Massachusetts, before she "escaped" in 1834, wrote a scathing "exposé" of life in the convent. *Six Months in a Convent* detailed numerous humiliations and instances of abuse to which she, the other students, and some of the younger nuns had supposedly been subjected (Schultz 4, 134). Shortly thereafter, in 1836, an author who identified herself as "Maria Monk" authored *Awful Disclosures of Maria Monk, or, The Hidden Secrets of a Nun's Life in a Convent Exposed* (also known as *Awful Disclosures of the Hotel-Dieu Nunnery in Montreal*) (Schultz 132). The book, with its descriptions of torture, murder, and illicit sexual acts taking place behind convent walls, became a standard anti–Catholic text and continued to be sold and read well into the twentieth century (Blee 90–91). Books such as these formed the original "scripts" of Roman Catholic horror.

Although anxiety of Roman Catholicism had been a part of the Protestant American landscape since the founding of the country, fear of Roman

Catholics themselves was perhaps at its most virulent in the first few decades of the twentieth century, following a wave of immigration from eastern and southern Europe which brought to the United States millions of new immigrants—many of them Catholic Austrians, Italians, Poles, Czechs, Slovaks, Croats, Hungarians, and Lithuanians. This surge in the fear of Roman Catholics coincided with both the growth of the American movie industry and a renewal of interest in the defunct Ku Klux Klan. Having originated in the late 1860s as a secret society dedicated to terrorizing freed slaves in the former states of the Confederacy, the Klan had largely vanished in the 1870s as a result of federal prosecution and the return of southern state governments to the rule of white men. The Klan was reborn in 1915, but this new Klan, while not abandoning its hatred of African Americans, took on a new series of targets—recent European immigrants, especially Roman Catholics and Jews. Catholics, the Klan preached, imprisoned young girls in convents "to feed the lust of [its] adulterous bachelor, overfed, drunken priesthood" and took vows to "burn, waste, boil, flay, strangle and bury alive" Protestants (Blee 75, 91). Indeed it was an intense hatred of Roman Catholics and a desire to drive them from public life that characterized the Klan of the 1920s and 1930s, a Klan that spread beyond the states of the old Confederacy to nearly every state in the nation. At its height, the new Klan boasted some six million members in states as diverse as Connecticut, New York, Pennsylvania, Ohio, Iowa, Illinois, Indiana, Michigan, Wisconsin, Minnesota, West Virginia, Maryland, Oklahoma, Kansas, Nebraska, Colorado, Washington, Oregon, and California (Blee 30; Horowitz 3, 4).

As might be expected, this dread of the Roman Catholic Church and its beliefs, rituals, and followers found expression in American movies of the period. This was especially true of American horror films, and, while not every film followed the same conventions, many such movies used Roman Catholic characters, motifs, and images to evoke a sense of fear in the audience. Chief among the movies incorporating Roman Catholic elements were vampire films. This is, perhaps, not surprising given the close connection between the folkloric figure of the vampire and the beliefs and rituals of the Roman Catholic Church.

The vampire (at least the vampires of Bram Stoker's *Dracula* and the vampires that appear in early twentieth-century films) is, in essence, a horrific, perverted representation of Roman Catholic beliefs and practices. Indeed, as some historians and folklorists have argued, the vampire is a creation of Christianity and, more specifically, of Roman Catholicism. Although a belief in creatures resembling vampires had existed in Europe (most notably in Greece) in pre–Christian times, the arrival of Christianity (in the form of the Church of Rome) significantly changed the nature of the vampire. Early Greek myths, for example, told of a creature that drained the life from human beings. This female creature (called a *lamia*) was depicted as a demon of purely supernatural origin (Beresford 22–23). After the arrival of Christianity in Greece, however, the vampire began to take on decidedly Christian characteristics. The vampire was now no longer a demon from a supernatural realm but a reanimated corpse, a dead person who retained a semblance of life and could leave its grave — much in the same way that Jesus had arisen after his death and burial and appeared before his followers. The transformation of vampire myths to include Christian elements happened throughout Europe; as various regions converted to Christianity, their vampires also became "Christianized" (Beresford 42, 44–51).

Perhaps the strongest link between vampires and Christianity is the importance of blood in the Christian, especially the Roman Catholic, tradition. Just as the vampire must consume blood in order to continue its unnaturally eternal life, so must Christians consume the blood of Jesus to be granted salvation and life after death. Indeed, in the traditional Roman Catholic liturgy, when the time arrives for communion, the following passage is recited in memory of Jesus' directions (according to the Gospel of Luke) to his followers at the Last Supper: "Take this [the chalice], all of you, and drink from it: this is the cup of my blood, the blood of the new and everlasting covenant. It will be shed for you and for all so that sins may be forgiven." While Protestant sects have interpreted what it means to drink Jesus' "blood" in various ways, the general Protestant belief is that Jesus is present in the wine *in spirit*. The Roman Catholic Church, however, has always clung to the belief that at the moment of transubstantiation the wine in the chalice *literally* becomes the blood of Christ, and this is what Catholics consume in obedience to the will of Jesus.

Although the attainment of eternal life through the consumption of the blood of an immortal being is surely the most important similarity between vampire mythology and Christian belief, other Christian/Roman Catholic beliefs also seemingly influenced ideas regarding vampires. For example, in many European folklore traditions, a common way for people to become vampires was to violate the laws of the Roman Catholic Church. In many parts of Europe, children born out of wedlock (especially to parents who were themselves illegitimate), children conceived during one of the many holy periods during which the Catholic Church outlawed sexual intercourse (especially Christmas Eve, Easter, and Pentecost), and people who had committed suicide (a mortal sin in Catholic belief) were all commonly believed to become vampires after death (Beresford 59). Methods for dispatching vampires also became

Christian in nature. For example, nailing vampires to walls or piercing the suspected vampire's feet with nails, in a manner suggestive of the torture of Christ, were said to be very effective at ending vampire attacks (Beresford 26). Even more suggestive of the link between Jesus and the vampire was a burial ritual that called for binding the body of the potential vampire with thorns, as the head of Jesus had been bound (Barber 158).[2]

All of these aspects of vampire lore developed during a period when the Church of Rome was the only Christian Church in western and central Europe and in some parts of Eastern Europe as well. At this time in these places, being Christian was the same as being Roman Catholic. There was simply no alternative form of Christianity. Although Protestants, as Christians, share many of the same beliefs as Roman Catholics (e.g., the death and resurrection of Jesus, the sacred nature of the blood of Jesus), these beliefs arose at a time when Rome controlled the meaning of Christianity in most of Europe. Vampire beliefs were thus by default associated with Roman Catholic beliefs and practices. Furthermore, following the Protestant Reformation, many of the "Christian" elements of vampire lore came to be identified either primarily or exclusively with Roman Catholicism and not with the various Protestant sects that spread throughout Europe. For example, the crucifix, the image of the tortured, pierced body of Jesus on the cross, which was believed to be especially effective in warding off vampires, came to be associated primarily with Roman Catholicism as most Protestant churches adopted the "empty" cross, emphasizing the resurrection and not the death of Jesus, as a symbol of their beliefs.

Indeed, continued belief in the existence of vampires was itself fostered largely by the Roman Catholic Church. Among the teachings of the Protestant Reformation was that demons (such as vampires) did not exist and that religious charms had no efficacy in casting out evil. Furthermore, Protestant churches preached that evil forces of supernatural origin could not harm man (Thomas 490). As a result, belief in both vampires and the magical-religious methods of destroying them or protecting oneself against them seem largely to have disappeared in Protestant communities. In Roman Catholic regions, however, such beliefs persisted. This was especially true of the Catholic regions of Eastern Europe. Indeed, there is evidence to suggest that the Roman Catholic Church may have promoted beliefs in vampires and demons in an effort to prove the superiority of evil-vanquishing Roman Catholicism over Protestantism (Thomas 491). Undeniably, the attachment of Roman Catholic writers to the vampire remained fairly constant over time. In 1746, for example, Dom Augustine Calmet, a Benedictine monk who had studied reports of vampires from throughout Europe, authored a book in which he accorded some veracity to the numerous legends concerning the undead. So influential was Calmet's book on vampirism that a character in the horror film *The Vampire Bat* (1933) actually consults it to learn more about the vampires that are supposedly terrorizing the town where he lives. As late as the twentieth century, one of the foremost "authorities" on the undead was a Roman Catholic convert (and self-proclaimed priest) Montague Summers who wrote extensively about vampires in such books as *The Vampire, His Kith and Kin* (1928) and *The Vampire in Lore and Legend* (1929) (Bartlett 7).

The characteristics of vampires that are clearly associated with Roman Catholicism are numerous, and it is these characteristics that received particular emphasis in early twentieth-century vampire movies. First, most vampire films were set in parts of Europe with large Catholic populations or in areas otherwise associated with Roman Catholicism. *Dracula*, for example, is set in Transylvania, a region of Romania with a large Roman Catholic Hungarian population, and the film clearly positions vampire lore as part of eastern European and Roman Catholic belief. The film opens with Renfield, an Englishman, traveling to meet Count Dracula, a Transylvanian aristocrat who has hired him to arrange a trip to England. Renfield arrives in Transylvania on the eve of Walpurgis Night, when evil spirits are believed to roam the earth freely. It is a night, the Hungarian Catholic peasants whom he meets inform him, when people hide within their houses "and to the Virgin we pray."

Dracula's Transylvanian abode is also very much Roman Catholic in nature. The main hall of Dracula's castle resembles the interior of a Gothic cathedral. The lofty ceiling, the walls lined by rows of arched windows, Gothic arches leading to the main staircase, and the castle's flying buttresses are all reminiscent of medieval church architecture. Dracula's home in England also has a connection to Roman Catholicism. Renfield, before becoming Dracula's deranged servant, has rented Carfax Abbey, an abandoned Catholic monastery that was later turned into a country estate, for Dracula to use as his residence. In the novel, Dracula remarks that, as a member of a very "old family," he "rejoice[s] that there is a chapel of old times" (Stoker 35). Furthermore, in both the novel and the film, the doomed ship that transports Dracula to England lands at Whitby. Although Stoker presumably chose to set the story in the neighborhood of Whitby because he was familiar with the area (having spent summers there), Whitby was also the setting of a meeting at which the future of Christianity in England was decided. At the Synod of Whitby in 664, King Oswiu of Northumbria decided that Christian practice in his realm would follow the example set by the Church of Rome and not the Irish Church.

Other vampire films also had "Catholic" settings. Tod Browning's *Mark of the Vampire* (also known as *Vampires of Prague*), a 1935 remake of his now lost 1922 vampire film *London After Midnight*, is set in an unspecified Roman Catholic region of central or eastern Europe. The film opens with a scene of gypsies praying and making the sign of the cross before a cathedral in the town square as darkness falls. When Western tourists scoff at the local "superstitions," a village woman shakes her head at their foolishness and crosses herself. Frank R. Strayer's *The Vampire Bat* (1933) has a similar setting, a small, central European community named Kleinschloss. Once again, when evidence indicates that the town has been beset by a vampire, one of the townsmen makes the sign of the cross and implores, "God, save us. The Devil." The 1936 "spin-off" of *Dracula, Dracula's Daughter*, begins in London, where Dracula's offspring, the Hungarian Countess Marya Zaleska, maintains both a stylish apartment and a studio in Chelsea, a part of London with a significant Roman Catholic population. The film ends in a castle in Transylvania. Even the film *Son of Dracula* (1943), which was set in the United States, takes place on a plantation in the bayous (presumably in Louisiana, an area with a large Roman Catholic population of French descent). References to eastern European settings are also made in this film. Kay, the main character, is described as having met Dracula's son Count Alucard (Dracula spelled backwards) in Budapest. In one of the early scenes in the film, Kay is warned of impending doom by Queen Zimba, a Hungarian gypsy who tells fortunes in the swamps.

Not only are the settings of vampire films Roman Catholic in nature, but some movie vampires and their victims also resemble members of the Roman Catholic clergy in their appearance. Irena Borotyn, the vampire's intended prey in *Mark of the Vampire*, wears a "negligee" resembling a friar's robe bound at the waist with a cord. Countess Marya Zaleska also dresses in a manner reminiscent of medieval monks and nuns. She wears long, black dresses and robes and often covers her head with a hood resembling a monk's cowl. Much of Countess Zaleska's power also seems to derive from another accoutrement of Catholic clergy. She wears a large ring that gives her the power to hypnotize and manipulate others. The ring is the source of Zaleska's power much as the ring of a Roman Catholic bishop symbolizes his power within the Church.

Various elements of Catholic ritual are also incorporated in vampire films of the 1930s. In *Dracula's Daughter*, Countess Zaleska steals her father's body (driven through with a stake by Professor Van Helsing at the end of *Dracula*) from a police station and cremates the body in the forest. Dressed in black robes with a hood covering her head, Countess Zaleska conducts an exorcism. As her father's body burns, she commands, "[B]e now exorcised, oh Dracula!" Brandishing a wooden cross above his burning remains, she exhorts, "[B]e the evil spirit cast out until the end of time." Regardless of whether or not this is the form that an actual exorcism would take, it is significant that the film identifies the ritual as such, for exorcism has been, since the time of the Protestant Reformation, most closely associated with rather than the Roman Catholic Church but not by Protestant churches (Thomas 52, 54, 265, 479).

Other Roman Catholic elements appear in vampire films in the form of apotropaics or charms used to ward off vampires. Crosses (especially crucifixes, a specifically Roman Catholic "charm") are commonly depicted in films as providing protection from vampires. In the movies, making the sign of the cross is a typical response to any mention of vampires, and the wearing or brandishing of a crucifix is (usually) treated as a foolproof method of protecting oneself from the undead. In the film *Dracula*, when Renfield reveals to the Hungarian peasants that he is employed by the eponymous Count, a woman crosses herself and, upon hearing him insist that he travel on to meet Dracula that evening despite the warnings of the peasants, presents him with a crucifix to wear for protection. The crucifix does, indeed, prove to be effective, and Dracula recoils from it in horror. In the novel *Dracula*, the crucifix is even more explicitly identified as an element of Roman Catholic "superstition." When the innkeeper's wife presents Jonathan Harker with a Roman cross to wear, he records his unease in his diary: "[The peasant woman] then rose and dried her eyes, and taking a crucifix from her neck offered it to me. I did not know what to do, for, as an English Churchman, I have been taught to regard such things as in some measure idolatrous..." (Stoker 12).

The crucifix features prominently in other vampire films as well. In *Mark of the Vampire*, Professor Zelen, the requisite vampire expert, chides Irena Borotyn, the victim of a vampire attack, for not wearing "that cross I told you to wear" and orders a servant, "Put it about her neck." In *The Vampire Bat*, a large crucifix hangs from the wall in the room of a woman who has been attacked by a bat. Mumbling in her delirium, the sick woman, Martha, calls for her rosary, and the woman attending her explains to the doctor, "She won't let it out of her sight." After the doctor leaves, Martha implores her friend to "put [the rosary] on. Put it on." Obeying the sick woman's wishes, the attendant places a large rosary around the woman's neck. Later in the film, the crucifix from Martha's wall is found on the floor beside the bed of the doctor's housekeeper, who has seemingly been killed by a vampire.

Authority, indeed domination, over one's followers was another important characteristic of vampires. It was also identified by American nativists as a salient feature of the Catholic Church and its representatives. Many American Protestants believed that their Roman Catholic neighbors blindly followed the word of the Pope, even to the extent that they would willingly take up arms and kill their non–Catholic countrymen so that the Pope could invade the United States (Blee 92–93). Many early twentieth-century movie vampires were likewise foreign "invaders" who gained control over the local populace by transforming them into vampires. Dracula leaves Transylvania and travels to England for the purpose of feeding upon the English and manages to gain control over several English people. Dracula's daughter also "invades" England while his son attempts to transform Americans into vampires.

Movie vampires of the 1930s were also characterized by the same haughty, aristocratic attitudes that American Protestants attributed to the "rulers" of the Catholic Church, the same "elitism" that Kathleen Urda identifies with the Catholic Lady Marchmain in her chapter on *Brideshead Revisited*. Vampires demanded the same unswerving loyalty from their followers and supposedly gained an equally unnatural control over their "victims." Browning's Dracula served as the model for the aristocratic vampire who lorded his power over those beneath him. Dracula's first victim in London is a poor flower girl selling violets on the street. Dracula's daughter, Countess Zaleska, is an equally ruthless aristocrat. She associates with the elite members of London society, and her only contact with the lower classes comes when she preys upon them to satisfy her lust for blood. In one memorable scene in the film, Zaleska's servant Sandor approaches a desperate young woman about to commit suicide and lures her to the Countess's studio (the Countess fancies herself an artist) with promises of food, warmth, and money. The Countess feeds her and then kills her. Like the members of the Dracula family, the aristocratic doctor who is the villain of the film *The Vampire Bat* also preys upon the weak, including his own servants. The doctor's last victim is his housekeeper. The eponymous vampires of Prague are the cape-wearing aristocrat Count Mora and his daughter Luna who inhabit the local castle. The true villain of the film is also an aristocrat, Baron Otto.

These aristocratic vampires easily bend their victims to their will. Dracula demands complete obedience from those who "belong" to him. In the film, Renfield is first held hostage by Dracula and later killed when he betrays his "master." The villainous doctor in *The Vampire Bat* uses a form of mind control to force his manservant Emile to bring his victims to him. The vampires in *Mark of the Vampire* also easily gain control over the mind and will of Irena. As Professor Zelen explains, "Miss Borotyn is in their power. To save her we must break the spell."

One of the great dangers of falling under a vampire's control was the possibility of sexual victimization. Similarly, one of the great dangers that Roman Catholicism posed, according to American nativists, was the sexual domination of young women by priests and nuns (Blee 89–91). Not surprisingly given these anxieties (especially regarding nuns), vampires in American films of the 1930s, including female vampires, are fond of preying upon female victims. In Browning's film, with the exception of Renfield, Count Dracula's English victims are all women — the flower seller, Lucy, and Mina. Dracula's attentions to Mina serve both to drain her energy and to awaken her sexuality. The arousal of her sexual nature does not go unnoticed by Mina's fiancé, Jonathan Harker. "Mina," Harker remarks, staring lustfully at the clearly aroused young woman, "you're so — like a *changed* girl. Oh, you look wonderful!"

Dracula's daughter also preys sexually upon her female victims. When a desperate young woman is brought to Countess Zaleska's studio, Zaleska asks the girl if she would be willing to pose for her semi-nude. When the girl removes her blouse, the Countess advances upon her, her eyes glowing with excitement. The girl retreats in terror and announces her desire to leave. The sexual implications of the Countess's hobby of painting young girls, her delight at the sight of the girl's body, and the girl's discomfort at her approach call to mind the accusations of illicit sexual acts and the sexual torture of innocent girls attributed to nuns in anti–Catholic literature of the nineteenth and early twentieth centuries (Blee 89–91).

An even more overtly sexual predator is Luna, the young female vampire in *Mark of the Vampire*. Luna's first attack on Irena Borotyn resembles an aggressive embrace more than it does an act of violence. After she first bites Irena, Luna is shown spying on her, once as she sleeps and again when Irena talks to her fiancé, Fedor. When Irena goes to Luna's castle, Luna "attacks" her again. Pushing Irena almost gently into a seated position, Luna places her arms around her and bends down to place her mouth on Irena's throat. Irena, entranced, makes no effort to fight off her advances. When Luna is interrupted by the unanticipated arrival of Fedor, she becomes enraged, snarling and hissing like an animal at the male recipient of Irena's affection.

The movie image of the vampire as a robed aristocrat from Roman Catholic regions who possessed an unnatural control, often of a sexual nature, over his (or her) victims, undoubtedly awakened associations in American Protestant minds with Roman Catholic clergy. However, as has been mentioned, the most "Catholic" of all of the vampire's characteristics was undoubtedly the vampire's desire for blood to prolong its eternal life. As can be expected, this element of vampirism/Catholicism also played an important role in vampire films of the early twentieth century. Dracula's blood drinking tendencies and his obsession with the life-giving substance are emphasized repeatedly in Browning's film. When Renfield sits down to dine on his first evening at Dracula's castle, the Count serves him wine in a metal goblet that bears a strong resemblance to a chalice. Renfield wonders why his host does not join him, and Dracula informs him that (in one of the most famous lines of the film), "I never drink — *wine*," implying, of course, that he does drink other substances. This line is repeated in the film *Dracula's Daughter* when Countess Zaleska refuses a glass of sherry at a party.

Just as Roman Catholics must consume the blood of Christ, it is not enough for Dracula and other vampires merely to consume the blood of their victims; the vampire's victims must also consume the blood that grants eternal life. To be truly "saved," to be become "undead" (to be resurrected as it were), the chosen one must consume the blood of the master. In both the film and the novel, Dracula transforms Mina, the heroine for whom he yearns, into a living vampire by having her drink his blood. In *Dracula's Daughter*, Professor Van Helsing explains that Dracula "infused his own tainted blood" into his victims in order to transform them into vampires. Similarly, the bloodsucking doctor of *The Vampire Bat* drains the blood of his victims in order to feed the blood to the new life forms that he is creating.

The vampire films of the 1930s with their blood drinking and other Roman Catholic imagery were undoubtedly prototypes not only for later Hollywood vampire films but also for other American horror movies as well. In the hearts and minds of early twentieth-century native-born Americans, both Catholics and vampires awakened fears of invasion, sexual abuse, and domination by aristocratic foreigners. Although Roman Catholic imagery featured most prominently in vampire movies, Catholic symbols also appeared in other horror films of the time. In *White Zombie* (1932), for example, the villain (played by Bela Lugosi) lives in a home resembling a Gothic cathedral complete with pointed arches and trefoil stone carvings. The film *Bride of Frankenstein* (1935) contains even more Roman Catholic elements. Frankenstein's misunderstood monster, fleeing from vicious peasants who have bound him, Christ-like, to a pole, finds refuge in the home of a blind hermit dressed like a Catholic friar. The humble cabin features a large crucifix that is positioned over the monster's shoulder and bathed in light in the scene in which the creature shares a symbolic meal of bread and wine with his new companion. Chased from the hermit's cabin by men seeking to destroy him, the monster flees through a crucifix-laden church graveyard. Although Catholic imagery remains a feature of many contemporary horror films, in the 1930s such imagery must have evoked anxiety in many audience members who sincerely believed that the Roman Catholic Church was a "vampiric" institution that sought to drain the lifeblood of democratic, predominantly Protestant America.

Notes

1. *Dracula* was not the first vampire film. Fritz W. Murnau's *Nosferatu* (1922), an unauthorized loose adaptation of Bram Stoker's novel, is considered the first vampire film. *Dracula*'s director Tod Browning had also directed an earlier, silent film featuring vampires called *London After Dark*. Unfortunately, the only known print of the film was destroyed in a studio fire in 1965. Browning's later film *Dracula* is the first vampire film to leave an enduring mark (no pun intended) on American audiences.

2. Ironically, although the methods of killing or preventing the creation of vampires used by European peasants were probably thought of as attempts to banish evil by replicating the conditions of Jesus's sacrificial death, the manner in which Jesus was killed suggests, according to historian Paul Barber, that Jesus's Roman executioners treated his body as they did to prevent him (an executed criminal) from returning as an evil spirit. The "Christian" methods used to destroy vampires may thus actually be based on pagan Roman methods employed to destroy the original Christian vampire — Jesus (158).

Works Cited

Barber, Paul. *Vampires, Burial, and Death: Folklore and Reality*. New Haven: Yale University Press, 1988.
Bartlett, Wayne, and Flavia Idriceanu. *Legends of Blood: The Vampire in History and Myth*. Westport: Praeger, 2006.
Beresford, Matthew. *From Demons to Dracula: The Creation of the Modern Vampire Myth*. London: Reaktion Books, 2008.
Blee, Kathleen. *Women of the Klan: Racism and Gender in the 1920s*. Berkeley: University of California Press, 1991.
Bride of Frankenstein. Dir. James Whale. Perf. Boris Karloff, Colin Clive, Valerie Hobson. Universal, 1935. Film.
Croot, Patricia E.C., ed. "Religious History: Roman Catholicism." *A History of the County of Middlesex: Volume 12: Chelsea* (2004). British History Online. www.british-history.ac.uk. Web. 11 Feb. 2010.
Dracula. Dir. Tod Browning. Perf. Bela Lugosi, Helen Chandler, David Manners. Universal, 1931. DVD.
Dracula's Daughter. Dir. Lambert Hillyer. Perf. Otto Kruger, Gloria Holden, Marguerite Churchill. Universal, 1936. DVD.
Dracula's Son. Dir. Robert Siodmak. Perf. Lon Chaney, Jr., Robert Paige, Louise Allbritton. Universal, 1943. DVD.
Horowitz, David A., ed. *Inside the Klavern: The Secret History of a Ku Klux Klan of the 1920s*. Carbondale: Southern Illinois University, 1999.
Mark of the Vampire (Vampires of Prague). Dir. Tod Browning. Perf. Lionel Barrymore, Elizabeth Allan, Bela Lugosi. Universal, 1935.
Schultz, Nancy Lusignan. *Fire and Roses: The Burning of the Charlestown Convent, 1834*. New York: The Free Press, 2000.
Stoker, Bram. *Dracula*. New York: Penguin Books, 1993.
Thomas, Keith. *Religion and the Decline of Magic*. New York: Scribner's, 1971.
The Vampire Bat. Dir. Frank R. Strayer. Perf. Lionel Atwill, Fay Wray, Melvyn Douglas. Majestic Pictures, Inc., 1933. DVD.
White Zombie. Dir. Victor Halperin. Perf. Bela Lugosi, Madge Bellamy, Joseph Cawthorn. United Artists, 1932. DVD.

House of Horrors
Brideshead Revisited *at the Movies*
KATHLEEN E. URDA

Traditionally, many critics, while admiring Evelyn Waugh's elegiac novel *Brideshead Revisited* (1945), have struggled with its complicated but undeniable embrace of Catholicism.[1] Through the eyes of the agnostic Charles Ryder, we learn about the Marchmains of Brideshead, and their strange, and then ultimately moving and powerful, Catholic faith. While Waugh does not shy away from realistic and critical portraits of devout Catholics, neither does the novel hide its own belief.[2] The beloved 1981 serialization of *Brideshead Revisited* for Granada Television presents the Catholic Church much as Waugh's book does. Julian Jarrold's 2008 movie, *Brideshead Revisited*, is, quite literally, another story. Jarrold declares about the screenplay by Jeremy Brock and Andrew Davies, "It seemed to look at the whole world of Brideshead in a different light."[3] In particular, this streamlined, 134-minute vision of the novel looks at Catholicism in a different light. I argue that the film grapples with Catholicism by essentially transforming *Brideshead Revisited* into a horror story in the English Gothic tradition with Lady Marchmain, the matriarch of Brideshead, Brideshead itself, and the Catholic Church as the monstrous villains of the piece. I will also speculate about why the filmmakers may have chosen a Gothic mode as the best way of presenting this story to a twenty-first century audience.

"Gothic" is a term that is now broadly applied to many different works and, as a result, its meaning is difficult to state definitively. However, I am primarily using Gothic here to refer to the literary movement sparked in the eighteenth century by Horace Walpole's *Castle of Otranto; A Gothic Story* (1764) and popularized further by Ann Radcliffe, Matthew Lewis, and their many imitators. While major differences exist among these works, there are certain common denominators:

> A Gothic tale usually takes place ... in an antiquated or seemingly antiquated space.... Within this space, or a combination of such spaces, are hidden some secrets from the past (sometimes the recent past) that haunt the characters, psychologically, physically or otherwise at the main time of the story [Hogle 2].

Generally, an innocent or group of innocents find themselves and their sexuality endangered in this space by oppressive forces, frequently patriarchal and at times apparently supernatural.

Though the Catholic Church is not always the source of these forces, Catholicism was tied to the Gothic novel from its beginnings. The very word Gothic originally refers to architecture identified with the medieval Church,[4] and *The Castle of Otranto* supposedly is a translation of a priest's text. In eighteenth-century England, after over two centuries of political and cultural reinforcement, the Catholic Church, its denizens and accoutrements, automatically evoked an ancient, mysterious, perverted, irrational, and powerful threat (Kendrick 41). Novels like Lewis's *The Monk* (1796) and Radcliffe's *The Italian* (1797) strategically heighten such associations with lurid and often unapologetically inaccurate portrayals of Catholic practices inside abbeys and convents. Though *The Monk* embraces a satanic explanation for the crimes perpetrated therein, whereas *The Italian*, like all Radcliffean Gothic, offers rational explanations for such wickedness, in both novels the secrecy and hypocrisy of the Church produce sexual perversions while preventing normal romantic happiness and sexual fulfillment.

Several points of contact exist between Waugh's novel and this Gothic tradition. After all, *Brideshead Revisited*'s narrator, Charles Ryder, recounts the story of how, as a young innocent at Oxford, he becomes involved with Sebastian Flyte and his family, the Marchmains, who are exotic to him not only because of their wealth and charisma but also because of their Catholicism. The family matriarch, Lady Marchmain, is a devout Catholic whose control is resisted and feared by her family. As in many traditional Gothics, this family has a great old house, Brideshead, where the narrator finds himself drawn at several important times in his life. At the start of the novel, a much older Charles, now a captain in the British Army during World War II, finds himself unexpectedly encamped with his company at Brideshead and reflects on his history with it. It is fair to say then, that Charles is a man haunted by the past and by an old estate, which, while not an abbey, does boast a Catholic chapel. And yet, *Brideshead Revisited* far from being a novel of Gothic fears is a complex and nostalgic look back at a past that is, for Charles, bittersweet in its beauty and loss. Characters do not fit easily into categories, either good or bad. Troubles and tragedies unfold without clear perpetrators, and despite Charles's ambivalence, the Catholic faith emerges as a compelling reality that stands apart from any one character. I will show how the film refashions the novel into a story that bears all the marks of Gothic horror: a dark tone, an oppressive villain associated with an irrational and often inaccurate Catholicism, persecuted innocents, and an ancient and haunted space from which escape is unlikely, if not impossible.[5]

Almost immediately, the film has a more ominous tone than the book. At the novel's start, a world-weary, disillusioned Charles, suddenly returned to Brideshead, feels as if he has awakened in a dream and his mood is yearning. In this section, entitled "Et Arcadia Ego," which suggests a hearkening back to a golden age, Charles confides to readers, "I had been there before; first with Sebastian more than twenty years ago on a cloudless day in June ... a day of peculiar splendour, such as our climate affords once or twice a year, when leaf and flower and bird and sun-lit stone and shadow seem all to proclaim the glory of God; and though I had been there so often, in so many moods, it was to that first visit that my heart returned on this, my latest" (21). In contrast, the film's opening mood is dark, an air siren sounding as the credits roll. While Charles (Matthew Goode) remains the observer through whom we learn about Brideshead, we hear his narration only at the film's beginning and end rather than throughout, which has the effect of making him a more enigmatic character. There is also a total change in the narration we do get to hear. He tells us, "One emotion remains as pure as that faith from which I am still in flight: guilt." Goode emphasizes the word guilt, and though this emotion's source is unknown, what is unambiguous is the film's insistence on Charles's anxiety about his past rather than his attraction to it.

The film blames such a response primarily on Lady Marchmain and the Church she symbolizes, again a significant departure in many ways from Waugh's novel. There, Lady Marchmain is a complicated figure, and Charles, while not swayed either by her Catholicism or her charm, tells us, "She accepted me as Sebastian's friend and sought to make me hers also, and in doing so, unwittingly struck at the roots of our friendship. That is the single reproach I have to make of her abundant kindness to me" (109). Though the waspish Anthony Blanche, a boyhood friend of Sebastian's, describes Lady Marchmain as a "pious" bloodsucker who has played the martyr and destroyed her family, this portrait (like many of his others) maliciously caricatures Waugh's more fully rounded character (53). Lady Marchmain does indeed try to control her family through means both subtle and unsubtle, with often disastrous results — her failed attempt to curb Sebastian's drinking by having him watched by the Oxford don Mr. Samgrass springs to mind. But Waugh also reveals this truth as partial.

Charles and others acknowledge Lady Marchmain's real desire not merely to control her children but also to ensure their happiness. She tries to persuade Julia, her eldest daughter, out of marriage to Rex Mottram, even before his divorce is known, because she understands, as Julia does not, Rex's character and what that might mean for her child. As she tells Julia, "Your happiness is [my business]. If you must know, I think Mr. Mottram a kind and useful friend, but I wouldn't trust him an inch" (187–8). Similarly, Lady Marchmain is upset by Sebastian's drunkenness not just from a sense of propriety or morality but because it signals his deep misery. She says to Charles after a drunk Sebastian makes a scene, "I do not mind the *idea* of him being drunk. It is a thing all men do when they are young. I am used to the *idea* of it.... What hurt last night was that there was nothing *happy* about him" (136). All of this is not to deny Lady Marchmain's domineering tendencies, but rather to point out that Waugh draws a multi-layered woman who tragically cannot help those she loves most despite her best intentions.

Also subtle is Waugh's picture of Lady Marchmain's Catholicism. Admittedly, she is for many in the novel synonymous with the Church, as is Brideshead. Charles comments, "Religion predominated in the house; not only in its practices — the daily mass and rosary, morning and evening in the chapel — but in all its intercourse" (126), and Sebastian confides to Charles, "'Mummy is widely believed to be a saint'" (89). But the book itself rejects that belief. Waugh goes to some lengths to suggest that Lady Marchmain, while a sincere Catholic whose prayers and suffering undoubtedly contribute to her family's eventual return to the Church, also unwittingly drives them and others away from it precisely because of a deep piety that nevertheless falls short of true holiness. The youngest Marchmain, Cordelia, indicates as much to Charles: "'I sometimes think when people wanted to hate God they hated Mummy ... she was saintly but she wasn't a saint. No one could really hate a saint, could they? They can't really hate God either. When they want to hate Him and His saints they have to find something like themselves and pretend it's God and hate that'" (221). Cordelia's distinctions here are important given the temptation to identify Lady Marchmain too completely with the Church.

The film foregoes Waugh's complex approach, however, and makes Lady Marchmain (Emma Thompson) into the horror haunting Brideshead. Though Gothic villains are often patriarchal men, there is also a precedent for them to be evil or weak mothers.[6] In *The Italian*, for example, the Marchesa di Vivaldi, the hero's mother, and the Abbess, the spiritual mother of San Stefano, are the ones who most impede the lovers' union. During Charles's first surreptitious visit to Brideshead, Sebastian (Ben Whishaw) hears from his nanny that Lady Marchmain is about to return, and, immediately terrified, he rushes from the room. In the novel, it is Julia Nanny says is returning, not Lady Marchmain, and it is Julia, or we can imagine, any member of his family, from whom Sebastian flees. But the film is building up Lady Marchmain and the Church for which she is the human face as the only demons chasing Sebastian.

The film particularly symbolizes Lady Marchmain's demonic villainy and its entwinement with Catholicism through the figure of the Virgin Mary. Charles's first sight of the house's interior loveliness and grandeur includes a painting of a Virgin and Child, which dominates the room and to which the camera repeatedly returns. It is given further significance when Sebastian, seeing Charles's interest in it, announces, before hastening him away, "I loathe that painting." His loathing for and flight from the painting remind us of his loathing for and flight from his mother and associates the two mothers in our minds. The Virgin Mary iconography continues when Sebastian whisks Charles through the chapel. While a small crucifix hangs over the altar, a much larger statue of the Virgin and Child is the real focus of the chapel and the camera. With such images, the film identifies Lady Marchmain, the mother who oppresses her children, with the Virgin Mary, one of the most recognizable and positive symbols of the Church but also one historically misunderstood and despised as a figure worshipped in God's stead, "the mark of idolatrous Catholicism" (O'Malley 40). The heavy visual emphasis on the Virgin Mary, who is central to but not the center of Catholicism, is entirely the film's invention rather than anything Waugh describes. Interestingly, however, such a portrait does appear in *The Monk*.[7] Indeed, the introduction of Mariolatry provides another tie-in with early Gothic novels and their often mistaken depictions of Catholic devotions and practices as well as linking Lady Marchmain's twisted version of motherhood with (supposedly) that of the Church.

While the book refuses to explain completely the Flyte children's resentment of their mother, and by extension Mother Church, the film assigns it to a perverted desire to keep them sexually innocent children. Charles's first encounter with Lady Marchmain, again a scene absent from the novel, reveals her infantilization of Sebastian. Through a half-open door, Charles glimpses Lady Marchmain browbeating a weeping Sebastian whom she encourages to "be a good boy for God and for Mummy." Cara, Lord Marchmain's mistress (Greta Scaachi) further confirms Lady Marchmain's monstrous over-mothering, with a vituperative denunciation: "'Even when they [the Marchmain children] were tiny in the nursery they must do what she want [sic] them to do, be what she want them to be. Only then would she love them. It's not Lady Marchmain [sic] fault. Her God has done that to her.'" The film's determination to make villains of Lady Marchmain and "her God" becomes even clearer when we contrast this scene with Waugh's original one in which Cara sees Lady Marchmain as her family's victim rather than the other way around. There Cara marvels at Lord Marchmain's and Sebastian's detestation of Lady Marchmain: "'And how has she deserved all this hate? She has done nothing except be loved by someone who was not a grown-up.... She is a good and simple woman who has been loved in the wrong way. When people hate with all that energy, it is something in themselves they are hating'" (103). While the novel's Cara suggests that the family has unfairly scapegoated Lady Marchmain, the film embraces such scapegoating.

Jarrold and the screenwriters also reject much nuance in their portrayals of Sebastian and Julia who become the totally innocent victims of Lady Marchmain's Gothic villain. In the novel, Sebastian and Julia are both attractive and multifaceted characters, who are victimized at times, but who are also (sometimes disastrously) self-determining. Sebastian controls his friendship with Charles from its inception. If either is more dependent and infatuated, it is Charles. Sebastian is maddeningly, if charmingly, mercurial in his relations with him as with everyone else. For example, during a break from Oxford, he barely communicates with Charles and then suddenly demands his presence at Brideshead via an alarming telegram. In the film, Sebastian is still demanding but far less powerful. Though Sebastian's peremptory summoning of Charles remains, Sebastian's command of the friendship does not. Rather, the filmmakers make over this erotically-charged friendship into one in which Charles leads a besotted Sebastian on in order to gain an entre to Brideshead, even going so far as to show Charles allowing Sebastian to kiss him one wine-soaked, sunset night. Waugh presents Charles as an upper middle-class gentleman's son, certainly not of the Marchmains' lineage and wealth, but still a young man of good family whose love of Sebastian and Brideshead contains little hint of crass greed. In the film, Charles is almost a parvenu out of Stendhal, a schemer from a dingy middle-class background.

By definitively suggesting that Sebastian is in love with Charles and that Charles cruelly manipulates this love, the filmmakers make Sebastian's homosexuality, rather than his drinking, his main struggle. In the novel, the reasons behind Sebastian's heartbreaking fall into drunkenness are ambiguous. Sebastian's struggles have to do with his parents, with his faith, with his future, and undoubtedly with his sexuality, but his pain is never directly tied either to homosexuality or to unrequited love of Charles. Sebastian primarily likes

Charles because he represents an escape from his family, and as soon as Charles befriends them, he too becomes tainted. In fact, it is Charles, not Sebastian, who clings to their friendship until finally he asks Sebastian during a visit to Brideshead, "'Tell me honestly, do you want me to stay on here?'" and is told, "'No, Charles, I don't believe I do'" (168). While the film depicts Sebastian's growing alcoholism it eliminates the mystery of this self-destruction, blaming it on Lady Marchmain/the Church and Charles's cruelty, but especially on the former. As Charles tells Lady Marchmain, "You're the reason he drinks."

In similar fashion, the movie transforms Julia, whom the novel first introduces as a headstrong, capricious, and rather cold girl determined to overcome the "barrier" (181) her religion represents to a fine marriage. Despite Julia's beauty and triumph as a debutante, most aristocratic British families would refuse to have their oldest sons marry a Catholic and eligible Catholic men are few. Julia does not greet this problem passively. Rather, Waugh compares her thoughts about how to find someone to marry to those of a war strategist. When she does find someone whom she likes, Rex Mottram, a wealthy and worldly Canadian of murky background, Waugh describes Julia's "appetite" for him (184) and, despite the fact that her mother disapproves, Julia persists in the romance. Even when it emerges that Rex is divorced and thus cannot be married in the Catholic Church, Julia gets her father's approval and marries Rex in the teeth of opposition from her mother and the Church.

The film's conception of Julia (Hayley Atwell) deprives her of such agency, however. In perhaps the movie's most major plot change, Julia's love for Charles occurs much earlier than in the book where Charles emphasizes that when they first meet, she seems to have barely more than a disdainful and distant tolerance for him: "We pursued separate aims which brought us near to one another, but we remained strangers" (178). It is not until chance reunites Charles and Julia years later that they fall passionately in love. But the film suggests their passion is there from the beginning, a catalyst for Sebastian's despair, for Charles's ambitions, and for Lady Marchmain's cruelty. Lady Marchmain dictates that Julia must marry a Catholic and, in one of the film's more bizarre departures from the original, has picked Rex (Jonathan Cake) as the man. In a scene written for the film that directly contradicts Lady Marchmain's concern for Julia's happiness in the novel, Lady Marchmain tells a lovestruck Charles that "happiness in this life is irrelevant" and that she "must marry a Catholic ... her future is not question of choice; it is a matter of faith ... God commands and we obey." Rather than creating her own destiny as she does in the book, Julia is not even present for this conversation, nor does the film later show her participating in the decision about her marriage. She, like Sebastian, becomes a sacrificial lamb uttering barely a bleat as it is led to the slaughter.

Such alterations help the film to create a Gothic feel as pure-hearted young people are hemmed in on one side by a brutal world and on the other by a heartless authority who imprisons them in the Catholicism that also traps her. As Frederick S. Frank observes, "[From its beginnings, the Gothic asserted itself as the literature of collapsing structures, evil enclosures, forbidden feelings, and supernatural chaos. Its primary crisis would be entrapment or fear of entrapment for the innocent and evil characters alike" (6). This description could easily be applied to the film, especially to its portrayal of what happens to the family following Lady Marchmain's death. As in the novel, Charles and Julia meet again years later on board a ship and, both unhappily married, begin an affair. Here, the film departs once more from the book's interpretation of what follows. In both versions, Charles and Julia's affair is doomed, but the doom's source comes in the film from an ill-advised return to Brideshead, now fully a house of horror. Sebastian, exiled in Morocco, warns Charles that even after Lady Marchmain dies "the place would still be full of her" and "run far away and don't ever look back." Yet Charles, out of greed, suggests returning, though Julia, like Sebastian, reacts with terror, as if the house is a person who will punish her. Waugh, in contrast, does not have Sebastian mention anything about Brideshead and shows Julia longing for a life with Charles there. When it appears that her father means to leave the house to her rather than to her brother Bridey or Sebastian, she is thrilled and tells Charles, "'I think you and I could be very happy here'" (321).

The film allows for none of that. Though Gothic or horror are not words Jarrold uses, they fit how he envisions the house as the film continues: "Brideshead is initially this beguiling, stunning, mysterious but beautiful place ... but later on Brideshead itself has a slightly more sinister presence when you realize the characters are fatally locked into it and can't escape from it ... so we very much charted the look of the film to try and reflect that."[8] Indeed the house does darken visually and acquires even more of a life of its own. Julia and Charles return to a dimly lit Brideshead that holds a certain malevolent — and it quickly becomes obvious — maternal presence. Standing beneath the portrait in the Great Hall, Julia suddenly repulses Charles's embraces, saying, "Not here," and begs to leave. It is as if her mother's influence has already started to creep back over her. After her eldest brother, Bridey (Ed Stoppard), casually mentions to Julia that his fiancée will not be her guest because she is "living in sin," Julia goes to stand frozen underneath the portrait.

Later, she articulates the feeling that her mother possesses Brideshead in a radically altered version of her hysterical speech by the fountain. Waugh has a remorseful Julia, reacting to Bridey's comment, talk about how "sin" is "'[a] word from so long ago, from Nanny Hawkins stitching by the hearth and the nightlight burning before the Sacred Heart. Cordelia and me with the catechism, in Mummy's room, before luncheon on Friday's. Mummy carrying my sin with her to church, bowed under it... Mummy dying with my sin eating at her, more cruelly than her own deadly illness'" (288). Here Julia thinks about her childhood, mourns her actions, and recognizes her mother's suffering, but the film performs an oversimplified psychoanalysis of Julia's remorse; even she can see that her feelings are due to years of maternal conditioning:[9]

> I tried to be good.... But it's not enough; it's never enough. God had to punish me, so he took my child. With you [Charles] I thought I could really and truly be free, but coming back here, it's like a thread, an invisible thread drawing you back inch by inch[10] until all of a sudden you're a child again and that voice inside your head, the one that Mummy planted all those years ago in the nursery ... filling your head with it and the voice is telling you, whispering, "Wicked little Julia, bad little girl, living in sin," and here I am again with you, living in sin!

Horribly, the film suggests that Julia, especially now that she has returned to this house of motherhood and Catholicism, entangled together, can never be free of the horrifying voice "planted" so deeply within her.

The next scenes confirm this Gothic fear of lasting psychological entrapment and thwarted escape. Charles, stricken by Julia's hysteria, has agreed to leave Brideshead, and the lovers begin their flight away in an echo of Charles's first flight from Brideshead, spurred on by a desperate Sebastian. This time, however, the flight fails, as they see Lord Marchmain returning to die at Brideshead just as they are trying to escape it to live. This scene is wholly interpolated and mostly underscores again the impossibility of escaping the iron grip of Brideshead and by extension, Lady Marchmain and the Church. In yet another invented scene, Charles shares with Julia his belief that "that woman [your mother] is more alive now than she ever was. She's in every brick, every stone, every slit. Sebastian was right. We should run away." If Lady Marchmain was not a Gothic monster with almost supernatural and death-defying powers before this, she is now.

Such a monstrous presence renders Lord Marchmain's deathbed repentance ambiguous to say the least. While some readers dislike the novel's ending in which Lord Marchmain recognizes his betrayal of Lady Marchmain and ultimately signals his reconciliation with the Church through a sign of the cross, Waugh intends it to be the emotional climax of the novel and a testimony to the power of Providence.[11] Certainly for Julia and even for Charles, who senses that this reconciliation will end their affair and resists it, the actual moment is one in which they feel desire and awe. Charles thinks, "I suddenly felt the longing for a sign, if only of courtesy, if only for the sake of the woman I loved, who knelt in front of me, praying, I knew, for a sign" (338). When it comes, Charles realizes "that the sign I had asked for was not a little thing, not a passing nod of recognition, and a phrase came back to me from childhood of the veil of the temple being rent from top to bottom" (339). Whether one accepts divine intervention as Charles does here, Waugh clearly wants us to do so.

The filmmakers' intentions are considerably less clear. They do some work to make Lord Marchmain's deathbed conversion about more than just Lady Marchmain's final revenge by indicating that Marchmain's repentance is about Sebastian rather than his wife. He mourns, "I watched that woman crucifying my son little by little, and I was silent. What does that say about me?" This remorse over his failure to stop Lady Marchmain's crucifixion of their Christ-like son seems like the film trying to preserve the idea of final redemption so central to the novel, but the juxtaposition of this attempt with what comes before and after renders it incoherent at best. The deathbed scene itself feels foreboding from the thunderstorm brewing outside to the half-crazed expression Michael Gambon gives Lord Marchmain. And though his children are touched by his repentance, Charles, through whose eyes we see these events, only moves from dread to pained resignation.

Even more revelatory of the film's real attitude is that after Charles leaves the room, Julia follows and finds him gazing up at the Virgin Mary portrait accusingly. Just in case we have forgotten whom this portrait represents, Julia says, "Daddy gave it to Mummy as a wedding present." She then tells Charles that she cannot go with him, because she "cannot shut herself off from His [God's] mercy." Though these words are part of Julia's farewell to Charles in the novel, there the farewell occurs on the stairs. Locating this parting underneath the Virgin Mary portrait sends the message that the Omnivorous Mother has finally succeeded in devouring her family rather than that Lord Marchmain and Julia freely return to their faith.

The film's last scenes, which return us to Captain Ryder walking around a now-beleaguered Brideshead, do not dispel this feeling of inescapable entrapment. In the novel, Charles goes to the chapel to say "a prayer, an ancient, newly learned form of words" (350). Before leaving, he reflects on the sanctuary lamp burning before the tabernacle, the lamp that in Catholic churches is never extinguished and honors Christ's Real Presence[12]:

> Something quite remote from anything the builder intended has come out of their work, and out of the fierce little human tragedy in which I played ... a

> small red flame — a beaten-copper lamp before the doors of a tabernacle.... It could not have been lit but for the builders and the tragedians, and there I found it burning anew among the old stones [351].

This is a hopeful reflection. Charles is at the very least about to convert to Catholicism, if he has not already, and the implication is that despite all the mistakes and the tragedy of the past, God abides and is found in this chapel. One of his men, seeing Charles, remarks, "'You're looking unusually cheerful today'" (351) and on this note the book ends.

No such note of cheer mars the Gothic gloom of Jarrold's film. Standing again beneath the portrait, Charles muses, "Whether by fate or the divine ironies of some higher power, I find myself returned once more to Brideshead. Did I want too much? Did my own hunger blind me to the ties that bound them to their faith? Am I only now, shadowed by war, all moorings gone, alone enough to see the light?" When Charles goes to the chapel, the visit answers the question of whether he is now so "alone" and pathetic as to seek solace in the Church. The red candle burns not before the tabernacle but before the Virgin Mary statue. The single red flame has a specific meaning within Catholicism, but the film gives it another, preferring to suggest once more that "the ties that bound" the Marchmains to their faith can be found in the monstrous Mother's abuse. Charles dips his hand in the holy water, not to make the sign of the cross, but apparently because he intends to douse the flame of Lady Marchmain once and for all. As his dripping fingers hesitate over the flame, images of the broken Sebastian and the young Julia flash across his mind. For a moment, he narrowly stares at the statue and the flame. Then, as if he has been defeated or perhaps just can't decide what to do, he walks out of the chapel and the film fades to white.

This ending can be interpreted several different ways. Perhaps Charles represents secular twentieth-century man, skeptical of religion but unable to reject or replace it altogether. Or perhaps, given that Charles is a man whose greed for beauty and advancement make him too apt to use those he loves, it means that he accepts the "guilt" he mentions at the start of the film. While both of those ideas may partially explain what is going on here, the ending is also consistent with the film's Gothic perspective on *Brideshead Revisited*. Charles cannot extinguish the flame of the Monstrous Mother/Mother Church and the innocents remain entrapped.

The big question, of course, is why the filmmakers seem unable to envision *Brideshead Revisited* and its Catholicism as anything but a Gothic horror story, particularly given the radical alterations such a vision entails. In the eighteenth century, there were plenty of political and cultural reasons that Gothic novels looked to what Victoria Nelson calls "Faux Catholicism" as a source of villainy and mystery. It would be surprising if in this century or the last fears about the political threat and power of the Catholic Church motivate many Western works, but an ambivalent struggle with how to portray Catholicism in an increasingly secular society remains apparent, as many of the authors in the present volume demonstrate. For example, Christa Jones argues that had the filmmaker Maurice Pialat emphasized Catholic mysticism in *Sous Le Soleil de Satan* his 1980s audience would have laughed. The Gothic mode may still seem to offer a solution to this problem of Catholicism and the contemporary audience. Nelson writes, "Despite its faux Catholic trappings, the original Gothic is generally regarded by its critics as the first Western literary genre operating implicitly in the vacuum left by the departure of religious belief" (90). If anything, this vacuum gapes ever wider and the desire to fill it with compelling historical and psychological theories is big business. The massive popularity of works like *The Da Vinci Code* shows that a Gothicized tale confirming the deep-rooted suspicion about what actually enables the Church's claims to divinely-guided authority remains a bestselling concept.[13]

Thus by reimagining *Brideshead Revisited* from a Gothic viewpoint, which often walks the line between psychological and supernatural explanations, the film can retain and contain the novel's religious authority and themes in ways that might seem likely to appeal to contemporary audiences prone to distrust the existence of the supernatural, or at the very least its existence as a positive force. The authority and influence of the Church is reduced to Lady Marchmain's manipulations. Almost every character's faith is attributed to her psychological abuse while even Lady Marchmain herself is the battered victim of "her God." And though, as Charles intimates late in the film, the remarkable psychological influence she maintains after death seems almost supernatural, if anything it is a demonic, not a divine, power.

Like the earlier Gothic novel, this film's demonization of authority seems particularly connected to the Church's relationship with sexuality. Since the filmmakers make sexuality and love the central energies Lady Marchmain tries to suppress, it stands to reason that the ultimate drive behind the horror of this symbolic depiction of the Church might be its objection to the expression of sexuality in various premarital and extramarital forms. Patrick O'Malley remarks about the earlier Gothic, "For the Gothic novelists ... Roman Catholicism and sexual deviance were each suggestive of the other" (18). The belief in the eighteenth century was that repression and celibacy would cruelly prevent normal sexual expression causing who knows what evils as a result. While many in the twenty-first century would broaden the definition of what constitutes normal sexual expression, the Church's threat to it has only increased in some eyes. Circumstances might have changed, but the villain remains the same. So, by Gothicizing Waugh's novel and the Church's role in it, Jarrold and the screenwriters do succeed in making it feel contemporary.

Unfortunately, though the Gothic genre has produced fascinating and sophisticated engagement with Catholicism, rationalism, family, sexuality, and transcendence, this particular film uses Gothic tropes to create a simplistic tale that reflects more of a concern with current prejudices and preoccupations than it does with Waugh's actual novel, perhaps to the detriment of the film and its desire to attract contemporary audiences. While a majority of critics liked the movie, audiences did not, a contrast with the popularity of the more faithful television production and of the book itself.[14] The original *Brideshead Revisited* may at times enrage but also continues to engage people with its questions and answers about belief in a secularized world; the film misses an opportunity to do the same by rewriting rather than revisiting the novel.

Notes

1. Robert Murray Davis gives an excellent overview of some secular critics' dislike of the novel's religious elements (15–19). See Martin Stannard's *Evelyn Waugh: The Critical Edition* for a more general selection of reviews at the novel's publication in 1945 (233–87).

2. Waugh warns that *Brideshead Revisited* is "nothing less than an attempt to trace the workings of the divine purpose in a pagan world" (See Note 1 in Stannard 236).

3. "The World of Brideshead," featurette, *Brideshead Revisited* DVD, Miramax, 2008.

4. See Walter Kendrick's discussion in *The Thrill of Fear* about the term Gothic (42–47).

5. I am aware of Radcliffe's distinction between her more rational novels of "terror" and Lewis's supernatural tale of "horror." For this paper's purposes, however, I intend the phrase "Gothic horror" to mean works that employ features like oppressive mysterious villains, the Catholic Church, ancient spaces, imprisonment, etc.

6. See Deborah D. Rogers, *The Matrophobic Gothic and Its Legacy*, on maternal figures in the Gothic.

7. Antonio has an eroticized relationship with a portrait of the Virgin (40–1).

8. "The World of Brideshead" featurette.

9. In "The World of Brideshead" featurette, producer Robert Bernstein uses the word "conditions" in describing how Lady Marchmain raises her children Catholic and notes how hard the film worked to "develop" the idea of "how parents can destroy the children" through such conditioning.

10. In the book, "the invisible thread" phrase comes from one of Chesterton's Father Brown stories and refers to God's loving, persistent pursuit of the lost soul. Here, of course, the phrase is sinister.

11. In notes for a mostly positive unpublished essay on *Brideshead Revisited*, George Orwell mentions the deathbed repentance as evidence that "[o]ne cannot really be Catholic and grown-up" (as quoted in David Lebedoff, *The Same Man*, 173). Edmund Wilson felt the scene smacked of snobbery (Stannard 246).

12. The exception is after the Mass of the Lord's Supper on Holy Thursday when the tabernacle is emptied and the Blessed Sacrament reposed.
13. See Victoria Nelson on *The Da Vinci Code* phenomenon (94–107).
14. The film website *Rotten Tomatoes* reports that 64 percent of critics liked the film, but that box office was $6,359,742.

Works Cited

Brideshead Revisited. Dir. Charles Sturridge and Michael Lindsay-Hogg. Perf. Jeremy Irons and Anthony Andrews. PBS Great Performances, 1982. DVD. Acorn Media, 2006.
Brideshead Revisited. Dir. Julian Jarrold. Perf. Matthew Goode, Ben Whishaw, Hayley Atwell, Emma Thompson, and Michael Gambon. Miramax, 2008. Film.
"*Brideshead Revisited* (2008)." *Rotten Tomatoes.* 15 Feb. 2010. <http://www.rottentomatoes.com/m/brideshead_revisited/>.
Davis, Robert Murray. *Brideshead Revisited: The Past Redeemed.* Boston: Twayne, 1990.
Frank, Frederick S. "The Early and Later Gothic Traditions, 1762–1896." *Fantasy and Horror: A Critical and Historical Guide to Literature, Illustration, Film, TV, Radio, and the Internet.* Ed. Neil Barron. Lanham: Scarecrow, 1999.
Hogle, Jerrold E. "Introduction: The Gothic in Western Culture." *The Cambridge Companion to Gothic Fiction.* Ed. Jerrold E. Hogle. Cambridge: Cambridge University Press, 2002.
Kendrick, Walter. *The Thrill of Fear: 250 Years of Scary Entertainment.* New York: Grove Weidenfeld, 1991.
Lebedoff, David. *The Same Man: George Orwell and Evelyn Waugh in Love and War.* New York: Random House, 2008.
Lewis, Matthew. *The Monk.* 1796. Oxford: Oxford University Press, 1980.
Nelson, Victoria. "Faux Gothic: A Gothic Subgenre from Monk Lewis to Dan Brown." *boundary 2* 34:3 (2007): 87–107.
O'Malley, Patrick. *Catholicism, Sexual Deviance, and Victorian Gothic Culture.* Cambridge: Cambridge University Press, 2006.
Radcliffe, Ann. *The Italian or The Confessional of the Black Penitents.* 1797. Oxford: Oxford University Press, 1992.
Rogers, Deborah D. *The Matrophobic Gothic and Its Legacy: Sacrificing Mothers in the Novel and in Popular Culture.* New York: Peter Lang, 2007.
Stannard, Martin. ed. *Evelyn Waugh: The Critical Heritage.* London: Routledge & Kegan Paul, 1984.
Walpole, Horace. *The Castle of Otranto.* 1764. New York: Penguin, 2001.
Waugh, Evelyn. *Brideshead Revisited; The Sacred and Profane Memories of Captain Charles Ryder.* Boston: BackBay Books, 1973.

Drying Blood
De-sexualization and Style in Paul Schrader's Cat People

Marco Grosoli

The close connection between the horror movie and the many vicissitudes of sexual libido is an idea that by now does not need to be either explained or proven. Suffice it to mention one title: *The Exorcist* (William Friedkin, 1973), in which a priest is called to stem the explosion of (basically sexual) devilish energy bursting out of 12-year-old Regan MacNeil. Later (*Exorcist II, The Heretic*, John Boorman, 1977), the more the source of evil gets individuated and circumscribed in a piece of over-sexualized wild Africa, the more it is clear that what matters is no longer the horrifying, uncanny, wild abyss of sex. It is rather a matter of *images*, of images without any depth, pure surfaces. The second chapter of the Merrin saga is quite unmistakably an allegory about the power and the weight of *images*, present-day Evil from which none can escape. However, this attempt at shifting from the depth to the surface, from the dangerous abyss of sex to the impalpable omnipotence of images, was probably a failure. Box office was relentlessly poor. Everybody's *Exorcist* has been doubtlessly the first one, Friedkin's.

We should have learned the lesson. Anything that is repressed, returns. So, *that very shift*, that unlucky attempt to change the axis while passing from the first to the second chapter, i.e., shifting from the depth to the surface, was doomed to re-emerge. The present paper tries to analyze an occasion in which this preponderance of the surface found a way to emerge from oblivion. Again, Africa is involved as the primordial source of Evil, and not so curiously a priest is involved as the pivot of sexual repression/arousal: Paul Schrader's *Cat People* (1982).

My reading will not be a genre one, even though my investigation will start with a quick reminder of the basic horror genre traits. My second step will consist in moving away from genre paradigms in order to focus on the reasons why those horror paradigms are connected rather inevitably to Catholic topics. Only after a related and broader excursus on Catholicism will it be possible to understand why this crossing point between horror and Catholicism gives so much importance to surface rather than depth, and hence style over matter. In fact, Schrader is not a horror director at all: *Cat People* is his unique "pure horror" effort to date.[1] He is instead, and quite overtly, an *auteur* dealing critically with genre canons. Schrader's operation here is very evidently stylish, almost formalistic. That is why the shift in this chapter from genre to *auteur* perspectives *has* to be made. Then, a detailed analysis of the film will be developed.

"Apart from the Law Sin Lies Dead"

A true turning point for horror studies was certainly Robin Wood's *An Introduction to the American Horror Film*. Using Freud and Marx, Wood convincingly shows once and for all that the horror universe deals with energies that are sexual, social, and/or both. In horror films, these energies, having been primordially repressed in order to make way for civilization, return in uncanny, violent, uncontrolled forms. This is what the horror movie is about. Then, Wood proceeds to make a taxonomy out of many possible examples: the feared "Others" (incarnating that excessive primordial sexual/social energy) to keep safe from are, in turn, woman, the proletariat, different ethnic groups, and so on. "Normality is threatened by the Monster" (Wood 203). Between normality and the monster, of course, all sorts of perverted and complicated relationships can occur, starting from an ambiguous superposition (that typical point where the normal and the odd blur the reciprocal borders). Who is normal? Who is the monster?

Perhaps, Robin Wood himself was not so faithful to this principle, i.e., to this possibly infinite variety of ways to make normality and the monster relate to each other. Re-reading his fundamental essay from thirty years ago, one is probably struck by the way he radically and firmly separates the reactionary horror films from the progressive ones, the films preaching constriction vs. the ones supporting liberation.

This has, of course, already been noticed; for instance, from a more or less Foucauldian and/or Marcuseian point of view (Badley 13–4; Polan 126). According to the first, one of the most efficient tools employed by the official power in order to hold its grasp on people is the careful concession of accurately restricted spaces of transgression; the latter even used to refer (in his book of the same name) to *repressive tolerance* as a key feature of modern democracies. In other words, stemming the libido is not necessarily reactionary, just as supporting libido's liberation is not necessarily progressive. On the contrary, chances may be that a certain kind of libido release is solidly functional within the system: transgression does not necessarily break the rule, it might even be a regular means to reaffirm and confirm the validity of the rule. Foucault notwithstanding, the point is that an essential, substantial bond links the Law and its transgression. Innumerable teen horror films from the eighties, up to the self-referential *Scream* trilogy (Wes Craven, 1996, 1997, 2000), remind us that the more one tries to get rid of libido, the more "the monster" bursts out uncontrollably. And the other way around: the more one faces what cannot be faced, the more one "grows up" and becomes an ordinary subject. Prohibition generates its own transgression, reinforces it but is as well reinforced by it. We do not have the free and liberating power of libido on one side, and the constrictive prohibition on the other: there is a stern interdependency between the two.[2]

This is where Catholicism comes into question. It is very easy to see how, in contrast with the relatively more liberal and "algid" European Protestant cultures, in Catholic countries (i.e., in the Mediterranean area, or in the Latin nations) sex is a major taboo, but it is also a powerful collective obsession. While officially praising chastity, this kind of culture is patently carnal and over-sensual, if not over-sexual. Lately, philosophers such as Giorgio Agamben, Alain Badiou and Slavoj Žižek, have been engaged in a sort of rediscovery of the writings of Saint Paul. The interest in Paul's perspective resides especially in that it deals precisely with that genetic bond linking tightly the prohibition and the transgression, Law and Sin:

> What is sin exactly? It is not desire as such, for if it were one would not understand its link to the law and death. *Sin is the life of desire as autonomy, as automatism.* The law is required in order to unleash the automatic life of desire, the automatism of repetition. For only the law *fixes* the object of desire, binding desire to it regardless of the subject's "will." It is this objectal automatism of desire, inconceivable without the law, that assigns the subject to the carnal path of death. Clearly, what is at issue here is nothing less than the problem of the unconscious (Paul calls it the involuntary, what I do not want, *ho ou thelo*). The life of desire fixed and unleashed by the law is that which, decentered from the subject, accomplishes itself as unconscious, with respect to which the involuntary subject is capable only of inventing death. The law is what, by designating its object, delivers desire to its repetitive autonomy. Desire thereby attains its automatism in the form of a transgression [Badiou 79].

The law traces a border, and places the sexual/social repressed energy *on the other side*, beyond control. From this angle, it is easy to understand why the true Catholic act would not consist in erasing sin (since trying not to sin just produces the opposite effect), nor in erasing law, but rather in *breaking the relation itself between law and sin*, in breaking the link thanks to which law and sin are simultaneously generated from each other:

> St. Paul's problem is thus not the standard morbid moralistic one (how to crush transgressive impulses, how finally to purify myself of sinful urges), but its exact opposite: how can I break out of this vicious cycle of the Law and desire, of the Prohibition and its transgression, within which I can assert my living passion only in the guise of their opposite, as a morbid death drive? How would it be possible for me to experience my life-impulse not as a foreign automatism, as a blind "compulsion to repeat" making me transgress the Law, with the unacknowledged complicity of the Law itself, but as a fully subjectivized, positive "Yes!" to my Life? [Žižek 149–50].

Whatever the answer, it is clear that religion here meets psychoanalysis. In fact, just a few pages later Žižek (152–153) literally reports a passage from Jacques Lacan quoting word for word Paul's speech about the relations between law and sin from the Epistle to the Romans — with a little change: the word "sin" is substituted by Lacan with the word "Thing." In Lacanese, "The Thing" is the unbearable, excessive substance of enjoyment one cannot possibly deal with; to put it roughly, the term "Thing" designates the obscure and powerful energies from the unconscious in all their overwhelming fury. What is important here, is that Žižek (following Lacan) repeatedly points out that there is no such thing as a dreadful, horrifying primordial force that gets split, "repressed" and limited when the law (the language) shows up. What is really primordial is that immaterial split, generating *at the same time* the law and the ineffable depth it "limits." With respect to this, the Thing is a perspective illusion: it is but Law's necessary counterpart. Neither Law nor its transgression (the Thing) "comes first," because they just cannot help but being thought of as structurally relating to each other. So, neither of them is fundamental and substantial — but their relation is.

This is why Žižek distinguishes Badiou's Paul from Lacan's, despite their many convergences: for Badiou, "breaking the relation between law and sin" involves sticking to the positive, actual remainder that unpredictably exceeds that relation (in the Catholic parlance, "grace"), whereas for Lacan it can only consist in pure negativity, being sin (The Thing) not a self-consistent substance with an abysmal depth, but merely an *effect inconsistent in itself*. First comes the relation between Law and sin, and only *then* "Law" and "sin" as supposedly distinct entities.

Agamben's book on Saint Paul (evidently closer to Lacan's stance than to Badiou's) might make this notion of "pure negativity" clearer. As we have seen, law/language fixes both the identity of the subject and its "sin," the transgressive "Thing" as the absolute, terrifying and unbearable unconscious excess. This connection must be revoked. The split between what does pertain to the law/language and what does not, must be "as not" (*hos me*) separating what it separates:

> The Pauline *hos me* seems to be a special type of tensor, for it does not push a concept's semantic field toward that of another concept. Instead, it sets it against itself in the form of the *as not*: weeping as not weeping. The messianic tension thus does not tend toward an elsewhere, nor does it exhaust itself in the indifference between one thing and its opposite. The apostle does not say: "weeping *as* rejoicing" nor "weeping as [meaning =] not weeping," but "weeping *as not* weeping." [...] In this manner, it revokes the factical condition and undermines it without altering its form [Agamben 24].

This does not mean at all that what has been divided must be reunited: it rather means that the division itself must be divided, rendered "not operative" without erasing it. Law/language, as the basic negativity granting the subject its identity (and its own constitutive "sinful" excess), must undergo a "pure" negativity. It must be not just negated, but rather *deactivated*:

> "For when we were in the flesh, the passions of sin were enacted [*energeito*] through the law in our members to bring forth fruit unto death. But now we are de-activated [*katergethemen*, 'made inoperative'] from the law" (Rom. 7:5–6). The etymological opposition with *energeo* clearly demonstrates that *katergeo* signals a taking out of *energeia*, a taking out of the act. (In the passive, it means no longer being in the act, being suspended.) ... According to Paul, messianic power does not wear itself out in its *ergon*; rather, it remains powerful in it in the form of weakness [...] Just as messianic power is realized and acts in the form of weakness, so too in this way does it have an effect of the sphere of the law and its works, not simply by negating or annihilating them, but by de-activating them, rendering them inoperative, no-longer-at-work [*non-più-in-opera*]. This is the meaning of the verb *katargeo*: just as, in the *nomos*, the power of the promise was transposed onto works and mandatory precepts, so does the messianic now render these works inoperative; it gives potentiality back to them in the form of inoperativity and ineffectiveness. The messianic is not the destruction but the deactivation of the law, rendering the law inexecutable [*l'ineseguibilità della legge*] [Agamben 96–8].

Saint Paul has a precise name for this "transfiguration" of the subject *beyond* the barrier of law/language (i.e., of death) that constitutes him: resurrection. Not a positive vital substance "exceeding" the separation between law and sin, but rather what results from the separation of that very separation. Agamben then dedicates his final chapter to Walter Benjamin's "dialectic image" to fix a crucial connection between Pauline resurrection and *the image*

(Agamben 59–87 and 138–45). In fact, pure negativity is directly connected to image as such. "The Pauline passage on the *hos me* may thus conclude with the phrase '*paragei gar to schema tou kosmou toutou* [for passing away is the figure, the way of being of this world]' (1 Cor. 7:31). In pushing each thing toward itself through *as not*, the messianic does not simply cancel out this figure, but it makes it pass, it prepares its end. This is not another figure of another world: it is the passing of the figure of this world" (Agamben 24–5). "Resurrection" does not mean to leave this world for another: it means *getting transfigured into its own figure, into an image* rather than just sticking to an identity imposed by law/language (and subsequently falling into the charms of sin). On one side, the deathly alliance between the Verb (law/language) and the abysmal, ineffable depth of the Thing (sin). On the other side, *the image* as the nemesis of that alliance, as the "weakened" surface version of a de-activated depth, of a suspended energy which is now potential rather than actual, defused and pale rather that repressed and burning. The image (an epitome of Resurrection) as the breaking of the bond between law and sin.

Cat People is about a happy but painful de-sexualization through sex, instead of through the avoidance of sex: again, deactivation instead of destruction. A priest is the main character, because the priest embodies the vicious circle between lust and denial at the core of Catholicism (and faced in particular by Saint Paul) — and a great importance, in both form and content, is given to surfaces as such. Breaking the vicious circle between prohibition and transgression, the repression and the repressed (a vicious circle so typically belonging to horror films), abundantly involves the superficiality of the image as a fundamental condition. And this centrality of the image is deeply rooted in Catholicism (notoriously, the "religion of the image," whereas, for instance, the Hebraic tradition focuses a lot more on the Word), and especially in Saint Paul.

Cat People's Vita Nova

This paper began with a mention of "Africa as the primordial source of Evil." Indeed, *Cat People* starts with an African prologue, in which a beautiful girl is offered as a sacrifice to a black panther. Then, the main character is introduced, a blood descendant of that promiscuous man-animal relation: Irena (Nastassja Kinski). She lands in New Orleans, where his brother (a priest) lives. They both are "cat people," that is, people who turn into panthers after having sex, and who must kill in order to regain their human shape. Irena is a virgin, so she cannot know yet — but her brother does: we see him as a panther trying to kill a prostitute. She manages to escape, so he stays a panther, and is as such captured after a while and put into the local zoo. During the rest of the film, he (as a panther) eventually kills one of the zoo workers, rushes away leaving no traces, turns human again and kills another woman, and then gets killed in the end without having succeeded in getting his sister to make love with him, despite his constant attempts. Meanwhile, Irena falls in love with the zookeeper. In the end (and only in the end), she makes love with him, turns into a panther, disappears, kills someone and, once her lover has finally found her, asks him to kill her so that innocent blood will no longer be spilled. But he has a better idea: he ties her to the bed and makes love with her so that the panther in her can be caught and then kept in a cage. Jacques Tourneur's 1942 horror masterpiece from which Schrader's remake is taken is instead about a married couple who cannot really be as one, since Irena is not a woman, but a panther in the guise of a woman. Thus, there can be nothing sexual between the two; and whoever gets close to Oliver (the husband) has to face the fury of the panther-as-a-woman.

Decades of horror studies have recognized in this plot an example of how the male gaze is ready to make a terrifying and threatening monstrosity out of what it cannot understand — that is, female sexuality. Our usual deadlock: the Thing is nothing but a projection of the law banning it. Žižek (151) again:

> So the crucial point is that we have *two* "divisions of the subject" which should not be confused. On the one hand, we have the division of the subject of the Law between his conscious Ego, which adheres to the letter of the Law, and his decentred desire which, operating "automatically," against the subject's conscious will, compels him to "do what he hates," to transgress the Law and indulge in illicit *jouissance*. On the other hand, we have the more radical division between this entire domain of the Law/desire, of the prohibition generating its transgression, and the properly Christian way of Love which makes a New Beginning, breaking out of the deadlock of Law and its transgression.

This is why, forty years later in Schrader's film, we have *two* panthers. One is a priest named, of all names, *Paul*. There could not be a clearer example of the deadlock between law and sin: official chastity matches the unofficial "ultra-violence" (Paul is played by Malcolm McDowell, mostly famous for having played Alex in Stanley Kubrick's *A Clockwork Orange*, 1971). The other panther is his sister Irena, who turns down the zookeeper Oliver's love because she cannot have sex without being transformed into a ferocious panther. However, love will perform the miracle of breaking the bond between law and sin: Irena, a female version of Jesus Christ according to Schrader himself (Jackson 167), agrees to be tied to the bed to make love with Oliver, so that he can catch the panther and keep it inside a cage in his zoo, as a wonderful, terrible attraction. The fury of the panther is deactivated, made into a mere spectacle for the eyes.

Eyes are precisely the point. The African prologue ends with a woman staring a panther in the eyes with a shot-countershot between the two. Then the eyes of the woman dissolve into Irena's, just landing at New Orleans airport. The film's final sequence is again two close-ups of Oliver's and the panther's eyes staring at each other. In the middle of the film, the most violent confrontation between brother and sister is marked again by two subjective shots, through which the viewer's gaze coincides with Paul's and then with Irena's, while the two stare at each other and thus at the viewer himself. A veritable key-figure of the film, this matching of two gazes, represents the gaze that is no longer the agent of the splitting into the standard sexual difference, but *is itself redoubled and neutralized*. The exception confirming the rule: right before transforming into a panther and devouring his second woman (who is performing oral sex on him), Paul is framed with a close up of his gaze just before a black dissolve closes the scene with *no other gaze having matched his*. A gaze matching no other gazes is a devastating gaze, still fully inside the deadlock of sin/law; a redoubled gaze, a gaze meeting another gaze, is a neutralized gaze: it watches its own splitting.

In 1942, a brilliant Hollywood artisan (Jacques Tourneur) used an intelligently "hidden," invisible and highly refined style to better serve the story. Now the story is intentionally mechanical and rough, as it were: to express that Oliver loves Irena beyond sexual craving, Schrader portrays the zookeeper listening to a tape in which a male voice declaims Dante Alighieri's *Vita Nova* or "new life." (For some relaxation after a workday!) Besides the narrative often stopping and pausing, there are several parts of the film in which nothing happens — whereas, in other parts, tons of missing information is given all at once (as in the basement scene, or in the second African *intermezzo*).[3] Subsequently, the style does not "serve" the story anymore: Schrader, who generally does not like horror films and frankly dislikes Tourneur's *Cat People* (Jackson 167–172), rather indulges horizontally and statically in a constant visual magnificence. In other words: the style becomes strongly independent from the story, it is itself overtly an object to be contemplated and admired, as a *deactivated gaze*, no longer integrated in a narration. Tourneur moved his camera to follow action and characters, Schrader indulges in (gorgeous) camera movements which are completely arbitrary and gratuitous: suffice it to mention the complex movement of the first zoo scene, moving from the window to Oliver with two officials, abandoning them to frame the caged beasts on the lower floor, and then returning to Oliver (and the officials) having descended the stairs in the mean time. Or when the camera slowly explores the room after Paul has killed his second woman, framing fluidly and calmly a series of objects, among which is a bleeding torn-away arm. During both these gentle, caressing, refined camera movements the Thing (the beasts, the arm) is just an object among many others: all its excessive traits have been literally flattened away by style. Indeed, *Cat People* the remake is hardly scary, hardly an horror film anymore. It is rather a matter of style.

This meta-stylistic aspect is conscious, and deeply influences the development of the basic antagonism between brother and sister. When Paul kills his first woman, she (a prostitute) enters an empty room where Paul is supposed to be, talks a little bit assuming he is in the adjacent room, and then sees a black tail sticking out from under the bed. She touches it, and this is enough to make the panther come up and attack her legs. The point here is that we *never* see the panther: we just see some glimpses of its tail and claws in a quick montage of very tight close-ups. This use of the "partial objects" building up the filmic space recalls unmistakably Robert Bresson, someone whose style Schrader has tried to emulate more than once. But somehow it also alludes to the predominance of off-screen space, and thus to the outstanding (and so efficiently terrifying) use of the off-screen space of Tourneur's film (Fujiwara 72–84), as does the fact that throughout the film Paul's metamorphoses are systematically hidden from the viewer's gaze. We do not see Paul turning into a panther: we see Paul, then we see something else, and later on we see the panther he has become in the meantime (or something signaling the presence of a panther). Thus, Schrader seems to trace a parallel between Paul's laceration between law and sin, and a filmic texture radically split between in- and off-screen space: in the film, what the viewer does *not* see is given a huge importance. On the contrary, we do see the panther rising from Irena's skin and breaking it from the inside — and every time Irena is feeling she is transforming into the animal, the film literally stops and indulges, following her while she walks, undresses, looks around and so on. She is literally overexposed to the camera gaze. Hence, the pressure of off-screen space is drastically reduced in comparison with the original film — also because of the abundance of master shots from above, embracing the entirety of a given place. The 1942 version showed Irena grabbing a caged canary which, however, always stayed off-screen: we only were able to see Irena's gleeful face while moving her hand inside the (unframed) cage. In 1982, Irena devours a rabbit after having lengthily looked at it — or better: after yet another gaze-to-gaze close-up confrontation. And if in the original piece the dichotomy between in- and off-screen space was mirrored by the one between light and shadow (again Fujiwara 72–84), whose subtle interplay inside the frame prolonged somehow the hesitation between the known and the unknown operating between what was inside and outside the frame, the 1982 version flattens it all up, preferring strong chromatic dominances: several violently reddish or greenish frames, without any nuance complicating the frame chromatically.

No nuance anymore. Away with any ambiguity: all is displayed and shown. The vague allusions to the Serbian origins of the 1942 Irena become two long African sequences in which all the genesis of the man-panther mutation is carefully explained. And, by the way, in order to make everything clear, the film now lasts almost twice as long. Everything is reduced to inert surface (Romney 149), starting from the "abysmal depth" of sin (the Thing) — and this is why there is such an abundant use of mirrors re-framing the characters. This of course does not mean that sex is cancelled — after all, Schrader's flamboyant style itself is very sensual, not "chaste" at all. Trying to renounce sex would still mean falling into the vicious circle of repression-arousal. No repression and no release: sex is defused by *facing* it, by frankly staring even at its darkest sides (or, as Barbara Creed — the author of *The Monstrous Feminine*— would probably add, at the very dangerous Medusa's gaze) in order to reduce it to just a visible object, like the final panther in the cage stared at by Oliver. In fact, the film seems to end with the freeze frame of the panther, but the panther roars another time before it gets "frozen" again right before the end credits. In his *The Transcendental Style*, Schrader says that stillness in film is the quintessential way the form manages to transcend the conflicts — however, "transcend" here does not mean to solve conflicts, but rather to defuse the tension between the conflicting terms: stillness *and* movement still both exist, they are just no longer at war. Equally, the Thing here is not eliminated: sex is not overcome by chastity, but by *even kinkier sex*, i.e., by a strange combination between bondage and zoophilia, finally liberating the panther in Irena. When sex is so deliberately faced, it loses all its mystery; there is just no need to repress it anymore, no matter how "perverted" it is. Both Paul and Oliver keep the "beast" separated — their gaze keeps it distant, as underlined by an editing cut connecting Paul and Oliver each snapping a photo. Whereas Paul represses the separation (with the result that the beast overwhelms him), Oliver accepts the separation, and consciously embraces it: he watches the beast from outside its cage.

What must be released, is not the supposed depth of sex/sin/the Thing (inevitably linked to repression): it is the separation itself. As in Saint Paul, the separation must be itself separated: this is what *Cat People* is about. Paul's repressed separation is consciously embraced by Oliver for the love of Irena. "Oliver is in some ways crazier than Irena and Paul in his ultimate decision to love the woman in the panther as much as, if not even more than, he ever loved the panther in the woman" (Sarris 43). Oliver's Irena is *in* the panther, not *apart* from the panther. The basic separation of the male gaze, woman/panther, is not revoked by attempting a unity, but thanks to a further separation, the one looking for the woman inside the panther. After all, only in 1982 (and not in 1942) did *Cat People* show a scene in which an arm sticks out of a panther undergoing an autopsy. If the 1942 film is about a tragic separation, forty years later this separation is itself separated. The lacerated, Bresson-like montage of the Paul-as-a-killer-panther scene, with all its tension between in- and off-screen space, is thoroughly reproduced in the final bondage sex scene (much like the one in *American Gigolo*, Paul Schrader, 1980), but with a major difference: we do have a series of tight close-ups fragmenting Irena's body, but *we also have the shots of her face, connecting them together organically*. Again: the separation is still there, but this time it is not "traumatic"; it is instead consciously assumed and looked at. What operates the separation, i.e. the gaze (Irena's face), is no longer hidden/repressed: it is fully part of it, as just one of the fragments gathered together by the series of close-ups.

A few seconds before staring at "his" panther in the finale, Oliver is asked something by a colleague: "The crows are plucking the quills out of the porcupine." "Separate them." "Oh." "Brilliant."

Conclusion

The horror genre itself is separated between repression and the return of the repressed. And, even more than that, it deals with the vicious circle between the two. *Cat People* confirms that this vicious circle has a lot to do with Catholicism, whose authentic kernel consists in breaking that deadlock. A closer analysis has proven a deep affinity with Saint Paul's perspective on the subject. With regard to narrative, the film revolves around the (Pauline) separation of the separation, and implies somehow that religion as an institution must be dialectically overcome in order to reach the "fundamental" (Paul's, for instance) Christian values: the plot shows the negation of priesthood and of the separation between law and sin that it stands for. But all this would have no importance without a formalistic tendency to transfigure depth ("the Thing") into a deactivated surface. It is this stylistic attitude that reveals the true relevance of this film inside Catholicism, the "religion of the image."

Notes

1. With a significant exception: *Dominion: Prequel to the Exorcist* (2005), also shot in Africa, was intended to be the official prequel for the Merrin saga, if the

production hadn't decided to turn it down and make Renny Harlin shoot another one (*Exorcist: The Beginning*, 2004).

2. Vogel, the former priest in Jess Franco's *Exorcism* (1974), is a perfect embodiment of such a vicious circle: he indulges in excruciating tortures to punish (female, especially) sinners. A Sado-Kantian (and Lacanian) analyses of Vogel's deadlock and its eventual resolution is offered within this book by David Annandale ("Dark Imperative").

3. This deliberate *roughness* of the writing by such a highly refined scriptwriter as Schrader unquestionably is, strikes as significant. Isabella van Elferen, in her "Bloody Liturgy" essay contained within this book, acutely demonstrates that there is a strong relationship in vampire fiction between Catholic and Protestant ideological sources. The primitive and carnal fury represented by Catholic imagery in that kind of fiction is a "Gothicized" Catholicism, i.e., it can be depicted in that gruesome way only in relation to the rigor of European Protestant (and Enlightenment) culture. It is the Protestant *scriptura sola* that makes the incandescent surfaces of all Catholic paraphernalia (i.e., rituals) both the poison of man's soul and its own antidote. Now, Paul Schrader has been a Calvinist Protestant throughout his childhood and youth. So the rigid traits of his scriptwriting in *Cat People* should be regarded, according to the very same dialectic pointed out by van Elferen, as the Protestant counterpart allowing images to embody the ambivalence of Catholic guilt being guilt's own antidote.

Works Cited

Agamben, Giorgio. *The Time That Remains. A Commentary on the Letter to the Romans.* Stanford: Stanford University Press, 2005.
Badiou, Alain. *Saint Paul. The Foundation of Universalism.* Stanford: Stanford University Press, 2003.
Badley, Linda. *Film, Horror, and the Body Fantastic.* Westport, CT: Greenwood Press, 1995.
Creed, Barbara. *The Monstrous Feminine: Film, Feminism, Psychoanalysis.* London: Routledge, 1993.
Fujiwara, Chris. *Jacques Tourneur: The Cinema of Nightfall.* Jefferson, NC: McFarland, 1998.
Jackson, Kevin (Ed.). *Schrader on Schrader and Other Writings.* Boston: Faber and Faber, 1990.
Marcuse, Herbert. "Repressive Tolerance." *A Critique of Pure Tolerance.* Ed. Robert Paul Wolff, Barrington Moore, Jr., and Herbert Marcuse. Boston: Beacon Press, 1969. 95–137.
Polan, Dana. "Eros and Syphilization: The Contemporary Horror Film." *Mass Culture and Everyday Life.* Ed. Peter Gibian. London: Routledge, 1997. 119–27.
Romney, Jonathan. "New Ways to Skin a Cat. Paul Schrader's *Cat People.*" *Enclitic* 8.1–2 (1984): 148–55.
Sarris, Andrew. "Old Movies, Old Times." *Village Voice*, April 13, 1982: 43.
Schrader, Paul. *Transcendental Style in Film: Ozu, Bresson, Dreyer.* New York: Da Capo, 1972.
Wood, Robin. "An Introduction to the American Horror Film." *The American Nightmare: Essays on the Horror Film.* Ed. Richard Lippe and Robin Wood. Toronto: Festival of Festivals, 1979. 7–28. Rpt. in *Movies and Methods, Volume II.* Ed. Bill Nichols. Berkeley: University of California Press, 1985. 195–220.
Žižek, Slavoj. *The Ticklish Subject: The Absent Centre of Political Ontology.* London: Verso, 1999.

Something in the Dark
Race, Faith, Horror and the Other
RALPH BELIVEAU

Noel Carroll, in his book *The Philosophy of Horror*, argues that meaning in the horror genre requires an understanding of two related relationships. First the potential for fear is grounded in the relationship between the viewer and the monster or the source of evil. Second, and of equally important consideration, is the relationship between the viewer and the protagonist (Carroll 59–96).

But the context becomes interestingly complicated if we focus on horror and ethnicity, particularly in relation to Roman Catholicism. Horror in these contexts tells us much about the struggle over power, the definition of Self and Other, the implications of purity and adaptation, and the hybridizing of genres and politics. As had happened with science fiction writing in the 1950s and early 1960s, alternative social politics could be most easily expressed in a genre that was thought to lack serious social importance. Similarly, much important discussion about race and faith has taken place in the horror genre. As Martin Norden points out, horror and the depiction of evil often serves two agendas; reinforcing racial, ethnic and other hierarchies by establishing punishments for the transgression of social boundaries, and to "maintain the mainstream's cohesion by inscribing extremely untoward qualities and behaviors onto 'Others'" (Norden xviii).

Thus it becomes essential to look at the multiple positions of African American, Latino/a, Haitian, and *Other* identities in the context of film and media industries still dominated by white male American and European power structures. Often these positions reflect the way culture has been transformed by the influence of Catholic rituals and practices, but the transformation displays a complex interaction of the new and old. Horror media provides a particularly useful means to see these discussions since thematic concerns do not automatically require high budgets, complex effects, expensive stars, etc. Horror arises out of particularly low-rent tombs sometimes but still has presence in the mainstream film and television industries where higher budgets are not unknown. Mainstream perspectives suggest that horror is a cheap-to-operate money machine, trading on scare tactics to bring a paying audience into the tent. Fortunately, horror is often the place where the industry's smugglers can find the space to discuss particularly complex social anxieties, since even the basest of motives for the production of horror media reveals details about the areas of culture from where these images emanate. The social anxieties are particularly meaningful at the intersection of Catholic belief and threats to human identity.

Self-Possession and Colonial Exorcism: Is the Other of the Other the Self or Another Other?

Horror films offer a unique place to consider the relation between the Self and the Other. Both become complex constructions in the harsh realm of a horror text. As Self/Other relations are determined by both what is presented on the screen and what we make of it, several ways of seeing this relationship emerge. How the self is defined by extension defines the terms of "humanity" extended by the viewer.

For example, in the film *The Exorcist* (Friedkin) two different ideas of the experience of evil are offered as alternatives for the viewer, set out in this dialogue:

> KARRAS: I think it might be helpful if I gave you some background on the different personalities Regan has manifested. So far, I'd say there seem to be three. She's convinced...
> MERRIN: There is only one.

For Father Karras, the young(er) but world-weary Jesuit going through a crisis of faith, evil is as much a psychological as a spiritual problem. For Father Merrin evil is a single Other, one personality. The film plays on the conflict by creating a slippage between thought, word, and image. Who is *The Exorcist*, after all? Merrin is clearly the center, the elder expert called in because of his experience with exorcism rituals. But Karras is the agent ultimately responsible for completing the exorcism. His aggressive efforts take the evil presence out of the girl Regan, accepting it (or them) into his own body and identity. His sense of Self is in conflict with the immediate presence of the Other. His body contains two contradictory polarities, which struggle for control. The struggle ends when Karras asserts his own self over the invading presence of the Other and throws himself out the window and down the stairs to martyr himself in the destruction of the Other.

The film leaves the singularity of the Other in question, presenting no particular evidence that the invading entity is either a single or a multiple agent. Mark Kermode's book on *The Exorcist* brings this out. William Peter Blatty, author of the original novel as well as the film's screenplay, felt it was important that Karras' action at the end not be misunderstood. The editors at Harper and Row wanted Blatty to make the end less obvious and more ambiguous, leaving a suggestion that Karras was thrown out of the window by the demon that was possessing him as strongly as the possibility that Karras sacrifices himself to kill the demon (Kermode and British Film Institute 81). This clarity of the dualism between good and evil is aligned to the way moral trajectories are expressed from the perspective of melodrama (see Heller-Nicholas, this volume).

But of greater importance for the way we might think of the race and horror we can look at another brief discussion in a break in the exorcism between the priests, which was initially cut by William Friedkin because he thought it made too fine a point of the whole film:

> KARRAS: Father, what's going on in there? What is it? If that's the devil, why this girl? It makes no sense.
> MERRIN: I think the point is to make us despair, Damian — to see ourselves as animal and ugly — to reject our own humanity — to reject the possibility that God could ever love us [Kermode and British Film Institute 79]

Merrin's account for the possession sheds a bright light on the questions of representations of race in horror media. Humanity is opposed to the animal inside, and the question of what constitutes our humanity is determined by our control over ourselves. The animal is instinct, biology, and survival. The human is control, restraint, and ultimately self-sacrifice. This strategy of effacing the notion of humanity, restricting access to the position, and tying it to despair and disempowerment simultaneously brings this distinction into the center of the social constructions of Self and Other.

Self and Other are distinguished through a combination of outward and internal characteristics. People who look different are taken to be different in a fundamental way that questions their belonging to "humanity" as conceived by the self (Rothenberg 42–44). They become Other, and the desire for protection and survival for whatever group stands in for the Self drives a wedge between the full recognition of the humanity in the Other and the Self. Catholic doctrine suggests the existence of multiple Others, under the sway of Satan or Lucifer as the central controlling agent. But of great significance both to Catholic doctrine and our considerations of race here is the idea that "the Devil and the other demons were created by God good in their nature but they by themselves have made themselves evil" (Kent).

A spiritual linkage is made between self-determination and evil in this explanation of the idea of the Other. The despair discussed in the script of *The Exorcist* grounds the notion of separation from having a good "nature," where nature is a quality of the spiritual essence of humanity rather than an opposition along the lines of the culture vs. nature split. The humanity of Self is goodness, provided we do not avoid the possibilities for salvation from the influences of the Other that has made itself evil.

This theological designation of the relationship of Self and Other has one particular set of designations in Catholicism and horror, but in the sociocultural context these notions take on a different complexity since questions of race swirl around notions of Self and Other. In the broadest sense, Self accumulates the central assumed characteristics of personhood such as whiteness, maleness, the normalcy of heterosexual monogamous desire, middle class values, and a Judeo-Christian belief system. Things other than this Self are defined as *Other* in a multiplicity of different ways, and the process of exclusion has been called *Othering*, where differences and distinctions are identified, and a movement away from the identified difference is enacted. But the terms of Self and Other are destined to shift and alternate, providing different ways of considering the notion of belonging with the body of the self or the body of the Catholic church, or existing apart, in a state that starts as separation, moves through exile, and ends as a negative or negation of self, an antagonist who is different, misunderstood at best and inhuman in the most racist of conceptions. We can see race oriented versions of this transformation in the two prequels to *The Exorcist*.

About thirty years and two sequels after *The Exorcist*, a prequel was produced that set out to tell the back story of the central elder priest character, Father Lankester Merrin, which deployed notions of race and Other in the context of a horror film. *Dominion: Prequel to The Exorcist* (Schrader) tells the story of how the banality of evil caused Father Merrin to lose his faith.[1] In 1944, while still a priest Merrin is forced by a Nazi captain to point out which members of the gathered villagers will be immediately executed. Three years later, no longer thinking of himself as a priest, he has exiled himself to an archaeological dig in East Africa where a church has been discovered that appears to have been built and then immediately buried. Excavation shows that the church sits on top of a pre–Christian shrine, and the church gives every indication of having been built as a prison for what turns out to be an evil force.

What gives the film a particularly significant place in the relationship between Catholicism, race, and horror is the way it uses the notion of race and culture as the door through which evil gains access to the actions of humans. The main story of the film is set in British-colonized Kenya, a subtle echo of the prologue in Nazi-occupied Holland. The center of this colonial situation is the conflict between British civilization and the Kenyan indigenous African people the Turkana. Some of the Turkana have been Christianized, becoming the apparatus that allows for both the colonial occupation as well as the day-to-day operation of a hospital, a school, and Merrin's archaeological dig. The Turkana who operates the hotel where Merrin stays is proud of his conversion to Christianity. Merrin's driver appears to have converted as well, and takes the role of a "fixer" who negotiates between Merrin and the other non–Christian Turkana who are hired to dig out the buried church. Of course the spiritual evil in the pagan temple below the church is soon set free by the excavation. This sets in motion a series of events that require a troop of British soldiers to arrive to maintain order, and the possibility for a slaughter between the Turkana and the British is set in motion.

The horror in *Dominion* is grounded in notions of alienation, exile, and racial conflict. The Nazi commander who forced Merrin into grotesque evil calls to mind Arendt's notion of the banality of evil (Arendt 250), where awful acts are perpetrated not by monsters, but by bureaucrats. The commander tells Merrin, "God is not here today." The film argues that exile from God (or the threat of it) echoes in Merrin's alienation from his God and his faith. The Nazi soldier bureaucrat translates in the main action of the film into the British colonial soldiers, who act under bureaucratic order to maintain civilization in the colony by seeing Turkana actions as savage, calling for the civilized response of random execution and a potentially bloody suppression of a rebellion. The British commander's treatment of the unconverted Turkana turns out no different than his treatment of the Christianized and "civilized" black faces; he treats them with a similar condescension and distain.

But what is the "nature" of evil and its depiction in this film? It could be accused of a lowbrow oversimplification that desensitizes an audience to evil (Alford 13). Or it could be a more complex notion of evil that engages both the emotional and the intellectual aspects of a willing audience (Freeland 3). Most importantly for considerations here, however, evil is implanted as much in attitudes toward race and the construction of Self and Other as they are in the potential threat against self alone. But this is dependent on how the relationship between Merrin's central character arc and the question of colonialism are interconnected.

The title *Dominion* emphasizes the notion of control, but specifically the notion of an area being controlled from an outside power. British rule over Africans is haunted by the notion of the demonic dominion over all people in the area, just as Merrin is haunted by his experience with the Nazis and his exile from God. The evil force is as much colonialism as the more theatrical notion of the possessing demon, as well as the more naturalistic evil demonstrated by the Nazi incident. To the extend that a "dominion" is a notion of control, the opening of the church designed to contain the evil parallels the way the racism in the words and politics of the British troops spills into violent aggression.

So the film's main articulation parallels racial dominion with the Othering of evil. To the extent that the central drive in the plot is Merrin's lost faith, the resolution is satisfying in his return to the Priesthood and the Catholic communion. But of course the problem with colonialism remains. That aspect of the film remains unsatisfying, since all of the racial politics that Schrader introduces do not amount to a resolution of the capacity of bureaucratic banality to hold the door open for evil. Perhaps this is also suggested in the way the possession subplot works. During the dig we are introduced to Cheche, a young man with severe disabilities on one side of his body. He is exiled from the Turkana, and Merrin eventually brings him into the encampment hospital after finding him severely injured. Cheche becomes possessed by the evil force unleashed, but rather than becoming profane and corrupt as the Regan character in the original *Exorcist*, at the point of Baptism the demonic force inhabits him and his body attains a kind of physical perfection. His first statement as a possessed entity is "I am perfection."

The casting of Cheche was a choice that reinforced the issue of race at the center of the film. Cheche does not look African, but he also does not look like a white European.[2] He is Other to both the African Turkana and the white British and other Europeans. At the same time, he is a sympathetic young man suffering from severe disabilities, a victim, alienated from God by virtue of the demonic possession. The possessing Other tells Merrin that it can offer him freedom from guilt:

CHECHE/DEMON: You hate God, Merrin. And why not? God gives you guilt. The guilt in unbearable.
MERRIN: I do not curse God.
CHECHE/DEMON: But ... there is one thing you can do. You can cease to care.
MERRIN: That is your offer?
CHECHE/DEMON: I offer freedom.

Under the larger issue of colonialism, the demon is offering a bargain that many have taken. The ascendant political power of Europe and America were founded on a bargain struck with a history of racist exploitation through enslaving, colonizing, and even exterminating the Other. In the era of late modern empire any guilt over this exploitation is disavowed. Schrader's film can be credited with exploring a precursor to the current ability to deny any guilt or responsibility for this history of exploitation, frequently expressed by separating one's self from the actions of one's ancestry ("I didn't own slaves or kill Indians, so why should I pay or feel guilty?"). Is Schrader's film a criticism of this point of view? This becomes a question of whether the film's depiction of Self is conclusively multicultural. The resolution of the plot is Merrin's return to faith, a return from exile. But the situation of colonialism remains a secondary concern. It scratches at the surface in dealing with so many incomplete or split identities. Merrin is introduced as half–Dutch and half–English, Cheche is half disabled, and the demonic force is half lies and half-truth, again echoing the construction from Blatty and Friedkin's original demonic force.

In the end, Merrin sacrifices his doubt to chase the evil demonic Other out of the Turkana valley. But the Turkana leader tells him that Merrin is now its adversary, and that Merrin will be pursued. He heads away from Kenya, to return to Rome and his role as a priest. Oddly the last shot in the film calls to mind the last shot of *The Searchers*, where Ethan Edwards, far too corrupted by his own wildness and hatred, no longer fits in the idea of home and hearth. "In this context the final image of Ethan, for whom there is no place in this integrated world, evokes considerable pathos as the door is shut upon him" (Card 8). Merrin no longer fits into the world of the hospital, or even the world of Kenya; he has an appointment with an Other that will, we know, eventually take him to a final confrontation in Georgetown. We learn from this film that evil is clearly multiple, since the adversary demon is gone, but the system of colonial exploitation remains, even if not for much longer.[3]

Purity Control: Zombification, Hybridity and Syncretism

The travels of Catholicism have subjected the faith to all sorts of different contexts, where questions of culture and race are centrally significant. In horror films, this is arguably most common in the conflict between cultures underneath a superstructure of faith. Where the depiction of race and colonialism in *Dominion* led to ambiguous notions of Self and Other, the interactions shift to questions of purity when race and horror combine. Though the differences might be overlooked, the loss of self under demonic possession is fundamentally different from the loss of self under markers of zombification.

To discuss these ideas from a perspective of race and ethnicity suggests attention be paid to the films produced in the so-called "Blaxploitation" era. The controversy surrounding this era remains alive and well with both advocates and detractors establishing different arguments for the movement. Ed Guerrero notes how right from the start these films were controversial in the African American community (93). But they offered a fundamentally new position for Black faces in front of the camera, as well as an occasional possibility of writing or directing.

Less controversial was the need to offer a counter-narrative of the African American religious heritage. West African religious expression is more complex and less systematic than some of the early 20th century descriptions admitted (Apter 160), but the significant notion for the discussion of these films was the struggle to understand Western European Catholic and West African religious practice as a site of conflict and negotiation, reflecting not only the racial, but also the class and power dimensions that were being negotiated. This framework is an important part of African American history, though it's depiction in film was predictably loaded with racial fear. The opportunity came in the 1970s to speak to a Black audience about this experience.

The first was *Sugar Hill* (Maslansky) in 1974. The title is the name of the central character, whose relationship with a club owner is cut short by a set of mostly white thugs who tire of trying to get him to sell and try to take the club through killing him. Hill goes to see a voodoo priestess, Mama Maitresse, who warns Sugar Hill of the danger, but assists her in calling up Baron Samedi, a voodoo Loa (or saint) representing the dead. Hill offers herself in exchange for assistance in avenging her dead lover. Samedi obliges, raising a force of dead slaves who had been buried in the swamp over the centuries.

Where the previous generations of zombies were presented as bodies shambling along at the will of another, the zombies in *Sugar Hill* represented agents of justice. In this sense they stand in as a reaction to the reductionist treatment of African religious influences in previous horror tales with zombie antagonists. As slaves, they share the identity of the exploited Other with the dead in the 1966 film *Plague of the Zombies* (Gilling), but the politics of revenge are an essential component of their function on screen. They arise with eyes that look like miniature mirrors, reinforcing the idea that the souls of the people they will attack are in danger, not just their lives. The character of Sugar Hill also displays a consciousness of her African heritage. Her hair appears straight when she is in the city context, but turns to an Afro whenever she is in the swamp.

Sugar Hill bears many of the signature traces of what came to be known as the "Blaxploitation" era of films. These films, produced between *Sweet Sweetback's Baadasssss Song* (Van Peebles) and *Shaft* (Parks) in 1971, and the collapse of the classic Blaxploitation era in the later 1970s, remain controversial in relation to the development of cinematic expressions that empower African Americans. But perhaps a stronger argument can be made about the potential positive forces that these films represented. The film industry had (and largely still has) tight restrictions on access to the power to make films, restrictions that included retaining writing and directing control in the hands of white men. Although one could certainly reduce these films to their most prurient side, they also represented a new way of conceiving of action on the part of African American characters.

The plot of revenge and control and the plot of Voodoo and Catholicism are brought together in *The House on Skull Mountain* (Honthaner), also released in 1974. In this film a wealthy African American Matriarch, Pauline Christophe, is on her death-bed. She summons four great grandchildren, her only relatives, to hear the reading of her will. She dies and the four distant relatives arrive — Lorena Christophe, Phillippe Wilette, Harriet Johnson, and Dr. Andrew Cunningham. The first three appear black, while Cunningham is white. As they wait a couple days for the return of the family lawyer, spirits appear in conjunction with some voodoo activity on the part of the couple who were servants to Pauline. Thomas, Pauline's caretaker, wants to control the house and is using Voodoo to do it. He eventually kills Phillippe, Harriet, and the other servant, and attempts to possess Lorena, when he is thwarted by Cunningham who researches and uses a countering voodoo spell.

At the very beginning of the film is a tableau that sets out the challenge of thinking of the position of spirituality to African Americans. Pauline's bed has two tables next to it, one containing the symbols of her Catholic faith, the other containing the signs of her voodoo practice. Her position between the two is unresolved, in a state that sees the influences of both in contention. Her ability to balance the power of both forces is set out as her strength. Thomas only takes up the voodoo side, and wreaks havoc on the relatives, even leading to the death in a voodoo ritual of his companion in plotting the deaths of the newly arrived relatives.

House on Skull Mountain plays on this contrast between balance and extremity. Phillippe is motivated by his own desire to indulge. He drinks to excess and attempts to seduce Lorena, and is subsequently killed. Harriet, who leads a very pious life, is nevertheless overtaken and killed by the power of Voodoo. The remaining two relatives — Cunningham and Lorena — are attracted to each other. Their different racial appearances seem not to be an obstacle (though, truth be told, their being related doesn't seem to, either).

These Blaxploitation era films find different ways of negotiating conflict in substance. Zombie cinema and voodoo cinema offer different ways to consider the question of purity versus change. Built into an era that was offering an enhanced sense of power over representation (even if that power didn't always include writing and directing control), these films took the anxieties of the white audience of 1930s and 1940s zombie cinema, and recast it as anxieties over African American purity and power.

Ethnicity and Race Sit at the Table

Can the European dominance in the Catholic Church accommodate a different approach grounded in non–European cultures? Can horror filmmaking alter its own dogmatic system of conventions to accommodate the conventions of an artistic vision grounded in the experience of marginalized ethnicities? To conclude this discussion of Catholicism, race and horror, I would like to examine an instance that reflects the conflict of ethnicity and faith.

One of the more overlooked gems in the history of race and horror is the anthology project *Cosmic Slop* (Hudlin, Hudlin and Sullivan), which originally aired on HBO in 1994.[4] Directed by Reginald Hudlin, Warrington Hudlin, Kevin Rodney Sullivan, and produced by Ernest Johnson, *Cosmic Slop* presented a trilogy of fantastic stories in an anthology format. Though compared with *Twilight Zone*, it more closely resembles *Night Gallery* in presenting three stories that fall in relatively different genres. It leads off with an adaptation of Derrick Bell's "Space Traders," which uses a science fiction setting to consider what would happen if somebody offered to buy all of America's black citizens. The last story is a striking adaptation of a suspense/thriller social commentary based on a Chester Himes story called "Tang" about a woman living with an abusive partner in an inner city neighborhood who receives a package with instructions for "the revolution."

But of central importance for this discussion is the middle section, an original story called "The First Commandment." In this story, Father Carlos administers to a community that has combined aspects of their African religious background with Roman Catholicism. Spivey, an administrator from a city museum wants to pay the Catholic Church a significant amount of money for a statue of the Blessed Virgin of Charity, but Father Carlos is resisting:

SPIVEY: The point I am trying to make, your eminence, is that this statue is a great work of art. It should be on display in a museum along with other art treasures.

> FATHER CARLOS: the blessed virgin of Charity represents compassion and belongs in a church. If the people want to see it they're welcome to our church.
>
> SPIVEY: Well if your church were ... a little more accessible I could see your point Father Carlos, but I mean who's going to travel all the way to the South Bronx just to see this statue?

The Cardinal makes the deal, but is questioned by Father Carlos. The cardinal indicates his displeasure that some of the parishioners in Father Carlos' church practice Santería, saying that the parishioners cannot combine these forms of worship, but must choose.

"The First Commandment" treats Santería in a way markedly different from traditional representations. Whether in newspapers or as treated in the 1987 film *The Believers* (Schlessinger), Santería is translated into more of a religious cult, occupied with a foreign need for animal sacrifice (Krzywinska 175). *The Believers* translates still further into mainstream perceptions be casting the supernatural as a Devil-like evil recognizable in Christian traditions. Instead, "The First Commandment" grounds notions of good and evil in the struggle over self-determination vs. the need for authority and purity as markers of belonging to the figurative Catholic communion. The hierarchy of the church, represented by the Cardinal, is insensitive to the history or cultural complexity of the South Bronx parishioners. Father Carlos is torn. After losing the argument to his superior, he then must make the decision palatable to the members of his church who venerate the Blessed Virgin. To them she represents not just charity, but also the African Orisha called Oshun, representing love, maternity, and marriage.

Here the conflict appears more directly not just in terms of representation, but also in the negotiation of meaning. Padrino, who runs a store selling Orisha material, is shown heading Santería ceremonies. He asks Father Carlos:

> PADRINO: Santería has accepted the saints. Why is it that Catholicism cannot accept the Orishas?

To this question, Father Carlos has no answer, but to say:

> FATHER CARLOS: There is one true God.
> PADRINO: OK, *tambíen*, I agree. But what is his name?

The politics of ethnicity in this episode circulate around different notions of power. Catholic obedience in mind as well as name causes a conflict in Father Carlos, who must also come to understand how the marginalization of his parishioners and their beliefs can still fit into a Catholic context. The story brings to its center the conflict between two different supernatural systems when the statue disappears in transit. As the Catholic Church seeks a natural accounting for the disappearance, the answer is, of course, in the realm of the supernatural. The statue has come to life, both Blessed Virgin and Oshun. She moves into a crack house, cleans it up, and proceeds to see people from the neighborhood. Padrino brings Father Carlos to the site, but the Priest looks skeptical:

> PADRINO: You do believe in miracles, don't you?

Carlos is once again frozen by his position. Initially he cannot enter the building at Padrino's urging. The publicity brings the Cardinal to the scene, who wants the person to stop "the charade." But when Father Carlos enters and speaks to her, she says she will only tell him what she wants if he addresses her by her true name.

When she tells him that her true name is Oshun, she transforms from the Catholic version of the Blessed Virgin to the ancestral African version of the Orisha. Father Carlos is starting to feel the connection to his ancestry, but the cardinal tells him:

> CARDINAL: This is not about ancestors or race. This is about faith.

The conflict surrounds the possibility of a hybrid identity, both for Oshun and for Father Carlos. The statue is returned to the museum (after Oshun presumably reverted), and Father Carlos returns to his duties saying mass. But at the sacrament of Communion, the African version of Oshun appears and disappears where the statue once stood, and on receiving communion several of the parishioners are possessed by Orisha spirits.

In what we might call the Rod Serling–like twist ending, the hybridity of Catholicism and Santería are materialized in the totality of the ceremony. Father Carlos' attempt to be obedient in the face of miracles, and to maintain his faith in the mission of the hegemony of Catholicism fails — when it tries to obliterate traces of the other cultures onto which it has been thrust.

In the same way, "The First Commandment" demonstrates that the conventions of a genre can be recast to discuss issues that are otherwise marginalized. It is conventional in horror to refrain from too obvious a position in relation to political issues; however in the right context and with the possibility of different points of view in control of the creative process, work can be created that provokes new ways of thinking about the relationship between race and Catholicism.

Conclusion

Noel Carroll's discussion of the paradox of horror asks how we can be so moved (to fear or terror) by experiences we know to be fictions. He suggests that it's not really a question of whether we believe in what we are seeing, even in the sense of suspending our disbelief (Carroll 65). It is instead an argument that it's the thought that counts:

> We are not pretending to be horrified; we are genuinely horrified, but by the thought of Dracula rather than our conviction that we are his next victim ... (this) solves the problem of how it is we can be authentically horrified by fiction at the same time we do not believe in the existence of the monsters in the text. For we can think of the Green Slime without subscribing to its existence, and we can be horrified by the context of that thought [Carroll 86].

We ought to consider this possibility not just in the context of being horrified, but also of being negotiators of racial and religious politics. Discussion of the films here requires the ability to have the thought of Catholic faith as well as having the thought of ethnic and racial conflict. These pull in different directions. To know something about faith should not require participating in that faith, but sharing the thought of what faith means. To know something of the politics of race is to know of the existence of injustices with only faith to keep us imagining a future where the injustices are minimized.

Notes

1. Though space only allows for a discussion of Schrader's film, there were actually two prequels shot. Morgan Creek Productions, unhappy with what Schrader had shot and was completing, took the unusual move of re-filming almost the entire film, with many of the same actors, directed by Renny Harlin. Many of the same attitudes toward race and colonialism are in both films, but Harlin's has some significant differences. Neither did particularly well either critically or financially.
2. He was played by Billy Crawford, a Filipino-American pop singer and actor.
3. Kenya became independent on 12 December 1963.
4. *Cosmic Slop* was available for a brief period on VHS tape, but has not at this writing been given a DVD release. Even so, the project was celebrated as the "First Offering" of the 35th Annual Newark Black Film Festival in 2009, featuring a new print courtesy of HBO and a discussion with Warrington Hudlin.

Works Cited

Alford, C. Fred. *What Evil Means to Us*. Ithaca: Cornell University Press, 1997.
Apter, Andrew. "Herskovits's Heritage: Rethinking Syncretism in the African Diaspora." *Syncretism in Religion*. Ed. Anita M. Leopold and Jeppe S. Jensen. London: Equinox, 2004.
Arendt, Hannah. *Eichmann in Jerusalem: A Report on the Banality of Evil*. London: Faber and Faber, 1963.
The Believers. Dir. John Schlesinger. Perf. Martin Sheen, Helen Shaver, Robert Loggia. Orion. 1987.
Card, James Van Dyck. "The Searchers: by Alan LeMay and by John Ford." *Literature Film Quarterly* 16.1 (1988): 8.

Carroll, Noël. *The Philosophy of Horror, or, Paradoxes of the Heart*. New York: Routledge, 1990.
Dominion: Prequel to the Exorcist. Dir. Paul Schrader. Perf. Stellan Skarsgard, Gabriel Mann, Clara Bellar. Morgan Creek/Warner Bros., 2005.
The Exorcist. Dir. William Friedkin. Perf. Ellen Burstyn, Linda Blair, Max von Sydow, Jason Miller. Warner Bros., 1973. Film.
Freeland, Cynthia A. "The Naked and the Undead: Evil and the Appeal of Horror." *Thinking Through Cinema*. Eds. Murray Smith and Thomas E. Wartenberg. Boulder, CO: Westview Press 2000.
Guerrero, Ed. Framing *Blackness: The African American Image in Film. Culture and the Moving Image*. Philadelphia: Temple University Press, 1993.
The House on Skull Mountain. Dir. Ron Honthaner. Perf. Victor French, Janee Michelle, Jean Durand. Chocolate Chip, 1974. Film.
Hudlin, Warrington, Reginald Hudlin, and Kevin Rodney Sullivan. *Cosmic Slop*. HBO, 1994.
Kent, William. "Devil." *The Catholic Encyclopedia*. New York: Robert Appleton, 1908. February 10, 2010.
Kermode, Mark, and British Film Institute. *The Exorcist*. 2nd ed. London: British Film Institute 1998.
Krzywinska, Tanya. *A Skin for Dancing In: Possession, Witchcraft and Voodoo in Film*. Trowbridge, England: Flicks Books, 2000.
Norden, Martin F. *The Changing Face of Evil in Film and Television*. At the Interface/Probing the Boundaries v. 41. Amsterdam, NY: Rodopi, 2007.
Plague of the Zombies. Dir. John Gilling. Perf. Andre Morell, Diane Clare, Brook Williams. Hammer, 1966. Film.
Rothenberg, Paula. "The Construction, Deconstruction, and Reconstruction of Difference." *Hypatia* 5.1: 16p.
Scorsese, Martin, Michael Henry Wilson, and Florence Dauman. *The Century of Cinema: A Personal Journey with Martin Scorcese Through American Movies, Volume 2*. Videorecording. British Film Institute, England, 1995.
Shaft. Dir. Gordon Parks. Perf. Richard Roundtree, Moses Gunn, Charles Cioffi. MGM, 1971. Film.
Sugar Hill. Dir. Paul Maslansky. Perf. Markey Bey, Richard Lawson, Robert Quarry. American International, 1974. Film.
Sweet Sweetback's Baadasssss Song. Dir. Melvin Van Peebles. Perf. Melvin van Peebles. Yeah, 1971. Film.

SECTION THREE

Ridiculous and Monstrous Catholicism

Reversing the Gospel of Jesus
How the Zombie Theme Satirizes the Resurrection of the Body and the Eucharist

JANA TOPPE

The fantastic both in literature and film is a product of upheaval and crises: when traditions become questionable, and the current order is declared null and void, the fear of mankind's ultimate obliteration arises along with the disorientation such turmoil brings. The French Revolution called the institutions of State and Church into question, the Enlightenment and later Nietzsche's analysis of nihilism decentralized man and replaced belief in God with a pessimistic, fatalistic nothingness. The Industrial Revolution accelerated life in general, and technological progress along with urbanization and modernization caused the fear of an impending, man-made apocalypse to rise, with its peak yet to come. Even in recent times, the ultimate cataclysm is perpetually blueprinted within fiction. With its portrayal of an unfathomable other invading our rational world, the fantastic expresses these human fears of a sudden, uncontrollable disaster. Some texts revolve around a small-scale catastrophe, like a single person possessed by a demon, or a house haunted by a curse, while others devise total annihilation. The depicted apocalypse is no longer a wholly biblical one, devised by God to cleanse the world of sinners and bring peace to mankind. Ever since religion was declared an instrument of the un-enlightened and misty-eyed, the end of man has been turned into a homemade problem. Man's hubris, his ever-pressing urge to discover and excel, catapults him into his doom.

The zombie motif adopts an interim position: something (sometimes a man-made virus, other times an inexplicable and thus all the more disturbing phenomenon) causes the dead to rise and brainlessly walk the streets. Since the resurrection of the dead is part of Armageddon as prophesied in the Bible, this is evidence of the end of the world. Contradictorily, these raised bodies seem to be without a soul or consciousness of the self, therefore initiating a Godless world without reparation. Man dies and returns, but in between life and death he loses himself, recoiling as an empty shell driven by base instincts only. With rising numbers of infected, the prospect of God's helping hand moves beyond reach.

The zombies' origin is partly Catholic in itself, as it stems from the voodoo religion, which is a product of the combination of Roman Catholicism with West African tribal rites; this merger took place on account of the introduction of slaves to the region. While the Spanish conquistadores brought Catholicism to the Caribbean country of Haiti, the slaves brought along their own beliefs and practices, which then combined over the years to form the voodoo religion. As a matter of fact, Lucio Fulci's 1978 film *Zombie* integrates this into the plot when a character quickly summarizes the origins of voodoo. One could postulate that the cinematic zombie myth in itself is already rooted in Roman Catholicism, and was amalgamated in the course of the years, withdrawing from the Haitian myth and adopting (pseudo-)scientific elements. Whereas the Haitian zombies — according to the voodoo belief— are confined to one location due to their relationship to a witch doctor, and cannot transmit their condition, the modern cinematic zombies that developed over the course of the time became viral, deadly, and usually a symbol of hopelessness, despair, and last but not least, the end of the world.

For decades of cinema, the evil that humans were faced with could be banished, be it by anathema, apotropaic powers, or blessed instruments. Dracula, the werewolves, Frankenstein's monster, the Mummy: even in their presupposed immortality, their susceptibility to at least one type of malediction enabled the hero to defeat them and restore order in the world by the end of the story. Films such as Victor Halperin's *White Zombie* (1932) applied the Haitian zombie myth of corpses resurrected with the help of black magic and then put to work as henchmen, exposing the human abuse of will control and the ever-prevailing topic of megalomania. These walking dead are by no means contagious, their state is induced by a witch doctor and occurs only in a limited (and exotically foreign) space. George A. Romero transformed the horror genre by making his walking dead appear with no real explanation, and by giving the viewers no hope of a happy ending (*Night of the Living Dead*, 1968). The film closes with shots of the protagonist's (and last survivor's) dead body being dragged onto a pile of zombie corpses with a meat hook to be burned. A lynch mob, ridding the area of the living dead, shot him point blank as he tried to leave his hideaway, relieved that the end of the nightmare was in sight. Other films such as Roman Polanski's *Rosemary's Baby* (1968) installed comfortless endings of this kind as well, depicting a dreary world that no man could save. This notion gives way to a nihilistic worldview, in which there is no order that can be restored, as all is hopeless. The hope for a glorious life after death is destroyed as soon as the dead rise from their graves, bloodthirsty, hungry for human flesh, and by no means ready to be judged or to ascend to Heaven. Hell on earth is now the status quo.

In a world struck by the viciousness of a virus that raises the dead, turning them into a brain dead threat, there is no hope, no God, no Savior. The gospels promise that Jesus died and was raised from the dead to give humankind the gift of immortality. When a human turns into a zombie, he dies by the virus and then rises from the dead, only to create others like her/him through his bite. Whereas Jesus created a movement of the living spirit, accompanied by His disciples, these beings create a movement of the living dead; masses of what were once humans now stalk the living, a grotesque form of proselytization. The zombie motif can be considered a permutation of the anastasis of Christ. As a direct opposition to the tales of Lazarus and Jesus Christ, the zombie does not return with any sense of identity or even an intact body.

This chapter will focus on the zombie as depiction of the formerly human, flesh-eating animated dead, which arose from the amalgamation of the Haitian original zombie myth with the ghoul and were made into a lasting tradition by Romero's *Night of the Living Dead*. Also, the definition of the zombie in this context only includes persons that were raised from the dead or infected by a bite that killed them and then re-animated their corpse. The antagonists in *28 Days Later* and *28 Weeks Later* do not qualify as "zombies" by this definition, as they do not fulfill the premise of dying and then returning to life in a changed state of existence. While their theme of feeding on others relates to the discussion of the Eucharist, it is not applicable in my examination of the Resurrection.

Resurrection of the Body, Resurrection of the Flesh

Resurrection, the resumption of life after death, is commonly referred to the as "resurrection of the body," on account of the soul's immortality and according inability to die along with the body.[1] The resurrection of Christ is the hope of all Christians in that it allows them to anticipate their own resurrection, the triumph over death with the help of God's power. Jesus will return to Earth, eliminate every authority and subject all His enemies, and finally destroy death in general. The most prominent explanation of the resurrection of the body, its purposes and principles, is given by the Apostle Paul in the book of First Corinthians, on which this article will focus. In First Corinthians 15:12ff, the Apostle Paul addresses the doubts in Christ's resurrection, proposing a directly proportional relationship between the resurrection of Christ and the resurrection of the dead. If Christ had indeed not been resurrected, no one would be able to rise from the dead, therefore rendering all faith futile. Doubting the resurrection of Christ is seen as bearing false witness to God, since the reciprocal then would infer that there is no resurrection of the dead. This clearly states that the resurrection of the dead is an affirmation of God's raising Christ from the dead, and in extension, the reassurance of God's eschatological plan (and maybe even his existence in general!).

Hence, the existence of the walking dead alone is not a sign of a nihilistic world; it in fact proves the opposite. It is the utter absence of aid and succor that calls the significance of resurrection into question: if God exists, and has indeed raised the dead, why is the situation so desolate and why are their bodies continuously decomposing? They are brain dead, and their immortal soul seems to have evacuated the body, leaving an empty shell with only primal urges driving it onward.

The body that is raised after death is said by Paul to be different from that during living times. Paul's eschatology posits dichotomies such as flesh and glory as well as natural and spiritual (bodies). Murdoch E. Dahl proposes a view he calls "hetero-somatism" (Dahl 8), which contends that "Christians in the general resurrection will not have their physical bodies restored in a glorified form, but will be provided with new ones like their Lord," assuming the body of Christ after resurrection was not the same body that was hung on the cross. One of the possibilities Dahl examines is that "although the resurrection body will not be *materially identical* with the one we now possess, it will be [...] *somatically identical*" (Dahl 10). The opinions of theological scholars vary on this subject matter, with some arguing that the body laid in the grave is not the body that will be resurrected, and that existence will then pass into a spiritual plane. Therefore the resurrected body will be a spiritual one, while the present body is merely the seed of another plane of existence, which is sown and from whose decay in the ground grows a new entity, as stated by the Apostle Paul in the book of Corinthians: "What you sow does not come to life unless it dies" (*NIV Bible*, 1 Cor. 15:36). According to Paul, while the body is "sown in dishonor, [...] it is raised in glory" (1 Cor. 15:43), a spiritual, powerful body is to be revived, the opposite of the weak, natural body. Human life can thereby be considered part of a process, whose ultimate destiny is in Christ, in the spiritual existence. The inability to attain salvation without aid is part of human nature, and "flesh and blood cannot inherit the kingdom of God" (1 Cor. 15:50).

Several texts of Scripture propose the risen bodies to have certain characteristics, three of which — identity, entirety, and immortality — are ascribed to both the righteous and the wicked. The bodies of the just are bestowed with four additional qualities: impassibility, brightness (or glory), agility, and subtlety. Impassibility renders them immune to all pain, brightness endows them with a glorious appearance ("it shall rise in glory," 1 Cor. 15:43), agility frees them from the confines of their naturally slow motion and renders them capable of "moving with the utmost facility and quickness wherever the soul pleases" (Maas, "General Resurrection"), as "[i]t is sown in weakness, it shall rise in power" (1 Cor. 15:43), while subtlety infers that the body submits itself to the sovereignty of the soul ("It is sown a natural body, it shall rise a spiritual body" 1 Cor. 15:44; an example for this quality is Christ's passing through material objects) (cf. Maas). A comparison of these qualities with the characteristics of the resurrected bodies in popular culture, namely those of zombies, leads to the astonishing revelation that they can actually be applied, with the exception of subtlety, which would be more fitting for the revenant theme or even vampire stories. While some of the qualities are transcribed almost literally, others are a mere satire of the Scripture. Superficially, the walking dead bear the three characteristics all resurrected bodies are given, as they retain identity, and entirety, and attain immortality. A closer look reveals the inherent sarcasm: the identity they restore is merely an outward appearance, as their brain functions have decreased so far as to erase all forms of self-awareness, volition or thought process; the proposed entirety cannot be achieved, as their bodies are decomposing, some of them even falling apart (in the 2007 remake of *Dawn of the Dead*, a legless zombie attacks the protagonists in the parking garage; other films show a hand chasing a character, or detached heads still snarling and snapping at people). Immortality is a quality only sustainable until the brain is destroyed. While their bodies seem to be immortal, or at least inviolable, urged onward even if limbs are lost, they have no immortal soul, and they can be stopped with a single shot to the head. The bodies are not impelled onward by an immortal soul, they are instinct-driven, or perhaps incited by some other evil life force that is not their soul.

The four qualities bestowed upon the righteous are present in the walking dead as well, although these resurrected bodies can hardly be considered as "just," unless one would like to consider them just in the sense that they are impartial with regards to whom they attack. Since the resurrection of the dead in this context is carried out regardless of good or evil, they are all rendered equally harmful. Their bodies are impassible: they can be physically attacked without feeling pain. Their outward appearance has most definitely changed, but in satire of the sacrosanct risen. There is no brightness or glory to be found, as they are decaying. Their agility differs from era to era and from filmmaker to filmmaker. While George A. Romero's implementations of the living dead display the walking dead as slow, staggering and fittingly corpse-like creatures, the zombies of the new millennium, namely after *28 Days Later* and especially Zack Snyder's remake of *Dawn of the Dead*, are dangerously quick and agile.

The orthodox perception of the resurrection of the body differs from the teachings of the Apostle Paul in that it refers to the resurrection of the *flesh*. This entails that the natural body of all men, righteous and wicked, is to be restored; the latter will be resurrected to spend their days in misery, while the righteous are animated into blessedness. Most modern exegeses of 1 Corinthians 15 insist that the resurrection only refers to Christians. The traditional view interprets Paul's notion of the two Adams as a result of original sin.[2] "Adam infected the whole race with sin and death, while Christ, the second Adam, is the cure of the disease" (Dahl 39). Paul's illustration of the resurrection of the body, following verse 35 of 1 Corinthians, is considered to discuss a transformation rather than a variation of the existing body. The emphasis here lies on man's general physical superiority over all the beasts, derived from the superiority of his soul. However, the outcome remains the same: as the body is resurrected, it is on its way to the Kingdom of Heaven (or, respectively, the depths of Hell).

In Christian thought, ultimate redemption must include the physical body as well as the soul, the Cartesian *res cognitans* and *res extensa* form a steadfast unity: the immaterial substance cannot exist independently from the extended body.[3] Man is only a complete creature of God if his body and soul are connected, even if it is his soul that renders possible his entry into heaven. In the case of the zombie, the body is resurrected, but the soul's location is untraceable. There is no judgment upon them or the remaining survivors, and the authorities are incapable of halting the social and physical decay, or the spread of the disease. Man's order becomes inefficient, as it is prophesied in Revelations,[4] but there is no Savior in sight. In *Dawn of the Dead*, the former policemen may help restore order within their group of survivors, but their jurisdiction ends there.

The body that is raised after death in the films dealing with zombie outbreaks is also in a different state than before, not only in that it is decaying progressively, but also because its brain functions and all that once made it human have ceased to exist. "And just as we have borne the likeness of the earthly man, so shall we bear the likeness of the man from heaven" (1 Cor. 15:49). The walking dead, however, do not. They retain their fetid, disintegrating human shape, which is slowly becoming less and less human due to its lack of humanity (read: brain function, volition, emotions, self-awareness, and all that which makes us so unique as humans), and more and more abhorrent. Therefore, these bodies never reach the heavenly plane described by the Apostle Paul. They lack all the splendor of the grace of God. With the crucifixion and subsequent resurrection and ascension of Christ, death has been defeated in the sense that it may still be inimical, yet it is now in the hands of the Christ, and not the Devil. "The last enemy to be destroyed is death" (1 Cor. 15:26), and it "will be overcome only through the resurrection or transformation at the end of time," meaning that no one but Jesus has the ability to conquer its "cosmic power" (Holleman 65). So the Second Coming of Christ entails that the Christians who have died will be raised, and those alive will be transformed, resulting in the destruction of death and the implementation of immortality. The defeat of death is thematically broached in one of George A. Romero's most recent installments, *Diary of the Dead* (2007), where the characters chronicle the resurrection of the soulless dead in a documentary they fittingly name "The Death of Death." Romero inserts a short analysis of the endless cycle brought about by this new situation in a conversation that takes place between the characters Debra and Tracy. Since every dead person means a resurrected body that attacks the living, death has been conquered in the most unsettling way, as Debra explains, pressing that this will repeat itself for eternity. Obviously the resurrection of the body occurred without the presence of Jesus Christ. Although death per se no longer exists as a finite state, it is ever present. "Every time we walk in somewhere, somebody dies," Tracy says, and Debra adds, "Or somebody's already dead. It's gonna be the same everywhere we go."

While the zombie theme satirizes a large number of Biblical elements, it does take one rather literally: "For since death came through a man, the resurrection of the dead comes also through a man" (1 Cor. 15:21). In this passage, the Apostle Paul is obviously referring to Christ, while the motif of the zombie might be seen as its verbatim transcription, as well as its darkest farce. The resurrection that ensues in these films does come through man, usually by means of nuclear fallout or viruses. Assuming the dead are made alive in Christ,[5] it is a fair question in this construct why God's creation will have to face him not in the promised splendor but in a decaying, revolting state of brain death and decomposition. The zombie sneers at Creation, having to be eradicated by force, thereby putting man into a position he was not intended for by Christian thought: deciding over life and death.

If "flesh and blood cannot inherit the kingdom of God" (1 Cor. 15:50), the resurrection displayed in these fictional worlds is not one of hope and redemption. These creatures will only inherit the earth, and be bound to it, to a world without hope or preternatural aid. It is as though all human beings have been condemned to an eternity in damnation, the righteous and the wicked, or as though there is no metaphysical plane at all, thereby leaving them transcendentally homeless in Georg Lukács' sense, to wander the world mindlessly forever. While it is true that the dead have been raised and the remaining others "changed" (1 Cor. 15:52),[6] this transition is by no means heavenly. It is only spiritual or, respectively, psychological in the sense that it leaves the survivors shaken and traumatized, immobilized by fear. There is no glory in these worlds. Earth is no longer the battleground in the fight over the souls of men; it has become a desolate and hopeless *locus horrendus*.

In George A. Romero's 1978 classic *Dawn of the Dead*, and even more so in the 2004 remake by Zack Snyder, the world is an empty place. As the sinners walk the Earth, no one invokes the help of God. Both movies use the line "When there's no more room in Hell, the Dead will walk the Earth",[7] alluding to a number of passages in the Bible,[8] while simultaneously picturing a Godless world. Romero's 1978 original of *Dawn of the Dead* bears several scenes in which it is difficult to even tell the difference between the undead and the living, seeing how neither really lives meaningfully. It is as if the resurrection of the body without the prospect of the Day of Atonement is punishment for their wasted lives. Zack Snyder's remake insinuates the biblical topoi in a subtle manner, as in "Crossroads Mall" and "Hallowed Grounds Coffee."[9] While it is possible to make out redemptive deaths in both versions, literal religious belief is hard to come by. Several characters sacrifice themselves so that the others can live, and even self-inflicted deaths only occur out of this sacrificial impulse, which points to a relativization of the inherent deadly sin. In several other films of the genre, characters are shown to make the sign of the cross prior to committing suicide, hoping to find forgiveness for their escape from the hellacious existence that would await them otherwise. However, most characters in this specific film display a fittingly nihilistic mindset with their hopes first set on help coming in human form, and later accepting the desolation. While the policeman Kenneth can be seen as one of the few Christian characters in the remake, even he does not believe in redemption, as he is the one holding the sign expressing the hopelessness of the situation (that there is "no help coming") to Andy, who is trapped across the street in his gun shop. When confronted about the end of times, he reacts tensely and derogatorily, having to come to terms with the fact that the walking dead are not a sign of the New Jerusalem after all, but a sign of global decay.

An irrevocably forlorn world is the setting for the third and final part of Romero's *Dead* trilogy, *Day of the Dead*,[10] where the few survivors have escaped to subterranean bunkers in order to survive. In this case, military officers and scientists are living underground, experimenting on the walking dead. It is particularly interesting to see that many films of this genre show characters increasingly seeking shelter in places that are not their natural habitat, like the air (by trying to remain airborne as long as possible) or underground. The film's exposition gives the viewer an impression of the world's emptiness: Miguel's pleading calls through the megaphone, "Hello!" and "Is anyone there?" echo through the abandoned streets and remain unanswered. "There is no one," except a staggering horde of walking dead that is drawn to the sound of his voice.

When the undead take over the military facility, ripping most of the humans to shreds and devouring their flesh, we glimpse several shots of the zombies in Dr. Logan's testing room. The three connected wooden contraptions built to constrain the test subjects appear like three crosses standing in a row, with blood and body parts thrown all across the room. The walking dead are now defiling this likeness to the cross and its connotations with their mere existence, their stance between life and death, and their self-sufficient decision to take the lives of others. It is also here that one of the soldiers shoots himself, crossing himself beforehand.

Whereas the films in the late 1960s up to the early 1990s depict a Godless world overrun by completely mindless and unintelligent monsters, an adaptive turn took place around the 2000s (considering the apocalyptic panic surrounding this recent turn of the century, this date is not entirely surprising). In several films the zombie becomes an educable and fast-learning individual that is able to follow its own needs (a topic started in *Day of the Dead*, where the zombies in the underground testing facilities are successfully subjected to task-based learning). In *Land of the Dead* (2005), George A. Romero's undead are politicized once again, but this time they portray an underprivileged class initiating Marx's and Engel's prophesied class war. This film politicized the zombie even further than Romero's earlier films have done — while simultaneously adding Christian elements — in that it applies the belief that "the meek shall inherit the Earth."[11] While the few survivors are shut off in small, hierarchically structured cities, with the rich living in their type of ivory tower atop the city (known here as "Fiddler's Green"), the less privileged — in the shape of the undead — gather under a leader to march on the town and take what they are entitled to. They are therefore no longer the ungodly creatures ringing in an apocalypse without relief; moreover, they are representatives of the hope that one day justice will come, and the oppressed will be freed while their oppressors will be punished. The first shall be the last... In a way, this development reinstated the Catholic belief in the resurrection of the body, as the undead return to life in order to bring about judgment. There is one twist however: the zombie's bite is not selective. In this version of Judgment Day, there is still no God, and New Jerusalem is the world in which all humans, good or evil, are turned into zombies, forced to live among the ruins of their past for all eternity. The outlook remains bleak, and the speck of original Catholic belief that has been restored only functions to further satirize the topic.

Andrew Currie's *Fido*, a humorous cross between the zombie genre and the *Lassie* films, re-introduced Christian values to the topic by instilling the nuance of a soul in the undead. In this film, set in the idyllic 1950s, the undead have been domesticated by a device that suppresses their urge to kill humans and eat their flesh, turning them into placid housekeepers and pets. Yet some of these formerly soulless and remorseless undead are capable of developing amorous feelings, even loyalty and a feeling of belonging towards the family that owns them; the household helper Fido turns into a surrogate father for Timmy and husband for Helen Robinson, thereby replacing the absent father, who is a representative of cold-hearted corporate America, and therefore a detriment to Christian family values. Helen's love for the zombie Fido however is not a case of adultery, which would be highly unchristian, because the zombie's undead and decaying nature makes him less of a threat, less of a "man," since a dead man can hardly be a competition for a live — and potent — man. The affection between the undead housekeeper and his owner really just displays the deep meaning of compassion and friendship, which is valued over the capitalist virtues of profit and gain. The zombie is a non-sexual being, who can only threaten the psychological relationship between husband and wife, or father and son, more a good friend than a lover. Like the dog Lassie, he represents deep friendship and love in a non-sexual way, therefore approving the old Christian worldview of the *Lassie* films. Seeing how *Lassie Come Home* (Fred M. Wilcox, 1943) is considered a "Christian film" in several interpretations[12] this can partly be said of *Fido* as well. Even though the comical aspect blurs this image, one look beyond the mask of the parody reveals deep-seated conservative roots with its themes of family and love.

The Eucharist

Connected with the hope of the resurrection of the dead, the Eucharist, also known as the Lord's Supper, commemorates Jesus' Last Supper with His disciples on the night before His crucifixion. This conjunction is pointed out in John 6:54–56:

> Jesus said to them, "I tell you the truth, unless you eat the flesh of the Son of Man and drink his blood, you have no life in you. Whoever eats my flesh and drinks my blood has eternal life, and I will raise him up at the last day. For my flesh is real food and my blood is real drink. Whoever eats my flesh and drinks my blood remains in me, and I in him."

The Nicene Creed, the profession of faith recited during the Eucharistic rite, connects the Eucharist with the Last Day and the resurrection of the dead: "We believe [...] (i)n one holy catholic and apostolic Church; we acknowledge one baptism for the remission of sins; we look for the resurrection of the dead, and the life of the world to come" (Schaff 29).

The institution of the Eucharist has caused disunity within the Christianity on account of the varying interpretations, even though the participation is meant to enhance the communion among Christians as well as with Jesus. In Roman Catholicism there exists the belief in the transubstantiation of the consecrated bread and wine, according to which the bread and wine transforms into the body of Christ, His Real Presence, while the outward appearance of both bread and wine remains the same.

The eating of the flesh is inextricably connected to the resurrection of the body, both in the Catholic practice and in the zombie theme. As seen in all of the films discussed above, the zombies' urge to feast on the living, or to at least bite them, is part of the resurrection procedure. The virus of course resurrects the dead in general; yet a large number of the characters throughout the film that are infected and return to life enter this state of existence through an assault by a zombie. The anonymous hordes of walking dead may or may not have been bitten; most of them probably rose from the grave or the morgue. The non-anonymous characters however, the ones we see as living human beings before they "turn," procure their resurrection after a bite.

The zombie theme turns the transubstantiation proposed to take place in the Eucharist into a general cannibalistic feast. Interestingly enough, in Scripture itself, the phrase "to eat some one's flesh," has a figurative meaning, namely, "to persecute, to bitterly hate some one [sic]" (Pohle, "The Real Presence"). This is one of the reasons eating and drinking is to be understood literally, as partaking of the body of Christ. If we were to complicate this statement, it is possible to draw a rather complex conclusion regarding the zombie theme: the flesh eating in this case is like a literal transcription of the figurative meaning presented in Scripture. The creatures are fiercely persecuting their victims, all the while their goal being to bite them, to tear their flesh and rip them apart. Furthermore, the victims are infected with this hatred, the "spirit" of this grotesque Eucharist being passed on through the bloodstream. No longer are the followers of Christ consuming His body: instead of many eating the flesh of one, many are now eating the flesh of many, arbitrarily chosen.

Conclusion

Man's everlasting wish to defeat death could so far only be fulfilled, and his fear of dying only be consoled by religious faith. Where religious belief once promised re-animation and atonement after death, science now researches for methods of prolonging life and conquering mortality. The "resurrection panic" shown in the discussed films is a sign of the times: an expression of the hopelessness of a world without religious faith, where the defeat of death does not entail a better world but rather an ongoing cycle of dying and returning to life without an identity.

The zombie can be so many things: Whether the films aim to disturb the audience with their expression of nihilistic hopelessness or intend to criticize the general population's consumerist behavior, whether the concept is to scare or to be political, the zombie is a regular projection screen. Yet no matter what individual films determine to express, the roots of the zombie genre can be found in Roman Catholicism, not least due to its Voodoo origin. The resurrection of the body as the Catholic faith expects it is satirized at great length by the concept of the zombie alone, and even further mocked by most modern zombie films. The world cannot hope for the re-animated dead to bring about the Second Coming of Christ and with it a better world. The resurrection of the dead is only the tip of the iceberg, demonstrating that there is no end in sight, and that there is "no help coming."

Notes

1. "As the body is the partner of the soul's crimes, and the companion of her virtues, the justice of God seems to demand that the body be the sharer in the soul's punishment and reward. As the soul separated from the body is naturally imperfect, the consummation of its happiness, replete with every good, seems to demand the resurrection of the body" (Maas).

2. "'The first man Adam became a living being'; the Adam, a life-giving spirit. The spiritual did not come first, but the natural, and after that the spiritual" (1 Cor. 15: 45–46).

3. "Neither can exist in completeness without the other and therefore they must be united in resurrection" (Dahl 42).

4. Or as predicted by the Apostle Paul: "Then the end will come, when he hands over the kingdom to God the Father after he has destroyed all dominion, authority and power" (1 Cor. 15:24).

5. "[...] so in Christ all will be made alive" (1 Cor. 22).
6. Cor. 15:52: "We will all be changed. [...] the dead will be raised imperishable, and we will be changed."
7. The 1978 version has this for a tagline, whereas the remake incorporates it into a TV segment showing a televangelist who warns the viewers of the impending Judgment Day.
8. Such as Revelation 20:13: "And the sea gave up the dead which were in it; and death and hell delivered up the dead which were in them: and they were judged every man according to their works."
9. For a hardly politically correct but religious interpretation, see Adam H. Becker's review of the film in the online version of *The Revealer*. Becker attempts to steer clear of racial categorization but has no problem referring to a character as "faggy" and in his opinion "immoral."
10. It is important to keep in mind that the Day of the Dead, also known as All Souls' Day, is an official holiday of the Catholic calendar, commemorating the faithful departed; the film's title serves as a further permutation of Roman Catholic components.
11. The film's tagline is "The dead shall inherit the earth" (imdb.com).
12. For instance, see Greg Tubbs. "Movie Review: Lassie." The United Methodist Church. Web. 12 Jan. 2010.

Works Cited

Becker, Adam H. *The Revealer*. 12 April 2004. Web. 12 Jan. 2010.
Boon, Kevin Alexander. "Ontological Anxiety Made Flesh: The Zombie in Literature, Film and Culture." *Monsters and the Monstrous. Myths and Metaphors of Enduring Evil*. Ed. Scott Niall. New York: Rodopi, 2007. 33–43.
Brittnacher, Hans Richard. *Ästhetik des Horrors*. Frankfurt/Main: Suhrkamp, 1994.
Dahl, Murdoch E. *The Resurrection of the Body. A Study of 1 Corinthians 15*. London: SCM Press, 1962.
Dawn of the Dead. Dir. George A. Romero. Perf. Ken Foree, David Early. Laurel Group, 1978. Film.
Dawn of the Dead. Dir. Zack Snyder. Perf. Sarah Polley, Ving Rhames, Jake Weber. Strike Entertainment, 2004. Film.
Day of the Dead. Dir. George A. Romero. Perf. Lori Cardille, Terry Alexander, Joseph Pilato. Dead Films, Inc., 1985. Film.
Diary of the Dead. Dir. George A. Romero. Perf. Michelle Morgan, Joshua Close, Shawn Roberts. Artfire Films, 2007. Film.
Eucharist. Encyclopædia Britannica. Encyclopædia Britannica Online, 2009. Web. 08 Nov. 2009.
Fido. Dir. Andrew Currie. Perf. Carrie-Anne Moss, Billy Connolly, Dylan Baker. Lions Gate Films, 2006. Film.
Freund, Winfried. *Deutsche Phantastik: die phantastische deutschsprachige Literatur von Goethe bis zur Gegenwart*. München: Fink, 1999.
_____. *Literarische Phantastik: die phantastische Novelle von Tieck bis Storm*. Kohlhammer: Stuttgart, 1990.
Gelder, Ken. *The Horror Reader*. New York: Routledge, 2000.
Greene, Richard, and K. Silem Mohammad. *The Undead and Philosophy: Chicken Soup for the Soulless*. Chicago, IL: Open Court, 2006.

Holleman, Joost. *Resurrection and Parousia: A Traditio-Historical Study of Paul's Eschatology in 1 Corinthians 15*. New York: E.J. Brill, 1996.
The Holy Bible, New International Version. Grand Rapids, MI: Zondervan, 2001.
Knox, Vicesimus. *Considerations on the Nature and Efficacy of the Lord's Supper*. London: Charles Dilly, 1799.
Laguerre, Michael S. *Voodoo and Politics in Haiti*. New York: St. Martin's, 1989.
Land of the Dead. Dir. George A. Romero. Perf. Simon Baker, John Leguizamo, Dennis Hopper. Universal Pictures, 2005. DVD.
Lassie Come Home. Dir. Fred M. Wilcox. Perf. Roddy McDowall, Elizabeth Taylor, Elsa Lanchester. Loew's, 1943. DVD.
Maas, Anthony. "General Resurrection." *The Catholic Encyclopedia*, Vol. 12. Robert Appleton Company, 1911. Web. 8 Nov. 2009.
McSweeney, Bill. *Roman Catholicism: The Search for Relevance*. Oxford: Basil Blackwell, 1980.
Night of the Living Dead. Dir. George A. Romero. Perf. Duane Jones, Judith O'Dea, Karl Hardman. Image Ten, 1968. DVD.
Pohle, Joseph. "Eucharist." *The Catholic Encyclopedia*, Vol. 5. Robert Appleton Company, 1909. Web. 8 Nov. 2009.
_____. "The Real Presence of Christ in the Eucharist." *The Catholic Encyclopedia*, Vol. 5. Robert Appleton Company, 1909. Web. 8 Nov. 2009.
Schaff, Philipp. *The Creeds of Christendom: with a History and Critical Notes. Vol. I. The History of Creeds*. Grand Rapids, MI: Baker Book House, 1905.
Seeßlen, Georg, and Fernand Jung. *Horror: Grundlagen des populären Films*. Marburg: Schüren, 2004.
28 Days Later. Dir. Danny Boyle. Perf. Cillian Murphy, Naomie Harris, Noah Huntley. DNA Films, 2002. Film.
28 Weeks Later. Dir. Danny Boyle. Perf. Robert Carlyle, Rose Byrne, Jeremy Renner. Fox Atomic, 2007. Film.
Wainwright, Geoffrey. *Eucharist and Eschatology*. London: Epworth Press, 1971.
White Zombie. Dir. Victor Halperin. Perf. Bela Lugosi, Madge Bellamy, Joseph Cawthorn. Edward Halperin Productions, 1932. DVD.
Zombie. Dir. Lucio Fulci. Perf. Tisa Farrow, Ian McCulloch, Richard Jonson. Variety Film Production, 1979. DVD.

Kin Dza Dza!
Christianity and Its Transformations Across Space

MARGARITA GEORGIEVA

Kin Dza Dza!: *An Introduction*

In 1965 appeared *33 (A Non-Science Fiction)*—Georgi Daneliya's first attempt at directing a speculative fiction comedy. It was considered anti-Soviet, was banned and shared the fate of many science fiction films produced during that period. *33* is among those peculiar examples of Soviet cinema that make one wonder about the success of well-accepted films like *Kin Dza Dza!* Almost immediately after its release in 1986, three years before the fall of the Berlin Wall, Daneliya's *Kin Dza Dza!* was serialized as a television show and thus became a cult film in Russia and the Communist Bloc countries. Since then, the movie has passed largely unnoticed by the rest of Europe and the Americas. The Second Life Conceptual blog defines *Kin Dza Dza!* as "the best sci-fi film that nobody has ever heard of"[1] and Amazon customer reviews call it a "truly amazing and overlooked film" that "virtually nobody in the western world ha[s] seen."[2] In fact, the film has received numerous awards for having the best music (1987), for being the best international fantasy film (1988) and a legend of the science fiction genre (2002). The *Kin Dza Dza!* passion has nowadays spread to cyber space. A DVD has been released and, to complete this 24-year success story, an animated 3D remake is on its way. This is how Daneliya's work withstood the cultural and political trials of the last decade of the 20th and made it into the first decade of the 21st century.

Kin Dza Dza! has been presented as cyberpunk fantasy before its time, as allegorical science fiction and dystopian satire, grotesque comedy and "post-apocalyptic anti-utopian sci-fi comedy."[3] In fact, it is all of these at once and much more. The film tells the story of Gedevan Alexandrovitch, the Georgian, and Vladimir Nikolaevitch, the Muscovite, who travel to the desert planet Pliuk[4] in the galaxy Kin Dza Dza. They meet the telepathic Mr. Wef and his mindreading companion Bi, traveling artists by profession, from whom they learn that the promiscuous races on Pliuk are color-coded and that the ruling Chetlanian classes exercise their power over low-class Patsaks via uncontrollable state police. This complex society is exclusively based on moneyed transactions and exchanges of much-praised matches. Gedevan and Vladimir find their way back to Earth with difficulty, after a series of adventures involving episodes in a Pliukian prison and a meeting with the magnificent but senile Pliukian leader P.J. Once Gedevan and Vladimir set foot back on Earth, they realize that the experience has changed them forever.

Kin Dza Dza! has been defined and redefined many times. It is important to note, however, that the Soviet science fiction which came out in print was bonded to filmography from its earliest beginnings. Our analysis of Daneliya's film takes into account the fact that image and word are complementary. It should be remembered that the film director also worked on the script. The study of both the dialogue and the film's cinematographic aspects is fundamentally important. To fully grasp the complexity of the seemingly incongruous and bizarre succession of events, we should bear in mind that Russia has a long tradition in science fiction with a golden age taking place during the 20th century, somewhere between the rise of the Iron Curtain and the fall of the Berlin Wall. At that particular moment in history, Soviet science fiction writers explored the themes of space pioneering and scientific adventure as inseparable from the social and political changes resulting from a comparatively radical communist regime. The clashes between different worlds and political systems alluded to the real world and Soviet science fiction progressively acquired two faces — the widely accepted progress-oriented facade and the more obscure, critically subversive one. Partly on account of this duality and partly because of their European heritage, many authors produced communist utopias and satires of capitalism and/or contemporary society, frequently alluding to the real world. Thus, science fiction became an outlet for the serious disguised as amusing, entertaining or humorous. The displacement of the actual from the real world to a distanced fictional plane became a means of discussing politics and power without having to fear censorship. To a certain degree, the humorous touch explains both the success and the acceptance of *Kin Dza Dza!* The film might have also escaped censorship because of the *perestroika* and *glasnost* policies of the 1980s.

The Soviet Union: Politics, Science Fiction, and Religion

Before presenting and analyzing some of the most prominent Christian symbols in *Kin Dza Dza!*, we shall attempt to explain the interrelations between politics, religion and science fiction at the time and country of its production. Two things should be remembered here. Firstly, it is important to note that both Daneliya and Gabriadze are Georgian by birth but have been citizens of the USSR. It is equally important to remember that Georgia has frequently been in opposition and/or open conflict with Russia. In addition, the country was Stalin's homeland and became, for a certain period, the birthplace of the dictator who ruled the Soviet Union. Secondly, Georgia was one of the first states to officially adopt Christianity around A.D. 300–330, recent research suggesting that this might have happened earlier with Christianity spreading since the first century A.D. At the basis of Georgian identity lie repetitive political and religious confrontations with other countries, traditions and religions. *Kin Dza Dza!* deals with Georgian dependency and the power conflicts between the ruled nation and the ruling union or as the Pliukians put it, it is a question of who will kneel in front of whom.

It is believed that religion and communism are incompatible, that Soviet propaganda and the cult of the personality excluded the possibility of a Christian cult. In fact, the explicitly antireligious Marxist-Leninist interpretation of communism could not be conciliated with faith. Indeed, Karl Marx justifies "the abolition of religion" and terms it "the illusory happiness of the people" (Marx 244).

> The Communist Party destroyed churches, mosques, and temples; it executed religious leaders; it flooded the schools and media with anti-religious propaganda [...], introduced a belief system called "scientific atheism," complete with atheist rituals, proselytizers, and a promise of worldly salvation [Froese 35].

Quoting Moroz's *Istoriia "Mertvoi vody"* (2005), Laruelle points out that from the second half of the 1930s, the rebirth of Russian nationalism supported by Stalin seems to denounce Christianity "for accepting justifications for class division" (Laruelle 286). The tendency continued during the 1960s with Khrushchev. The middle of the 20th century saw a progressive renewal of skepticism, of enlightened atheism and faith in scientific development, all of these combined with an active rereading of various pre–Christian traditions. Telling examples are the plenary sessions of the CPSU Central Committee where plans for technical progress and high efficiency were made. A strengthening of the anti-faith struggle was called for. What is then the link between the Soviet political regime and Christianity? Since Orthodox Christianity was suppressed, the state had to offer an alternative and a replacement for it. In fact, according to Shnirelman and Froese, the party's ideological commission encouraged the establishment of new, non-religious rituals (Shnirelman 231) to the point of becoming an alternative religion itself (Froese 37). Thus, several ambitious clergy abandoned the old religion for a new one and became "atheist proselytizers for the League of Militant Atheists" (Froese 37). In that climate, the sole legal political party excluded all other organizations, having other leaders at their head, and public worship was redirected from the wholly spiritual to the scientifically tangible.

Science fiction comes in adequation with these ideas because it supposes that the truth, which certainly is out there, is necessarily a scientifically explainable one. Spirituality is reconsidered and transformed into a combination of assurance, conviction and inquisitiveness. The unknown is explained. The skies are no longer inhabited by an omniscient God but by beings, some of them rather different from the ones that can be found on Earth, but beings nevertheless. In this sense, Soviet science fiction provokes a rethinking of the myths of creation and offers an alternative to the fundamental questioning concerning the human genesis. It is difficult to judge whether these themes are addressed intentionally in *Kin Dza Dza!* The initial direction of the script might have had a covertly political target rather than a religious one. The spiritual touch is probably a resultant repercussion. However, there is a clear-cut link between religion and the scenario of *Kin-Dza-Dza!* The film is concerned with Christian myths without showing it directly, intentionally or explicitly. It addresses and confronts three societies and three examples of morality whose sentiments of primacy and superiority clash with one another. The concern of all three is to find out who comes first in the universal experiment of creation. The men from Earth carry a very complex politico-religious heritage that tells them that they are the chosen ones. Therefore, they feel the need to prove themselves the more compassionate and benevolent nation after discovering that the Pliukians are manifestly the more technologically advanced civilization, i.e., the Pliukian primacy in terms of scientific evolution is unquestionable. The emotionally primitive and barbaric men from Pliuk, devoid of all sensibility, exercise their destructive technological power on everyone and everything in a vain attempt to assert their own authority over the known universe. After their passage everything turns to dust and their home planet has become a desert. On the other hand, the enlightened, falsely saint-like inhabitants of the Edenlike planet Alpha take themselves for gods, thinking that they can have a say in the personal destiny of each and every one. They are completely withdrawn but are omnipresent and intimidating in their robes of immaculate white. The name of their planet is indicative of their claim to the position of firstborn.

In *Kin Dza Dza!*, the encounter of two Soviet Union citizens with other beings can be interpreted as an attempt to strengthen the idea that the Soviet system of ethics is the right one, confirming the scheme of progressive secularization of the communist state. Vladimir and Gedevan are very incredulous by nature and can be said to represent the archetypes of the enlightened atheist—one is a construction engineer and the other a student. Things like art and faith lie in a completely different sphere for them. When they meet the two extraterrestrial artists, their first impression is that they are in a "capitalist country"[5] where spirituality has become a caged moneyed performance executed on the front seat of a popemobile (the vehicle is called "pepelats" on Pliuk, can also fly and has the form of a wine bottle opener). The moral decay and fall of the Pliukians comes as a confirmation of the greater potential of scientific atheism. This is why in the first part of the film, Gedevan and Vladimir feel superior and express their moral ascendancy openly by refusing to obey Pliukian police, the guardians of the P.J. cult. On the other hand, other scenes in the film seem to claim the inverse, more specifically that a society without faith becomes a lost world. The Pliukians have lost "of all the commandments [...] the most important one" and that is the decree to "love your neighbor as yourself."[6] Hence, they have lost all the values of a functioning society—tolerance, charity, democracy—and have replaced them with active segregation and simulacra of controlled religion. In this sense, *Kin Dza Dza!* might also be interpreted as a warning that the eventual extreme of scientific atheism can lead to complete loss of faith and from there, to an ecological, economic, political, linguistic and moral apocalypse. The ambiguity of Daneliya's critical stance resides in his treatment of politics as organized religion and in the distanciation of this experiment from Earth and its country of origin.

Another parallel that can be drawn between the political and religious aspects of *Kin Dza Dza!* and Soviet reality is the personality cult. "The godlike worship of Communist elites appears the most ironic twist of Soviet communism" (Froese 43). It allowed the state to play on the Catholic and Orthodox belief of "incorruptibility" of the body by exposing the embalmed corpse of Lenin before the public to adore and worship. Likewise, an important part of *Kin Dza Dza!* deals with the powerful, enigmatic, threatening father figure of P.J. who seems to have always been the one and only leader, as if touched by immortality. The two space travelers Gedevan and Vladimir are confronted with a world from which religious devotion has decayed into idolatry but, in reality, the truth is more complex. True faith has been replaced by a form of "direct ideological indoctrination" (Schwartz, Bardi 387) and an enforced worship of P.J., the unfathomable leader of the Pliukians whom nobody has seen because he is dead, whose last breath is conserved in a huge red balloon in the center of the capital and whose holograms can appear randomly and unexpectedly anywhere on the planet.

> MR. WEF: This isn't a dirigible, you simpleton. This is Mr. P.J.'s last breath.
> GEDEVAN: Nonsense. How can a person have so much breath? That's absurd.
> BI: Don't blaspheme! P.J. is alive! And I am happy.
> MR. WEF: And I'm happier still.[7]

One of the most memorable phrases in the film is, "Say 'Kou' to worship!"[8] Both the Chetlanian and Patsak inhabitants revere the images of their leader much like Orthodox Christians venerate icons with the only difference that on Pliuk, they have to conform or else spend the rest of their miserable lives in a coffin lined with nails in an institution strongly reminiscent of the Catholic Inquisition. Several scenes in *Kin Dza Dza!* expose the strange extraterrestrial rituals of preserving a person's last breath, depicting pale balloons of yellow parchment and of varying sizes. These float above ground and their size is indicative of the person's social status in life. The color of the scenery is always in unison with these floating graveyards. The rolls of film for *Kin Dza Dza!* were selected in view of this. The initial idea was to use high quality Kodak film but the decision to replace it with rolls of lower quality was intentional, creating the impression of a burning heat. The occasional pastel red and orange colors are mixed with pale yellow and grey. The atmosphere is otherworldly and the impression is that of looking upon a scorched photograph through a thin veil. Pliuk is a planet where the white is yellow and the black — dark grey.

Biblical Elements and Christian Symbolism in Kin Dza Dza!

There is no way of knowing whether the Christian symbols and Biblical elements in *Kin Dza Dza!* were used intentionally. The initial significance of the script might have targeted the political rather than the religious. The spiritual touch is probably a resultant repercussion. Yet, many Christian symbols are apparent and occur in key moments of the plot. The spiritual and ethical dimensions of the terrestrial-extraterrestrial encounter are never tackled overtly but they are frequently alluded to with the help of Christian symbols and images. Another particularity of the film is the mixture of allusions to both Catholic and Orthodox Christianity. The numerous resemblances between the two currents of religious thought and their common but elusive Pan-European Christian heritage may be the reason for this.

Among the Christian sacred writings, The Book of Revelation is one of the most frequently referred to in Soviet science fiction. For instance, it is used as the motto of Arkady and Boris Strugatski's *The Doomed City* (1970s). It is a justification for the "door standing open in heaven,"[9] revealing dystopian or apocalyptic visions of imaginary or parallel worlds. *Kin Dza Dza!* opens one such door. The planet Hanut, the home of all Patsaks, has gone blank, being drained of light, water, and air. Simultaneously, Gedevan Alexandrovitch and Vladimir Nikolaevitch discover that they too are Patsaks by nature. The discovery brings them to the question of their origins. If the post-apocalyptic landscape of Hanut had once been the home of a flourishing civilization of which they are the ancestors, would it mean that humanity has been given a second chance on Earth? Gedevan and Vladimir have the privilege of standing on what is left of Eden after the fall of man and are offered the possibility to recreate it. The importance of their names — all of them from the Greek and Slavic semantic fields of "conquest" and "victory" — is revelatory. However, they refuse to collaborate. Their vision of paradise differs greatly from the much less egalitarian Pliukian conception of it:

> BI: Now, the planet Hanut is very cheap.
> MR. WEF: 63 chatl.
> BI: We'll sing around the Galaxy for a month and the planet is ours. And within a month, we'll buy the air too.
> MR. WEF: 93 chatl.
> BI: If anyone comes on the planet, they won't have any air because we'll own it all.
> MR. WEF: They'll crawl in our feet and we'll be spitting on them.
> GEDEVAN: Why?
> MR. WEF: For pleasure.
> GEDEVAN: Where's the pleasure of spitting on people?
> BI: (laughs) He's so young...[10]

Similarly, their conception of performing and singing is different. The two couples can agree neither about the songs' contents and corresponding dance movements nor about whether to sing in a cage or out of it. Their quarrel on the subject might be taken as an allusion to the Orthodox and Catholic differences in liturgy. However, it is unclear to what extent this allusion was conscious during the filming of *Kin Dza Dza!*

Partly on account of the political regime in the USSR, if anything was to be said about religion, it had to be done by circumventing straightforward declarations. Hence, Christian symbolism is most usually revealed by the shot structure. The triangular forms and the pyramid are recurring elements in the film. Originally the symbol of the Trinity, here the triangle is used to signify centralized power impersonated by the father figure of the dictator who is always dressed in white. When P.J. appears, he is always accompanied by a kneeling Patsak servant and, inevitably, the positioning of their bodies forms a triangle. The structure of several group shots is triangular and more particularly, the scenes involving musical performances. The pyramidal constructions symbolize the structure of Pliukian society which is organized in four strictly color-coded strata — the Patsak masses, the Etsilop police, the Chetlanian who wear yellow trousers and those who wear red ones are the four bases of the pyramid and on its top stands P.J. He is also the one who detains an unlimited right over water, the source of all life and sustenance. The pool scene in the second part of the film is reminiscent of a baptism ceremony with a slight tinge of homoeroticism. Naturally, as everything else on Pliuk, the ceremony is twisted and perverse. The satire of organized religion contains several layers of Christian elements, which are separated from the intended purpose of their usage. A case in point is the usage of bells, generally used as a call for prayer and a reminder of the origin and greater purpose for the things of this world with their sound being likened to the music of heaven. On Pliuk, they are used as a sign of submission and all Patsak are required to wear them on their nose.

The principal setting of *Kin Dza Dza!* is a desert. The film is structured along a series of exoduses from a city into the desert and back to a city. The two men from Earth and their extra-terrestrial companions cross the desert together then cross it again to the West (and the direction is of symbolic and historical importance) two by two in father-son figure couples. These are announced by extensive landscape shots of the Pliukian wasteland, followed by portrait shots of the protagonists. Initially a symbol of purification, the desert landscape in *Kin Dza Dza!* is representative of the spiritual condition of the protagonists. Just as the planet Hanut, plunged in permanent darkness, is indicative of their slavery and the obscurantism of the P.J. cult, the Pliukian desolate wasteland is suggestive of the population's moral dissolution. The two-part structure of the film replicates the Biblical structure into an Old and New Testament. Likewise, the first part of *Kin Dza Dza!* is about the origin and history of things — it tells the story of the first exodus from Earth, the history of the Pliukians and the plagues that turned their planet into a desert, the lack of light on Hanut being reminiscent of the Plague of Darkness. The second part of *Kin Dza Dza!* is built on St. Peter's "*Domine, quo vadis?*" When Vladimir and Gedevan cross the desert, Vladimir is portrayed as the leader, the man of faith, while Gedevan remains the Doubting Thomas for a while. Vladimir chooses the direction with assurance and determination. Gedevan walks behind and his questions are but a reformulation of St. Thomas's "Lord, we don't know where you are going, so how can we know the way?"[11] The second part is also about choices—the two Earthmen are confronted with the dilemma to go back to Earth or save their imprisoned Pliukian friends. They confront this dilemma twice and always prefer exile to disloyalty. In this sense, the second part is also the place for ethics and moral lessons as it "seriously questions or rejects outright the scientific culture because it is the clearest manifestation of man's flawed, fallen nature" (Born 252).

Kin Dza Dza! is about brothers in conflict and about the encounter between Self and Other, two entities that diverge only in the outcome of their history after their separation. *Kin Dza Dza!* supposes that a schism occurred at a particular moment in time on a certain planet. Its inhabitants settled in two different galaxies and evolved differently from the point of their separation onwards until the day their paths crossed again only to find that they are "living in profound tension with scientific knowledge that makes certainty in Christianity impossible but which in itself is an inadequate source of meaning—thus, both science and faith are rigorously examined and each found unsatisfactory" (Born 252). Hence, the film is not only a story of the boundaries between a Soviet satellite and the Soviet state but also confronts capitalism with communism, the East with the West. In addition to that, it tackles, somewhat accidentally, the severed links between the Roman Catholic and the Orthodox countries, presenting the European territories as partitioned into sections of religious and political influence. The film is an example of the partitioning between Roman Catholic and Orthodox countries which P. Gunst sees as "overlap[ping] other lines of demarcation" including their differences in scientific adaptation on a global level and their technological development. If the home country of Vladimir and Gedevan is an Orthodox one, the planet Pliuk corresponds to the Catholic society of Western Europe and the planet Alpha, situated midway between the two, is the substitute for the Catholic Central European countries under Soviet influence. The leader of Alpha is dressed like a pope; he talks and behaves like one and his body language is that of a Catholic priest blessing the multitudes. According to P. Gunst, "Catholic countries formed a Central European region whose socioeconomic development and agricultural adaptation to world markets placed it midway between East and West" (Gunst 53–91). Indeed, this can be inferred from the difference in clothing and from the technological development on Alpha, which is the land in the middle. From there one can either return back to Earth or go back to Pliuk. Moreover, on account of its particular system of ethics, Alpha is characterized by greater opposition to the penetration of Pliukian modes of life. The planet is likened to Central European countries, which were resistant to communism and had stronger oppositional movements (Ascherson 221–237). Undoubtedly, the variation along economic and sociopolitical lines relates to the differences in value priorities (Schwartz, Bardi 388) — while the survival of nature and resistance to Pliuk are the predominant concerns on Alpha, the survival of man with or without nature is of importance on Pliuk.

The models of society used in *Kin Dza Dza!* have been transposed into the film from the map of a partitioned, divided Europe. Hence, *Kin Dza Dza!* addresses the divisions and clashes between individuals, originating in a profound divergence of ideas and mindsets. The construction of a national identity within a multinational union of Soviet states is presented as impossible via the idea of the broken nation of Hanut. The role of religion as ethnic solidarity is absent because the film is built on series of doubles and mirror images of separate worlds — the Soviet state and Georgia, the Communist Block and the rest of Europe, communism and capitalism, Orthodoxy and Catholicism. The worlds of *Kin Dza Dza!* are mirror images of one another and, at the same time, of the 1980s European political map. The terrestrial and extra-terrestrial clashes with the Other reveal a profound likeness.

> BI: Is it true that nobody sings in cages on Earth?
> GEDEVAN: Mr. Bi, on Earth only animals are kept in cages.
> BI: Are these animals Chetlanian?
> GEDEVAN: Don't know. Chetlanians are like animals sometimes.
> MR. WEF: Is the nightingale Patsak?
> GEDEVAN: Why should it be?
> MR. WEF: It was you who said it sings without a cage!
> GEDEVAN: Well, then it is.
> BI: See? You have the same open racism as here on Pliuk. But on Earth it is the Patsak who detains power. Not the Chetlanian! Just like you and your friend the nightingale.[12]

Conclusion

As Need and Evans justly point out, it is not always certain what "the impact of seven decades of atheistic communism" (299) might be when differentiating between the Orthodox and the Catholic denominations. For example, it could have provoked the change in religious affiliations noted during the 1970s when only 28 percent of the population declared themselves Orthodox and 31 percent declared themselves "other professing Christians" (Froese 39). It might also explain the two simultaneously occurring, seemingly contradictory developments — secularization and religious revival (Agadjanian 351). While those changes operated in society, the importance of science fiction seemed to grow. The phenomenon might partly explain why the Golden Age of Soviet science fiction occurred when it did to become an outlet for religious and/or existential concerns.

As part of that movement, *Kin Dza Dza!* is a film about changes and the imminent confrontation with the Other. It attempts to deliver a "conscious or unconscious moral message," to awaken a sense of common history and transform it into spectacle, a "moral spectacle" according to Heller-Nicholas in this volume. In that, the film is representative of the 1980s. Through the eyes of space travelers, the universe is seen as the harmonious unity it was before a great schism split it apart. The Earth, Hanut, Pliuk and Alpha counterbalance each other and despite the colossal dissimilarities of their fates, their populations have the same origins. The film enacts the reunification of brothers, at the same time suggesting that Christianity can also be reunited. It upholds the idea that man is capable of the best and the worst, that integrity and spirituality are not innate but acquired.

In an interview, Daneliya defined film directing as "making something punkish."[13] *Kin Dza Dza!* is punkish in its satirical and political aspects and because it addresses social injustice and economic disparity. In addition, the film represents an attempt to end the inequalities and cross the border with the West, to have a look at the other side, to gather enough courage and feel free to tell that story back home. Illustrated by Gedevan's remark that it is "just because you say what you don't think and think what you don't think, that you sit in cages,"[14] the transformation of the freedom ideal in the USSR, and more specifically the freedom of speech, acquires a multitude of dimensions. On the political, as well as the spiritual level, it is linked to the evolution of the Catholic clergy's understanding of liberty and to its relationship with the rest of the Christian (here Orthodox) world.

> One thinks immediately of the Church's movement from her initial rejection of the idea of religious liberty to Vatican IPs embrace of a human right to religious liberty as a defining element of a rightly ordered polity [...] one thinks of the transition from the nineteenth-century Church's initial posture of suspicion towards "rights talk" to her contemporary affirmation of the existence of an order of human rights and insistence that protection and promotion of these rights lies at the very heart of the government's responsibilities [Grasso 45].

In Russia, as one of the three countries persecuting Christians and, more specifically Catholics, and called by Pope Pius XI the "terrible triangle," science fiction became a form of "inner emigration" through which writers were seeking to escape the government as well as the intellectual signification of communism by withdrawing into their spiritual world (Agadjanian 351). Within the terrible triangle, mass religiosity was rendered impossible by a conspiracy of silence and the regime provoked an intellectual schism where the writing/filming/directing persona became separate from the persona of the Soviet citizen. Science fiction was then "ripe for making observations about religion and spirituality because it lent itself to parable-telling and myth-making" but it also "create[d] a mystic point of view that [did] not deny the other side of the world, the devil's madness" (Winston 35). Both remarks apply to *Kin Dza Dza!* which is partly a parable — it has a simple setting (a desert planet), focuses on the actions of the participants, shows the results of these actions and their moral implications. The only deviation from the parable is that Daneliya's lessons are very ambiguous. It still remains to be seen which side in the film is indulging in "the devil's madness." It is impossible to take a side as to who criticizes whom; that instability seems to be a move towards reconciliation of the three worlds in *Kin Dza Dza!*

Notes

1. Tony Fawl, "Kin Dza Dza — Strange Russian Science Fiction," Science Fiction SadCAST Review, http://slconceptual.wordpress.com/2007/08/03/kin-dza-dza/, accessed 03 Jan. 2010.
2. Ryan Ward, "A truly amazing and overlooked film!" Amazon Review, May 2006, http://www.amazon.com/Kin-dza-dza/dp/B00024MH8C, accessed 03 Jan. 2010.
3. Fawl.
4. Most translation and transcription difficulties reside in the linguistic crisis of the Pliukian world. Daneliya and Gabriadze imagined an extra-terrestrial language for their script, much in line with what Orwell (*1984*) had done before them and what Burgess (*Clockwork Orange*) would later do. Words denote this or that, imply both one thing and its opposite; expressions containing extra-terrestrial terms can take a variety of meanings.
5. *Kin Dza Dza!* part 1, 10:41 min.
6. "The Greatest Commandment," *The Holy Bible* — NIV, Mark 12:28–31.
7. *Kin Dza Dza!* part 2, 16:08 min. Translation is mine.
8. The linguistic crisis on Pliuk is so deep that the language has only two words — "kiu" and "kou." The first is a socially acceptable swear word, while "kou" stands for all other words.
9. "Throne in Heaven," *The Holy Bible* — NIV, Revelation 4:1.
10. *Kin Dza Dza!* part 2, 45:19 min. Translation is mine. "Chatl" is Pliukian money.
11. "Jesus the Way to the Father," *The Holy Bible* — NIV, John 14:5.
12. *Kin Dza Dza!* part 2, 08:30 min. Translation is mine.
13. "Kin-dza-dza," Russian Cinema Council, http://www.ruscico.com/dvd.php?lang=en&dvd=316, accessed 23 Jan. 2010.
14. *Kin Dza Dza!* part 1, 42:05 min. Translation is mine.

Works Cited

Agadjanian, Alexander. "Public Religion and the Quest for National Ideology: Russia's Media Discourse." *Journal for the Scientific Study of Religion* 40:3 (2001): 351–365.

Ascherson, N. "1989 in Eastern Europe: Constitutional representative government as a 'return to normality?'" J. Dunn. *Democracy: The Unfinished Journey 508 bc to ad 1993*. Ed. Oxford: Oxford University Press, 1992.
Born, Daniel. "Character as Perception: Science Fiction and the Christian Man of Faith." *Extrapolation* 24:1 (1983): 251–271.
Dudley, Joseph M. "Transformational SF Religions." *Extrapolation* 35:4 (1994): 342–350.
Froese, Paul. "Forced Secularization in Soviet Russia: Why an Atheistic Monopoly Failed." *Journal for the Scientific Study of Religion* 43:1 (2004): 35–50.
Grasso, Kenneth L. "A Distinctive Idea of Freedom: Francis Canavan and Contemporary Catholic Social Thought." *The Catholic Social Science Review*, Vol. 2 (1997): 45–53.
Gunst, P. "Agrarian Systems of Central and Eastern Europe." *The Origins of Backwardness in Eastern Europe: Economics and Politics from the Middle Ages Until the Early Twentieth Century*. Ed. D. Chirot. Berkeley: University of California Press, 1989.
The Holy Bible (New International Version). Biblica, 1984, available online http://www.biblegateway.com/. 17 Jan. 2010.
Kin Dza Dza! Dir. Georgi Daneliya. Perf. Stanislav Lyubshin, Evgeni Leonov, Yuriy Yakovlev. Mosfilm Studios, 1986. Film.
Laruelle, Marlène. "Alternative Identity, Alternative Religion? Neo-Paganism and the Aryan Myth in Contemporary Russia." *Nations and Nationalism* 14:2 (2008): 283–301.
Marx, Karl. "Introduction to a Contribution to the Critique of Hegel's Philosophy of Right." *Early Writings*. London: Penguin Classics, 1992.
Moroz, Evgueniy. *Istoriia "Mertvoi vody"— ot strashnoi skazki k bol'shoi politike. Politicheskoe neoiazychestvo v postsovetskoi Rossii*. Ed. Andreas Umland. Stuttgart: Ibidem-Verlag, 2005.
Need, Ariana, and Geoffrey Evans. "Analysing Patterns of Religious Participation in Post-Communist Eastern Europe." *British Journal of Sociology* 52:2 (2001): 229–248.
Rutledge, Amelia A. "*Star Maker*: The Agnostic Quest." *Science Fiction Studies*, Vol. 9 (1982): 274–283.
Schwartz, Shalom H., and Anat Bardi. "Influences of Adaptation to Communist Rule on Value Priorities in Eastern Europe." *Political Psychology* 18:2 (1997): 385–410.
Shnirelman, V. *Intellectual Labyrinths: Essays on Ideologies in Contemporary Russia*. Moscow: Academia, 2004.
Winston, Kimberly. "Other Worlds, Suffused with Religion." *Publishers Weekly* (April 2001): 35.

Murder Mystery Meets Sacred Mystery
The Catholic Sacramental in Hitchcock's I Confess

BARRY C. KNOWLTON *and*
ELOISE R. KNOWLTON

Religion is a problem for filmmakers. Regardless of the faith tradition depicted, and regardless of the way in which a faith is depicted, the potential for incomprehension or offense is enormous. When it comes to religion, emotions run high, and viewpoints tend to be hardened. Catholicism, a religion that is complicated theologically and intimidating culturally, is especially problematic. When depicting Catholicism, filmmakers have had to tread lightly. They have had to both avoid giving offense (unless, of course, that is what they wanted to do) and generating incomprehension (unless, that, after all, is the way they wanted to do it). The typical, and comfortable, way to represent the Catholic religion has been to focus on the good works, pious sentiments, and ethnic charm of Catholics, often Irish, as in *Boys' Town* (1938), *Men of Boys' Town* (1941), *Going My Way* (1944), and *The Bells of St. Mary's* (1945). Spencer Tracy's Father Flanagan and Bing Crosby's Father O'Malley are nearly always shown in Roman collars, but never in liturgical vestments. Their priestly ministry is represented as generically pastoral, but never sacramental. In short, a mainstream Hollywood film that takes Catholic theology seriously, and that centers its action uncomfortably on the fantastical efficacy of a sacrament, is a rarity, and a problem. Alfred Hitchcock's *I Confess* (1953) may have been "neglected" (Keyser and Keyser 135), precisely because it dares to make this sacramental investment.

Hitchcock was raised Catholic and educated by Jesuits. He and his family never abandoned their faith, a fact that biographer Donald Spoto points out and then ignores. Other critics are less dismissive; Eric Rohmer and Claude Chabrol's overview of Hitchcock's first forty-four films reads Catholicism, or more broadly, Christianity, throughout the works, identifying themes of providence, satanic possession, and the complexities of communities of sin. Hitchcock himself did not make an issue of his religion, and rarely spoke of it. It plays no overt role in his films until *I Confess*, the most clearly Catholic film in his *oeuvre*. *I Confess* tells the story of a murderer who admits to his crime in the confessional. Because he has heard it in the context of a sacramental confession, the priest can tell no one, even when he is himself suspected of the crime. This was a very personal project for Hitchcock — the criminal's wife shares his wife's name, Alma — and the film bears the marks both of Hitchcock's distinctive technical skill, and the stresses of a project he came to believe was a mistake. In an interview with Francois Truffaut, Hitchcock said,

> That's the trouble with *I Confess*. We Catholics know that a priest cannot disclose the secret of the confessional, but the Protestants, the atheists, and the agnostics all say, "Ridiculous! No man would ... sacrifice his life for such a thing" ... we shouldn't have made the picture [Truffaut 204].

In this "ridiculousness," one feels the rub of the rational against the sacramental, friction that is at the heart of the film's ambition as well as its perceived failure. A standard murder mystery is the dramatization and valorization of rationality acting in the world; Catholic sacramentality, having at its heart a divine power acting in the human world, is a far more difficult and uncomfortable thing to attempt to dramatize. If one works, as Hitchcock did, in a realist mode, one cannot rely on gaudy special effects to depict the power of God. How then to make a movie about sacramental power that is neither reductive nor ridiculous? Hitchcock thought he failed, but if he failed, his failure is instructive not only of the degree to which Hitchcock's Catholicism is at work in his films, but of the problem all his films in one way or another can be seen to take up: the problem of unseen and inner forces at work on humans. In *Psycho* and *Vertigo* we are to understand that these forces are psychological, and if the actions of the characters are irrational, we as the audience are those characters' rational judges. In *I Confess*, a far more daring, unbelievable, and even uncanny force subtends the film's central character and his actions.

If the challenge of the film is to dramatize a particular kind of silence, to give it weight and edge when what is at stake is a peculiarly Catholic thing, how does the film make visible this silence, and to what extent are those efforts successful? If the film rests on this need, then one of the first distinctions to be made for the viewer is that between crime and sin. Audiences are comfortable with the former. How can they come to understand the latter, and in a peculiarly Catholic fashion?

Crime vs. Sin

Crime and punishment on the one hand, sin and repentance on the other: one of the central problems of *I Confess* is how to dramatize the tension between a civil notion of crime and a religious notion of sin. The conflict between the two authorities — human and divine — lies at the center of Jesus' story. Jesus was killed because he posed a threat to Roman authority. Asked whether or not Christians should pay tax, Jesus replies, "Render to Caesar the things that are Caesar's and to God the things that are God's" (Luke 20:25). Confession in the civil valence is rational and instrumental, based on the need for evidence of the crime. While a confession is not conclusive — how many murder mysteries have someone confessing to the crime to protect someone else — it greases the wheels of civil jurisprudence. A confession leads to a guilty plea, avoiding an expensive trial and mitigating the severity of punishment. Justice is a matter of legal punishment, to preserve the body politic's good order, and to uphold the secularly established law. According to civil authority, the priest in *I Confess* is withholding evidence, and could be prosecuted under the law as an accessory after the fact. Hitchcock, in his interview with Francois Truffaut, points this out: "I think this is a fundamental fact: any priest who receives the confession of any killer becomes an accessory after the fact" (Truffaut 202).

Confessing to a sin is different from confessing to a crime, and is understood differently by Catholics and Protestants. All Christians share the Judaic notion of sin, deriving from humanity's disobedience to God, as represented in the Genesis story of Adam and Eve. But the two traditions part ways after that. The Protestant view is that the sinner must be inwardly repentant, and if forgiven, is forgiven directly by God. The Catholic view holds that a priest, as the successor of Jesus, the judge of souls, is the medium through which forgiveness (absolution) is granted. The corruption of indulgences, where sins were forgiven in exchange for money, was one of the points on which Martin Luther critiqued the Church: justification, that is, salvation, was by faith alone, not by cleaning the soul's slate by means of a mediating, score-keeping church authority.

While the Catholic view also requires sincerity in repentance, the repentant sinner must confess to a priest and receive the forgiveness (absolution) only a validly ordained priest can confer. The efficacy (effectiveness) of this aspect of the Catholic sacrament depends on the action of the priest, through whom God's forgiveness is granted. If he absolves the sinner of his guilt, the sinner is absolved. If not, not. This belief in priestly power derives from the passage in scripture where Jesus confers the Holy Spirit on his apostles (the first priests) such that "whosoever sins ye remit, they are remitted unto them; and whosoever sins ye retain, they are retained" (John 20:23). A brief review of the film's intertwined storylines may serve to demonstrate some of the means by which the film seeks to negotiate the tension between the rational investigation of crime, and the divine expiation of sin.

Doubles

The story has two threads, closely knotted in a tight Hitchcockian twist. The first, in the filmic present, is the story of a young priest's implication in a murder his parishioner has committed and confessed to him. Here we see again what might be called the quintessential Hitchcockian situation, played here in a religious key: the innocent man falsely accused. Fr. Michael Logan (Montgomery Clift) is a decorated World War II veteran. The murderer, Keller (O.E. Hasse), is a German refugee whom he has helped emigrate to Quebec, where the film is set. Logan now employs Keller and his wife Alma (Dolly Haas) in the parish rectory. Even before the murder has occurred, the relationship between the two is in place by means of their nationalities: guilty German, forgiving priest. (Remember, this is 1953.) Our introduction to Logan shows him as a doer of pastoral good works, returning good for evil. Clift's ability to convey wordless inner conflict serves as a visual means of conveying the weight of this silence.

The second plot line, revealed through a police interrogation and depicted through flashbacks, is the story of Logan's earlier romance with Ruth (Anne Baxter), a childhood sweetheart whom he declined to marry before going to war. She married conventionally but without love while he was away, and seeks him out on his return to renew the relationship, failing to mention that she has been married during his absence. In a pivotal scene, Ruth and Michael are driven by a rainstorm to spend a night together in a summer house. Sex is delicately but definitely signified by the tie on Ruth's blouse. In the morning, the two are challenged by the owner of the property: none other than Vilette, the very man whom Keller will later murder for an unrelated reason, and who will in his final weeks try to blackmail Ruth and Logan about the summer house event. With Vilette's denunciation, Ruth's marriage is revealed to Logan. When next she sees him it is years later, at his ordination.

Hitchcock's orderly mind was given to doubles and doubling, never more apparent than in *Vertigo*, but clearly at work here as well. Keller disguises himself on the night of the crime by donning a cassock, throwing suspicion on a priest. Whether or not he intended suspicion to fall on Logan is uncertain: he could have known he was out that night. Suspicion does fall when witnesses report seeing a priest leaving Vilette's, and is strengthened when Inspector Larrue (Karl Malden) learns of Logan's relationship with Ruth, of Ruth's blackmailing by Vilette, and of the consequent motive for murder in Logan's desire to free her, and himself, from persecution.

Vilette's false priest is doubled by the false priest imagined by Larrue, who can only understand Logan as a man. As his name would suggest, Larrue is the man on "the street," a tough figure of worldly rationality. For him the cassock is an empty signifier. It means "priest," but no more than that: a detail in the suspect's description. He knows someone dressed as a priest committed the crime, and that Logan is hiding something. Why? Normal motivations are clear enough: to protect a woman he loves. For a layman, that would be a noble reason. Larrue serves as the vehicle through which the audience (now in the know and positioned as Catholics) witnesses the education of secular authority in the ways of the Church. Malden, with his inexplicable and wholly undisguised American accent, gives the American audience a familiar grounding as it, too, investigates a mystery. But while for Larrue it is the identity of the murderer, for the audience it is now the unaccustomed theological concern for a priest's fidelity to his vocation. Hitchcock has us asking not "whodunit?" but "will Logan crack?"

The fact that, in this case, Hitchcock has revealed — to us — the identity of the murderer at the outset of the narrative deserves some comment. Ordinarily, a Hitchcock film holds truth in abeyance, offering incidental revelations and red or reddish herrings, until a climactic *denouement*. This kind of narrative inequity between audience and film is part of the vertiginous discomfort of experiencing a Hitchcock tale: you don't know, and you know you don't know, what will happen next. You do know, however, and are always painfully aware, that there is a somewhat sadistic *raconteur* in charge, and he's going to make you suffer before he reveals all. Those fleeting glimpses of Hitchcock's portly figure are more than signatures. They serve to remind us that the artifice in play is not controlled by the viewer. We are granted a glimpse of the puppeteer, and the puppets are not all on the screen.

But in *I Confess* the truth is out in the first minutes of the film. Clear signposts, literally street signs, point us in the right "direction," the Francophone equivalent to "one way." We move closer and closer to the scene of the crime, and finally peek in through a wide-open window to see the murder victim, the murder weapon, a bead curtain set in motion by the just-departed murderer, and then, a dark figure leaving the house. Compare these opening shots with those of *Citizen Kane*, which they clearly echo both in visual composition and in sound track. In *Kane*, we similarly creep past signs, but they tell us to stay away. We similarly peek through a window to witness the founding mystery of the film: Charles Foster Kane's deathbed intonation of "rosebud." While the Kane exposition sets mystery in motion, the Hitchcock exposition confesses all from the outset. In the next shots we see the murderer remove the priestly disguise. We see his face, and that he is not wearing a Roman collar. We follow him back to the church. Now we know who did what to whom. But we cannot tell Larrue what we have heard and seen that night any more than Logan can.

Three Kinds of Confession

A close parsing of the scene of Keller's confession reveals Hitchcock's thorough understanding of the refinements of Catholic theology. In reading the following scenes, we have consulted and quoted a 1923 (pre–Vatican II) catechism in an edition published for the use of priests. This might well have been the text a priest such as Logan could have used in his ministry. The theological doctrine, without the priestly directives, would have been that studied by a youthful Alfred Hitchcock.

From the window of his room, Logan sees someone entering the church. It is late, after eleven. Logan investigates and comes upon a distressed Keller kneeling in a pew. Questioned, Keller says he wanted to pray. This implies the "interior penance" which "consists in turning to God sincerely and from the heart, and in hating and detesting our past transgressions, with a firm resolution of amendment of life, hoping to obtain pardon through the mercy of God" (263). We are to understand that it is a good thing that Keller ("Killer") feels remorse for killing Vilette. His conscience is alive and his reason is functioning: the conditions for absolution exist.

The penitent Catholic is drawn to confession (more formally called the sacrament of penance) by faith in the power of forgiveness, and this faith is what grounds the efficacy of the sacrament. Initially, however, Keller is more than just remorseful: he is despairing. When Father Logan asks him whether there is anything he can do to help, Keller says that no one can help him. While "it is a virtue to be sorrowful at the time, in the manner, and to the extent which are required" for the sacrament of penance, Keller seems to have given himself "to such melancholy and grief, as utterly to abandon all hope of salvation" (Catechism 264). Logan acts to reassure him, and to reassert the faithful belief that nothing is beyond God's power to forgive. "If, then, the pastor happens to encounter those who seem to distrust the infinite goodness and clemency of God, let him endeavor to inspire their minds with confidence, and raise them up to the hope of obtaining the grace of God" (Catechism 267). In order for the sacrament to take place, Keller must move from the fear that no one (not even God) can help him, to an affirmation in the power of the sacrament to overcome any sin, however grievous.

Before he gets there, Keller occupies an intermediary state, and one that would be perfectly readable to the audience: "I must tell someone," he says. More confiding than confessional, this appeal to Logan would appear to be on the basis not of their relationship as priest and parishioner, but as friend to friend. Part of the seriousness of Keller's situation is that, in murdering Vilette, he has betrayed Logan's trust in bringing him into this community and giving him and his wife a place there. Keller knows that what he has done has damaged not only his relationship with God, but with Logan, and with Logan not as a priest but as a friend and benefactor. Had Keller gone on at that point, the valence and weight of his words would have been very different. Does a friend turn in a friend? A serious moral question, and one that Logan would have been free to ask. Had Keller disclosed rather than confessed the murder, Logan would have been duty bound as a citizen to turn Keller in to the authorities. Keller's disclosure bespeaks the guilt he feels toward Logan for having "abused [his] kindness." But he doesn't continue to speak as an erring friend. Hitchcock clearly distinguishes the personal from the penitential by having Keller rise to his feet, saying, "I would like to make a confession," signifying that he is asking a priest for the sacrament of penance. He is so understood by Logan, who says nothing but heads for the confessional, the sacramental rather than legal or interpersonal space of disclosure.

In the confessional, Logan dons the stole that signifies his priestly authority and composes himself to hear Keller's confession. The Catechism explains that "the matter ... of the Sacrament of Penance is the acts of the penitent—namely, contrition, confession, and satisfaction" (268). Contrition is regret, signified in the confessional by a statement of remorse, often a set statement called an "act of contrition." Confession is naming what it is one did: one must speak it, and speak it all. Satisfaction is penance proper: what one does in expiation, as directed by the priest, such as prayer or reparation. Keller begins with an act of contrition ("I confess to almighty God and to you that I have sinned..."), but doesn't finish. He admits to sin, but does not express a determination to do penance and sin no more. Keller's confession is incomplete, both in form and in intent. "Proper contrition," the Catechism explains, "involves a detestation of all past sins, an intention to confess them and render satisfaction for them, and a firm purpose of amending one's life" (278). Keller cuts past Logan's inquiry as to the date of his last confession, and blurts out: "I have killed Mr. Vilette. Vilette, the lawyer. I went to his house tonight," Keller explains. "I went to steal his money. I wore a cassock, to avoid attention. He surprised me. He was going to call the police...."

At this point, as if the film must avert its eyes from the privacy of the confessional, the scene dissolves to the Kellers' room in the rectory. The sacramental confession that Keller had wanted to make gives way to an interpersonal confession — one tells one's spouse what one must tell someone — and in what he says to his wife the tension between the sacramental and legal notions of confession is reiterated. If Keller had confessed to the police, it would have been entirely proper for him to try to mitigate his guilt. Though the Church also would make a distinction between premeditated and unpremeditated murder, the purpose of sacramental confession is to take full responsibility for one's sinfulness. That Keller has not done so is evident in his observation that Vilette was rich, and in his firm purpose of stealing Vilette's money so that he and Alma can "start a new life" in a secular sense.

Here we learn what satisfaction Keller is supposed to render for the sin he has committed: he must return the money he has stolen. "Well known to all is the maxim of St. Augustine: *The sin is not forgiven unless what has been taken away is restored*," the Catechism reminds us (279). But it also tells us that "since the Sacraments signify what they effect, the words, *I absolve thee*, signify that remission of sin is effected by the administration of this sacrament; and hence it is plain that such is the perfect form of the sacrament" (269). Again, there is a distinction to be made between the guilt that has been absolved and the satisfaction that must still be rendered. Before he has been absolved of his guilt in the killing of Vilette, Keller is liable to the punishment of eternal death. In other words, if he had died without making his confession, he would have gone to hell. This is suggested by the soundtrack, which, as Keller leaves the scene of the murder and returns to the church, and until he enters the confessional, quotes from the "Dies Irae" or "Day of Wrath," the section of the Requiem Mass that represents the Last Judgement with an emphasis on those who will be damned. Having been absolved, if Keller had died without rendering satisfaction, the temporal punishment would have to be worked out in Purgatory, but he would then be eligible for heaven.

But an inability or unwillingness to render satisfaction would also indicate a disposition to sin again, and this is what we see in Keller. Logan has told him that he must return the money he has stolen, but he confesses to Alma that he cannot do it. He has been sacramentally forgiven his sin, but still fears the legal punishment for his crime. "It is so dangerous," Keller says. "They will catch me — they will hang me!" His fear is understandable. Less so is Alma's fear: "Father Logan will go to them — he will tell them!" Whatever has made her fear that Logan will do this, it is what makes her husband realize that he can't. "He will tell them? He cannot tell them what he heard in confession." On the one hand, this affirms Keller's contrition because he confessed without considering that by confessing his sin he might be able to avoid punishment for his crime. On the other hand, his realization that Logan cannot tell anyone what he has done is the beginning of Keller's firm purpose of getting away with murder.

Logan cannot tell the police or anyone else what Keller has told him, because of what is called the "Seal of Confession." "By the Seal of Confession we understand the obligation to keep secret whatever has been revealed in sacramental confession," begins a 1927 history of the sacrament, explaining that "the importance of the seal for the Sacrament of Penance follows from the nature of things. Without strict silence the administration of Penance would be impossible" (Kurtscheid 1, 2). If a person commits a sin that is also a crime, and if confession of the sin entails a revelation of the crime, then the person would not confess. But the Church considers that the forgiveness of the sinner is more important than the punishment of the criminal, and so

> The faithful are to be admonished that there is no reason whatever to apprehend that what is made known in confession will ever be revealed by the priest to anyone, or that by it the penitent can at any time be brought into danger of any sort: the laws of the Church threaten the severest penalties against any priest who would fail to observe a perpetual and religious silence concerning all the sins confessed to them. *Let the priest,* says the great Council of Lateran, *take special care, neither by word or by sign, nor by any means whatever, to betray in the least degree the sinner* [Catechism 292].

The exigency of the Seal of Confession generates most of the film's dramatic tension. Not only can Father Logan not tell the police that Keller is the murderer, he cannot by anything he says or does help the police solve the mystery. When questioned, he cannot even say, "I can't answer that question because to do so would violate the Seal of Confession." He must say only that he cannot answer the question. Even with Keller, Logan cannot re-open the discussion. In a scene unfolding on the day after the confession, Logan stands on a ladder, painting. (He's covering something up.) Keller wants to continue to discuss their situation, and to renegotiate the penance. "Hasn't God forgiven me, thanks to you?" Keller asks Logan, and if he had been able to answer, the answer would have been "yes." But outside the confessional the seal of confession constrains Logan, even if such a discussion might lead to a more satisfactorily penitent Keller. "I know what you must think of me," Keller says, but if Logan thinks any less of him after hearing his confession, he will have to be sure not to let on, for that too would compromise the seal of confession. He replies to Keller's urgent pleading with, "I don't know what you are talking about." This not very compassionate response is the only thing he can say in such a situation. Keller had told Alma that he could not return the money, because he did not want to be caught by the police. In asking Logan for another penance, Keller seems to think that the penance imposed was to confess to the police. But this has to be a misunderstanding on Keller's part, though, again, Logan can say nothing to clarify the matter. "There is nothing I can add to what I have already said." But he can't have told Keller to turn himself in, because the seal of confession would have prevented him from imposing a penance that would expose the penitent.

In asking for another penance, Keller is demonstrating his willingness to do penance, in conformity with his initial contrition, but his unwillingness to do the penance imposed shows a disposition to sin again, which he indeed does. He speaks, and acts, with Germanic *sang froid*, as a man who had nothing to do with Vilette's death. Francois Truffaut has followed this development, and comments that "the turning point in Otto Keller's attitude is when he instructs his wife not to clean up the bloodstained cassock. At that moment he relinquishes any claim to being a naïve and deeply religious man: he is deliberately trying to destroy his confessor and benefactor; he's become diabolical and evil" (Truffaut 204).

The drama of Logan's silence — a silence shared by the audience and misunderstood by Larrue — darkens as Hitchcock's plot turns the screw tighter and tighter. As Larrue's evidence mounts against him, Logan's fidelity to his ordination is tried higher and higher, until that fidelity threatens to cost him his life. Here a reading invoked by Rohmer and Chabrol is especially suggestive: "let us join Jacques Rivette," they say,

> in emphasizing the idea of *confession*, already encountered in *Under Capricorn*. "The guilty person understands by remission of sin that he is totally discharged of it, and that his confessor is obliged, if necessary, to take the sin on himself and expiate it in his place... In a variety of manners, the couples obsessed by guilt (the heart of all Hitchcock films) live through the same experience: they manage to make the sin hesitate between two souls until it is abolished by the irremediable confusion of their destinies" [Rohmer and Chabrol 115–116].

Parallels with a Christ-like sacrifice emerge and are touched up with shots of an agonized Logan walking past a statue of Jesus carrying the cross, escorted by Roman soldiers. Like Jesus, Logan undergoes a passion that combines theologically significant suffering with prosecution by civil authorities. At this point, the police are looking for him, and wonder whether he has fled to avoid arrest. As he walks the streets of Quebec, Logan retraces the path Jesus takes in his passion story. Like Christ in the garden of Gethsemane, he appears to be hoping that "this cup may pass him by." His perambulations take him to the church in which he was ordained, where he evidently accepts that it will "be as God wills." He turns himself in to Inspector Larrue. The trial follows, ending in his acquittal for insufficient evidence. Logan leaves the courtroom to face an accusing mob outside, which shouts at him to remove his Roman collar. Innocent but reviled, Logan's real exoneration and near-apotheosis depend not on civil authority, but on two more revelatory confessions in the final scenes.

Concluding Confessions

In the penultimate scene, the three forms of confession converge: the legal, the interpersonal, and the sacramental. The film's pace accelerates as the trial is swiftly followed by Logan's public denunciation, Alma's literal fingering of Keller as Vilette's killer, and her shooting. Mortally wounded, Alma is laid along the running board of a car, where Father Millais, Logan's pastor, cradles her head and begins mumbling Latin. Logan stands by, concerned. Into this scene of pastoral care Inspector Larrue intrudes, demanding, "What is she saying?" Alma, looking at Logan, her friend and benefactor, whispers, "Forgive me," and dies.

Alma's death scene is perhaps the fullest collapsing of the sacramental, legal, and personal aspects of confession. She seems to be asking Logan for his personal forgiveness, because she had known that it was her husband who had killed Vilette, but had said nothing and so allowed Logan to be tried for the murder. During the trial she is shown distressed but silent. Only when she sees the hostile crowd besieging Logan does she break silence and declare him innocent. As she dies, Father Millais pronounces absolution. Larrue has learned only that what she was saying had something to do with Vilette. The police are in pursuit of Keller because he has just shot his wife, but Larrue presses Logan for information about Keller and Vilette. Logan is still bound to maintain the seal of confession, and, as Larrue's questioning becomes more insistent, we are reminded that to maintain the seal of confession, Logan has to avoid indicating in any way that Keller confessed to him.

When Keller is cornered, and Larrue asks him, "What about Vilette?"

Keller assumes that Logan has told the police about his confession. He reproaches Logan for giving him away, and so reveals that Logan has been resolutely and absolutely faithful to his priestly obligation. Keller's statement also solves the mystery of Vilette's murder, but what registers on the faces of Larrue, Father Millais and Ruth is not surprise but admiration and amazement that Logan has been faithful through such a trial. Larrue realizes that Logan's strength and fidelity transcend his detection. Father Millais, who knew that even though Logan had been acquitted he would be unable to function as a priest given the hostility of the laity, now understands better than any layman just how Christ-like Logan has been.

We are left with Keller, who has one last confession to make in the final scene. But he is not at all properly disposed. He continues to taunt, and then to threaten Logan. Logan shows the physical courage he must have shown during the war. As Keller is about to shoot Logan, he is shot by the police. "Oh, Father," Keller says, as he drops his gun and starts to fall, "Help me — quickly!" Logan rushes forward and takes Keller in his arms. "Forgive m..." Keller says, and dies. Logan looks at him with sadness and compassion, and absolves him.

This final confession and absolution may seem as ridiculous to some as had the idea that a priest would not disclose the secret of the confessional. We would in the ordinary run of ordinary plots expect to see the bad guy gunned down by the police and justice thereby done. Dirty Harry would have given us far more satisfaction in this sense. Hitchcock piles on Keller's evilness: he taunts and is on the point of killing his friend and benefactor. Then the film shows him receiving forgiveness from the man he has wronged, the priest to whom he has made this last confession. How does Logan do it? How can he? Hitchcock had intended for Keller to kill Logan, but the Motion Picture Production Code insisted that the film not end with the killing of a priest. Had Hitchcock's preference been honored, the messianic parallels would have been limned more boldly. This ending, more acceptable to the censor, is also in keeping with the film's commitment to show Logan's greatness of heart and fidelity to his calling. He risks his life to preserve his vows; he risks his life to help the guilty man, and even at gunpoint his care for Keller does not wane.

Hitchcock's *I Confess* concludes with revelation, but not, as in *Psycho* or *Vertigo*, of a twisted, horrible truth we understand rationally. Instead, we find ourselves abruptly confronted with something both fantastic and ridiculous, something we cannot rationally understand, confirm, or feel as satisfying. Keller's absolution, like Logan's silence, is problematic, uncomfortable and even offensive to our sense of justice. This may be Hitchcock's most daring directorial moment. He bets the film on the audience's ability to see beyond the easy comprehension of heroism to the uneasy apprehension of a sacred mystery: that God's forgiveness so far exceeds our own.

Works Cited

The Bible. Revised Standard Version. Ed. Herbert G. May and Bruce M. Metzger. New York: Oxford University Press, 1962.
Catechism of the Council of Trent for Parish Priests. Trans. John A. McHugh and Charles J. Callan. New York: Joseph Wagner, 1923.
I Confess. Dir. Alfred Hitchcock. Perf. Montgomery Clift, Anne Baxter, Karl Malden. Warner Bros, 1953. Film.
Keyser, Les, and Barbara Keyser. *Hollywood and the Catholic Church.* Chicago: Loyola University Press, 1984.
Kurtscheid, Bertrand. *A History of the Seal of Confession.* Trans. F.A. Marks. St. Louis: B. Herder Book Co., 1927.
McDannell, Colleen, ed. *Catholics in the Movies.* Oxford: Oxford University Press, 2008.
Rohmer, Eric and Claude Chabrol. *Hitchcock: The First Forty-Four Films.* New York: Frederick Ungar, 1979.
Spoto, Donald. *The Dark Side of Genius: The Life of Alfred Hitchcock.* Boston: Little, Brown, 1983.
Taylor, John Russell. *Hitch: The Life and Times of Alfred Hitchcock.* New York: Pantheon, 1979.
Truffaut, Francois. *Hitchcock.* New York: Simon and Schuster, 1983.

Catholic Moral Teaching as a Fantastic Element in *Gone Baby Gone*

BRETT GAUL

Gone Baby Gone (2007) is the story of the search for missing four-year-old Amanda McCready.[1] Amanda lives in Boston, Massachusetts, with her mother Helene, a woman who abuses alcohol and uses illegal drugs. When Amanda goes missing, Helene's brother Lionel and his wife Beatrice hire private investigators Patrick Kenzie and Angie Gennaro to assist the police in the search for Amanda. The police are not thrilled to have external help, but Captain Jack Doyle instructs officers Remy Bressant and Nick Poole to meet with Patrick and Angie and share whatever information about the investigation that the police have gathered. The story continues as Patrick, Angie, Remy, and Nick track down leads and attempt to find Amanda. The film has a number of twists and a thought-provoking, surprising ending.

Although *Gone Baby Gone* is an overtly realist film, one way in which it retains a sense of the fantastic is by including Catholic symbols. While the symbols in the film are standard Catholic ones, their inclusion merits being called "fantastic" because their use often seems to be a deliberate attempt to draw a contrast between an idealistic, fanciful world of faith and the actual world.[2] For example, after Lionel and Beatrice hire Patrick and Angie, they all meet with Helene. Helene is watching *Jerry Springer* with her friend Dottie. When Lionel suggests that Dottie should leave the room, he and Helene get into an expletive-laden shouting match. Three of the characters — Patrick, Beatrice, and Helene — are wearing necklaces with crosses on them. Patrick's necklace also has a religious medallion on it. These Catholic symbols stand in stark contrast to the unsavory scene depicted. Later in the film at Amanda's memorial service, the small room in which her casket is displayed also contains a statue of Mary and a statue of an angel. Although these Catholic symbols are appropriate for the setting, viewers later discover that the memorial service itself was entirely fictitious. Another Catholic symbol used in the film that draws a contrast between the idealistic world of faith and the actual world is a medallion of Saint Christopher, the patron saint of those who need protection from harm. The use of this symbol is particularly effective in calling attention to the contrast between the world of faith and the actual world because it was worn by Johnny Pietro, a seven-year-old boy who disappeared a few weeks after Amanda did. Once viewers are told that Pietro disappeared while wearing this medallion, they naturally wonder why he was not protected from harm. Finally, a scene near the end of the film featuring Lionel uses a variety of Catholic symbols to show that Lionel has not lived up to the standards of his faith. After Patrick discovers that Lionel knows some vital information about Amanda's disappearance that he has not previously shared, he calls Lionel to set up a meeting. Upon hanging up the phone Lionel sits silently in his easy chair looking straight ahead. As he does this, the camera pans around to show a small bust of Jesus, some statues of cherubs, a picture of Amanda, and a framed copy of a "Family Prayer" that includes a picture of Jesus, Mary, and Joseph. The last shot of the scene, though, is the framed face of a cherub whose eyes and expression hauntingly imply that he knows what Lionel has done and that the actual world is not the ideal world.

The most interesting way in which *Gone Baby Gone* retains a sense of the fantastic, however, is not through its use of Catholic symbols, but through Patrick's references to his priest and Catholic moral teaching. In fact, the film opens with Patrick recounting a conversation that he had with his priest when he was young. He says he asked the priest "how you could get to heaven and still protect yourself from all the evil in the world?" The priest replied by quoting from Matthew 10:16: "You are sheep among wolves, be wise as serpents, yet innocent as doves." Throughout the film Patrick relies on his Catholic upbringing to guide him through various ethical dilemmas. However, many of the main characters in the film — Remy, Captain Doyle, and Angie — regard Patrick's faith-based ethical system as fantastic because they allege that it reflects a fanciful view of the world rather than one based on reason and experience. The depiction of Catholic moral teaching as a fantastic element in the film focuses on two important ethical issues. The first issue is whether people can ever do anything so heinous that they forfeit their right to be respected as persons such that it is morally permissible to execute them. Remy thinks so, but Patrick is not so sure. "Murder's a sin," he says. The second issue, and main focus of the film, is the question of what exactly determines whether a particular action is morally right. According to Remy, Captain Doyle, and Angie, the right action is that which produces the best consequences for those affected by the action. Patrick—echoing the Catholic Church's teaching on this issue—argues otherwise. He contends that some actions (for example, killing an innocent person), because of their very nature, are inherently wrong and therefore morally impermissible. Such actions ought not to be performed even if they would produce the best consequences. The film's final shot shows Patrick contemplating whether Remy, Captain Doyle, and Angie's view of Catholic moral teaching was correct after all.

When Amanda is discovered to be missing, her Uncle Lionel and Aunt Beatrice hire private investigators Patrick and Angie to augment the police department's investigation because both possess local knowledge which could be useful in finding Amanda: they know people who do not talk to the police. One person in the neighborhood Patrick knows who does not talk to the police is Bubba Rogowski, a drug dealer. When Patrick and Angie learn that one of the police's lead suspects is Corwin Earle, a convicted child molester who may be living with former convicts Leon and Roberta Trett, Patrick and Angie visit Bubba to see if he knows the Tretts. Although Bubba asks Patrick "[w]hat makes you think I know people like this," Patrick responds that he knows Bubba does not pay his rent "doing people's taxes." When Bubba finds out from one of his street dealers that Leon and Roberta are in the neighborhood, Bubba tells Patrick and the two pay the Tretts a visit.

During their visit they discover that Earle is indeed living upstairs in the same house as Leon and Roberta. After Bubba and Patrick leave, Patrick calls Remy and Nick to tell them that he has found Earle, and the officers later meet Patrick outside the house. Instead of waiting for additional police support, though, Remy and Nick decide to split up and storm the place themselves. In the course of doing so, Nick is shot on the front porch and wounded badly. Upon seeing Nick get shot, Patrick attempts to provide aid and is shot at himself. After calling 911 and reporting that a police officer has been shot, Patrick returns gunfire and enters the house. He immediately encounters an angry and pistol-wielding Roberta who chases him up the stairs to the second floor and into a room. He shuts and locks the door and proceeds to search the room. Another door, this one slightly ajar, leads out of the room. Patrick opens the door, enters this room, and sees Earle sitting on the floor with his arms wrapped around his knees. "It was an accident," says Earle. When Patrick checks the bathroom he looks into the bathtub and finds the dead body of a young child. Although he has not found Amanda, Patrick has found Johnny Pietro, the boy who disappeared a few weeks after Amanda did. As Patrick puts his handgun to the back of Earle's head, Earle says "Wait!" but Patrick nevertheless pulls the trigger.

While Remy is happy that Patrick killed Earle, Patrick is not sure that he did the right thing. Maybe he should have let the police take Earle into custody and prosecute him for the rape and murder of the boy instead of taking the matter into his own hands. The issue here is whether Earle, because of his heinous crime, has lost his right to be respected as a person and can therefore be justifiably killed. Angie and Remy think so, but Patrick is not so sure. At Our Sister of Infinite Mercy Hospital where Nick is being treated, Angie tells Patrick that she is proud of him for killing Earle. "That man killed a child," she says. "He had no right to live."

Later, as Patrick leaves the hospital, he meets Remy. In the hospital's parking lot, where Remy has been drinking rum, the two talk about what happened and Remy also says that Patrick should be proud of himself. When Patrick says he does not know whether he should feel proud because "[m]y priest says shame is God telling you what you did was wrong," Remy shows nothing but disdain for the priest. "Murder's a sin," insists Patrick. "It depends on who you do it to," replies Remy. "That's not how it works," says Patrick. "It is what it is."

Remy then tells Patrick how he "planted evidence on a guy once." An informant told Remy that a man had drugs in his apartment, but as Remy and Nick take inventory of the dumpy place, they find only rats and roaches. In the course of their search, they discover a boy in one of the bedrooms. The father has the boy "in this crack den subsisting on Twinkies and ass-whippings...." "You're worried what's Catholic?" asks Remy. "I went back out there, I put an ounce of heroin on the living room floor, and I sent the father on a ride, seven to nine." When Patrick questions how that could have been the right thing to do, Remy responds, "You gotta take a side. You molest a child, you beat a child, you're not on my side. If you see me coming, you better run.... Easy." Though Patrick protests that performing such actions does not feel easy, Remy counters by asserting that the kid is better off without his father.

In both of these scenes characters argue that Earle has forfeited his right to be respected as a person. In the first scene, Angie tells Patrick that she is proud of him for killing Earle, essentially arguing that because Earle sexually assaulted and killed a child he has forfeited his right to be respected as a person and can therefore be justifiably executed. He no longer must be treated as an end in himself. In the second scene, Remy sides with Angie as well. He too contends that Patrick was justified in killing Earle because Earle was a child molester and a murderer. On Remy's account, anyone who beats, molests, or kills a child forfeits his right to be respected as a person and can rightly be harmed. Thus, both Angie and Remy take the position that a person's right to be respected as a person can indeed be forfeited. They argue that reason and experience demonstrate that Patrick was justified in killing Earle.

Patrick disagrees (or at least thinks that it was wrong for *him* to kill Earle). He contends that his killing Earle was wrong because murder is a sin. Indeed, the *Catechism of the Catholic Church* states that "[t]he fifth commandment forbids *direct and intentional killing* as gravely sinful. The murderer and those who cooperate voluntarily in murder commit a sin that cries out to heaven for vengeance" (547). However, the Catholic Church's official teaching on the question of whether someone's right to life can be forfeited is "Yes." The Catechism states that "[l]egitimate public authority has the right and the duty to inflict punishment proportionate to the gravity of the offense" and that "the traditional teaching of the Church does not exclude recourse to the death penalty, if this is the only possible way of effectively defending human lives against the unjust aggressor" (546).[3] Nevertheless, it is clear that on the Catholic Church's account Patrick's killing Earle was wrong because Patrick is not a legitimate public authority and killing Earle was not the only possible way of effectively defending human lives. Because Patrick directly and intentionally killed Earle, then, he did in fact sin.

In *Ethical Argument: Critical Thinking in Ethics*, Hugh Curtler also addresses the issue of forfeiture of rights. Curtler supports Patrick's position, arguing that a person's right to be respected is absolute; it cannot be forfeited. He admits that there are problems with this claim but notes that "there are problems with the idea of forfeiture as well" (48). One problem Curtler raises with the idea of forfeiture is the issue of exactly *when* a person forfeits his right to be respected as a person (46). Curtler asks, "What constitutes a serious enough breach of respect for others to warrant the loss of one's 'personhood,' one's right to be respected by others?" (46). Another problem Curtler identifies with the concept of forfeiture "is whether or not forfeiture is final" (47). If one has forfeited his right to be respected as a person, is there really nothing he can do to regain that right? Curtler concludes his discussion of these two problems by saying that they "go to the heart of the doctrine of forfeiture, and they raise serious questions about whether or not the doctrine makes any sense. I consider them serious enough to argue that a person always has the right to be respected and can never lose that right no matter what he or she does, appears to have done, or is charged with doing" (47). Although it is unlikely that Patrick's position regarding whether one's right to be respected can be forfeited is as well thought-out as Curtler's is, Patrick — siding with the Catholic Church — nevertheless thinks that his killing Earle was wrong.

While both Angie and Remy think that Patrick was justified in killing Earle because Earle forfeited his right to be respected as a person, Remy also implies, however, that it can be legitimate to disrespect someone as a person even if that person has *not* forfeited his right to be respected. This is a different issue altogether because instead of focusing on whether an individual can ever do something that results in his forfeiting his right to be respected as a person, it focuses on whether it is ever justifiable to violate one's *non-forfeited* right to be respected as a person. This issue is raised by Remy's telling Patrick about the time he planted evidence and introduces the second ethical issue of the film: does anything other than the consequences matter for determining whether an action is morally right? Because Remy planted evidence on a suspect, the suspect was sent to prison. In Remy's mind, this act was justified because the individual used drugs and beat his son. Here Remy is endorsing John Stuart Mill who famously says in *Utilitarianism* that "actions are right in proportion as they tend to promote happiness; wrong as they tend to produce the reverse of happiness" (7). With the father in prison, the boy would be better off. Remy seems to be saying that Patrick was likewise justified in killing Earle because with Earle dead, young children will be better off; there will now be one fewer pedophile roaming the world. For Remy, then, reason and experience should lead one to the conclusion that only the consequences of an act matter for determining whether it is right or not. Moral philosophers call the view Remy articulates "act consequentialism" because it holds that what is right is a function of the consequences of a particular act. According to act consequentialism the right action is that action which, of all the alternatives available to the agent, produces the greatest net sum of happiness in the long run for everyone affected by the action. But when Patrick expresses uncertainty with Remy's reasoning and alludes to the teaching of the Catholic Church, Remy incredulously asks, "You're worried what's Catholic?" He simply cannot believe that Patrick would cling to Church teaching when — in his mind anyway — reason and experience are overwhelmingly on the side of such actions as killing pedophile murderers and planting evidence on certain suspects when doing so will produce better consequences than not doing so. On Remy's account, Patrick's belief is fantastical because it is naïve and unrealistic to adhere to this Church teaching in the real world.

Although the question of whether anything other than the consequences matters for rightness is first raised in the scene between Remy and Patrick outside the hospital, the question is raised even more dramatically a second time when Patrick finally puts the pieces of the puzzle together. He eventually figures out that Amanda was actually taken by her Uncle Lionel — with the help of Lionel's old friend Remy — and entrusted to Captain Doyle in order to get Amanda away from the adverse environment in which she lived. Upon confronting Doyle and seeing Amanda with Doyle and his wife at their country home, Patrick and Doyle discuss whether it is right to keep Amanda from Helene. "Does it make you feel better?" asks Patrick. "Telling yourself you did it for the right reasons? That you took her to be saved. From her own mother?" When Doyle responds that they are just trying to give Amanda a better life, Patrick argues that they should have talked to social services instead of kidnapping her. "You turn around," says Doyle, you go back to your car "and you wait thirty years. You don't know what the world is made of yet." After Patrick informs Doyle that he is going to call the state police, Doyle tries one last time to dissuade Patrick from turning him in.

> DOYLE: Thought you would've done that by now. You know why you haven't? Because you think this might be an irreparable mistake. Because deep inside you, you know it doesn't matter what the rules say. When the lights go out, and you ask yourself, "Is she better off here or better off there," you know the answer. And you always will. You... You could do a right thing here. A good thing. Men live their whole lives without getting this chance. You walk away from it, you may not regret it when you get home. You may not regret it for a year, but when you get to where I am, I promise you, you will. I'll be dead, you'll be old. But she... She'll be dragging around a couple of tattered, damaged children of her own, and you'll be the one who has to tell them you're sorry.

Even though Angie also agrees with Captain Doyle, Patrick nevertheless calls the state police and tells them that Doyle has Amanda. The police soon come to Doyle's house, take him into custody, and return Amanda to Helene. It is not clear what Patrick's ethical perspective is other than that he is not a consequentialist. He alludes to the Catholic Church a few times in the film, but it is unclear whether he holds a full-blown Catholic ethic. According to the *Catechism of the Catholic Church*, "[t]he morality of human acts depends on: [i] the object chosen; [ii] the end in view or the intention; and [iii] the circumstances of the action" (433). At any rate, Patrick is in agreement with the Catholic Church's teaching that "[a] good intention ... does not make behavior that is intrinsically disordered ... good or just" (Catechism 434). In attempting to cover up the kidnapping of Amanda, Lionel, Remy, and Captain Doyle have good intentions because Helene clearly is acting like an unfit mother, but their good intentions cannot make kidnapping morally right. While the Catholic Church teaches that consequences "contribute to increasing or diminishing the moral goodness or evil of human acts" and "can also diminish or increase the agent's responsibility," consequences "can make neither good nor right an action that is in itself evil" (Catechism 434). In short, "[o]ne may not do evil so that good may result from it" (Catechism 435).

Regardless of his particular ethical perspective, though, it is obvious that most of the major figures in the film think that Patrick does the wrong thing by calling the state police and are horrified by his point of view. According to Remy, Angie, Lionel, and Doyle, only the consequences matter for rightness. They think that leaving Amanda with the Doyles is the right thing to do because it is the action which produces the best consequences. As Captain Doyle says himself, "[I]t doesn't matter what the rules say." For act consequentialists like Doyle and Remy, rules are merely rules of thumb. They can be broken whenever doing so will produce more good than following the rules would. Since kidnapping Amanda and giving her to the Doyles is the act that produces the most good, that is the right action. According to the *Catechism of the Catholic Church*, however, kidnapping is "morally wrong" because it brings on "a reign of terror" by subjecting its victims to "intolerable pressures" (553). Thus, one may not do it even if it will result in good.

In one moving scene near the end of the film, Patrick sits alone at his kitchen table flipping through a magazine and watching a story about Amanda's return on the local television news. As the anchors wrap up their story, one of them says, "How about that? A great end to that story. Good news for everybody." However, it is clear that the story is not good news for everybody — especially Patrick. Almost all of the main characters are appalled by his decision to call the state police. Angie now hates him and has moved out. Additionally, the Doyles are not happy because Jack is now in jail. Even Beatrice is mad at Patrick and will not pay his bill because Lionel is also in jail.

The final scene shows Patrick dropping by Helene's place to see how things are going. Helene is getting ready for a date with a guy who saw her on television and wrote letters to her. When Patrick asks who is going to watch Amanda, Helene replies that her friend Dottie is. "Does Dottie know that?" asks Patrick. "She will in five minutes," replies Helene laughingly. Helene then asks Patrick if he would mind babysitting Amanda. After he agrees Helene calls him "a godsend" and hurries out the door. In the final moments of the film, Patrick and Amanda sit on the couch watching cartoons on television. Patrick asks Amanda if the doll she is playing with is "Mirabelle," the doll Helene told police that Amanda had with her when she was abducted. "Annabelle," Amanda corrects him. The film then ends as Patrick— sitting silently on the couch — appears to come to the realization that Helene did not even know the name of her daughter's favorite doll.

The viewer is left wondering whether Patrick still thinks he did the right thing. He promised Helene that he would find Amanda and kept his promise, but looking strictly at the likely consequences of Amanda's growing up with Helene or the Doyles, it seems clear that Amanda would be better off without Helene — in fact, in Latin "Amanda" literally means "about to be loved." It is as if Amanda was about to be loved but then she was returned to Helene. Although Helene swore that she would stop using drugs and going out, she goes out with a guy she hardly knows without making plans for Amanda's care. If Patrick had not stopped by, would Dottie have been able to watch Amanda on such short notice? Even though Amanda was only with the Doyles a short time, she seemed to like it with them and seemed to be genuinely loved by them. When the state police come to take Captain Doyle into custody, they have to pry Amanda from Doyle's wife because Amanda will not let go of her. Perhaps this was because Amanda was scared, but perhaps it was also because she did not want to leave the Doyles. When Amanda is returned to Helene, she does not appear excited about it at all.

While some viewers think that Patrick obviously did the right thing by calling the state police, others think that Patrick obviously did the *wrong* thing. Some defenders of Patrick's action essentially agree with the Catholic Church's position and say that although those responsible for kidnapping Amanda had good intentions, they nevertheless performed a wrong action. Those criticizing Patrick's action, however, question how returning Amanda to Helene can possibly be the right thing to do when Helene clearly appears to be an unfit mother. They, like Remy, Angie, Lionel, and Doyle, argue that Patrick's action is horrific because it flies in the face of reason and experience. Although Patrick himself struggles with the question of whether only the consequences matter for rightness, guided by his Catholic faith he ultimately decides to defy those around him and return Amanda to her mother. This may not be the act that will produce the best consequences, but it is the act which the Catholic Church regards as morally right.

In *Gone Baby Gone* the use of Catholic symbols and Catholic moral teaching itself allows an overtly realist film to retain a sense of the fantastic. While such symbols as crosses, medallions, and images of Jesus, Mary, and cherubs are used to draw a contrast between an idealistic, fanciful world of faith and the actual world, the use of Catholic moral teaching itself is the main way in which the film draws attention to the differences between the world of faith and the actual world. In particular, the film questions Catholic responses to the ethical issue of whether it is possible for people to forfeit their right to be respected as persons and the issue of what exactly determines whether a particular action is morally right. Overall, the film depicts Patrick's Catholicism-based morality as fantastic because it appears to reflect a fanciful view of the world rather than one based on reason and experience.

Notes

1. The film is based on the novel of the same title by Dennis Lehane. Other films based on Lehane novels of the same title are *Mystic River* (2003) and *Shutter Island* (2010).

2. For another discussion of Catholic symbolism in fantastic film, see Christopher McKittrick's chapter in this volume titled "Blasphemy in the Name of Fantasy: The Films of Terry Gilliam in a Catholic Context."

3. For more on the Catholic Church's position on the death penalty, see pages 173–175 of *Compendium of the Social Doctrine of the Church*.

Works Cited

Catechism of the Catholic Church. 2nd ed. Citta del Vaticano: Libreria Editrice Vaticana, 1997.

Compendium of the Social Doctrine of the Church. Washington, D.C.: United States Conference of Catholic Bishops Publishing, 2004.

Curtler, Hugh Mercer. *Ethical Argument: Critical Thinking in Ethics*. New York: Oxford University Press, 2004.

Gone Baby Gone. Dir. Ben Affleck. Perf. Casey Affleck, Michelle Monaghan, Morgan Freeman, Ed Harris, John Ashton, Amy Ryan, Amy Madigan, and Titus Welliver. Miramax/Buena Vista, 2007.

Mill, John Stuart. *Utilitarianism*. Ed. George Sher. Indianapolis: Hackett, 1979.

The "Fantastic" Roman Catholic Church in Italian Cinema

VICTORIA SURLIUGA

Modern Italian filmmakers have often associated the fantastic with dream-like and surreal visions of religious rituals and, as a result, have portrayed the Catholic Church in two fundamental ways. Some of them, such as Federico Fellini (1920–1993) and Marco Bellocchio (1939–), describe the Catholic Church as a political institution whose mission involves the use of superstition and fantastic imagery to make the word of God understood in populist terms by non-elites. As examples of this category, I will consider two Fellini films, *La dolce vita* (1960) and *8½* (1963), and also one Bellocchio production, *In the Name of the Father* (1972). A second stream of development includes the works of directors Pier Paolo Pasolini (1922–1975) and Ermanno Olmi (1931–), respectively a non-believer and a believer who use Catholic fantastic symbols to explain the occurrence of minor miracles in daily life. I will consider Pasolini's *Hawks and Sparrows* (1966) and *Theorem* (1968), and Olmi's *The Legend of the Holy Drinker* (1988) and *One Hundred Nails* (2007).

Altogether, this selection covers a relatively long period in the history of Italian cinema, from 1953 to 2007. It explores four powerful directorial gazes on the ritualistic, superstitious, and supernatural aspects of the Catholic Church. It also highlights the effects of the Catholic symbolic apparatus on the personal and collective history of the Italian people. In Fellini, the supernatural elements are tamed down by dreamlike visions and sarcastic commentaries. In Bellocchio, the most common religious rituals acquire a certain blasphemous uncanniness. In Pasolini and Olmi we experience the miraculous in the faith of simple people who follow saint-like figures or a modern mystic who may or may not be the Messiah. In the works of all these artists, spirituality is juxtaposed to superstition, and faith to politics. Often this result is achieved by constructing a sarcastic outlook that tames the fantastic elements so abundant in the self-representation of the Catholic Church; at other times a precarious balance is reached between faith and the fantastic.

The term "fantastic" refers to a literary genre defined by Tzvetan Todorov in the volume *Introduction à la littérature fantastique* (1975). I will adapt Todorov's category of fantastic to a series of Italian films, as a theme and as a genre characterized through specific images and structures. Since cinema demonstrates the working of the fantastic through narrative and figurative structures, a film belongs to this genre when it represents in a recognizable way an unexplainable series of events and thereby creates a sense of displacement. Here, the borderlines between emotion, imagination, and reality are often crossed. Each viewer must decide to what extent the events are illusions since it is precisely the missing link between reality and imagination that constitutes the realm of the fantastic.

According to Todorov, in "the heart of the Fantastic [...] occurs an event which cannot be explained by the laws of this same familiar world" (25). When a person experiences the fantastic, on one hand, "he is the victim of an illusion of the senses, of a product of the imagination — and laws of the world then remain what they are." On the other hand, "the event has indeed taken place [...] but then this reality is controlled by laws unknown." In conclusion, "the Fantastic occupies the duration of this uncertainty." Another key term used by Todorov is "hesitation," which explains the momentary lack of conscious understanding that is based on fear and insecurity about our abilities to draw a sharp line between "real" and "fantastic" (26). The "inexplicable" suddenly confronts us, creating doubts as to what we are really seeing.

In 1970, the Italian novelist Italo Calvino helped sharpen these concepts when he responded to a survey on fantastic literature on *Le Monde*, replying to four questions about the definition of fantastic, the existence of fantastic literature, the relation between his works and the genre itself, and models of fantastic novels and tales. In his written replies, Calvino explained that the fantastic as a genre can be applied to 19th century horror narratives, requiring from the reader an act of belief followed by a reaction of fear. After a general introduction to the genre itself, Calvino pointed out that in 20th century writing there is a more intellectual, and less emotional, use of the fantastic, in which playful and ironic twists combine to reveal the nightmares and repressed desires of contemporary subjects. The fantastic is no longer an event or perspective that we cannot explain. For this reason, it can be argued that as viewers of cinematic representations of the fantastic, we benefit from the detachment of knowing that the plot-line and all events can be interrupted, read fictionally, immediately analyzed, and completed by the figurative element of the moving image. The filmic images created by the Italian directors under study here remove the need for the audience to undertake an act of faith in the writer's ability to create a terrain of uncertain knowledge.

When looking at the representations of the Catholic Church in the films mentioned above, we spot recurrent fantastic elements. First of all, while bringing forth the belief that some elements of its spiritual mission are not accomplished by the ecclesiastic structures, the Catholic Church is nevertheless implicitly accepted as the bearer of spiritual power. In the essay "On the Catholic Irrationality of Fellini," Pasolini unites Gadda the writer and Fellini the director in their acceptance of the institutions of Church and state. The same can be said about Bellocchio and Olmi, as directors who "do not subject their structures to examination and [...] accept them as almost absolute and unchanging givens." Furthermore, "they even place themselves in a constant opposition that is based on their individual, infantile temperaments" (Pasolini 1984: 69). Their blind acceptance of a structure such as the Church will produce some analogies, according to Pasolini. First, there is an automatic connection between an act of faith and a complex belief in the Church. The considerations around the fantastic proceed from the questions: "reality or dream? Truth or illusion?" (Todorov 25). In *In the Name of the Father* (1972), when we see Friar Matematicus sleeping in a coffin in order to become acquainted with death, we can immediately associate the ritual of burial with a feeling of uneasiness. Is Bellocchio portraying something that could really happen? Considering the auto-biographical tone of the film, maybe the director experienced something similar or heard of a similar instance. But most importantly, it is precisely in this moment of doubt that the Fantastic operates.

Federico Fellini

An example of the fluctuating border between the illusions of the fantastic and reality can be found in the films of Federico Fellini, and especially in *La dolce vita* (1960) and *8½* (1963). Fellini's films all share a dreamlike quality that constitutes the director's aesthetics, a phenomenon that has been labeled as "Felliniesque."

Confused mysticism is portrayed in *La dolce vita*. Here, the religious icons leave a sense of confusion about their intended use. When the statue of an angel appears flying over Rome, are we supposed to see a sign of God? Another statue of an angel is used in *The Young and the Passionate* (1953). In that film, first Fausto (Franco Fabrizi) and Moraldo (Franco Interlenghi) steal the statue, then they try to sell it, and altogether the angel does nothing but create problems for the protagonists. In both films, the appearance of an angel signifies the characters' moral confusion. This psychological trait can also be said to characterize Marcello Rubini (Marcello Mastroianni) in *La dolce vita*. The film describes his increasing awareness of the squalor underlying his superficial existence as a socialite and journalist in Rome. Rubini's job obliges him to bear witness to a false miracle, when he is called to write about apparitions of the Virgin Mary in the suburbs of Rome. The children who witness this "miracle" are the instruments of a fraud that their parents have planned in order to attract the press and make some quick money. When Rubini arrives on the scene where the apparitions are taking place, he is deeply depressed and upset about his empty life, and it seems that only a miracle of some kind could give him a sense of hope. Even while it is clear to him that the children's parents have organized a fraud, as viewers we are left with a sense of hope that at some point some other miraculous event will take place and Rubini will be saved from his constant depressive state.

Commenting on *La dolce vita,* Pasolini believed that "this work of Fellini fully belongs to the great productions of European decadence," because of "the enjoyment of sound itself" and "a visual enjoyment in which the image goes beyond its function and becomes the *pre* image," through a process of "semantic amplification" (68). Pasolini reads Fellini's work as a manifesto of Catholic ideology mainly because of the constant association of sin and innocence in the presence of grace. Indeed, Fellini represents the Church as an institution with an ambiguous secular side that leaves room for individualized beliefs, because there is always room for a personal miracle or for the hope that one will take place. At the same time there is an understanding that conventional faith could be misdirected. It is in this provision for the miraculous that Fellini's fantastic operates because it derives from assumptions and desires that are based on an illusory interpretation of the filmic images.

In Fellini's *8½*, the Catholic Church is represented in contradictory ways united by the institution's mission to exert secular authority. In this film, a director named Guido Anselmi (Marcello Mastroianni) is unable to make his latest film. On one hand, the Catholic Church is portrayed as an institution that regulates acceptable behavior, and whose representatives are in charge of detecting the presence of evil forces. This is the meaning of the disciplinary measure imposed on the young boys who are caught enjoying the dancing of Saraghina, a prostitute who lives in a hut on the shore. As a punishment, the priests running Anselmi's school make him kneel on dry chickpeas facing his school-mates, subjecting him to a devastating combination of public humiliation and physical pain.

On the other hand, the priests are also in charge of the spiritual side of personal improvement. A good part of the film portrays Anselmi's encounters at a spa with various representatives of the Catholic Church, with whom he discusses the role of the Church in his films. When he is summoned by one of the cardinals, Anselmi is reminded of the fact that having the grace of the ecclesiastical higher authorities means everything in life. The director approaches the cardinal with mixed feelings: while he would like to genuinely believe that the Church controls some unknown point of access into supernatural knowledge, Anselmi cannot help being skeptical. When he is summoned into a sauna to talk with a cardinal about his films, he expresses his unhappiness and is told in response that being happy is not his mission in life. Instead, the cardinal maintains: "Extra ecclesiam nulla salus" (there is no salvation outside of the Church). This saying comes from Origen, one of the early Church's key theologians, but the Cardinal repeats the message in various ways, using expressions such as "extra ecclesiam, nemo salvatur" (no one is saved outside of the Church) and "salus extra ecclesiam, not est" (salvation cannot be found outside of the Church) which are combined with another saying, attributed to Saint Augustine: "he who is not in the City of God, belongs to the *Civitas Diaboli*," or the "City of the Devil."

As a result of these litanies, both Anselmi and the film's viewers may think that perhaps the cardinals really know something about evil and satanic forces. This fear of the unknown still makes us uneasy when we hear about the ecclesiastical endorsement of priests who specialize in exorcisms, such as the well-known 20th century Italian charismatic Father Gabriele Amorth. In his representations of the Catholic Church, Fellini brings forth some of the Catholics' main superstitions. These are linked by the belief that the Church accurately interprets apparitions of the Virgin Mary, manages holy or sanctified sites like Lourdes and Medjugorje, and has countless exorcist priests at work around the world, while at the same time it owns banks and plays a very powerful role in the complexities of contemporary Italian politics. Very similar arguments can be brought forth about the role of the Fátima apparitions and miracles in Portuguese cultural and social history. In "Our Lady of Fátima and Marian Myth in Portuguese Cinema," a chapter in this volume, authors Paulo Cunha and Daniel Ribas trace the chronology of Portuguese films that describe or show aspects of the apparitions and miracles of the Virgin Mary, witnessed by three children, to whom she transmitted social and political messages. In Fellini's work the fantastic continually operates like a pendulum, swinging from the secular and back again to the spiritual. Superstitious elements are simultaneously interesting narrative elements and possible points of entry into the unknown. Fellini's films are based on the clash between the characters' individual superstitions about the Catholic Church and the reality of the dogma. This creates a visual moment where the viewers cannot immediately distinguish between the characters' point of view and the "real" world that surrounds them. It is in this narrative twist that Fellini most fully applies Todorov's concept of fantastic.

Marco Bellocchio

Among contemporary Italian filmmakers, Marco Bellocchio stands out for his remarkably gloomy and *noir* vision. Educated in religious institutions, Bellocchio posits a Marxist ideology that borders on an anarchical view of the world. The director was trained at the Centro Sperimentale di Cinematografia in Rome and, after studying at the Slade School of Fine Arts, made his debut at the Venice Film Festival presenting *Pugni in tasca* in 1965. Later, he directed *La Cina è vicina* (1967), *Nel nome del padre* (1971), *Sbatti il mostro in prima pagina* (1972), *Enrico IV* (1984), an adaptation of a Luigi Pirandello play, *L'ora di religione* (2002), *Il regista di matrimoni* (2006), and *Vincere* (2009). Bellocchio's main themes in most of these films are the disintegration of the middle-class family and a sharp criticism of the Catholic Church.

Bellocchio criticizes the corruption of the ecclesiastic structure because of the contamination of the spiritual realm with secular acquisitions resulting in the accumulation of temporal power and material goods. His work includes elements of the fantastic when his treatments of faith and Catholic rituals come together. In *In the Name of the Father* (1972), Bellocchio describes how the arrival of Angelo Transeunti (Yves Beneyton) at a Catholic boarding school disrupts everyone's lives. The events take place in 1958–1959. Transeunti is placed in this rigorous school because of his behavior: he has been habitually insulting and slapping his father. As a believer in the Nietzschean theories of the "superman," he manipulates one of his schoolfellows into killing his annoying mother, drives another one to commit suicide, and creates all sorts of commotion in the school.

There are three moments in the film when Bellocchio presents rituals and themes of the Catholic Church (mass, burial, and apparitions) with the clear intent of first desecrating them, and then annihilating and replacing them with new practices that are based on the internal logic of the film narrative (Aprà). The first episode refers to Matematicus, one of the priests who will later die, and to his habit of sleeping in a coffin in order to be more in touch with dying. When he emerges from the coffin to interact with the students, he sits up like Count Dracula rising at midnight. Up to this point Bellocchio's narrative had been entirely secular. This image adds a fantastic dimension that deliberately mystifies what would otherwise be a conventional pedagogical setting.

The priests are seen as corrupted characterizations of the stereotypical holy attributes that are associated to their behavior. In "Killer Priests: The Last Taboo?," a chapter in this volume, Shelley O'Brien addresses the cinematic representations of deviant behaviors in priests. While traditionally they display strength, compassion, and all the pious qualities associated with priests, O'Brien considers two Italian *giallo* films by Lucio Fulci and Antonio Bido, and a British production by Pete Walker to describe the opposite, which includes greed, desecration of religious objects, homicide, and deceitful behavior.

The second episode in Bellocchio's schema, however, is even more striking. One of the students is sitting in the school's private Church during Mass, and suddenly his attention is captured by a vision. A statue representing the Virgin Mary or a female saint suddenly comes to life, walking towards him and embracing him. As viewers, we are forced to question the images in which the fantastic is operating through otherworldly or superstitious elements that impart a horrific tone to the film. A third fantastic episode is presented by Bellocchio in the description of a miraculous pear tree that blooms during winter. A young woman, dressed in white, summons crowds to witness the miraculous blooming of the tree that accompanies the apparition of the Virgin Mary, who can only be seen by her. Following a structured logical system that can be associated with both a paranoiac attitude and a tendency to compulsion and control, Transeunti witnesses the event and later goes back to cut the tree. The girl at the center of these miraculous events does not show any emotion and is not even angered by his act. She limits herself to following him to the garden's entrance. Here he turns around to advise her to get a job as a factory worker. Thus, we are torn between the two different points of view, one of them supporting the idea of the miraculous and the other one censoring it.

Bellocchio shows how the rituals of the Catholic Church are often ingrained in the Italian Catholics, whose faith tends to be based largely upon superstition and much less upon the Church's theology and dogma.

Pier Paolo Pasolini

In Pier Paolo Pasolini's films a fascination with simple acts of faith and a belief in the miraculous are central themes. Pasolini attributes fantastic elements to the Catholic Church by giving life to hagiographical narratives, as in *Hawks and Sparrows* (1966), and in analyzing to what extent faith operates in an unseen way, as in *Theorem* (1968). Both films present Pasolini's views on the decadence of the middle-class, whose members are victims of *petit bourgeois* values and are doomed to be excluded from understanding the presence of the sacred in daily life. *Hawks and Sparrows* brings together an unusual comedic couple: Totò (playing the parts of Totò Innocenti, Ninetto Innocenti's father, and of a Franciscan friar, Brother Ciccillo) and Ninetto Davoli (playing the parts of Ninetto Innocenti, Totò Innocenti's son and another friar, Brother Ninetto). Totò and Ninetto are pictured on a walk in the countryside. They are accompanied by a talking raven, who introduces himself by saying that his country is "Ideology," and that he lives in the capital, the "City of the Future," in "70 times 7 Karl Marx Street." His parents are "Mr. Doubt" and "Mrs. Conscience." Totò and Ninetto explain that they live in the neighborhood of "Trash," in "23 Famished Street" under "Mount Ditch," well-known all over the world as the site of the martyrdom of "Saint Illiterate." Ninetto says that he is son of Totò Innocenti, "Totò the Innocent," and Grazia Semplicetti "Grace the Simpleton."

As they walk on, the raven starts narrating the story of two Franciscan friars, Brother Ciccillo and Brother Ninetto, who are ordered by Saint Francis to go and preach God's love to hawks and sparrows. The two itinerant friars figure out the language spoken by the birds, which consists of a high-pitched whistling accompanied by the text in the subtitles that explain what they are preaching. A full dialog between the friars and the birds takes place, and as a result they accomplish their mission to convert the animals. After the raven's story finishes, Totò and Ninetto continue their journey. At first, they are unsuccessful in collecting money that is owed to them, but then the roles are reversed, and they are not able to return money that they owe. In this swift change of circumstances, they become victims themselves. However, when they realize that they no longer have anything to eat, they kill the raven to provide food for their journey. Through its sacrifice, the raven becomes first a victim and then a saint.

A similar mechanism of self-sacrifice and canonization occurs in *Theorem* (1968). A middle class family is thrown into confusion by the arrival of a visitor (Terence Stamp), a blond non-talkative man who has sexual encounters with each family member, including the maid, and thereby triggers both neuroses and potential. The maid Emilia (Laura Betti) is the first character to be seduced by him. As a consequence, she resigns from her job and moves to the Lombardian farm owned by her family where she starts experiencing mysticism. Dressed entirely in black, Emilia sits on a bench in the farm's courtyard, and she only eats chicory. Shortly after arriving in Lombardy, she starts performing miracles, first by making the red spots of chicken pox on a young boy's face disappear, next by levitating on the roof, and finally by changing her tears into a healing river when she is buried in dirt. Pasolini portrays these supernatural events without passing any judgment. These miraculous events contain referential elements that would be understood by a Catholic audience. The sacred, represented by the miracles, is nevertheless contaminated at its source, because the events have been triggered by a systematic series of sexualized seductions. Sacredness is never achieved and we witness the anxious pursuit of the discovery of God (Gardy 64) through the appearance of a Christ figure who is androgynous, composed of both male and female elements, respectively through the Visitor and Emilia (Gardy 65).

Emilia and Paolo, the father (Massimo Girotti), are the only two characters in the family whose neurosis is tamed by mysticism. As a result of his sexually suggestive acquaintance with the visitor, Paolo decides to transfer ownership of his factory to the workers. At the end of the film, he is depicted as a naked figure, walking on a dune, after having undressed in the middle of the Central train station in Milan, a filmic echo of Saint Francis' act of undressing in Assisi's main square. His son Pietro (Andrés José Cruz Soublette) has a more neutral reaction to the Visitor's departure, and he continues painting; however, he soon destroys his artwork. Pietro's sister Odetta (Anne Wiazemsky) has a mental break-down, and she is hospitalized in a psychiatric clinic. After her own sexual liaison with the Visitor, their mother Lucia (Silvana Mangano) begins randomly picking up younger men in the suburbs of Milan for sex. Here, experience parallels director Pier Paolo Pasolini's own habit of picking up young men in the suburbs of Rome.

With *Theorem,* Pasolini attempts to provide a portrayal of the seismic changes taking place in Italian politics in 1968, the year in which the film was produced. Casarino has suggested that in order to provide a solution to Italian society's chaotic problems, a theorem's axioms need to be precisely identified, and here they converge in Terence Stamp's character (98). Interpretations of the figure of the Visitor have been varied and contrasting, but have generally revolved around the concept of the sacred. Terence Stamp's character represents God, and his actions demonstrate how divinity affects the lives of those who are touched by sacredness. Cesare has noted that critic Enzo Siciliano suggests that "the theorem of Pasolini's *Teorema* (1968) is the idea of an incarnation, an appearance of the sacred in reality and that reality itself possesses the quality of being sacred" (Cesare 22). However, the opposite view, suggested by Cesare, is that to Pasolini "the theorem is a materialist one about the disappearance of the sacred from reality" (*ib.*) By presenting miracles, supernatural events, and radical spiritual changes, Pasolini is operating on the Fantastic effects of simple acts of Catholic faith by eliminating the institutional presence of Catholicism itself. The Church, therefore, no longer has a space in the collective imagination and unconscious that gives birth to the Fantastic ramifications of the Catholic dogma.

Ermanno Olmi

The cinematographic career of Ermanno Olmi, a Catholic filmmaker, began with documentaries. His first feature film, *Il tempo si è fermato* (1959), describes the friendship between a dam's keeper and a student. In 1961, with film-critic Tullio Kezich and others, he set up the production company "22 dicembre." In 1963 he directed *I fidanzati*, then in 1965, *E venne un uomo*, a documentary on the life of Pope John XXIII. Olmi's most well-known feature films are *L'albero degli zoccoli* (1978), *La leggenda del santo bevitore* (1988), *Lunga vita alla signora!* (1987), *Il mestiere delle armi* (2001), *Cantando dietro ai paraventi* (2003), *Centochiodi* (2007). In 1994, Olmi also produced *Genesi: la creazione e il diluvio*.

Olmi's fantastic description of the Catholic Church again centrally situates belief, or faith, in the institution's complex web of dogmas and rituals. In *The Legend of the Holy Drinker*, Olmi adapts Joseph Roth's 1939 novel *Die Legende vom heiligen Trinker*. Andreas Kartak (Rutger Hauer) meets a distinguished yet, like him, homeless man (Anthony Quayle), under the bridges of the French river La Seine. This man gives him two hundred francs on the condition that he will deliver the money to the Church of Sainte Thérèse of Lisieux. More unexpected events then begin to occur, such as Andreas' meeting with old friends, some of them interested in Andreas' money, others in giving him more cash. Because of these interruptions, Andreas finds himself unable to give back the money until the end, when he collapses in a coffee house located right across from the Saint's Church, and then he delivers the sum to the priest.

Throughout the narration, Andreas sees Sainte Thérèse in apparitions as he dreams while sleeping under the bridges. During the day, she also appears when he is getting drunk while waiting for the Mass to start at the Saint's Church where he must turn over the money to the priest. The saint always appears as a young girl and talks to him, reminding him of the promise that he has made. Every aspect of the film is linked to the miraculous, or, what Carl Gustav Jung would call "synchronicity," meaning the link that unites various events that are not necessarily associated with one another. Andreas' benefactors appear to him first in the form of the man that he meets at the beginning of the film, and then as his childhood friend, a boxer named Daniel Kanjak (Jean Maurice Chanet) who gives him clothes. Each encounter can be read within the Catholic context as a miracle, an unpredictable, irrational, and surprising event that fulfills Andreas' needs.

Meaningful apparitions constitute the chief vehicle for a Catholicism of the fantastic in another film directed by Olmi, *One Hundred Nails*. A successful and scholarly professor (Raz Degan), who teaches at Italy's University of Bologna, reaches the conclusion that books alone cannot entirely teach about life. He decides to put his newly-found scorn for books into dramatic action in an ecclesiastical library of rare manuscripts. He removes the books from the shelves and hammers one hundred coarse Christological nails into them, leaving them open on the floor, where they are found by the librarian the following day. The professor decides to leave the city and drives into the countryside along the Po River, where he meets a group of local people who interpret his Middle Eastern looks as evidence that he is Christ. The fantastic operates in this misunderstanding on the part of the Northern Italian peasants, who start asking the Christ-like figure to advise them about problematic situations and to narrate stories from the Bible. Some of the people start asking questions and making comments: "Where have they taken the nails out of this Christ?"; "You, who have been an altar boy, what do you say?"; and "Maybe he is a priest who has thrown his gown away!" They compose themselves around a table, like nine apostles, asking the professor, "Ehi, Jesus Christ, can you turn water into wine?" and receiving the response, "Let's see what I can do." The peasants reply, "Very well. If you know how to do it, we have an abundance of water," since they live next to the Po River. The professor first narrates the parable of Jesus Christ turning the water into wine at Cana, then the one of the Prodigal Son. Through the lenses of the fantastic we can detect a parallel between the transformation of water to wine and the two other transformations: that of the peasants into apostles, and of the professor into a Christ like figure.

The police come to arrest the professor as a result of his desecration of the books, the existence of which has become completely meaningless to him as a scholar, to the point that he explains during the interrogatory that all the volumes in the world are not worth a coffee with a friend. He explains his point of view by saying that God does not speak through writing. The written word as speech is juxtaposed to silence. According to critic Clodagh Brook, the point is that even the most erudite texts do not contain truths, and the professor, having recognized this, chooses, instead of a life dominated by books and writing, "a harmonious life dominated by silence and the dialect of the simple people he encounters" (270). In a way, the professor's conclusion is not particularly original. Books can serve all masters and any god. The librarian argues that God has placed in books words addressing eternal life for the salvation of His children. The professor replies that God is the butcher of human kind as he has not even saved his own son. The librarian replies that on Judgment Day the professor will have to answer for this, to which the professor says that it will be God who will have to account for all the suffering of the world. In the end, the professor will never go back to visit his new friends/apostles, who will continue waiting for him and his return. They will keep on catching false sights of him, saying that "Jesus Christ was seen walking on the provincial road," and that "nothing more was heard about that guy who was called Jesus Christ by everyone."

Conclusion

Across all these powerful films by Italy's leading directors, priests and ecclesiastical institutions, as the obsolete representatives of the Catholic Church, are presented as carriers of a message that can no longer find a relevant and modern venue of expression. Instead of the Church, it is the operation of the fantastic which becomes the necessary footbridge to link ordinary humans to God, even as the representations of the fantastic in these films rely upon the Catholic Church's own legacies of "miracles," otherworldliness, and wonderment. The filmic works of Fellini, Pasolini, Bellocchio, and Olmi in this way share a representation of the Church's spiritual impotence, while exhibiting different levels and sorts of resistance to the inability of the Church to fulfill its spiritual mission. The emphasis on the Church's political and secular agendas is seen as having removed all spiritual significance from its rituals. The possibility of providing spiritual comfort has quickly been replaced by fantastic representations of superstition, and a magical belief that rituals will somehow tame all fears and connect those who practice them to a divinity that has otherwise become remote and unknown.

Works Cited

Brook, Clodagh. "Beyond Dialogue: Speech-Silence, the Monologue, and Power in the Films of Ermanno Olmi." *Italianist* 28.2 (2008): 268–280.
Calvino, Italo. *Una pietra sopra: Discorsi di letteratura e società*. Torino: Einaudi, 1980.
Casarino, Cesare. "Pasolini in the Desert." *Angelaki: Journal of the Theoretical Humanities* 9.1 (2004): 97–102.
Cesare, Tony. "Pasolini's *Theorem*." *Film Criticism* 14.1 (1989): 22–25.

La dolce vita. Dir. Federico Fellini. Perf. Marcello Mastroianni, Anita Ekberg, Anouk Aimee. Riama Film, 1960. Film.
8½. Dir. Federico Fellini. Perf. Marcello Mastroianni, Claudia Cardinale, Anouk Aimee. Cineriz, 1963. Film.
Fists in the Pocket. Dir. Marco Bellochio. Perf. Lou Castel, Paolo Pitagora, Marino Mase. Doria. 1965. Film.
Gardy, Kim. "A Controversial Figure: Ambiguity and Allegory in Pasolini's Christ." *Studi d'Italianistica nell'Africa Australe / Italian Studies in Southern Africa* 4.2 (1991): 64–80.
Hawks and Sparrows. Dir. Pier Paolo Pasolini. Perf. Toto, Ninetto Davoli, Femi Benussi. Arco Film, 1966. Film.
I vitelloni. Dir. Federico Fellini. Perf. Franco Interlenghi, Alberto Sordi, Franco Fabrizi. Cite Films, 1953. Film.
In the Name of the Father. Dir. Marco Bellochio. Perf. Yves Beneyton, Renato Scarpa, Piero Vida. Vides Cinematografica, 1972. Film.
The Legend of the Holy Drinker. Dir. Ermanno Olmi. Perf. Rutger Hauer, Anthony Quayle, Sandrine Dumas. Cechi Gori Group, 1988. Film.
One Hundred Nails. Dir. Ermanno Olmi. Perf. Raz Degan, Luna Bendandi, Andrea Lanfredi. Cinemaundici, 2007. Film.
Pasolini, Pier Paolo. "The Catholic Irrationalism of Fellini." *Film Criticism* 9.1 (1984): 63–73.
Theorem. Dir. Pier Paolo Pasolini. Perf. Silvana Mangano, Terence Stamp, Massimo Girotti. Aetos Produzioni Cinematographiche, 1968. Film.
Todorov, Tzvetan. *The Fantastic: A Structural Approach to a Literary Genre.* Trans. by R. Howard. Ithaca: Cornell University Press, 1975.

The Satanic Saint in Maurice Pialat's *Sous le soleil de Satan*

CHRISTA JONES

Though France has been known as the oldest sister of the Church, religious films have never enjoyed much popularity there, in particular during the 1960s and 1970s, which were marked by *cinéma d'auteur*, the *Nouvelle Vague* and realist filmmaking rather than mysticism (Prédal 10). The mid-eighties, however, witnessed a revival of religious cinema in France—and indeed throughout Europe—perhaps in part due to the breakdown of upper middle class values and the rise of consumer culture (Williams 398). Religious French films of the second part of the twentieth century include Robert Bresson's *Journal d'un curé de campagne* (1950) about a young French priest, *Mouchette* (1967), *Le diable probablement* (1977), Jean-Luc Godard's *Je vous salue, Marie* (1985), Alain Cavalier's *Thérèse* (1986), Jean-Pierre Mocky's anti-clerical *Le miraculé* (1987), Jean Delannoy's *Bernadette* (1988) and, last but not least, Maurice Pialat's *Sous le soleil de Satan* (1987), considered the "least uplifting, most circumspect film ever made about sainthood," or rather, false sainthood (Jones 48).[1]

In the United States, meanwhile, popular films such as Roman Polanski's *Rosemary's Baby* (1968) and William Friedkin's *The Exorcist* (1973) mixed religion with the fantastic. In France in the 1980s, renewed enthusiasm for the Catholic Church and Catholic priests translated in both cinemas and on television, given the enormous popularity in France of the Australian series *The Thorn Birds* and a number of commercials featuring monks and nuns. The cinematic scenery changed again in the early nineties as themes related to immigration and violence in France's suburbs took center stage, and the rise of feminism, boosted by a growing number of women filmmakers (Multeau 258). The genres of French religious cinema vary depending on the subject, ranging from biblical illustrations to the life of Jesus and his saints, to a positive or negative evocation of the church and its priests, and to that of Satan and the presence of evil in our world which easily leads to atheism (Schneider 60).

French filmmaker Maurice Pialat (1925–2003) directed several short films and ten feature films, including *L'Enfance nue* (1968), *Nous ne vieillirons pas ensemble* (1972), *La Gueule ouverte* (1974), *Passe ton bac d'abord* (1978), *Loulou* (1980), *À nos amours* (1983), *Police* (1985), *Sous le soleil de Satan* (1987), *Van Gogh* (1991), and *Le Garçu* (1995). *Sous le soleil de Satan* (1987) — his eighth full-length feature — is based on the eponymous novel by Catholic writer Georges Bernanos, which appeared in 1926 and was followed by the best-selling novel *Diary of a Country Priest* in 1936. In France, Pialat was one of the most interviewed and acclaimed French film directors during his lifetime, though the French did not initially honor him as one of the "greatest French filmmakers" (Billard 57). This deliberate neglect was in part due to his notoriously choleric personality; the press usually portrayed him as a misanthrope. Regardless, today he is widely recognized as the "most important of the French film makers of the late twentieth century" in the Francophone world (De Baecque 13).

Turning to the Anglophone world, Pialat was outright ignored by Anglophone film critics during his lifetime (Magny 11). In his 458-page book *Republic of Images: A History of French Filmmaking*, Alan Larson Williams dedicates less than one page to Maurice Pialat's films and ten lines to *Sous le soleil de Satan*, which he dismisses as a "retro" work, harking back to the "Tradition of Quality" (340). He downplays Pialat's films noting that they explore the "once-discredited cinema aesthetic of the 1950s" (399). In her book *Maurice Pialat* film scholar Marja Warehime attributes the dearth of Anglophone criticism to the director's idiosyncratic character. This deliberate neglect of his work in Anglophone criticism might be due to the fact that Pialat's films are indeed difficult to classify. They do not completely fit in with the category of the *Nouvelle Vague*, which they miss by about a decade and which Pialat despised, nor do they constitute a return to classical or traditional French cinema or so-called *cinéma vérité* (Fontanel 17).

Though he was a self-proclaimed agnostic, Pialat nonetheless appreciated a highly religious Catholic author like Georges Bernanos whose novels he deeply admired to the extent that he even decided to make a film adaptation — his only adaptation from a novel — of Bernanos' eponymous novel. *Sous le soleil de Satan*— both novel and film—portray Donissan, a Catholic priest who struggles to cope with the existence of evil and the physicality of Satan himself who tempts him to abandon all hope for life, redemption and sainthood in favor of evil. In return, the priest is given the power to read people's minds and souls. He can foresee the future, an ability that he mistakes for sainthood, and secretly instinctively knows but refuses to admit to himself that these powers are not God given. If one appellation applies to *Sous le soleil de Satan*, it would be the cinema of cruelty, given that Pialat unveils "reality in its harshness, thus fashioning hypersensitive characters that can do nothing but tear each other apart" (Magny 59; my translation). Though Pialat's film adaptation won the prestigious *Palme d'Or* at the Cannes Film Festival, its reception was "mixed" when it premiered. In fact, large parts of the audience booed and jeered when Pialat stepped forward to accept his award:

> There were those who said it was because the critics found the film static and verbose; equally likely is that beneath the jeering were generations of Catholicism woven profoundly into the fabric of the essentially European audience. Pialat, who was there to nurse his latest offspring, raised his fist to them and cried out: "You don't like me and [well, let me tell you] I don't like you [either]." The film's producer, Daniel Toscan du Planter, made an official statement about how the film was "completely French, a work deeply rooted in our traditional culture" and added that it was the "eternal story of our 'captive souls,' of man's divinity in the middle of his own shit and mud" [Gray 143].

Pialat's belligerent and self-denigrating attitude toward his own work certainly exacerbated the audience's hostile reaction but the film was also widely criticized for its academicism (Philippon 2).[2] Most importantly, critics deplored the fact that the film failed to do justice to the novel by eliminating all elements of mysticism, spirituality and transcendence. They argued that Pialat deliberately edited out the very ingredients that had been so important to Bernanos, in particular the communion between saints — a fundamental element of the novel — and that he limited the film to the visible world (Multeau 245, Serre 79). To some extent this harsh criticism is justified. However, in my view, stressing elements of mysticism as Robert Bresson did in his 1950 adaptation of Bernanos' novel *Diary of a Country Priest* and the mystical experience of its eponymous character, Father d'Ambricourt, would have been untimely in the 1980s. Pialat's film is a work of art in its own right; though based on Bernanos' novel, it represents Pialat's interpretation of it and should be taken as such. Pialat was also criticized for not portraying accurately the devastation of the post–World War I Artois region. Indeed, though the film spans approximately the period from 1890 to 1920–1930, the war is curiously absent from the film. Metaphorically, the war is very much present given the darkness, hopelessness and cold that pervade this small countryside world ruled by Satan and his human messengers. The film is dominated by an all too visible oppressiveness, reinforced by a low, overcast sky and the predominance of dark colors, in particular black and brown reflected in the rainy, muddy French countryside and a number of night scenes (Jousse 37). Despite the films' shortcomings to render the complexities of the human soul to the extent described in the novel, Pialat's interpretation is accurate: by casting Gérard Depardieu as the main character, Father Donissan, he chose to highlight the novel's main messages — human weakness and corruption of the human soul, by highlighting the portrayal of human desperation in the absence of God and in the face of constant temptation of evil.

Clearly, the depressing microcosm portrayed in the film is marked by sacrificial violence in the name of evil (Martini 174). This pessimism also reflects a lack of spirituality among the wider population and a progressive desecration of French society. The character Gallet, an adulterer who has an extramarital relationship with sixteen-year-old Mouchette, illustrates the increasing secularism of society. The desecration of post-war French society also shines through in Menou-Segrais' dialogue, which captures the deterioration of religious belief: "Today, what do people make of spiritual life? The gloomy battlefield of instincts. What do people do of morals? A hygiene of senses. Temptation is nothing more than a little carnal appetite. Men only seek pleasure and utility." In my viewing of the film, Pialat succeeded in conveying this key message.[3]

The film contains four episodes. It opens up with a dialogue between Donissan and his superior Menou-Segrais, and also shows Donissan alone in his room, trying to pray and flagellating himself. The second part tells the tragic story of Mouchette, focusing on her perverse — satanic — femininity, masterfully interpreted by a very young Sandrine Bonnaire. The third part — Bernanos' "The Temptation of Desperation" — features the pivotal roadside encounter between Satan and Donissan that takes place at Berck, between Étaples and Campagne while Donissan walks to his new parish "La Trappe," as well as Mouchette's suicide. The final part, "The Saint of Lumbres," culminates in Donissan's death.[4] All four parts underline the absence of piety and genuine religious feelings among the population, as the fantastic takes the place of a divine order that ought to be the backbone of Christian faith in Donissan's parish. As Joël Magny has pointed out, Pialat made a *cinéma du corps*, given the physicality of his films (80). Throughout the film, the fantastic is made visible in physical wrestling with the devil as well as a physical battle of Donissan himself who though ironically played by a slightly overweight Gérard Depardieu, keeps fainting as his belief in the goodness of his parish and the very existence of God falters, as made clear when Donissan exclaims: "What God? What a laugh. God doesn't mean anything."

The dark atmosphere of the film — shot mostly at dawn or nighttime — truly reflects the miserable state of the *Pays d'Artois* and Boulonnais in the Pas-De-Calais region then still weakened from the bloodletting of the First World War. From the start, the film music, the *intermezzo* of Symphony No. I composed by Henri Dutilleux sets a dark, ominous mood. In the first scene which depicts Menou-Segrais — interpreted by Maurice Pialat, the pastor of the parish Campagne — shaving young Father Donissan's tonsure, his *protégé*, the latter already expresses his despair: "When I am with you, everything appears simple. When I'm alone I'm worth nothing. I am like the zero, which only has value next to other numbers. There is nothing more miserable than a priest," Donissan states, remarking that he is forced to see God humiliated on a daily basis. "I can't say anything, all I can do is absolve or cry," he laments. Clearly, Donissan is a tortured soul with very low self-esteem. He desperately wants to become a saint but sainthood appears out of reach. As a result, he seeks punishment as evidenced in his repeated sessions of self-flagellation, which provide him some temporary relief from the guilt he feels for being unable to communicate with God. Unable to study the Bible, he throws it to the floor, as he needs physical relief to clear his mind and face his anguish. In the self-flagellation scene, Donissan's room bathes in pale blue light suggesting the presence of Satan (Buchman 51). In Catholic tradition, however, pale blue is also the color of the Virgin Mary, making it unclear to determine to what extent Donissan has been "infected" by evil at this stage. As his confession reveals, however, he feels that he is no longer innocent and pure. The devil has started to take possession of his soul and mind, while God fails to manifest himself. Perhaps, however, this absence of the divine is part of a larger scheme in which God still pulls the strings; a test Donissan must take to see the divine light. As Geoffrey Cubitt notes with regard to the French Revolution which was by many Frenchman viewed as a satanic act, Satan's status in Christian thought was traditionally ambiguous: "On the one hand, he was God's opposite and antagonist; on the other, at least according to one interpretation of his biblical role as a tempter, he was an agent whose vile actions were subordinate to a broader and more mysterious divine scheme" (141). Just as some viewed the French Revolution as divinely arranged, Donissan's abject suffering, his feelings of self-doubt and insufficiency could be viewed as part of a divine scheme to test his faith, a cruel but necessary transition to achieving sainthood. The hero in *Sous le soleil de Satan* wonders why he cannot have a good relationship with God. In my viewing, Donissan's predicament is that he has no relationship whatsoever with God. God has abandoned him, while he keeps desperately trying to communicate with him. Donissan's self-perceived failure to communicate with God and to become a saint himself translates into feelings of despair and acute restlessness, which urge him to move to a different parish in his quest for sainthood. Typically, Pialat's films depict characters that are either on the run, de-centered or in transit (Magny 52). This particularly applies to Donissan who is unable to sit still, read the Bible or pray, as emerges in one scene when he throws the Bible to the ground or in the self-flagellation scene when he seeks to relieve his tension by replacing his psychological despair with physical pain.

From the start, the relationship between Donissan and his superior Menou-Segrais is ambiguous. While throughout the film, Menou-Segrais is portrayed as a father figure who ludicrously calls Donissan "my little one," he also confides his dependence on his protégée and is reluctant to set him free by letting him go to Étaples, a parish of his own where he will be unprotected. However, eerily, Menou-Segrais has the ability to read Donissan's mind, an indication that Satan might also control him as it becomes clear that it is he who gives people the ability to read other people's minds. Surprisingly Menou-Segrais — knows or guesses? — that Donissan views him as a mediocre person, an ability that makes him a diabolical character. When Donissan begs Menou-Segrais to release him by allowing him to transfer to a different parish, Menou-Segrais finally agrees, stressing that Donissan must follow his vocation on his quest for sanctity. Before agreeing to let him go, Menou-Segrais predicts Donissan's future, again an indication that he is diabolical: "I give you to those who are waiting for you and whose prey you will be." Clearly, Menou-Segrais appears to know that Donissan will suffer immensely and yet he sees him off.

Mouchette — Donissan's *alter ego* — is also a messenger of the prince of evil. Unlike Donissan, she does not believe in God, as she tells Donissan in a seven-minute scene, which immediately precedes her suicide: "God? What a joke!" Mouchette and Donissan are physically opposites — Mouchette is young and frail but mentally strong and determined to live her short life to the fullest, while Donissan is physically strong yet mentally weak; somehow they are evil twins given their intuitive familiarity with evil: "both share, for their misfortune, the same secret, both have to deal with madness (be it named God, Satan, Vice, murder)" (Philippon 3). Mouchette accuses both of her lovers of weakness for failing to openly proclaim their love for her. In her first appearance on screen, she shoots her first lover, the marquis de Cadignan whose unborn child she bears. The murder is an act of revenge for his refusal to commit himself to her by leaving the village of Campagne with her, leaving behind her hated father. Interestingly, the murder is filmed as an *acting out* and even though she screams after he falls to the ground dead — she did not know that the hunting gun was loaded — the viewer has no indication as to what her true feelings are when she holds the gun to his chest. As Joël Magny points out, the *hors champs* of the murder scene suggests that Mouchette is in fact innocent, given the absence of any premonitory signs. This is Donissan's interpretation of the murder as he tells her in their brief encounter: "You are not in God's eyes, guilty of this murder. You are but a toy in Satan's hands." However, her scream might also be interpreted as a scream of revenge or surprise at her unexpected, sudden empowerment when she realizes that she has the power to give life — to her unborn baby — and death — to her weak lover. After leaving the scene of crime at dawn, Mouchette washes her muddy shoes in a stream to remove any murder evidence; as in other scenes the blue light suggests the presence of evil. The young girl then fully confides her murder to her second lover, the *docteur* Gallet who dismisses her behavior as delusional. Though Mouchette longs for redemption, she is again and again encouraged to sin. In her conversation with Gallet, Mouchette discloses her real — satanic — identity: that of a suicidal disturbed compulsive liar, unpredictable, evil and dangerous person. She also confesses her madness to him. Mouchette is possessed by Satan who makes her act the way she does. She senses that she has no power to act and even her suicide is not an act of free will. In one scene we see Gallet looking around quickly as if he had sensed a dangerous presence — Satan, his wife? — Mouchette asks him:

MOUCHETTE: "Are you afraid of hell?"
GALLET: "Mouchette, this is not the time to blather."
MOUCHETTE: "Oh stop it, you'll put on your airs and get mad. Answer me: do you fear Hell?"
GALLET: "Of course not."
MOUCHETTE: "I was sure of it. You are afraid of your wife but you are not afraid of hell. How stupid you are."
GALLET: "Mouchette, enough. Either be quiet or leave." [...]
MOUCHETTE: "You are afraid of your wife but you are not afraid of me?"
GALLET: "Because you are a nice girl, Mouchette."
MOUCHETTE: "Undoubtedly... So, with Mouchette you take pleasure but not the rest?"

The scene shows that Mouchette is as tormented as Donissan. She is scared to death yet cannot stop playing with fire as she engages in this adulterous relationship with Gallet.

Another crucial scene that reveals Satan's presence happens after the Mouchette-Gallet sequence. After celebrating Mass with Donissan, Menou-Segrais tells him that he will send him to Etables. As Donissan sets out on the thirteen-kilometer journey to Boulincourt, walking into dusk, the dark, ominous musical theme reflects his utter despair and announces his crucial meeting with Satan — a horse seller — interpreted by Jean-Christophe

Bouvet. Pialat brilliantly lets viewers believe that this character is an ordinary, in fact rather well meaning and nice person. In the film, realism gives way only gradually to the fantastic, which is presented as reality. This interpretation of the fantastic is in line with Pialat's philosophy since he did not believe in the supernatural (Estève 91). Consequently, the fantastic in the film masquerades as reality and is indeed difficult to discern. In the novel, there is thus no mistaking that Satan exists while in the film, diabolical happenings — murder, suicide, resurrection — are shrouded in the fantastic. In the film adaptation, the fantastic is very subtle but all the more eerie and shocking. It is usually introduced by an ellipsis as evidenced by the sudden apparition and disappearance of the devil, as in the powerful scene of the encounter between the horse seller and Donissan — filmed in the style of Truffaut's *American Night*. Satan's appearance is announced by the use of a blue filter, which remains in place even after his disappearance, indicating that Donissan has been infected by evil. In this key scene, Satan takes on the human form of a homosexual horse seller who acts like an ordinary man, helping lost Donissan to take a shortcut. Donissan's solitary walk begins in fading afternoon daylight which gives way to a blood-colored sky in this long-shot sequence that makes it appear like a somber painting of human despair. Daylight is fading as Donissan stumbles over the fields, exhausted and lost, when suddenly a man appears out of nowhere offering to accompany him to the village of Campagne. As they walk across fields and climb over fences, Donissan collapses and is helped back to his feet by his companion. The priest then opens up to him, telling him God sent him to help him since he spent the "longest and hardest imaginable night." When it is pitch dark, the devil gradually discloses his true identity and invites Donissan to sleep with him. Utterly exhausted from the long walk and his mental failure of communicating with God, who he tells the devil "abandoned him," Donissan fully confides his weakness and despair to Satan who, holding him in his arms fondles and cradles him, saying that he loves him tenderly and kissing him on the lips. Donissan's bondage and dependence on Satan is striking. He has lost all agency and fully obeys his orders to take a rest and lay down without any protest. "I love you tenderly," Satan says, to which Donissan replies: "I have no friends." Satan continues, "I have looked for you well, I have chased you," as he starts petting Donissan voluptuously and gives him the "kiss of a friend." Only then does he disclose his identity and starts denigrating the priest as "mud brain, sleeping dog, submissive animal," and warns him that he will test him until his death. In denial, Donissan replies that the test will come from God, but the devil makes Donissan look at him, recognize himself and take note of his own transparency. In a panic, Donissan starts yelling: "Retreat Satan! Bearer of hatred retreat!" but his pleas come too late. Donissan now bears the sign of the devil. The film does not answer the crucial question whether Satan is part of a bigger divine scheme of testing Donissan — God's puppet — or whether he is an independent satanic power with his very own satanic sun. Donissan's answer suggests that there is no link between the powers of good and evil, and outright rejects the power of evil. Later on however, as he is inhabited by these evil powers that give him the power to read other peoples' minds, he does not refrain from using the immense powers Satan gave him.

The fantastic also occurs in the suicide scene when Mouchette slits her throat with a razor blade. While we see her looking at herself in the mirror and putting the razor to her throat, the actual suicide is not filmed. The ellipsis is filled with the noise from a loud bang that coincides with her death as Donissan kicks in the bathroom door, picks up the corpse and carries it to the altar of the cathedral, a symbolical gesture of redemption. He crouches down over the corpse and looks up at Mouchette's mother, his mouth and chin covered with Mouchette's blood, suggesting that he is partially guilty of her death since, in a previous encounter, he told her all her sins. Still, Donissan could not possibly know that Mouchette had killed herself and yet he wastes no time claiming the body, another hint that he knew of her scheme and did not want to save her in time. Though Pialat privileges realism in large parts of the film, Donissan's intuitive knowledge of Mouchette's suicide pertains to the realm of the fantastic. The scene leading up to her suicide — crouched on her bed, holding on to the bedding as if crying out for help — also suggests the presence of Satan taunting her and holding the razor to her throat as she looks at herself in the mirror terrified.

Following his scandalous gesture of trying to redeem Mouchette's soul by putting her corpse on the altar, Donissan is transferred to another parish, "La Trappe," in an effort to defuse tension in the parish. Speaking with his mentor Menou-Segrais as he is getting ready for his departure, his mentor tells him that "the spirit of evil has entered his life," that he is virtually hopeless and that he "will be alone on his chosen path," comments that suggest an intriguing familiarity with evil. Upon his arrival at his new parish and as he stands in his small bedroom, Donissan's confession that he is incapable of loving and longs to die is followed by a fantastic spectral apparition of Mouchette victoriously walking towards him while he retreats to the wall, scared.

Finally, Donissan's fantastic resuscitation of a young boy who died of meningitis, while greeted by the mother's crying, "You are a saint," appears to be the work of Satan, given the yellowish glare of the boy's eyes against a black and white background. In view of his superhuman fantastic abilities, the members of the parish are obsessed with Donissan and worship him like a superhero, while his fellow priests are unsure what to make of him — a condemnation of the Catholic Church for failing to recognize evil. Donissan's stardom recalls that of Italian films by Pasolini and Olmi where, as Victoria Surliuga outlines in her chapter, viewers experience the miraculous in the faith of simple people who follow saint-lie figures who may or nay not be the Messiah. Donissan feels abandoned despite his dedication to the parish, which resembles an evil "fan club" of sinners all of whom aspire to be pure. At the end of the film, Donissan's death in the confessional, a "vertical coffin" seems ambiguous as it shows the cadaverous pale face illuminated with a cold light against a dark backdrop, suggesting that even in death, Donissan has failed to find God, that throughout his life, he had been illuminated by the sun of Satan (Durier 87).

To conclude, the film chronicles troubled Donissan's voyage towards self-knowledge and evil, his failed efforts to embrace his Catholic faith and not give in to temptation. Evil materializes in the form of the fantastic, a supernatural power, which is mistaken as a sign of sainthood by the members of Donissan's parish who interpret the resurrection of the dead boy as a heavenly miracle. Pialat's adaptation, however, suggests that the little boy's resurrection is not the deed of a saint — a miracle — but rather a diabolic act, thus casting doubt on the superiority of sainthood in a world ultimately dominated by weakness and evil. Thus, in the scene where Donissan lifts the heavy corpse of the little boy up high the corpse plunges into obscurity while Donissan is illuminated, reversing classical convention. This reversal suggests that Donissan is dominated by evil, even if he might be blind enough to deny this very fact. Again, the scene of the miraculous intervention is filmed as an elliptic cut which goes hand in hand with a change of perspective. The ellipsis suggests a fantastic — evil — presence. In this low angle shot, Donissan is seen picking up the corpse and holding it up high, utterly exhausted. Finally, the camera veers down, zeroing in on the possessed boy opening his eyes.

While Donissan can perform miracles such as reading Mouchette's mind and seeing her sins, including the murder of her lover, this ability is not a mark of sainthood but a trait of evil, as evidenced by her suicide — a logical consequence of a devilish inspired life devoid of all hope of divine redemption. In Pialat's film adaptation, it is striking that God is absent — Donissan's despair is caused by his inability to communicate with God — while Satan's suffocating presence is palpable throughout the film. Donissan's lucid moments intermingle with spells of confusion and despair, which gradually lead him to give in to Satan and blasphemy, professing that the prince of darkness determines each and everybody's lives and that all men, including Catholic priests, are devoid of any self-determination, mere toys of his evil desires.

242   Section Three. Ridiculous and Monstrous Catholicism

Notes

1. See René Prédal's article "Cinéma français des années 80: Le retour du religieux" for a discussion of religious films in France and in other European countries. Also see Olivier Serre's article "Les prêtres des salles obscures" and his filmography for an overview of twentieth-century French religious films. See Henri Agel's article "Quand Satan mène le bal. Une valeur sûre" for an overview of French, Italian, German and American twentieth-century films portraying Satan.
2. For an account of the difficult circumstances under which the film was shot and to understand Pialat's dislike of the ceremonial circus of the Cannes Film Festival and his controversial reaction, see Toubiana's interview with Maurice Pialat "La ligne droite" and Pascal Mérigeau's *Pialat*, pages 259–71.
3. Pialat's primary concern was to keep the intensity of Bernanos' verbal exchanges in the dialogues on screen while eliminating the heaviness of the literary dialogues, which he brilliantly succeeded in doing.
4. See Bruno Durier's article "*Sous le soleil de Satan*: De Bernanos à Pialat ou d'une écriture à l'autre" for a detailed comparison of the novel's and the film's plot structures.

Works Cited

Agel, Henri. "Quand Satan mène le bal. Une valeur sûre." *CinémAction* 49 (1988): 94–8.
De Baecque, Antoine. *Le dictionnaire Pialat. Clamecy*. Éditions Léo Scheer, 2008.
Bernanos, Georges. *The Diary of a Country Priest*. Trans. Pamela Norris. London: The Religious Book Club, 1937.
Billard, Pierre. "Pialat: L'enragé d'absolu." *Le Point* 780 (31 August 1987): 57–8.
Buchman, Sonia. "Bleu." *Le dictionnaire Pialat. Clamecy*. Ed. Antoine De Baecque. Éditions Léo Scheer, 2008. 50–2.
Durier, Bruno. "Sous le soleil de Satan: De Bernanos à Maurice Pialat ou d'une écriture à l'autre." *La Revue des Lettres Modernes*. Paris: Minard, 1991. 65–90.
Dutilleux, Henri. "Première symphonie." Arles: Harmonia Mundi France, 1992. CD.
Estève, Michel. "*Sous le soleil de Satan*: Du roman au film: Note sur le surnaturel et le démoniaque." *La Revue des Lettres Modernes*. Paris: Minard, 1991. 91–9.
Fontanel, Rémi. *Formes de l'insaisissable: Le cinéma de Maurice Pialat*. Lyon: Aléas, 2004.
Gray, Marianne. *Depardieu*. London: Warner, 1991.
Jones, Kent. "Under the Sun of Satan." *Film Comment* 40.3 (2004): 48.
Jousse, Thierry. "La France de Pialat." *Maurice Pialat: L'enfant sauvage*. Ed. Sergio Toffetti and Aldo Tassone. Torino: Lindau, 1992. 37–43.
Magny, Joël. *Maurice Pialat*. Paris: Editions de l'Etoile & Cahiers du cinéma, 1992.
Martini, Andrea. "Depardieu dans l'univers Pialat." *Maurice Pialat: L'enfant sauvage*. Ed. Sergio Toffetti and Aldo Tassone. Torino: Lindau, 1992. 167–75.
Mérigeau, Pascal. *Pialat*. Paris: Editions Grasset & Fasquelle, 2002.
Multeau, Norbert. *Les caméras du diable: Chroniques cinématographiques*. Paris: Éditions Dualpha, 2001.
Oms, Marcel. "Quatre Bernanos au cinéma: La grâce sous la braise." *CinémAction* 49 (1988): 89–93.
Prédal, René. "Cinéma français des années 80: Le retour du religieux." *CinémAction* 49(1988): 10–6.

Philippon, Alain. "Description d'un Combat." *Cahiers du Cinéma* 399 (September 1987): 2–5.
Schneider, Roland. "Des Genres en tout genre!" *CinémAction* 49 (1988): 58–61.
Serre, Olivier. "Les prêtres des salles obscures." *CinémAction* 49 (1988): 75–91.
Sous le soleil de Satan. Dir. Maurice Pialat. 1987. Perf. Gerard Depardieu, Sandrine Bonnaire, Maurice Pialat. Gaumont Vidéo, 2003. DVD.
Toubiana, Serge. "Un film de foudre." *Cahiers du Cinéma* 397 (June 1987): 6–7.
_____. "La ligne droite." *Cahiers du Cinéma* 399 (September 1987): 60–2.
Warehime, Marja. *Maurice Pialat*. Manchester: Manchester University Press, 2006.
Williams, Alan Larson. *Republic of Images: A History of French Filmmaking*. Cambridge and London: Harvard University Press, 1992.

Dark Imperative
Kant, Sade and Catholicism in Jess Franco's Exorcism

DAVID ANNANDALE

Reviewing William Friedkin's *The Exorcist* in 1973, Pauline Kael witheringly called the film "the biggest recruiting poster the Catholic Church has had since the sunnier days of *Going My Way* and *The Bells of St. Mary's*" (339). Whether the adaptation by Friedkin and producer/screenwriter William Peter Blatty of the latter's self-described "apostolic work" (cited in Kael 337) was successful in the recruiting sense or not, its incontestable financial triumph attracted plenty of disciples, and numerous low-budget imitators followed it into the theaters. These cinematic offspring (considered in more detail by Alexandra Heller-Nicholas in this book) generally mimic Friedkin and Blatty's work both in their approach to spectacle (grotesque make-up, vomiting, enthusiastic deployment of obscenities and blasphemies, sexual taboo-busting, and so on) and in their ultimate allegiance to a conservative Catholic morality. In stark contrast is a 1974 effort by the extremely prolific Spanish director Jesús (Jess) Franco. Given that the Vatican once condemned Franco and Luis Buñuel as "the most dangerous filmmakers in the world" (O'Neal), it should not be a surprise that, despite its title, Franco's *Exorcism* (AKA *Exorcisme et Messes Noires*) is less a cash-in on *The Exorcist* than it is a ferocious riposte to the latter's project. As such, it dramatizes the encounter, courtesy of Jacques Lacan, of Immanuel Kant and the Marquis de Sade, and suggests, amid all the spectacle of blood and torture, the outline of an emancipatory agenda.

Lacan formulates his thesis in "Kant with Sade" thusly: "*Philosophy in the Bedroom* came eight years after the *Critique of Practical Reason*. If, after showing that the former is consistent with the latter, I can demonstrate that the former completes the latter, I shall be able to claim that it yields the truth of *the Critique*" (*Écrits* 646). No small part of *Exorcism*'s force lies in the fact that its relationship with *The Exorcist* is similar to that of Sade and Kant. *Exorcism* attacks *The Exorcist*'s overt goals, while revealing the truths that *The Exorcist* must, for the sake of those goals, deny about itself.

In an unusual move for a horror movie, *The Exorcist*'s title and ominous poster point to the hero, and not the villain, of the piece. Franco reverses the reversal in *Exorcism*. The would-be exorcist of this film is Paul Vogel (played by Franco himself), a defrocked priest. "I was expelled from the priesthood," he laments. "Those idiots thought I was too severe. They were wrong. My heart was pure and just and ... and intransigent in dealing with sin." Sexually frustrated, obsessed with sin, he writes lurid torture tales for the press run by Raymond Franval (Pierre Taylou, playing a character named after Sade's *Eugénie de Franval*). Vogel is also a serial killer, picking women up and then, convinced that their sexuality and the lust they inspire within him are the work of the devil, "exorcising" them by stabbing them to death. He becomes infatuated with Anne (Lina Romay, Franco's partner and artistic collaborator). Anne is part of Raymond's stable of performers who put on elaborate S&M/black mass shows for well-heeled audiences. Vogel kidnaps and tortures Anne, and, aghast by the black masses, murders some of their participants before finally being gunned down by the slow-on-the-uptake police.

The title of *Exorcism*, then, refers to a threat, rather than to a promise of salvation. Franco keeps the premise of Friedkin's film in his sights, however, since Vogel honestly believes that he *is* saving the souls of his victims (almost all of whom, significantly, are female). Franco's strategic move is simple but devastating: by removing all trace of the supernatural, he reveals the truth of exorcism (and thus the fact that *The Exorcist*'s poster is unintentionally revealing). If there is no devil, the ritual becomes an act of torture whose goal is to punish and control women's bodies. *The Exorcist* reads the onset of puberty and adolescent rebellion as clear signs of demonic possession, which is itself the inevitable result of the collapse of the nuclear family (Ellen Burstyn's Chris Mac Neil is a single mother with an active career) and the turning away from the Church (Chris is not religious). By contrast, the victims in *Exorcism* are happy until Vogel comes along, and their sexuality, which would appear nightmarishly promiscuous and beyond the pale in William Peter Blatty's world, is, in Franco's presentation, cheerfully polymorphous. If unfettered sexuality is the good, and there is no devil, how could an exorcism be anything other than insane, hateful and deadly? Franco underscores this point during a crime scene investigation. The audience has just seen Vogel stab a couple to death. He calls on the Trinity while doing so, but his actions consist of little more than vicious knife blows and a disembowelment. The police arrive, and Malou (Roger Germanes), the intelligent assistant to the thick-headed Inspector Tanner (Olivier Mathot) takes one look at the murder victims and announces, "The form of the wounds and the depth of the incisions — everything seems to point to the exorcism ritual of the early Inquisition." In the terms of *Exorcism*'s film world, then, Vogel's crimes are not atrocities that he happens to think of as exorcisms, but are, rather, accurate recreations of the ritual, which is monstrous in and of itself. It would seem, then, that there is more than mere self-delusion to Vogel's claim that he was too rigorous in his adherence to Catholic dogma. In other words, he applied the law to the letter, and thus revealed its monstrousness. The Church must expel Vogel. In his extreme fidelity, he is what must be disavowed. He is the truth that cannot be admitted or faced. He must be cast out, or the repressive, brutal acts he commits, so redolent of a misogynistic terror of the female body and sexuality, must be recast, via the introduction of supernatural entities, as the acts of salvation Vogel so devoutly believes them to be.

Opposed to Vogel's serial killer are Anne and friends. That these characters are the agents of good in the film is crucial to *Exorcism*'s agenda, as is how they are presented to the audience, especially since it is through them, and not Vogel, that Sade enters the picture. The opening scene of the film appears, at first, to be set in a dungeon. Anne, naked except for fetish boots, is spread-eagled and chained to an A-frame. Rose (Nadine Pascal), also naked, sacrifices a bird and tortures Anne with a whip and knife. Shortly after the scene begins, Franco reveals that one's initial impression of the setting is wrong. Anne and Rose have an audience: well-dressed couples sitting at tables in darkness and watching intently, as if studying the scene. Anne's screams become moans as she responds to Rose's kisses. Has the victim been seduced by the torturer, or was the torture only for show? In mid-embrace, Rose stabs Anne, who slumps dead. There is one more reversal: the lights go up, the audience applauds enthusiastically, and Anne rises from the dead. She and Rose hold hands, bow, and happily scamper off the stage.

The sequence announces both the film's allegiance to Sade and the way in which it intends to deploy him. Sade repeatedly constructs "sexuality as a site of public performance and contemplation" (Mendik 10), as does Franco. Asked about the similarity, Franco concurs: "Yes, this is so. With that film [*Lady Porno*], I intended it to be theatrical, in the same way that Sade's work is theatrical. I think of the cinema as a show, and the show must be good as a show" (qtd. in Mendik 23–4). Almost every one of *Exorcism*'s sex scenes involving Anne or Rose is a performance of one sort or another, even if the audience is limited to Vogel's voyeuristic imagination, as he feverishly visualizes what, it turns out, actually *is* going on in Anne's apartment. The presence of an on-screen audience is, of course, a reminder to the film's actual viewers of their own role in the voyeuristic economy of cinema, and thus underscores the fact that *every* sex scene in the film is, by definition, a theatrical performance. The fact that Anne's torture and death are a piece of theater permits Franco to present what Slavoj Žižek, following Lacan, indicates as "the Sadian fundamental fantasy: the fantasy of another, ethereal body of the victim, which can be tortured indefinitely and nonetheless magically retains its beauty (see the standard Sadian figure of a young girl sustaining endless humiliations and mutilations ... and mysteriously surviving it all intact)" ("The Ideal Couple"). Thus, over and over again, Anne and her cohorts are ritualistically slaughtered, only to cheerily come back for more. Here Franco offers a possible way out of one of Sade's impasses: "The work never presents us with a successful seduction in which [Sade's] fantasy would nevertheless find its crowning glory—that is, a seduction in which the victim, even if she were at her last gasp, would consent to her tormentor's intention, or even join his side in the fervor of her consent" (Lacan, *Écrits* 665). Anne, here, consents and embraces Rose. The obvious objection, of course, is that Anne's torture is not real, and so her consent is meaningless, but this misses the nature of Franco's achievement, which is to find, in Sade, a kernel of emancipation at the center of the nightmare. It is here that the encounter between Sade and Kant is most important.

One form this encounter takes is political. Like Blatty, Franco was reacting to the socio-political state of his homeland. But where Blatty was recoiling from the unrest and social transformations that the 1960s wrought in the United States, Franco was responding, as he did for much of his career, to a lack of positive change in Spain. Here he discusses *The Sadist of Notre Dame* (*Le Sadique de Notre-Dame*), the 1979 revision of *Exorcism*:

> [I]t was a liberation for me to make that. In a sense, my own story is that I am always going and coming back and going and coming back. Each coming back means a kind of deception when I come back to Spain. Because the promise I believe might be in Spain is never here.... And so, frustrated by Spain, I get the desire to—POW!—explode and make something strong and *Le Sadique de Notre Dame* was one of those cases [Collins 9].

Though, by 1979, Francisco Franco was dead, it would seem that Spain's transition away from fascism was neither fast enough nor dramatic enough for Jess Franco. Furthermore, the rawness of his films (*Exorcism*'s coarse, authentic grime is aesthetic light years distant from the studied, big-budget grit of *The Exorcist*) "links them [within Spain] historically to an antifascist aesthetic, a subversive tradition of controlled resistance" (Hawkins 113). And indeed, Franco notes that *Le Sadique de Notre-Dame* was popular in Spain (censorship prevented *Exorcism*'s release there) as film audiences rebelled against the previously enforced Catholicism (DVD Commentary). Given the political impulse it seems fair to say lies behind *Exorcism*, the fact that Horkheimer and Adorno, in *Dialectic of Englightenment*, see Sade as a prophet of fascism is suggestive. For them, Sade follows the logic of Kantian Enlightenment all the way to the end, and there finds totalitarianism. Sade and other "dark writers of the bourgeoisie, unlike its apologists, did not seek to avert the consequences of the Enlightenment with harmonistic doctrines. They did not pretend that formalistic reason had a closer affinity to morality than to immorality. While the light-bringing writers protected the indissoluble alliance of reason and atrocity ... by denying that alliance, the bearers of darker messages pitilessly expressed the shocking truth" (Horkheimer 92). For Horkheimer and Adorno, then, Sade's atrocities are not celebrations as much as they are revelations of the darkness that is inherent to the very ideologies they pretend to attack.

One could, then, align fanatical ex-priest Vogel with Sade's collection of monstrous popes and bishops, and Franco states that he was interested in people who lose control through being too religious and take disavowed pleasure in the tortures they meet out (DVD Commentary). Furthermore, Vogel is a personification of fascist Spain, committing murder in the service of enforced Catholicism. However, Sade's clergy denounce the religion they are supposed to defend, and are unapologetic in the delight they take in their crimes. Vogel honestly believes (or at least desperately wants to believe) that his actions are righteous, necessary, and holy — a stance that would provoke gales of contemptuous laughter in a Sadian libertine. There is also the fact that, as we have seen, Franco's libertines and their rituals are nightmarish only from Vogel's point of view, and they are in fact presented as the identification figures for the audience. So though fascism (and to be more precise, its Catholic variant that would rule over Spain through the middle of the 20th century) and Sade encounter each other in *Exorcism*, Franco uses Sade less as an anatomist of fascism, and more as a counter to it.

It is in the service of deploying Sade as a counter to repressive forces that Lacan is most useful. Certainly, like Horkheimer and Adorno, he shows Sade working out the darker implications of Kantian philosophy. But if Horkheimer and Adorno see the Sadian nightmare as the inevitable result of Kantian ethics, Lacan, if one is to follow Žižek, suggests that "Sade articulates what happens when the subject betrays the true stringency of the Kantian ethics" ("The Ideal Couple"). If this is so, Žižek continues, "then Kant is the antitotalitarian par excellence." One way to this antitotalitarian position is through Lacan's presentation of the Sadian transformation of Kant's categorical imperative.

Lacan provides a couple of variations of that transformation. In his 1959–60 *Seminar VII*, Lacan says that the categorical imperative — "[a]ct so that the maxim of thy will can always at the same time hold good as a principle of universal legislation" (Kant 31) — becomes, in Sade's hands, "Let us take as the universal maxim of our conduct the right to enjoy any other person whatsoever as the instrument of our pleasure" (*Seminar* 79). But in the version of "Kant with Sade" that appears in *Écrits*, Lacan's restatement of Sade's law is a bit different: "'I have the right to enjoy your body,' anyone can say to me, 'and I will exercise this right without any limit to the capriciousness of the exactions I may wish to satiate with your body'" (648). The difference (and its importance) is made all the more apparent if we consider the phrasing in the version of "Kant with Sade" that appeared in the September 1962 issue of *Critique*. The 1966 Lacan replaces "I can say to anyone" ("dirai-je à qui me plaît" [*Critique* 3]) with "anyone can say to me" ("peut me dire quiconque" [*Écrits II* 247]). What might look, at first blush, like a reversal does not, in fact, indicate a change in position, but merely a refinement of thought through a shift in emphasis. The revision implies the consent of the victim (if "victim" is really a valid term in this context), and is a more generous phrasing of the maxim. It is still an accurate representation of Sade. In "Yet Another Effort, Frenchmen, If You Would Be Republicans," the manifesto contained within *Philosophy in the Bedroom*, the Chevalier de Mirvel reads: "If we allow, as we have just done, that all women must be subjugated to our desires, then surely we must similarly permit them to satisfy all of theirs.... [Just as] they must surrender themselves to all who desire them, they must equally have the freedom to enjoy all those they believe worthy of satisfying them" (516–7, translation mine). Implicit here is the surrender of the speaker himself to a system where all must permit everything to all.

And indeed, Sade's libertines freely give themselves to each other, and make demands that are freely granted. The victims of the libertines, are, of course, not so lucky, but within the circle of executioners there is an uncommon harmony and consensus. This is also the situation that exists between Anne, Raymond and the rest of Franco's libertines. Where Franco breaks from Sade is that these libertines have no victims. They take on all the roles in their sex games themselves. To return to the objection that the deaths and torture Anne and company subject themselves to are theater, therefore not real, and thus the break from Sade is too great for Franco's project to be authentically Sadian in any sense, the answer is that there is a level where what is going on is entirely real. Setting aside the fact that, as we have seen, theatricality is a vital part of the Sadian project (and, after all, *Philosophy in the Bedroom* is written in the form of a play), Franco's characters do seek authenticity. For all their amusement, they nonetheless refer repeatedly to their black masses as "real." It is the *ritual*, not the sacrifice, that is real, and it is treated as such by both the participants and Vogel. Raymond muses that the murders "have something to do with our quest for excitement in the domain of black magic." But the goal of the black magic is not to raise the devil, but to explore the participants' sexuality. The sex acts, then, like Sade's perversities, are so many points in the construction of an argument.

Following Sade and Kant, Anne and friends have also eliminated virtually every trace of sentiment. There is certainly nothing particularly emotional going on during the various and varied couplings and orgies the characters engage in. These people never seem to express anything deeper than an obvious pleasure in each other's company, though Raymond and Rose are worried when Anne goes missing, and they obviously want to save her from harm. There is very little sense, however, that this concern springs from a deep romantic attachment. And this, according to Kant, is as it should be: "It is of the greatest importance to attend with the utmost exactness in all moral judgments to the subjective principle of all maxims, that all morality of actions may be placed in the necessity of acting *from duty* and from respect for the law, not from love and inclination for that which the actions are to produce" (86, emphasis his). Rose and Raymond don't appear to love Anne any more than she loves them. But their duty to protect each other is assumed automatically, and if "to love one's neighbor means to like to practice all duties towards him" (Kant 88), then Rose and Raymond are, in Kant's terms, being properly ethical. By contrast, there is a character who expresses strong passions, and that is Vogel. He works himself up to an emotional frenzy that culminates in murder. He completely gives in to the pathological. Thus, given where *Exorcism's* moral center resides (and the fact that there even *is* a moral center), Franco is giving us, in line with Žižek's reasoning, not a Sadian Kant, but a Kantian Sade.

For Žižek, the point upon which hangs the question as to the incipient fascism of Kant's philosophy is the issue of responsibility:

> What we encounter here is the properly perverse attitude of adopting the position of the pure instrument of the big Other's Will: it's not my responsibility, it's not me who is effectively doing it, I am merely an instrument of the higher Historical Necessity... The obscene *jouissance* of this situation is generated by the fact that I conceive of myself as exculpated for what I am doing: isn't it nice to be able to inflict pain on others with full awareness that I'm not responsible for it, that I merely fulfill the Other's Will ... this is what Kantian ethics prohibits. This position of the sadist pervert provides the answer to the question: How can

the subject be guilty when he merely realizes an "objective," externally imposed necessity? By subjectively assuming this "objective necessity," i.e. by finding enjoyment in what is imposed on him. So, at its most radical, Kantian ethics is NOT "sadist," but precisely what prohibits assuming the position of a Sadian executioner ["The Ideal Couple"].

There is a potential problem here. Can one truly say that Sade's libertines are "instruments of the big Other's Will"? Isn't their utopia, where there are no limits to the enacting of desire, one of absolute freedom? In fact, it is not. Again and again, Sade presents characters like *Philosophy in the Bedroom's* Mme de Saint-Ange, who has no control over her lusts. "The pleasures I wished to deprive myself of," she says, "only returned to present themselves to my spirit with yet greater force, and I saw that when one is, as I am, born for debauchery, it is useless to dream of applying brakes [to desire]" (383, translation mine). Sade's monsters have little more freedom of choice than do their victims. "When jouissance petrifies in the object," Lacan writes, "it becomes the black fetish.... This is what becomes of the executioner in sadism when, in the most extreme case, his presence is reduced to being no more than the instrument" (*Écrits* 652). And further: "the fact that the executioner's jouissance becomes fixated there does not spare his jouissance the humility of an act in which he cannot help but become a being of flesh and, to the very marrow, a slave to pleasure" (652). Lacan and Žižek here give us the truth of Sade, and the point where the libertines do indeed fail to meet the strictures of Kantan ethics. To be a slave to physical necessity, writes Kant, "leaves no room for *transcendental freedom*, which must be conceived as independence on everything empirical, and, consequently, on nature generally.... Without this freedom, (in the latter and true sense), which alone is practical *à priori*, no moral law and no moral imputation are possible" (102, emphasis Kant's). The sort of freedom the libertines enjoy, then, "would at bottom be nothing better than the freedom of a turnspit, which, when once it is wound up, accomplishes its motions of itself" (Kant 103). Slaves to desire, Sade's libertines enjoy only this false turnspit freedom, along with a freedom from responsibility, and so fail the Kantian test.

Franco's libertines, on the other hand, follow a properly Lacanian-Kantian ethic. Žižek writes,

Lacan's "*ne pas céder son désir*" ("do not compromise your desire") involves [a] tautological injunction (a new corroboration of the fact that, as Lacan put it, Kant's moral law is simply desire in its pure state): it provides no positive guarantee or support of our desire, that is, the subject is not allowed to say: "I know this is reprehensible, but what can I do? This is what I desire, and I cannot give it up..." — the subject is fully responsible for what she or he desires [*Indivisible Remainder* 172].

However, he also argues that Lacan ultimately shows that "the Sadian Will-to-Enjoy ... is thoroughly 'pure,' ethical in the strictest Kantian sense. The imperative that sustains the Sadian subject's endless search for enjoyment fulfils all the criteria of the categorical imperative" (*Indivisible Remainder* 173). As we have just seen, though, the Sadian libertines might well not compromise their desire, but neither do they take responsibility for it. They are its happy slaves, embracing the license their enslavement to their nature entails. Franco's libertines bring Kant to Sade by neither compromising their desire nor denying their responsibility for it. There is never a sense in *Exorcism* that the manifold ways in which they enact their desire are the result of anything other than a conscious choice, one that smacks far more of unsentimental (yet joyful) exploration than a surrender to uncontrolled passion. What they do, they do from choice, and are never (unlike Vogel) driven to their acts. These characters, then, follow the categorical imperative far more rigorously than do Sade's.

In no way, though, does Vogel live up to the categorical imperative, and so comes much closer to embodying the nightmare vision that, as Žižek shows, Kant explicitly prohibits. Vogel will not take responsibility for his own desires, and punishes the women for the arousal he experiences. This punishment, however, is conceived of as a duty. He has no choice in the matter; the big Other (God in this instance, or, more accurately, given the stole he wears, the Church) has reduced him to an instrument. He is on a mission. "I fought with sin," he informs his first victim, "I fought with vice. That's why I will exorcise you." He is called by his faith to save the women from themselves by lethally mortifying their flesh. This, for Franco, the truth of exorcism: it is misogynistic male panic dressed up in the raiments of virtue. Stripped of its ceremonial paraphernalia, it is simply a violent assault. But that paraphernalia speaks powerfully to the mechanism that supports this assault. Through the ritual words and ritual raiments, the exorcist cloaks himself in the signs of the big Other, and rejoices that his desire is his duty, and his duty is the desire of the Other, and thus, once again, not his responsibility at all. "Do not despise my command because you know me to be a sinner," Father Merrin tells the demon inhabiting Regan in *The Exorcist*. "It is God Himself who commands you." The exorcist, then, can barely be said to be acting at all: it is God acting through his body who is responsible.

It is interesting, then, that for all that *The Exorcist* presents the Catholic Church as a force of unalloyed good, it also presents it just as clearly as the big Other. Damien Karras' adherence to his duty, as defined by the Church, numbers, among its consequences, the facts that he must continue in his role as psychiatrist and priest even as he loses his faith, and that he doesn't have the means to provide proper care for his ailing mother, who dies as a result.

The nightmare Karras has about his mother — where he futilely tries to catch up to her as she disappears into a subway station — tempts one to read it as Karras' unconscious rebelling at the impossible demands of the Other's desire. But the exorcism, which can only take place with the Church's permission and under its rules, shows Karras that his doubts are misplaced. The execution of the ritual itself is unsuccessful (though clearly it is the correct treatment, addressing the truth of Regan's symptoms, unlike conventional medicine), but Karras' self-sacrifice does save the day, as he calls the demon into his own soul and then hurls himself out the window to his death. Here, then, we see the ultimate surrender to the desire of the Other, the self-abnegation that is Karras' duty taken to its logical conclusion. It is a conclusion, furthermore, that *The Exorcist* supports. However tragic Karras' death might be, it is in a good cause: Regan is saved, and the truths of the Church's teachings are confirmed.

The portrayal of the Church as big Other is altogether different in *Exorcism*. Vogel, too, sees his duty all the way through to the end. As we have seen, Vogel is defrocked for being too faithful to Church teachings. In coming so close to actually fulfilling the big Other's desires, he makes those desires uncomfortably apparent. For the institution to continue to function, it must disavow the true nature of its desires, and thus expel its most faithful servant. So where *The Exorcist* advocates surrender to the big Other, and the fundamental lack of responsibility that involves, Franco strips away the crutch and comfort of blind belief, revealing its brutal core. In Franco's Kanto-Sadian world, true liberation is neither surrender to the Church nor to desire, but in the assumption of responsibility for one's own unfettered desire. In this light, Damien Karras is as pathetic and misguided a figure as Paul Vogel; he may not harm anyone, but he is Vogel's ideological and psychological cellmate.

So whither hope? It is to be found in the chains, knives, blood and happy perversities of Anne, Rose and Raymond. David Martyn writes of Sade's *The 120 Days of Sodom* that by "exhausting desire's stock of imagistic values and abandoning it to the sheer articulatory force of an algebra that would be total, the book creates the conditions under which a failure of totalization can occur" (212). Further: "The sublime failure I have been calling ethical is not something we can 'achieve'; it is absolute failure. But we can, perhaps, open ourselves up to it by accepting articulation, indeed embracing it, as it were, to the point at which it breaks, thereby breaking us as well" (213). Anne and her friends, through their unfettered sexuality and embrace of rituals that they evacuate of traditional meaning, threaten the social order represented by Vogel with total collapse. They do not bring about a new order, and where exactly they are going with their project seems as obscure to them as it does to the audience. But as Martyn points out, "we have to be constantly wary of ... action that would limit itself to the attainment of an *imaginable*, indeed of any *articulable* goal" (214, emphasis his). The breakthrough he gestures towards sounds very like Alain Badiou's Event, the system-transforming occurrence that cannot be articulated, or even conceived of, from within the system. Thus, Franco's characters' failure to reach or articulate a goal is itself a success. This might appear to be an endorsement of apathy, but it is not. If the failure in question were not reaching for the sublime, if it were just an ordinary failure, Vogel would not perceive a threat. Anne and her friends do not create an Event. They do not start a revolution. But they wrest the moral high ground from the Church while championing the diabolic, and they demonstrate care for their neighbor in rigorously Kantian terms while reveling in violence and laughing about murder. Finally, whatever actions they take, whatever acts they submit themselves to (whatever experiences they open themselves to), the responsibility is theirs. They do not, unlike Vogel and Karras, take refuge in duty to puppethood. The desire of these ethical libertines is their own, and none Other's.

Works Cited

Balbo, Lucas, et al. *Obsession: The Films of Jess Franco.* Berlin: Selbstverlag Frank Trebbin, 1993.
Collins, Kevin. "Interview with Jess Franco." *European Trash Cinema Special* 1 (1996): 5–36.
Exorcism. Dir. Jess Franco. 1974. Synapse Films, 2001. DVD.
Exorcism (DVD Commentary). Dir. Jess Franco. 1974. Synapse Films, 2001. DVD.
The Exorcist. Dir. William Friedkin. Perf. Ellen Burstyn, Linda Blair, Max von Sydow, Jason Miller, 1973. Warner Bros., 1998. DVD.
Hawkins, Joan. *Cutting Edge: Art-Horror and the Horrific Avant Garde.* Minneapolis: University of Minnesota Press, 2000.
Horkheimer, Max, and Theodor W. Adorno. *Dialectic of Englightenment: Philosophical Fragments.* Ed. Gunzelin Schmid Noerr. Trans. Edmund Jephcott. Stanford, CA: Stanford University Press, 2002.
Kael, Pauline. *Reeling.* New York: Warner, 1977.
Kant, Immanuel. *Critique of Practical Reason.* Trans. Thomas Kingsmill Aboott. 1909. Mineola, NY: Dover, 2004.
Lacan, Jacques. *Écrits.* Trans. Bruce Fink. New York: Norton, 2002.
_____. *Écrits II.* 1966. Paris: Seuil, 1999.
_____. "Kant avec Sade Version Publiée dans *Critique.*" DOC file.
_____. *The Seminar of Jacques Lacan, Book VII: The Ethics of Psychoanalysis 1959–1960.* Ed. Jacques-Alain Miller. Trans. Dennis Potter. New York: Norton, 1992.
Martyn, David. *Sublime Failures: The Ethics of Kant and Sade.* Detroit: Wayne State University Press, 2003.
Mendik, Xavier. "Perverse Bodies, Profane Texts: Jesus Franco, De Sade." *Necronomicon Book Two.* Ed. Andy Black. London: Creation Books, 1998. 7–29.

O'Neal, Sean. "Interview: Jess Franco." *Avclub.com*. *The Onion*, 27 Oct. 2009. Web. 12 Jan. 2010.
Sade. *La Philosophie dans le boudoir*. Oeuvres complètes du Marquis de Sade, Tome Troisième. Paris, Pauvert, 1986. 377–561.
The Sadist of Notre Dame. Dir. Jess Franco. Eurociné, 1979. Film.
Žižek, Slavoj. *The Indivisible Remainder: On Schelling and Related Matters*. 1996. London: Verson, 2007.
_____. "Kant and Sade: The Ideal Couple." Egs.edu. The European Graduate School, n.d. Web. 15 Feb. 2009.

Killer Priests
The Last Taboo?
SHELLEY F. O'BRIEN

The figure of the Roman Catholic priest has been employed as a character in cinema since the inception of the medium, and is often depicted in a positive, sometimes even heroic, light. Films such as *Angels with Dirty Faces* (Michael Curtiz, 1938), *Going My Way* (Leo McCarey, 1944), *The Mission* (Roland Joffé, 1986), and most famously, *The Exorcist* (William Friedkin, 1973), feature priests who offer up a broad range of characteristics which are traditionally associated with the Catholic clergy, for example, devotion, compassion, inner struggle, fortitude, martyrdom, and also humor. Some of these examples attempt to portray the priest as a complex character, others less so.

Alongside this more common representation of the Catholic priest, there are films that feature the priest as villain, as abuser, and, in extreme cases, as a murderer. These films tap into the common notion that those in a position of trust are all the more evil if they are discovered to have violated that trust. Therefore, it can be seen as even more shocking if a priest, a "servant of God," is discovered to be the wrongdoer. Arguably, the figure of the murderous priest is both fascinating and perverse, not least because it violates a major taboo. On the one hand, the representation of the priest as killer is outrageous, and on the other, it is a form of guilty pleasure, easily justified by the fact that some priests have indeed been the perpetrators of evil deeds.

This chapter then, aims to explore the representation of the Catholic priest as killer, looking in detail at two Italian *giallo*[1] movies and another key example made in Britain, Pete Walker's *House of Mortal Sin* (aka *The Confessional*, 1975). In relation to this, I will also examine how these films make use of the doctrine and ritual associated with the church, the narrative function of symbols closely associated with Catholicism, and how Catholic imagery is presented in the mise-en-scène. This chapter will also consider what might have inspired or influenced these filmmakers to create killer priest narratives.

Surprisingly perhaps, there are few examples of killer priests in films considering the horrific potential of this contradictory figure.[2] It is arguably unsurprising however, that the killer priest figure features in a group of Italian *gialli* from the 1970s — Catholicism being a dominant force in Italy, and most of the *gialli* directors having been raised as Catholics. Also, the *giallo*—with its graphic scenes of gory violence, multi-layered plots, and habit of deliberately misdirecting the suspicions of the viewer — is the ideal narrative form for the killer priest to inhabit. The two *giallo* films I will be discussing in this context are Lucio Fulci's *Don't Torture a Duckling* (1972) and Antonio Bido's *The Bloodstained Shadow* (1978).

It is notable that there are also *gialli* that on the surface appear to have priests as killers, but in fact they turn out to be impostors disguised as priests, for example, *The House with the Laughing Windows* (Pupi Avati, 1976), *Who Saw Her Die?* (Aldo Lado, 1972), and *What Have You Done to Solange?* (Massimo Dallamo, 1972). These films still have some relation with my discussion however — the mere fact that the killers in these two films choose to disguise themselves as priests in order to commit their crimes suggests something about the killer priest figure more generally, i.e., that his inclusion is often related to perceived immorality, the desire for retribution, and also as a device for misleading the audience. However, as stated earlier, it is not only Italian directors who use Catholicism and the killer priest figure as part of their narratives, hence the inclusion of Pete Walker's *House of Mortal Sin* in this chapter. This film features perhaps the most extreme example of a killer priest. Some would argue that the representation of the Catholic priest and the use of Catholic artifacts as murder weapons verges on blasphemy, for reasons I will discuss later.

Before examining this select group of films which feature a killer priest, it is important to consider why this figure was included at all. Fulci, Walker and Bido were all raised as Catholics — Fulci was lapsed (i.e., no longer a practicing Catholic) and had a somewhat difficult relationship with the church, as did Walker, although Bido does not appear to have had the same issues.[3] As they were also involved in the development of the storyline in these films, it is reasonably safe to assume that this impacted on the narratives and lead to the inclusion of the killer priest figure. It is also the case that both Fulci and Walker had a desire to shock in their taboo-trashing films[4] and that *gialli* and horror movies from other countries, especially those in the 1970s, were notoriously violent and downbeat in their style. Using a priest as a killer taps into the mood of this period — these films are not so much an all-out attack on the Catholic church, rather, they reveal a nihilistic view of the world in the same way as films such as *Last House on the Left* (Wes Craven, 1972) and *The Texas Chain Saw Massacre* (Tobe Hooper, 1974). Prior to the 1970s, priests were usually representative of what is supposed to be good in society, but by making him a killer it is a somewhat cynical and perverse way of revealing the corruption within society more generally — if a Catholic priest can be a killer, then what hope is there for the rest of us?

Fulci's *Don't Torture a Duckling* effectively sets the standard for the killer priest movie in more ways than one. The plot revolves around the investigation into the murder of several young boys in a Southern Italian village, and the eventual revelation that it is the local priest who is responsible for these terrible crimes. In this film, Fulci creates a vision of religion that has become twisted in such a way that it hurts rather than helps its followers. Don Alberto, seems deeply dedicated to the young boys in the village and devout in his faith, so the revelation that he is, in fact, a killer of the young boys in his care, is disturbing and yet tragic. Don Alberto epitomizes some of the contradictions inherent in Catholicism — in this particular case, he wants to preserve innocence, but in order to do that he ends up killing innocents. This can also be contrasted with the ways in which Fulci articulates the bigotry of the villagers. The brutal, vigilante chain whipping of Maciara being the most extreme example. Don Alberto is clearly deranged, and yet he is at least killing for what he believes is the "right" reason. Conversely, the villagers are presented as simply bigoted, trapped in the confines of a space that is archaic, and yet being forced to make the transition into the present. In this way, the film is a potent mixture of closed minded village mentality, and a misguided adherence to the doctrine of the church, which has become perverted through Don Alberto's very devotion to it.

There are several sequences that are enlightening in relation to the above — the dialogue between key characters and Fulci's use of the mise-en-scène constantly reinforcing what the film is about. Similarly, the opening shot of the film clearly indicates one of the key themes — the clash between the old and the new. Indeed, Mikel Koven argues that Don Alberto, "...murders young boys because he witnesses their increasing loss of innocence as outsiders become more and more frequent visitors to their Apulian village" (Koven). The camera tracks across the Southern Italian rural landscape that has been literally scarred by the imposing new highway. Despite this glaringly modern addition to the landscape, the surrounding scenery and pace of the tracking shot still suggest an overall feeling of tranquility. However, any sense of this rapidly disappears, and the peace is disrupted by a shot of frenzied hands digging up a tiny skeleton from the earth. The music score by Riz Ortolani is extremely unsettling here — the sound of echoing discords played on strings indicates that something is horribly wrong. The following shots of the simple, white painted village, Accendura, contradict what is happening underneath the surface — a surface innocence that will soon be shattered by a succession of terrible events. The final shot of the sequence is of young boys in church waiting for confession. They are overlooked by a "Grim Reaper" statue in the dark confines of the church, suggesting what is in store for them. It soon becomes apparent that the boys are also not as innocent as they might seem — they smoke and are fascinated by the opposite sex. For example, after confession they go to spy on out-of-town prostitutes having sex with two local men in an old building.

Throughout the film there are similar scenes that continue to expand on the themes of sexuality and the corruption of innocence. In relation to this Fulci often intercuts shots of sacred imagery with profane, constantly drawing parallels between Catholicism and elements of "black magic." For example, shots of Maciara, the local "witch," sticking pins into wax figures are intercut with sounds and images of young Bruno in church, where there are numerous lit candles. Maciara's room is then paralleled with the church images — her table is laid out like an altar and also has many lit candles. This "altar" is strewn with prayer cards featuring typical Catholic images, for example, the Virgin Mary, Madonna and child, and the crucifixion. As Stephen Thrower suggests, this kind of imagery "recalls the development of voodoo where African magic and Catholicism blended together, despite the organised church's disapproval" (97). This combination of both sacred and profane imagery gives way to young Michele being told to take a cold drink to Patrizia (who has recently returned to Accendura from the city). He discovers her naked, reclining under a sun lamp, and she teases him provocatively. When he says, "I'm coming — I don't want to spill it!" the sexual innuendo is all too apparent. The pedophilic undertones, and therefore corruption of innocence, become overt when Patrizia says, "Would you like to go to bed with me?" It is unclear as to whether she is simply teasing or if there is a hint of actual desire, but certainly Michele's eventual demise is related to his fascination with Patrizia. Later in the film, he mistakenly believes that she has asked him to meet her at night, and this is when he is murdered — but not before his friend, Bruno, has been murdered first.

Bruno has been missing for three days when his body is discovered buried in the woods — a scene which parallels the opening scene of Maciara digging up the skeleton of her own dead child. This effectively draws together the theme of innocence shattered by adult, outer forces, and it is further compounded by the arrival of Don Alberto. He is surrounded by a group of Bruno's friends, which on first viewing seems to be a sign of solidarity, but on reflection it is a cryptic lesson for the boys — they will be brutally punished if they stray from the path of innocence. Don Alberto is not a suspect at this point in the film, and Fulci takes the opportunity to present typical *giallo* red herrings in the form of Giuseppe, the "village idiot," and Maciara — both of whom suffer the bigotry of the villagers, mistakenly believing they are involved in the murders. Fulci also constantly reminds us of the archaic space of the village with long panning and tracking shots, which serve to underline the archaic beliefs of Don Alberto by representing Accendura as a place trapped in the past. His twisted and reactionary attitude is also compared to that of the bigoted inhabitants of the village — suggesting that his transgressions are neither worse nor better than theirs. The other key cinematic device, which Fulci uses to reinforce his themes, is the flashback. For example, when Torino's body is discovered in a water trough it is bloated and almost unrecognizable, his identity established by a brief flashback to his smiling face from earlier in the film. This may seem insignificant other than to establish identity, but in fact it supports the positioning of the boys as innocents, and it is a device that is used to this effect again at the end of the film.

As the narrative progresses, information about the killer is revealed by the police. The victims have not been molested before being killed and therefore the crime does not appear to be sexually motivated. Stephen Thrower doubts this and claims that, Don Alberto's crimes are "the evidence of repressed pederastic desires" (97). This is a rather obvious and somewhat trite reading, no doubt encouraged by recent revelations of priests being involved in sexual abuse. Thrower uses the fact that the boys have been strangled to support this claim, by noting that strangulation can be a sexualized crime.[5] However, this reading of Don Alberto's motive is problematic when considering the context of his crimes. He has to kill as quickly and quietly as possible out of necessity — Accendura is a small place, and suspicion would be easily aroused. Therefore strangulation is the most appropriate method, as "this mode of death ... [usually requires] a large disparity in physical strength between the assailant and victim."[6] There is certainly a disparity in physical strength between Don Alberto and the boys, so this is a practical solution rather than an expression of perverted desire. Furthermore, we are not witness to the killings, so there is no visible evidence for Thrower's claims either. It is therefore difficult to see Don Alberto's crimes as motivated by anything other than a horror of the corrupting influence of outside forces on the boys. In terms of narrative logic he is not a pedophile, it is rather that he cannot abide the thought of the boys becoming corrupted through engaging in sexual activity. The boys' interest in sexual matters is seemingly triggered by the arrival of outsiders in the small town, such as Patrizia and the prostitutes. Furthermore, as the murders only seem to have begun recently, this supports Koven's claim that Don Alberto kills the boys because their innocence is being corrupted by the outside world invading the space of Accendura. As I have already argued, the ways of the outside world are also encroaching on Don Alberto's own view of Catholic doctrine and ultimately will have an effect on his profession. This is highlighted when Patrizia asks him provocatively, "Well Don Alberto, what have they decided in Rome? Can you get married yet?"

Despite being insane, Don Alberto has not always been a murderer. Therefore it makes sense to argue that his sudden murder spree relates to these changes to his town and his life, rather than his own repressed desire for the boys as Thrower has claimed. Logically, if he were a pedophile, surely the murders would have been triggered sooner? This is further supported during a conversation between Don Alberto and the reporter, Martelli. Don Alberto suggests that the real culprit "is our would-be liberalism." This clearly hints at the motive behind his crimes, and it is reinforced when he makes it clear that he has dissuaded the local news vendor from selling "certain magazines" — another "arrival" from out of town bringing with it corruption.

The final revelation that Don Alberto is the murderer appears to be triggered by the murders of Michele and Mario — the last of the initial group of boys. As is common with serial killers the murders become closer together and intensify, and often come to an end with the killer revealing him or herself. After a struggle with Martelli, Don Alberto falls from a cliff, and an internal diegetic voice-over relates his warped reasoning for the murders, "It's not for myself that I do this — it is for them — for all those blessed innocent ones. I have to save them. They grow up — they feel the stirrings of the flesh and fall into the arms of sin."

The voice-over is accompanied by slow motion shots of the boys playing soccer. They are a clichéd picture of angelic innocence, dressed all in white. This sequence presents Don Alberto's "perfect" vision of them, and is not an actual flashback, so it serves to highlight the theme of innocence in a rather ironic way. A final flashback shows Don Alberto crying after killing one of the boys. He makes the sign of the cross over the body and absolves him of sin. This final sequence effectively binds together all the themes present in the narrative by referring to the sacrament of confession. Don Alberto cannot abide the thought of the boys no longer coming to confession and thereby not receiving absolution for their sins — better to preserve their innocence by killing them before they become corrupted! The Catholic Church teaches that the purpose of confession (now referred to as the sacrament of reconciliation) is "to acknowledge our sins, to repent of them, and to ask God's forgiveness. Then, in the sacrament of confession, grace can be restored to our souls, and we can once again resist sin."[7] Don Alberto's faith in the ritual of confession allows him to justify the killings to himself—despite the fact that he is the sinner—and by assuming that the boys will no longer go to confession and receive absolution for their sins, he believes he is protecting them from the torments of hell.

Stephen Thrower argues that "[the film] chillingly uncovers the sickness of the Catholic church's hatred of sexuality" (87) and certainly Fulci places the emphasis on this aspect of the church's doctrine, most probably due to his own problematic relationship with Catholicism. However, this alone cannot account for Fulci making the killer a Catholic priest and, as with many *giallo* movies, some elements in the story are only loosely explained. One thing we do learn is that Don Alberto's father killed himself. Suicide is regarded as a sin in the Catholic Church, and it could be argued therefore that he was traumatized to such a degree that he went insane attempting to reconcile his own Catholic beliefs with the "sin" committed by his father. As this is never explicated further it may not appear to have much credence as an analysis of Don Alberto's insanity, but equally, there is no evidence that he is motivated to kill due to a repressed desire for young boys.[8]

It is also possible that the explanation may be more prosaic and relate to the generic conventions of the *giallo*. The killer priest could simply be a convenient character to include in a *giallo* narrative — in the sense that their main purpose is to function as a form of "whodunit" featuring scenes of sex and violence. In the 1970s, a Catholic priest would be the last suspect for most viewers (although times have unfortunately changed in this regard), and the explanation for him killing in this case is logical in relation to his twisted take on Catholic doctrine. The film also works as a taboo-trashing exercise by making such a revered and trusted figure the culprit. In light of this, Antonio Bido notes that he employed the killer priest character in his film, *The Bloodstained Shadow*, because,

> The killer priest amused me because it was a way of saying that not all priests are saints. In short, there are priests capable of committing murder. I don't know but it's possible. Certainly there have been priests who have violated boys and girls and things like that. In a certain sense I did it to be a little blasphemous" ["Solamente Bido"].

Similarly, Pete Walker's *House of Mortal Sin* features a killer priest, Father Meldrum, who is motivated to murder his own parishioners for twisted reasons associated with innocence and sexuality, rather like Don Alberto. Steve Chibnall claims that "Father Meldrum is a pillar of the community who has been warped and cracked by maternal control and sexual denial" (Chibnall 164) and this is made more explicit as the narrative progresses, to the point where he commits matricide. Notably, despite Walker's own difficult relationship with the Catholic Church (Chibnall 157) he does not simply present a one-sided critique or an out-and-out attack on Catholicism. Indeed, he contrasts Meldrum's irrational and repressive views with Father Bernard Cutler's rational and progressive attitude throughout the film. However, although Walker's film has a somewhat balanced perspective, in many ways it is more openly taboo-trashing than Fulci's. This is mainly due to Meldrum's killings being presented with blatant relish by Walker, and also the fact that he is allowed to remain unpunished at the close of the film.

Early in the film, the principal character, Jenny, reveals to Meldrum in confession that she has sex with her boyfriend, Terry, and also that she has had an abortion. Meldrum does not offer absolution, instead he becomes fixated on Jenny and the idea of saving her soul, which in turn triggers a murderous chain of events. In his warped state of mind, Meldrum has no desire to see the church change its attitude towards marriage and celibacy. Indeed, he pontificates regularly about corruption and the "permissiveness of society." Notably, these themes can be seen as the common thread linking all three films under discussion. Indeed celibacy, sexual promiscuity, and abortion, are all common topics of debate amongst Catholics, even in the 21st century.

Unlike Don Alberto's covert killings, Walker does not hide the fact that the priest is the villain, and actively shows him killing and enjoying it. Meldrum kills in a variety of horrible ways — scalding coffee thrown in a character's face, suffocation, poisoned communion wafers, a barbaric attack with a lit censer,[9] and finally strangulation using rosary beads. Using sacred artifacts of the church as murder weapons can easily be seen as crossing into the realms of bad taste and irreverence on Walker's part, if not actual sacrilege — especially in the scenes showing the zealous nature of Meldrum's sacrificial killing of Terry with the censer[10] and his almost ecstatic strangling of Vanessa, Jenny's sister, with rosary beads. The height of bad taste is reached however when Meldrum laces the communion wafer with poison. The reception of the sacrament of the Eucharist — the eating of the host, which Catholics believe actually becomes Christ's body through the act of transubstantiation — is one of the most important rituals in the Catholic church. Desecrating the host and turning it into an instrument of murder can be interpreted as equivalent to defiling the body of Christ, and therefore it may well be read as a blasphemous representation. Meldrum even perverts the sacrament of extreme unction[11] when he gives his mother a poisoned host and anoints her with chrism as she chokes to death.[12] Arguably, the character of Meldrum is so warped that his choice of murder weapons could simply be passed off as being related to his insanity, but equally there is a sense of a desire to shock on Walker's part in these scenes.

By the end of the film Meldrum has killed, or been a factor in the deaths of, seven people. He even manages to put the blame on his housekeeper, Brabazon. As she reveals her undying love for Meldrum, he kills her and makes it appear that she is responsible for the murders. The film ends in a downbeat fashion with Father Bernard burning his resignation and leaving, Meldrum persuading him that, by covering up Brabazon's murders, "the Lord will forgive us for preserving the honour of his church." The final scene shows Meldrum pulling on his black leather gloves and preparing to go and kill Jenny. The rationale given for Meldrum's killing spree links back to his past. We discover that his mother maneuvered Meldrum into the church to keep him away from Brabazon, and hence away from committing sin. This irrational action by his mother led to his repressed sexual desires and, consequently, his warped mind. His justification for killing the girls is because they are a constant temptation for him. The other murders are a way of covering his tracks or — in the case of his matricide — a sort of frustrated revenge. Ultimately, the church's doctrine is changed by Meldrum into something perverted, just as it was by Don Alberto. Meldrum views everyone either as a permissive sinner or as a disrupter of his demented world, and therefore he uses the sacraments and symbols of Catholicism to engage in a form of twisted salvation. So, in Walker's film, we not only have a killer priest who enjoys killing, but also one who gets away with murder, unlike Don Alberto.

In Bido's *The Bloodstained Shadow* the killer priest, Don Paulo, like Don Alberto, does not get away with murder and dies at the end of the film — indeed, he pays for his own transgressions, unlike Meldrum. This is probably related to the fact that these are *giallo* movies and the killer has to be revealed and punished at the end of the film — even more appropriate when the killer is a Catholic priest. In the case of Don Paulo, he actively brings about his own death due to his torment and guilt over the murders. As Michael Mackenzie comments, "Father Paolo is himself revealed to be an extremely conflicted man: someone capable of murdering people in some of the most brutal ways imaginable, but all the time wracked with guilt" (MacKenzie). This is different from both Don Alberto and Meldrum, as they show no remorse for their killings and zealously justify them. Don Paulo kills in order to prevent the revelation of his earlier murder of a young girl (for which there is no explanation given), and yet he also states early on in the film that he regards these characters as transgressors — a doctor who was not convicted for his wife's murder, a woman who performs illegal abortions, and a rich pedophile, whom he describes as "a man without morals. It might be better if he'd disappear from the face of the earth. He's a mortal sinner." So perhaps there is a certain sense of justification by Don Paulo — he is covering his own tracks, but getting rid of immoral people at the same time!

The final sequence of the film sees Don Paulo confessing his sins to his brother, Stefano, in the church. Stefano says that he should have confessed the earlier murder, but Don Paulo believes that he would never have been forgiven. In a vision (or hallucination?) he witnesses himself giving communion to all the people he has killed, and sees the judgemental stares of the rest of the congregation. Believing that he has no way out of his desperate situation, he runs away to the nearby tower and throws himself from the top. This act of suicide, rather than confession and absolution, suggests that Don Paulo is quite a different character from Don Alberto and Father Meldrum. He is tormented by guilt over his acts of mortal sin and cannot live with himself, whereas Don Alberto and Meldrum show no remorse or guilt over what they have done. However, Don Paulo can see no way out of the trap he has created for himself, and also no way of assuaging his guilt. Therefore, tragically, he does not have faith in the sacrament of confession and the subsequent absolution that this offers, despite his devotion to the church, his parishioners, and his faith.

In conclusion, what is the actual purpose of the killer priest figure in these films and perhaps others? Firstly, it is a convenient and ingenious device used in the *giallo* movies to throw viewers off the scent of the murderer — a Catholic priest, in the 1970s, was an unlikely suspect. . Secondly, these three films featuring Catholic priests as twisted killers, rather than as trustworthy protectors of the vulnerable and innocent, also functioned as a taboo-trashing exercise for the filmmakers — the graphic murders and downbeat endings tapped into the misanthropic nature of the time. Thirdly, the killer priest can be seen as a general representative of the more repressive aspects of Catholic doctrine, for example, attitudes to the expression of sexual desire, celibacy for priests, contraception, and abortion. Indeed, when we also consider the recent revelations of sexual abuse covered up by church hierarchy, this figure takes on a significant metaphoric dimension and thus functions as a possible response to, and representation of, any aspect of the church which is either considered reactionary or, more shockingly, corrupt. In the final analysis, all these aspects combined can help to explain the existence of the killer priest figure. Representing someone who should be above corruption as corrupt, serves to remind us that we are all human, and therefore we are all capable of sin — including Catholic priests.

Notes

1. The term *giallo*—literally meaning "yellow"—stems from the violent Italian thriller stories which were published with lurid yellow covers. It was a term which became used for the cycle of movies beginning with Mario Bava's *Blood and Black Lace* (1964), which featured many of the key aspects now associated with these films, for example, the black gloved killer, a "whodunit" narrative, scenes of excessive violence, and often sexually provocative images.
2. This potential is realized in a gory fashion in *House of Mortal Sin*.
3. Information on Bido from the interview *Solamente Bido* included in the DVD extras for *The Bloodstained Shadow* (released by Blue Underground, 2008).
4. Walker is also notable for representing other supposedly morally upstanding members of the community as perverted and murderous in his films, such as judges and mother figures, while Fulci is notorious for his group of extremely gory horror films made in the 1970s and 1980s.
5. An obvious example of this would be the crimes of the notorious Boston Strangler in Boston, Massachusetts, in the early 1960s.
6. http://www.forensicmed.co.uk/strangulation.htm (accessed 3 March 2010).
7. Http://catholicism.about.com/od/beliefsteachings/p/Why_Confession.htm (accessed 24 September 2009).
8. Thrower's analysis of the film does not mention the suicide of Don Alberto's father at all.
9. Censers are any type of vessels made for burning incense, however, "in the Roman Catholic church a censer is often called a thurible," http://en.wikipedia.org/wiki/Censer (accessed 24 September 2009).
10. Note that the etymology of the word "thurible" derives from Greek "thuein" which means "to sacrifice," http://en.wikipedia.org/wiki/Thurible (accessed 24 September 2009). When Meldrum kills Terry it can be read as a sacrifice, made in order to "save" Jenny from sin.
11. Now known as Anointing of the Sick, but used to be known as extreme unction (commonly known as giving the last rites), that is the absolution of all sins for those who were in the process of dying. The sacrament can now be used for those who are seriously ill.
12. Consecrated oil, scented with balsam, and used in several Catholic rituals.

Works Cited

The Bloodstained Shadow. Dir. Antonio Bido. Perf. Lino Capolicchio, Stefania Casini, Craig Hill. Produzione Atlas Consorziate, 1978. Film.
Chibnall, Steve. "A Heritage of Evil: Pete Walker and the Politics of Gothic Revisionism." *British Horror Cinema.* Eds. Steve Chibnall and Julian Petley. Oxon: Routledge, 2002.
Don't Torture a Duckling. Dir. Lucio Fulci. Perf. Florinda Bolkan, Barbara Bouchet, Thomas Milian. Medusa Produzione, 1972. Film.
House of Mortal Sin. Dir. Pete Walker. Perf. Anthony Sharp, Susan Penhaligon, Stephanie Beacham. 1976. Film.
Koven, Mikel. "Italian Horror: Space, Modernity and the *Giallo.*" *Kinoeye: New Perspectives on European Film* Vol. 3, Issue 12 (27 Oct. 2003). http://kinoeye.org/03/12/koven12.php. Accessed 31 July 2009).

MacKenzie, Michael. Review of *The Bloodstained Shadow*. http://www.dvdtimes.co.uk/content.php?contentid+58973. Accessed 25 January 2010.
Solamente Bido, DVD extras for *The Bloodstained Shadow*. Blue Underground, 2008.
Thrower, Stephen. *Beyond Terror: The Films of Lucio Fulci*. Guildford, Surrey: FAB Press, 1999.

Mad Drunken Exorcists
The Decline of the Hero Priest

REGINA HANSEN

In the mid 20th century, the Gothic conception of the priest villain—detailed in the introduction to this volume—started to fade away. We see this mostly in American film, first in mainstream movies like *Boys Town* and *The Bells of St. Mary's* and by the 1970s in a whole host of horror films portraying Catholic priests as at least conflicted but well intentioned men—1976's *The Omen*—and at most as outright heroes, as in 1973's *The Exorcist*, which retains the Gothic emphasis on Catholicism, but is more fascinated than repelled by it. Possessors of secret knowledge, whose lives revolved around a daily mystic ritual, the Mass, Catholic priests as portrayed in much of 1970s horror film fulfilled the era's sense of spiritual thirst, the desire for real magic reflected in the explosion of works of fantastic literature—with Tolkien and his imitators—and later in the pop spirituality of *Star Wars* and "The Force." If not in the real world, at least on the American horror screen, Catholic priests were like wizards, but wizards you could meet at the local bingo hall or teaching at a university. Of course, while priests were often being portrayed heroically on screen, we now know— and many people always knew — that a significant number of actual priests were behaving not as heroes but rather exactly as the predators the early Gothic novels made them out to be. Between 2001 and 2002, the *Boston Globe* began extensive coverage of the child sex abuse scandal in the Catholic Church[1]—which was in the end found to involve 11,750 alleged victims between 1950 and 2004 (Cooperman) and 4 percent of Catholic priests and deacons nationwide — and exposed a cover-up that seems a classic example of Gothic mystification. So, since the scandal, has the Gothic portrayal of the priest been revived in supernatural horror? The answer is complicated and somewhat surprising.

The *Exorcist* came out in 1973 and features many elements of Gothicized Catholicism — orientalism with the opening in Iraq, nuns in full habit walking two by two, an atmosphere of dread surrounding the more shocking moments, an ancient looking church and creepy old seemingly "haunted" house. The film tells the story of a 12-year-old girl, Regan MacNeil, who is possessed by the ancient demon Pazuzu. There are two priests. The first, Father Merrin — is older, confident in both his faith in God, his belief in the supernatural and in his emotional (though perhaps not his physical) strength to face the demon — his old enemy, whom he has faced before. The other is Father Damien Karras — psychiatrist, rationalist, beer drinker, and boxer, working-class Greek with a New York accent, who is not confident either in his faith or in the goodness of his fellow human beings. When he is asked by Chris MacNeil, Regan's desperate mother, if he knows how to procure an exorcism, he looks at her in disbelief, saying flatly, "Beg your pardon?" (*The Exorcist*) and suggesting she get herself a time machine and go back to the Middle Ages. This seems to confirm what Regan's doctor has said earlier in the film, that exorcism has been discarded as a practice, "except for the Catholics who keep it in the closet as an embarrassment" (*The Exorcist*). Of course, that is the attraction for the horror filmmaker — the rite of exorcism is, though rare, still recognized and taught in the Catholic Church today.[2] Moreover, both the novel and film were said famously to be based on the exorcism of a boy in Silver Spring Maryland in the 1940s (McDannell 208).

By the end of the film, after seeing the way the possessed child behaves, and still more importantly, under the tutelage of Father Merrin — who is unironically portrayed as a man who has battled evil spirits and knows how to face them — Father Karras becomes a believer in the power of exorcism as well. He is the one who finally saves Regan, through his own suicide/martyrdom, a scene that continues to be argued about, but that director William Friedkin has repeatedly insisted is meant to show Karras' heroism.[3] A scene in the film's denouement underlines the idea of Karras (and Merrin as well) as a priest/hero, as the recovered girl sees Karras' friend Father Dyer, recognizes his Roman collar, and embraces him. An unironic scene of a child showing physical affection to a Catholic priest would probably be difficult to find in most films today, and for good reason, given recent events. Interestingly, *The Exorcist* not only sets up Merrin and Karras as wizardly figures, possessors of secret spiritual knowledge, doers of magic, but also as protectors of a child who is being spiritually but also sexually violated by an evil force. The shocking scene with Regan and the crucifix, as well as other scenes of defilement and desecration throughout the film underline that idea. Not only does *The Exorcist* turn the old Gothic and nativist image of the villainous rapist priest on its head, but it also clearly predates the current era, in which the child sex abuse scandal and the hierarchy's cover up of it has made it difficult for many people to see a priest as a protector of children's innocence. Today, the same evil Karras sees in the Demon Pazuzu many people have seen in the Church itself.

We might expect general American filmic portrayals of Catholic priests to be much less heroic since 2002, and that would be true — films on sex abuse by priests have existed since the 1990s, notably 1992's *The Boys of St. Vincent* which dramatizes an earlier scandal involving the Catholic order of Christian Brothers in the province of Newfoundland, Canada. The outrage at the abuse scandals has appeared across genres, in police procedurals like *Law and Order*[4] and *Without a Trace*,[5] and has even served to add an element of fantastical dread to otherwise non supernatural films — for instance, *Mystic River*, in which a boy is abducted and sexually abused by two men, including one wearing the ring of a Catholic religious order. Interestingly, though, rather than returning to the more salacious aspects of Gothicized Catholicism, supernatural horror films, at least those made for a more mainstream audience (or that might be viewed by such an audience) take a more complex — if sometimes puzzling — approach to their characterization of Catholic priests. Many horror films since 2002 continue their traditional association with Catholicism, and continue to have priestly protagonists, but now the priests are often on the sidelines, having failed in their holy work. We see this in the film *Constantine*, in which Father John Henessy, played by Pruitt Taylor Vince — he of the darting eyes — appears as a drunken and dissolute priest, burnt out from performing too many exorcisms, who now needs the help of non-priest John Constantine (Keanu Reeves) to fight against evil spirits. In *The Exorcism of Emily Rose* (2005), which — like *The Exorcist* 32 years earlier — is attractive to the horror audience because it is supposedly based on true events,[6] the exorcism has resulted in the death of the girl subject. The priest — Father Moore (Tom Wilkinson) is being held for negligent homicide. Sidelined in jail throughout the movie as only a witness to the narrative, Father Moore is only at the center of the action when seen in flashback. The central role goes to his defense attorney, the agnostic Erin Bruner (Laura Linney) who, interestingly, ends the film believing Father Moore's story of demonic possession. In both cases, these priests are not viewed as villains. In fact both are portrayed as essentially good but flawed men. They are not heroes either — they are failures, both of whom have lost the ability to successfully wield the power, the secret knowledge of the rite of exorcism. While they have influence, they have no agency.

An even more complicated current portrayal of a Catholic priest in recent

American horror is 2008's *The X-Files: I Want to Believe*, the second film based on the 90's television series, a blend of horror and science fiction. (This film — in which people are abducted, decapitated and their heads reanimated on new bodies — is definitely in the horror column, and of course alludes to one of the most important of all Gothic novels, *Frankenstein*.) Our heroes, Fox Mulder and Dana Scully, are called in to investigate the disappearance of an FBI agent. They are helped to solve this crime, plus a series of murders, by Father Joe Crissman (Billy Conolly) a convicted pedophile who reports having visions that tie him to numerous abduction victims. As viewers of the television series know, Scully is a skeptic in every way but one — she is a believing Catholic who in the film works at a Catholic hospital where she has to deal with a more mundane priestly villain, the bureaucrat Father Ybarra. In meeting Father Joe for the first time, Scully represents the voice of public outrage over the sex abuse scandal, refusing to accept either his visions or his self-stated repentance. Father Joe, on the other hand, sees his psychic visions as a way to redeem his past sins against the innocent boys he raped — perhaps a chance to redeem his priest hero status.

Like Father Henessy and Father Moore, Father Joe is not the center of the story. Like them, he is a failure (we meet him in his bathrobe saying a Rosary while a rerun of the 1970's sitcom *The Jeffersons* plays in the background). He has lost his sacramental right to priestly power through his vile crimes — he has been defrocked — but is even more than symbolically neutralized, since as he tells Scully, he castrated himself when he was 27 to try to control is pedophilic urges. He has neither magical nor masculine power. Still, the filmmakers do not seem to want to simply dispense with him. With his visions, Father Joe provides the film's central and sole supernatural element (unless we want to include the reanimated heads — but that is supposed to be science). He has psychic links with various victims throughout the film, links that even allow him to physically suffer what they are suffering. He develops lung cancer because one character has it and even dies at the same moment a character he is connected with dies. Mulder — who famously in the series believes in everything except Catholicism — finds one of the abducted women because he listens to Father Joe, and uncovers the film's whole abduction/decapitation/reanimation plot through following Father Joe's visions. Moreover, Scully is inspired to pursue aggressive treatment on one of her patients — not coincidentally a young boy of the age of Father Joe's victims — through the priest's admonition, "Don't give up" (*The X-Files: I Want to Believe*).

Though sidelined, Father Joe is given a lot of power in the film's narrative. In one of the film's closing scenes, Mulder and Scully even discuss the possibility of Father Joe's redemption:

SCULLY: "He told me ... don't give up, and I didn't, and it saved your life, but I put that boy through Hell, and I have another surgery scheduled for this morning, because I believed that God was telling me to ... through a pedophile priest, no less."
MULDER: "What if Father Joe's prayers were answered after all? What if he were forgiven, because he didn't give up?" (*The X-Files: I Want to Believe*)

Through the words of the main characters, the filmmakers seem to be allowing at least the possibility that the villain priest, whose crimes fulfill all the fears of the Gothic novelists and sadly also reflect present-day events, could be redeemed, and not only by his own repentance but through supernatural means. This plotline not only echoes Father Karras's regaining his faith at the end of *The Exorcist* but also actually reflects a real but for many people problematic element of Christian theology — especially Catholicism with its sacrament of Reconciliation/Confession — that anyone, even the vilest criminal and violator of innocence, can be redeemed, if they are genuinely contrite and perform the appropriate penance.[7] In the commentary to the DVD of the film, Chris Carter goes so far as to remark, "Father Joe is a vile character, but you kind of like him" (Carter). While one might question the possibility of "liking" such a character, the film — though in many ways flawed — offers a challenging portrayal of the Catholic understanding of redemption and divine forgiveness.

It remains to wonder why these recent American horror filmmakers have chosen not to vilify but simply demote and defang their priestly characters, or why even when they present us with a priestly villain they choose to potentially redeem him. There are plenty of villain priests in other genres. Moreover, in this volume, David Annandale, Shelley O'Brien and Christa Jones have shown us villain priests right out of the Gothic tradition in films from Spain, Italy and France. Still, those are historically Catholic countries. Maybe filmmakers there feel on firmer ground in their portrayals. Maybe American supernatural horror still "believes" in the secret and mystical elements of Catholicism enough to want to keep all options open for plot devices. Maybe these portrayals reflect a decline in the influence of organized religion. Whatever the case, the films above reflect yet another element of film's complex attitude toward the Catholic fantastic.

Notes

1. For an archive of the *Boston Globe*'s coverage of the scandal see http://www.boston.com/globe/spotlight/abuse/betrayal/.

2. Regarding the practice of exorcism, *The Catechism of the Catholic Church* states the following: "When the Church asks publicly and authoritatively in the name of Jesus Christ that a person or object be protected against the power of the Evil One

and withdrawn from his dominion, it is called exorcism. Jesus performed exorcisms and from him the Church has received the power and office of exorcizing. In a simple form, exorcism is performed at the celebration of Baptism. The solemn exorcism, called 'a major exorcism,' can be performed only by a priest and with the permission of the bishop. The priest must proceed with prudence, strictly observing the rules established by the Church. Exorcism is directed at the expulsion of demons or to the liberation from demonic possession through the spiritual authority which Jesus entrusted to his Church. Illness, especially psychological illness, is a very different matter; treating this is the concern of medical science. Therefore, before an exorcism is performed, it is important to ascertain That one is dealing with the presence of the Evil One, and not an illness (par. 1673).

3. In the 2000 DVD re-release of the film Father Karras's face morphs so you can more clearly see that he has chosen to save the child by killing himself. Friedkin made this addition as a way to remove doubt that what Karras has done is become a martyr, rather than simply commit suicide. The director has stated repeatedly that, although, people have a choice to think what they want about the ending, his intention (and that of the novelist/screenwriter William Peter Blatty) is to show Karras sacrificing himself for the sake of an innocent child, to save both her body and her soul, and thus also redeeming his own faith before he dies (Friedkin).

4. See "Revelations," *Without a Trace*, by Hank Steinberg, Perf. Anthony LaPaglia, Hector Elizondo, Poppy Montgomery. CBS, 2 October 2003.

5. See "Silence," *Law and Order: SVU*, by Dick Wolf, Perf. Christopher Meloni, Mariska Hargitay, Eric Stoltz. NBC, 17 May 2002.

6. The film is allegedly based on the story of a German woman named Anneliese Michel, but the interpretation is considered loose at best. See Sean Axmaker, "*Exorcism of Emily Rose* Strays Far from the True Story," *Seattle Post-Intelligencer* 9 September 2005, www.seattlepi.com/movies/239920_emily09q.html.

7. With regard to the spiritual effects of repentance, see *The Catechism of the Catholic Church* on the Sacrament of Reconciliation:

One who desires to obtain reconciliation with God and with the Church, must confess to a priest all the unconfessed grave sins he remembers after having carefully examined his conscience. The confession of venial faults, without being necessary in itself, is nevertheless strongly recommended by the Church" [par. 1493].

Also:

The spiritual effects of the sacrament of Penance are:
- reconciliation with God by which the penitent recovers grace;
- reconciliation with the Church;
- remission of the eternal punishment incurred by mortal sins;
- remission, at least in part, of temporal punishments resulting from sin;
- peace and serenity of conscience, and spiritual consolation;
- an increase of spiritual strength for the Christian battle [par. 1496].

Works Cited

The Boys of St. Vincent. Dir. John N. Smith. Perf. Henry Czerny, Johnny Morina, Brian Dooley. Canadian Broadcasting Corporation, 1992. Film.

Carter, Chris. "DVD Commentary for *The X-Files: I Want to Believe*." Twentieth Century–Fox, 2008. DVD.

Catechism of the Catholic Church. Tr. Libreria Editrice Vaticana. Liguori, MO: Liguori Publications, 1994.

Constantine. Dir. Frances Lawrence. Perf. Keanu Reeves, Pruitt Taylor Vince, Rachel Weisz. Warner Bros., 2005. Film.
Cooperman, Alan. "In 2004, 1000 Alleged Abuse by Priests." *Washington Post*, 19 February 2005. www.washingtonpost.com/wp-dyn/articles/A36324-2005Feb18.html.
The Exorcism of Emily Rose. Dir. Scott Derrickson. Perf. Laura Linney, Tom Wilkinson, Campbell Scott. Screen Gems, 2005. Film.
The Exorcist. Dir. William Friedkin. Perf. Ellen Burstyn, Linda Blair, Max von Sydow, Jason Miller. 1973. Warner Bros., 1998. DVD.
Friedkin, William. "DVD Commentary for *The Exorcist*." Warner Bros., 1998. DVD.
Mystic River. Dir. Clint Eastwood. Perf. Sean Penn, Tim Robbins, Kevin Bacon. Warner Bros., 2003.
Van Wormer, Kathryn. "Priest Abuse: Male Compared to Female Victimization Impact." *Psychology Today; Crimes of Violence: Analysis of High Profile Crimes of Violence of Psychological Significance*. 20 May 2010. Blog. http://www.psychology today.com/blog/crimes-violence/201005/priest-abuse-male-compared-female-victimization-impact.
The X-Files: I Want to Believe. Dir. Chris Carter. Perf. David Duchovny, Gillian Anderson, Billy Connolly. Twentieth Century–Fox, 2008. Film.

Otherness in *The Others*
Haunting the Catholic Other, Humanizing the Self

ANABEL ALTEMIR GIRAL *and*
ISMAEL IBÁÑEZ ROSALES

The Others (2001) is a psychological horror film by the Spanish director Alejandro Amenábar. The scene is set on the secluded Isle of Jersey in the immediate aftermath of World War II. Grace, the protagonist, is a strict Catholic mother who lives with her two small children, Anne and Nicholas, in a remote country mansion waiting for her husband to return from war. The children have an uncommon disease characterized by photosensitivity, so their lives are structured around a series of complex rules designed to protect them from exposure to sunlight. Curtains must be drawn at all times, and to ensure that no crack of light slips in accidentally, Grace carries with her a clanking ring of keys and locks every door behind her before she moves on to another room. The unlikely possibility of her husband's return, the malady of her children and the fact that the servants mysteriously disappeared make Grace's life desperate as she struggles to maintain her respectable household and her sanity. Three new servants arrive unexpectedly at the house to apply for the newly vacant positions. Housekeeper Mrs. Mills, mute maid Lydia and yard man Mr. Tuttle make up this eerie trio whose presence only increases tension and suspense while the audience try to focus on the real story: Grace's house seems to be haunted.

In particular, Anne is the first to notice "the intruders" and she even sketches them; Grace refuses to believe in ghosts but the evidence of another presence in the house grows too strong to ignore. Eventually convincing herself that they are not alone, Grace blames the servants for perpetrating some kind of hoax. So she decides to banish them from the house. However, locking the servants out only traps her inside with the intruders, which forces a confrontation that finally reveals the mystery behind the haunting.

The narrative of the film tells a problem of identity out of a lack apparently provoked by some dire circumstances, though not improbable, and a subplot in which elements of Roman Catholicism are negotiated in a fantastic setting. The film manages to create a haunted house story that takes all Gothic standard clichés — dark shadows, slamming doors, eerie voices, endless rooms, old graves — but the explicit and abundant use of these tropes leads the spectators' attention to the main narrative of the film: Grace's character development and the subsequent changing perception of herself. She appears as a fervent Catholic determined to stick to her faith in spite of the dramatic turns her life has suddenly taken. This move on the part of the director exposes the Catholic background that looms over the whole film and which defines Grace's attitude. By means of parody the excessive use of classic Gothic elements turns the horror scenes into the perfect locus where the main narrative, that is, Grace's search for identity, takes place. This clash of text and image gives the supernatural a familiar context introducing a sense of the uncanny. According to Botting, "the Gothic signifies a writing of excess ... [which] shadows the despairing ecstasies of Romantic idealism and individualism and the uncanny duality of Victorian realism and decadence" (1). Amenábar masterfully builds his film around a literary and historical Gothic context and on the other hand, combines his story with modern theories of Gothic such as those of Miles who claims that "the Gothic is ... a discursive site, a carnivalesque mode for representations of the fragmented subject" (28). From this angle, the film focuses on Grace's reconstruction of her own identity which is presented as an inner struggle between her predetermined Catholic beliefs and her unconscious refusal to accept her newly acquired condition.

The storytelling follows the Gothic framework in terms of constant oppositions: light and darkness, past and present, good and evil, male and female, human and monstrous, life and death and self and other. These confrontations can also be applied to the Catholic background as elements that constrain Grace's subjectivity as a result of her unnatural way of internalizing Catholic doctrines. Therefore the film develops this idea by the recurrent inversion of Catholic sacraments thus mirroring Grace's misconception of reality. In this line of argument Greeley states:

> Catholics live in an enchanted world, a world of statues and holy water, stained glass and votive candles, saints and religious medals, rosary beads and holy pictures. But this Catholic paraphernalia are mere hints of a deeper and more

pervasive religious sensibility which inclines Catholics to see the Holy lurking in creation. As Catholics we find our houses and our world haunted by a sense that the objects, events, and persons of daily life are revelations of grace [1].

However, considering herself a righteous Catholic, Grace seems unable to admit any manifestation of this "enchanted world" whose acceptance would mean that her earthly existence ended. The way she assumes and teaches her Catholic faith to her children through a personal interpretation and control of the norms leads her to haunt the Catholic as if it were an "other" instead of permitting herself to be haunted by the Catholic. So the objects, events, and persons of daily life in the house are not revelations of divine grace any more but mere "revelations of Grace." According to this, Catholic imagination is sacramental because Catholics can see created reality as a "'sacrament,' that is, a revelation of the presence of God. The workings of this imagination are most obvious in the Church's seven sacraments" (Greeley 1).

The film starts with a horrific scream. Grace seems to be awakening from a nightmare. With the camera close on her extremely pale face, she gasps for breath and then composes herself. Thus, Grace's "primal scream" represents her birth to a new form of existence and the bright light that covers her, when she appears dressed in white for the first and last time in the film, symbolizes her ceremony of baptism. According to Christian doctrine, through the sacrament of baptism people not only are freed from original sin and accepted as members of the Church but also are born to a life during which they will have to achieve God's grace. The problem is that the whole baptism scene seems to be an inversion of the sacrament since Grace, as we learn at the end of the film, is not being born to life but to some sort of otherworldly life.

Grace's obsessive observance of Catholic dogmas is based on fear which works as a driving force that severely represses and deprives her of her own identity. Besides, the dramatic circumstances that have recently taken place in her life push her to the limit thus resulting in her fall from grace. In other words, what she finds is not what she expects but the materialization of her terrors since her desire to live an extremely dogmatic Catholic life forces her to have a blurred conception of reality, thus living a gloomy and an almost spectral existence. The physical death of Grace's character stands for the symbolic death of her selfhood. As Beville puts it, "selfhood is a potential site for sublime experience, not just in the sense of the Gothic sublime as it relates to terror of death, but also in the sense of postmodernist terror as it relates to symbolic death" (95).

In this line of argument, Grace gets trapped in an "otherworldly experience" where she will be able to face her fears and past in order to become aware of her own identity. This experience may be considered as a "'third space' in literary representation, a site for fluctuations and metamorphoses, for labyrinths and the births of monsters" (Beville 96).

The first scene merges with the servants' laughs approaching the house. The fact of being present without being seen on screen makes clear their ghostly nature. As soon as they appear on the doorstep, they are portrayed as "other." In this way, the servants immediately focus the audience attention, arousing our concern about who they really are and what they are up to thus metaphorically invading Grace's space. Mrs. Mills' character exemplifies this invasion because she not only leads the crew of servants but also hovers in the hallways quietly observing everything Grace does. Soon Grace begins to resent, and feels alienated and judged by, Mrs. Mills, thus inverting both the class system order and the familial and domestic roles. This interference in the familial environment is a commonly used device by Gothic narratives to expose the vulnerability of one of the most traditional and powerful structures, the family understood as the only place where we feel completely safe:

> Although narratives of darkness ... may appear to suggest that the family is an all-powerful conglomerate, they also consistently present it as vulnerable to alien intrusions that threaten to rescind its authority at a moment's notice. The penetration of the familial space by disruptive forces has asserted itself as a familiar topos of suspense and horror cinema over the past few decades [Cavallaro 141–142].

The more Grace attempts to control the servants in taking care of both her family and home, the more she feels her authority is being threatened. Therefore, a rivalry is established between Grace and Mrs. Mills to occupy the predominant maternal position within the domestic structure. Narratives informed by Gothic motifs "use rivalries between women as self-perpetuating ruses. By extension, the female child and femininity itself come to be associated with evil as both the perpetrators and the victims of extreme atrocities" (Cavallaro 143). Mrs. Mills' main role in the film is to help Grace become aware of "the extreme atrocity" she has committed and the consequences her actions have brought about. So Mrs. Mills acts as a sort of comforter and spiritual guide who helps Grace to confront her destiny and face her fears. For this reason Grace simultaneously resents and depends on Mrs. Mills, who becomes her only confidante in the house. A parallelism can be established here between the Catholic confessor and the sinner as Mrs. Mills and Grace exemplify in the scene by the fireplace. Grace invites Mrs. Mills to sit by the fire. Although Grace is the actual owner of the house, Mrs. Mills seems to know everything about it and talks about the house as if she had never left it:

> MRS. MILLS: "Actually, we left too. Although when you leave a place ... it's like it's there with you, all the time. I always felt like I never left this house."

In the Gothic, the Haunted House is almost a character in its own right; in *The Others*, however, the mansion is obsessively controlled by Grace and, at the same time, imprisons its inhabitants. Her children's disease and the war have confined Grace in the isolated mansion which she used to share with her family and husband. Thus, deprived of any patriarchal authority and relegated to the "walled-in realm" of her home, Grace tries to control the house as an attempt to come to terms with her identity. Cavallaro comments on Gaston Bachelard's reflections on the affective properties of space; she argues that "the home is the point of departure of our negotiations between the inner realm and the circumambient universe. The parental residence may seem safe and comforting in comparison with the mysterious outside but its protective enclosures tend to breed not so much security as anxiety" (Cavallaro 147). Grace becomes a neo-gothic heroine whose confinement within the patriarchal structure of the house seems to infantilize her. This can be observed in the scene where she runs outside in search of her husband who, after his short visit has vanished again, and she stops in front of the iron gate. The shot from the other side of the gate pictures her literally imprisoned and her face looks like that of a scared little girl. According to Horner, "the heroine's attempts to escape from home indicate a desire to subvert a domestic ideology" (116). Traditionally, from a Roman Catholic perspective the house has been considered a patriarchal property and representation; therefore a parallelism may be established between the house as a familiar/familial space and the house as the Church, that is, the "Father's property." Thus, Grace not only feels imprisoned within her home walls but also within her strict Catholic belief which makes her unable to see alternative ways to evince it.

Anne and Nicholas are victims of their mother's troubled psyche. She uses them to project her fears and to continue her unnatural way of understanding Catholic doctrines as if they were somehow predetermined. The children become extensions of their mother and work hard at the school lessons and memorize Bible passages in order to please her. Most of the time, they whisper about their mother's recent "breakdown" and start to contact the "intruders." In particular, Anne is the first to interact with them, probably because she refuses to become a mere extension of her mother's psyche. The subverting role that Anne plays shows the perfect counter-narrative to Grace's symbolic blindness. Earlier in the film, we see how Anne questions the way her mother understands Biblical passages and a belief based on a constant fear of walking an alternative path to what is written or stated traditionally. While Grace is constantly preventing the light from slipping in, walking around with the clanking sound of the huge ring of keys as if she were a classical ghost, Anne opens her mind to the differences that her new condition implies.

This is clear in the scene where Anne tries on her First Communion dress. When Grace comes back to Anne's bedroom, she finds her daughter sitting on the floor playing with a puppet. Anne then turns her face to Grace and what her mother sees is the face of a blind old woman. On a second viewing of the film we learn that Anne is haunting the old woman, the medium in the séance. According to Warner,

> [Children tend to] make fun of intimidation and turn its threats hollow ... to play the bogeyman and scare themselves into fits. The pretence appears to match the observed pleasure in fright that children take: it defies fear at the very same moment as conjuring it. It exemplifies a defensive response that is frequently adopted in real experience: internalizing the aggressor in order to stave off the terror he brings [168–169].

This means that Anne has finally transcended the limitations of her ghostly state thus being unconsciously able to see the light. From Grace's perspective, however, the scene is a sort of mirror where she can face herself inverting the First Communion sacrament. She sees the loss of purity — an old woman in a white dress — while pulling the strings of her daughter's puppet. Unable to accept the idea, Grace attacks Anne, shouting, "You are not my daughter." However, she finds that she has actually attacked her daughter instead. Anne refuses to be near her mother. Mrs. Mills, usurping the maternal role and taking Anne's side, tells the girl that she too has seen the intruders but they cannot tell Grace because she will not accept what she is not ready for. As Mackenzie points out, "we use our kids to uncover uncomfortable truths that we don't dare to look at ourselves" because children know that "the nightmare is real [and] are much more prepared to confront these issues than adults" (16). Image and narrative merge in this scene to show how Grace is not able to understand the sacramental Catholic imagination. Thus Grace is caught between the desire to discover her new self and the fear of facing the monstrous other, which would mean death and consequently eternal damnation.

Grace constantly tries to erase the horrible memories of her "breakdown" refusing to see any alternative consequence but the one imagined by her. She has made up a convenient result to that macabre day: she thinks that God has granted her a second chance because she cannot face the idea of an end, the idea of death without God's grace. The first time that Grace begins to be aware of her numinous condition is during the scene in the attic. She goes upstairs and stops in front of the attic door. She can hear sounds inside and bright rays of light slip in under the door. When Grace enters the room she is scared of the sheets that cover furniture and images. In the same way that we feel along the film, she is afraid of what she cannot see. Suddenly, she feels a presence and steps backwards. Something touches her back: it is a Catholic statue. Quickly she turns round and uncovers the rest of things when she discovers a mirror. She stays looking at herself in the mirror for a while. Her expression tells us that she is looking at an "other" version of herself. As Cavallaro argues following the Lacanian concept of the mirror stage, "the mirror carries ambivalent connotations by operating as a metaphorical door to an alternative realm on the one hand, and by imprisoning the subject in the cage of her own narcissism on the other" (144). In the scene resembling a "madwoman in the attic" motif, Grace becomes framed as if driven inward trying to obtain a viable self but eventually finding oneself as belonging to an unknown Other. In other words, Grace experiences the horror of being aware that she has become someone else. Cavallaro goes on to say that "[the] specular image [is presented] as an illusory self and by ultimately making the image projected by the mirror literally and devastatingly alien" (144). Returning to the house as a metaphor of the Church, it is relevant that Grace's close encounter with her "other self" takes place in the attic as the high place at the top of the house. Similarly, in the structure of the Church, God occupies the highest position and it is precisely a religious statue "who" touches her so that she can find the mirror.

The scene plays with our deepest fears since most people have been in a similar place and have felt the same terror for things covered with sheets displaying the traditional image of the ghost. The same happens with religious statues. They can incite more fear than devotion in children and this unconscious feeling may endure through our adulthood. These frightening scenes are produced by hiding anxieties within the subject. Following Freud's theory of the uncanny, Jackson argues that the uncanny works at two levels functioning as a series of dualisms: things that are homely and familiar and their opposite, namely, unfamiliar, strange and alien. At a second level, the uncanny also means that which is concealed, secreted, hidden, and obscure; its negation functions to discover areas normally kept out of sight. "The uncanny combines these two semantic levels: its signification lies precisely in this dualism. It uncovers what is hidden and, by doing so, effects a disturbing transformation of the familiar into the unfamiliar" (65).

Amenábar skillfully displays the long Catholic tradition as a world of statues, rosary beads and votive candles — as Greeley said above — and connects them with a classical vision of belief based on authority and fear. Grace was probably taught through that interpretation. However, a literal and fearful observance of the precepts serves only to separate the self from the source of faith: a direct contact with the Holy. Thus deprived of a proper sacramental imagination, familiar objects have not a homely meaning for her but one that is strange and frightening. When she uncovers the objects in the attic, Grace symbolically turns the familiar into the unfamiliar as a reflection of the development in the discovery of her own identity. Morris points out that "the terror of the uncanny is released as we encounter the disguised and distorted but inalienable images of our own repressed desire ... not from something external, alien or unknown but — on the contrary — from something strangely familiar which defeats our efforts to separate ourselves from it" (307). Obviously, our very last repressed desire is the idea of death and we imagine multiple representations and rely on faith to find a satisfactory explanation for our contingent lives. This is the reason why Catholics find a direct way to be part of the Immortal through the sacraments. Victorian Gothic and a sacramental Catholic sensibility merge in the scene where Grace discovers the "book of the dead." Grace thinks that the people in the book are asleep but Mrs. Mills reveals that they are not asleep. They are dead. Grace finds it macabre but the servant explains the "sacramental" sense of such photographs. She says that "in the last century they used to take photographs of the dead in the hope that their souls would go on living through the portraits." Grace's reaction is congruent with her own way of understanding her faith: "How could these people be so superstitious?" Mrs. Mills' answer reveals and anticipates what Grace is to discover: "Grief over the death can lead people to do the strangest things."

When Grace finally accepts that there is some kind of presence in the house, she immediately considers the intruders as "not human," that is to say, as other, because they offer an unacceptable representation of being dead. The photographs could be labeled macabre but, in some way, they do not represent a menace. The intruders, however, are an almost physical materialization of our repressed images of death. Ironically, they represent a threat just because they are an anthropomorphic image of death. A ghost, then, is more human than any other representation of our ending. Thus the phenomenon of haunting is "a means of emphasizing the inevitability of human beings confronting the non-human that eludes explanation. The confrontation is inevitable because the inexplicable, though ostensibly non-human, is intrinsic to being human" (Cavallaro 61). Again, the familiar self becomes an unfamiliar other. Grace talks to Mrs. Mills about it:

> GRACE: "There was someone else there. And it wasn't human. There is something in this house. Something diabolic... I know you don't believe it, do you? No, I don't blame you. I used to not believe these things."
> MRS. MILLS: "I do believe, ma'am. I've always believed in those things. They're not easy to explain ... but they do happen. We've all heard stories of the beyond ... now and then. And I think that sometimes ... the world of the dead gets mixed up with the world of the living..."
> GRACE: "But it's impossible! The Lord would never allow such an aberration!

The living and the dead will only meet at the end of Eternity! It says so in the Bible."
MRS. MILLS: "Ma'am, there isn't always an answer for everything."

Grace is unable to understand that what is haunting her is part of her own self. The film is mostly seen from Grace's viewpoint and, as it happens with ghost stories, it is hard to know who is haunting and who is being haunted. With the benefit of hindsight, we learn that Grace is doing the haunting but she does not want to be aware of it and keeps on searching for the origin of the haunting. Symbolically, she is looking for herself. As the film advances, the manifestations of the intruders are more frequent while Grace's grasp on her environment is slipping away: the curtains have disappeared, the house is full of light, the servants lurk from the outside and her children think that she has gone mad again. Furthermore her religious belief cannot help her find a satisfactory explanation to the strange events so she finds herself again pushed to the limit. The night after Grace has banished the servants from the house, the children sneak out of the house and come across the hidden graves. Nicholas tells Anne to be careful just in case a ghost jumps out. His sister says that graves do not have ghosts, only skeletons. Anne then learns that the graves correspond to the servants. These appear and walk to the children who run back to the house. Nicholas asks how can they be ghosts if they are not wearing any sheets and clanking chains. It can be seen here again that the classical ghost is not an object of fear but a parodic representation of it. What really scares Anne is the human form of the ghostly trio of servants. Simultaneously Grace discovers a photograph of the servants from the book of the dead. Grace appears to stop the servants with the shotgun while the children run upstairs. Mrs. Mills tells Grace that tuberculosis killed them more than half a century ago. With the servants approaching the doorstep, the film closes a circle and comes back to the beginning. The servants' "mission" is clear:

MRS. MILLS: "We've been trying to make you understand."
GRACE: "Understand what?"
MRS. MILLS: "About the house. About the new situation."
GRACE: "What situation?"
MRS. MILLS: "We must all learn to live together. The living and the dead."

Grace now begins to understand. Upstairs, Anne and Nicholas discover that the old woman is acting as a medium in a séance with the "intruders." Grace appears and she and her children learn the awful truth: the old woman is not a ghost. They are the real ghosts who are haunting the house. Through this twist ending, the truth is finally revealed to Grace and the audience. Longing for the return of her missing husband and increasingly frustrated by her children's malady, she went insane, smothered them with a pillow and then, realizing what she had done, shot herself. When she awoke, she thought that God had given her a second chance through a kind of miracle. Once Grace consciously realizes that she is dead, Mrs. Mills offers her a cup of tea. For the first time in the film both women share a drink, not to say, viewpoint and condition. This communion between Grace and Mrs. Mills reassures that Grace has finally faced her other self.

In an interview by Jeffrey M. Anderson, Amenábar talked about the idea of the film: "When I was ten, I travelled to Chile with my brother and an aunt of ours had a séance in front of us. And it was quite impressive, but I can find out many explanations for it.... To me, this is a story about human ghosts. And that can be even scarier." Obviously, this forces us to think that Grace was already a ghost before dying. The whole film seems to make sense in retrospect. Conversely, we need to see it the way it is made in order to fully understand its meaning. The audience must take Grace's point of view and walk from room to room with her. As we find Grace at the beginning, in her daily life, she does her best to be a good, loving mother and to maintain her household alone. Then, what is the element that makes her a living ghost? The answer seems to be her faith, Roman Catholicism. Traditionally, Gothic narrative has been seen as anti–Catholic. Nowadays, as Jackson argues, "the modern fantastic, the form of literary fantasy within the secularized culture produced by capitalism, is a subversive literature" (180). The presence of Catholic elements in fantastic narratives is always interpreted as subversive, as going against the rules of an established set of norms. The fact that Grace is a Catholic may seem irrelevant for the success of the film's plot. Nevertheless, this move on the part of the director might lead us to look at Catholicism negatively thus identifying it with Grace, just as Kathleen Urda, elsewhere in this volume, comments on Lady Marchmain's character in Julian Jarrold's movie *Brideshead Revisited.*

In Amenabar's film, the protagonist is also portrayed as a cold and repressive character but in a different way. Grace and the Catholic Church do not appear as the monstrous villains but as the abject victims of the piece. During the first part of the film Grace does her best to be a loving and protective mother. Soon we discover that Grace's world is actually a reverted image of the mirror world in which she sees herself, the mirror which shows only what she desires to see. Her "Catholic mirror" turns horrifying when fantastic elements begin to appear thus proving it insufficient. What she perceives then is the uncanny sense of herself as other, the uneasy recognition of the unfamiliar in the familiar. Buber, following Heidegger's theories of the uncanny, argues that:

Uncanny [is] that empty space produced by the loss of faith in divine images. Unable to reach ... "God's sphere of being," man is left with a sense of vacancy.... The place which, metaphysically speaking, belongs to God ... can remain empty. Instead of it another, that is, a neither identical with God's sphere of being nor with that of man" [91].

This place seems to be the space where ghosts exist, the place that Grace, her children and the servants occupy. However, haunting stories are also a way to acquire identity out of an absence and to help us "to deal with the tangibility of our own mortality" (Cavallaro 62). Catholicism is rich in descriptions of places that one may find after death and there are several allusions to limbo, purgatory and hell throughout the film, establishing a clear connection between the ghost story and the Catholic sensibility. We can observe this association in the last scene. From the outside of the house the camera zooms through the window showing Grace who is embracing her children. Then they ask her: "if we're dead, where's limbo?" Grace answers: "I don't know if there even is a limbo. I'm no wiser than you are but I do know that I love you. I've always loved you. And this house is ours. You say it with me: this house is ours..."

This is an open and ambiguous ending which seems to offer two different meanings: on the one hand, Grace is portrayed as unburdened of her religious thoughts and occupying an empty space where God seems to be absent; on the other, we are left with the stained glass image of the familial trinity protected and embraced by the house as if it were a church, the place where revelations are made known. Finally, the House that imprisoned her is now the place where she is safe and complete and her Catholic belief, that early in the film dehumanized Grace, has now given her identity and a comfortable place to wait. No one knows what is to come for her but as Mrs. Mills said, "that's the way it's always been..."

Works Cited

Anderson, Jeffrey M. "Doing unto *The Others*." *Combustible Celluloid*. 20 July 2001. http://www.combustibleceluloid.com/interviews/amenabar.shtml.
Beville, Maria. *Gothic-Postmodernism: Voicing the Terrors of Postmodernity*. Amsterdam: Rodopi, 2009.
Botting, Fred. *The Gothic: Essays and Studies*. Cambridge: D. S. Brewer, 2003.
Buber, Martin. *The Eclipse of God*. New York: Harper, 1952.
Cavallaro, Dani. *The Gothic Vision: Three Centuries of Horror, Terror and Fear*. London: Continuum, 2002.
Greeley, Andrew. *The Catholic Imagination*. Berkeley: University of California Press, 2001.
Horner, Avril. "Heroine." *The Handbook to Gothic Literature*. Ed. M. Mulvey-Roberts. London: Macmillan, 1998.

Jackson, Rosemary. *Fantasy: The Literature of Subversion*. London: Routledge, 1988.
Mackenzie, Suzie. "Fear, Be My Friend." *Guardian Weekend*, 28 October 1999.
Miles, Robert. *Gothic Writing 1750–1820: A Genealogy*. London: Routledge, 1993.
Morris, David B. "Gothic Sublimity." *New Literary History* 16.2 (1985): 299.
The Others. Dir. Alejandro Amenábar. Perf. Nicole Kidman, Fionnula Flanagan, Christopher Eccleston. Warner Sogefilms, 2001. Film.
Warner, Marina. *No Go the Bogeyman*. London: Vintage, 2000.

About the Contributors

David Annandale, PhD, teaches literature and film at the University of Manitoba. His novels are *Crown Fire, Kornukopia* and *The Valedictorians* (Turnstone Press). He writes on film and video games, and he also reviews regularly for the Phantom of the Movies' VideoScope. He is at work on a book about video games.

Ralph Beliveau, PhD, teaches in the Gaylord College of Journalism and Mass Communication at the University of Oklahoma. His research focuses on critical media pedagogy, media criticism, film/video studies, popular culture, documentary theory, production and history, and rhetorical criticism. He has written about *The Wire*, African American biographical documentaries, Alex Cox, and media literacy.

Paulo Cunha is a PhD student at Coimbra University, a researcher at CEIS20 (Centre for 20th Century Interdisciplinary Studies) of the University of Coimbra, and a founding member of the AIM (Portuguese Association of Researchers of the Moving Image). He is responsible for the online databases *New Portuguese Cinema (1949–1980)* [http://ncinport.wordpress.com/] and *Film Criticism in Portugal* [http://criticacinport.wordpress.com/].

Brett Gaul, PhD, is an assistant professor of philosophy at Southwest Minnesota State University. His research interests include Augustine, ethics, and philosophy and popular culture. His work has appeared in *Augustinian Studies, Proceedings of the American Catholic Philosophical Association*, and *Just the Arguments: 100 of the Most Important Arguments in Western Philosophy*.

Margarita Georgieva is a freelance translator and doctoral student at the Université de Nice Sophia Antipolis (France). Her recent collaborations include *Nathaniel Hawthorne: Critical Insights* (2009) and *Encyclopedia of Themes in Literature* (2010). Her ongoing projects in collaboration with Udolpho Press (Germany) include a faithful translation of the Russian gothic *Don Corrado de Herrera* (1803) and a new edition of T. H. White's *Bellgrove Castle* (1803).

Anabel Altemir Giral is pursuing postgraduate studies at the University of La Rioja, researching her PhD on the Gothic and fantastic elements in the work of Scottish writer Muriel Spark. She teaches at the School of Modern Languages at the University of Zaragoza.

Marco Grosoli is a PhD student in film studies at Bologna University. As a film critic, he contributes regularly to "Cinergie" movie review and movie websites www.sentieriselvaggi.it, www.lafuriaumana.it and www.kinematrix.net. His essays have been published on "Fata Morgana," "www.zizekstudies.org," and in various edited collections nationally and internationally. He is editing a book about Guy Debord.

Regina Hansen, PhD, is a senior lecturer in rhetoric at Boston University's College of General Studies. She has published and presented on film and the fantastic, Neo-Victorian studies, and composition studies, and is the coauthor of the reader *Cultural Conversations: The Presence of the Past*. Her fiction has been recognized with grants from the Massachusetts Cultural Council, and by the PEN New England Children's Book Caucus.

Alexandra Heller-Nicholas is a PhD candidate in the School of Communications, Arts and Critical Enquiry at La Trobe University in Melbourne, Australia. She has published — on microhistory, horror and trash film cultures, sexual violence, aesthetics and ethics — in *Cinephile, Limina, Screening the Past*, and *Refractory*. Her book on the rape-revenge film is forthcoming from McFarland.

Ismael Ibáñez Rosales is currently head of the Language and Literature Department at Las Fuentes–Alcaste school in Logroño, Spain. At the University of La Rioja, he is a PhD candidate studying the British Catholic novel during the second half of the 20th century.

Christa Jones, PhD, is an assistant professor of French at Utah State University. Her articles, which focus on North African Francophone postcolonial literature, have appeared in *Al-Raida, Dalhousie French Studies, Francofonia, The International Journal of the Humanities, Expressions Maghrébines, MIFLC Review*, and *Women Studies Quarterly*, among others. She is writing a book on the cave in North African Francophone literature.

Barry C. Knowlton, PhD, teaches history and Latin at Stonehill College, and has published a variety of trifles on the linguistic turn (the relationship between philosophy and language), the Second World War, and the *Histories* of Herodotus.

Eloise R. Knowlton, PhD, is dean of undergraduate studies at Assumption College in Worcester, Massachusetts. She is the author of *Joyce, Joyceans, and the Rhetoric of Citation* (Florida University Press, 1998) and *Sweets of Sin*, a novel serialized in the *James Joyce Quarterly*. Her work has appeared in *Style, Mosaic*, and other publications.

Ann Kordas, PhD, is an assistant professor in the Department of Humanities at Johnson & Wales University, Providence campus. Her research interests are the history of occult beliefs in the United States and American childhood during the Cold War. Her primary field of interest is American cultural history.

Em McAvan, PhD, has taught literature and communication studies at Murdoch University, Western Australia. Her first book, *The Postmodern Sacred*, is forthcoming from McFarland, and other works on religion and literature have appeared in journals such as *Literature and Theology, The Journal of Postcolonial Writing* and *The Bible and Critical Theory*.

About the Contributors 289

Christopher McKittrick teaches English composition and literature at Long Island University and Suffolk County Community College in New York. His work has been published in *Newsday* and *Good Times Magazine*, and he is a regular contributor to MovieBuzzers.com. He has also spoken about film, literature, and graphic novels at academic conferences and his first short story was published in *By Mind or Metal: A Fantasy Anthology*.

Shelley F. O'Brien gained her MPhil in 2000 with a thesis entitled "Body Horror Movies: Their Emergence and Evolution." She has been teaching film for almost 20 years, and was invited to be a jury member for the Silver Méliès award at the 22nd Leeds International Film Festival in November 2008, and as guest speaker on "The Art of Sound" at the Cornwall Film Festival in 2009.

Rick Pieto, PhD, teaches in the Department of Communication at the University of Pittsburgh. He has published articles and given presentations on the Osbournes and reality television, horror fandom and Georges Bataille's book *The Dead Man*. His research interests include fan culture and genre, the politics of the attention economy and issues in online learning.

John Regan is senior lecturer at Boston University's College of General Studies. He has published numerous articles on literature and the teaching of writing, including an essay on the 1834 burning of the Ursuline Convent in Charlestown, Mass. His doctoral dissertation examined anti–Catholic literature in antebellum America and he has presented at many national conferences including MLA, SHARP, and the CCCC.

Daniel Ribas is a PhD student and a researcher at the University of Aveiro. He also teaches at the University of Applied Sciences of Bragança. He was, for several years, a freelance screenwriter and a film critic, and is a founding member of AIM (Portuguese Association of Researchers of the Moving Image) and the editor of the online magazine *Drama*.

Victoria Surliuga, PhD, is an assistant professor of Italian at Texas Tech University. She has written on Giambattista Marino, Federico Fellini's *Casanova* and the poetry of Andrea Zanzotto, and on the Italian contemporary poets Franco Loi, Giampiero Neri, and Giancarlo Majorino. She is writing a book on Italian stardom.

Jana Toppe is a PhD student in the Department of German Literature at the Free University of Berlin with a dissertation on the depiction of the crowd in German fantastic literature around 1900. Her research interests include horror studies, popular culture, and trauma studies.

Kathleen E. Urda, PhD, is an assistant professor of English at Bronx Community College, CUNY, in New York City. She received her PhD in 2007 from Fordham University, and her primary area of specialization is eighteenth- and nineteenth-century British fiction. Her research and publications focus particularly on how novel plots evolve and work and on Catholic literature and film.

Isabella van Elferen, PhD, is an assistant professor of music and new media at the Department of Media and Cultural Studies of Utrecht University. She has published widely on German Baroque music, film and TV music, videogame music, mobile phone ringtones, and Gothic theory and subcultures, and is writing a monograph on *Gothic Music: The Sounds of the Uncanny*.

Index

Act of Contrition 202–203
Amenabar, Alejandro 275, 276, 281, 282–283, 284
anastasis 171
angel(s) 29, 34, 36–37, 210
Angels with Dirty Faces (film, 1938) 256
Anglicanism 6
anti–Catholicism 7–8, 114–125
Antichrist 98–102, 111
Apostle Paul *see* Paul, Saint
Arendt, Hannah 156
Augustine, Saint 203, 223
The Awful Disclosures of Maria Monk 8

Badiou, Alain 142–144, 254
Baptism, sacrament of 277
The Believers (film, 1987) 162
Bell, Derrick 161
Bellocchio, Marco 219, 221, 224–225
The Bells of St Mary's (film, 1945) 196, 268
Benilde or the Virgin Mother/Benilde Ou a Virgem-Mãe (film, 1974) 88
Bernanos, Georges 233–234
The Bible 188–192
Bido, Antonio 257, 262, 264
Blair Witch Project (film, 1999) 107
Blatty, William Peter 68–69, 73, 76, 154, 158, 244, 247
"Blaxploitation" 159–161
blood 4, 5, 7, 97–112, 114, 117, 122–124; drinking of 99–102, 105, 117, 124; Jesus Christ and 4, 5, 99, 101, 117, 118, 124
The Blood Stained Shadow (film, 1978) 257, 262, 264–265
Boston Globe 268
Boyle, Danny 4, 17–19, 20, 23
Boys of St. Vincent (film, 1992) 270
Boys Town (film 1938) 196, 268
Bram Stoker's Dracula (film, 1992) 100, 110–112
Brazil (film, 1985) 30, 33–34, 35, 36, 37, 39
Breen, Joseph 9

Brideshead Revisited (film 2007) 12, 126–139, 284
Brideshead Revisited (novel, 1945) 12
Brontë, Charlotte, *Villette* 8
Brooks, Peter 69–71
Brown, Dan 4, 10
Browning, Tod 114, 119, 122–125
Buber, Martin 284–285

Call of Fatima (film, 2005) 92
Calmet, Dom Auguste 99
Calvino, Italo 220
Carmilla (novel, 1972) 97
Carroll, Noel 152, 163–164
Carter, Chris 272
The Castle of Otranto (novel, 1764) 7, 126
Catechism of the Catholic Church 213, 215–216, 272, 273
Catechism of the Council of Trent for Parish Priests (1923) 201–208
Catholic Church *see* Roman Catholic Church
Catholic moral teaching 210, 211, 213, 214, 217
Cat People (film, 1942) 146–147
Cat People (film, 1982) 140–141, 145–151
Christ *see* Jesus
Christians 4, 5, 6
Christmas, commercialization of 34–35
Christopher, Saint 210
Citizen Kane (film, 1941) 201
Clare of Assisi, Saint 3, 19–21, 11
Clergy 7, 8, 9, 14
comedy 19–21
Communion, sacrament of *see* Eucharist, sacrament of
Confession, sacrament of *see* Reconciliation, sacrament of
Confession, Seal of 204
The Confessional (film, 1975) see *House of Mortal Fear* (film, 1975)
Constantine (film, 2005) 270
Coppola, Francis Ford 100, 102–104, 105, 109, 110

Index

Cosmic Slop (TV program, 1994) 161–164
crime 198–199
Crosby, Bing 196
crucifix/crucifixes 5, 118, 121, 124
Currie, Andrew 178

Daneliya, Georgi 183, 185
Dark at Noon (film, 1992) 90–91
Dawn of the Dead (film, 1978) 176–177
Dawn of the Dead (film, 2007) 173, 174
Day of the Dead (film) 177
Depardieu, Gerard 235
Devil *see* Satan
Diary of a Country Priest (novel, 1936) 233, 234
La dolce vita (film, 1960) 219, 221–222
Dominion: Prequel to the Exorcist (film, 2005) 155–158
Don't Torture the Duckling (film, 1972) 257, 258–262
Dracula (film, 1931) 114, 116, 119–120, 121–124
Dracula (novel, 1897) 98–105, 107, 114, 116, 119, 121, 125
Dracula's Daughter (film, 1936) 120–124

8½ (film, 1963) 221, 222–23
Engels, Friedrich 177
England 9
Enlightenment 6–7, 8, 169
Erksan, Metin 72–74
Eucharist, sacrament of 13, 43, 178–180, 263; First Communion 286
Evangelical Protestantism 8
evil 4, 13, 29–33, 35, 36, 38, 39, 66, 67, 68, 69, 72, 76, 98, 99, 101, 103, 110, 156, 233, 235, 240, 241
Exorcism (film, 1974) 244–255, 269
exorcism, rite of 53, 56, 58, 67, 68, 70, 121, 269
Exorcisme et messes noires (film, 1974) see *Exorcism* (film, 1974)
Exorcism of Emily Rose (film, 2005) 270
The Exorcist (film, 1973) 4, 11, 13, 55–56, 57–59, 65–67, 67–70, 71, 72, 74, 76, 140, 153–155, 158, 244, 245, 252–253, 256, 269–270
The Exorcist (novel, 1971) 68–69, 154, 158, 232
Exorcist II: The Heretic (film, 1977) 140
Exorcist III: Cries and Shadows (film, 1975) 74–76

fado 91
Fatima (film, 1997) 90–91, 223
Fatima, Lady of *see* Mary, mother of Jesus
Fatima, Land of Faith/Fatima/Terra di Fe (film, 1943) 84–85
"faux Catholicism" 10, 136–137
Fellini, Federico 219, 221, 224–225
Fido (film, 2006) 178
The Fisher King (film, 1991) 30, 31–32, 35, 37, 39–40

"forfeiture of rights" 213–214
France: cinema 232–243; *nouvelle vague* 233
Francis of Assisi, Saint 18, 19, 21–22
Franco, Jesus (Jess) 244, 245, 247, 248, 251, 253
"free will" 29, 31–33, 35, 40
Freud, Sigmund 1, 21, 281
Friedkin, William 65, 66, 68–69, 72, 73, 74, 76, 140, 154, 158, 232, 244, 245, 256
Fulci, Lucio 257, 258

Genesis, Book of 198
ghosts 4, 11, 14, 275–286
giallo 225, 256, 257, 260, 262, 264, 265
Gilliam, Terry 29–40
Going My Way (film, 1944) 196, 256
Gone Baby Gone (film, 2007) 209–218
good 67, 69–70
good (charitable) works 17–18, 21–24, 26
gothic 7–8, 9, 10, 11, 14, 97–112, 126–128, 130–134, 136–139, 268–270, 276, 277, 278, 279, 282, 284
gothicized Catholicism 97–99, 101, 103, 105, 107, 109–112, 268–270
Grand Guignol 71
Greeley, Andrew 276–277

Haiti 170
Halperin, Victor 170
Harlin, Renny 164
haunted house 128, 275, 279
Hawks and Sparrows (film, 1966) 226
Hays, William 9
Hays Code *see* Motion Picture Production Code
Heaney, Seamus 5
Heelas, Paul 45
Heidegger, Martin 284
Hell 285
Hitchcock, Alfred 196–208
Holy Trinity 190
Honthaner, Ron 160
horror 4, 7, 8, 9, 10, 11, 12, 14, 53–63, 70–71, 75, 140–142, 145, 146, 147, 150, 257, 271, 276
House of Mortal Sin (film, 1975) 256, 257, 262–264
House of Skull Mountain (film, 1974) 160–161
Hudlin, Reginald 161
Hudlin, Warrington 161

I Confess (film, 1953) 196–208
Imaginarium of Doctor Parnassus (film, 2009) 34, 35, 39
immigration 7–8, 9, 12
In the Name of the Father (film, 1972) 219, 221, 224–225
Indulgences, selling of 32
Ireland 7, 196
Islam 73

Index   293

The Italian (novel, 1797) 127
Italy: cinema 219–231, 257

Jabberwocky (film, 1977) 30, 35, 38–39
Jackson, Peter 44, 46–47, 48–49
Jarrold, Julian 126, 131, 133, 138
Jesus 5, 18, 117–118, 125, 171, 175, 178–179, 180, 198, 205–206, 207, 210, 229–230, 233
John 20: 23 199
John 6:54–56 179
John Paul II, Pope 90
Joseph of Nazareth, Saint 18, 25–26
Judaism 8
Jung 228

Kael, Pauline 244
Kant, Immanuel 244–245, 247–252, 253
Kin Dza Dza! (film, 1965) 183–195

Lacan, Jacques 143–144, 244–245, 247, 248–249, 281
Land of the Dead (film, 2005) 177–178
Lassie Come Home (film 1943) 178
Law and Order (TV series) 269
Lefanu, Sheridan 97; *Carmilla* 97
The Legend of the Holy Drinker (film, 1988) 228–229
Lewis, C.S. 8, 44
Lewis, Matthew 126; *The Italian* 127; *The Monk* 98, 127
limbo 285
liturgy 102, 103–104, 109–112
The Lord of the Rings (film) 11, 41–42, 46–49
The Lord of the Rings (novel) 11, 41–42, 42–44
Lost Souls (film, 2000) 55, 56
Luther, Martin 31, 198

Marian apparitions *see* Mary, mother of Jesus
Marian myth 81
Maria's Hours (film, 1976) 88–90
Mariolatry 130, 135–136
Mark of the Vampire (film, 1935) 119–123
Marx, Karl 177, 185
Mary, mother of Jesus 8, 10, 130, 136–136, 210, 222, 223, 225, 236, 259; apparitions 12, 81–92; devotion to 6, 7; Lady of Fatima 81–92, 223; Lady of Medjugorje 223
Mass 4, 5, 13, 225, 268
materialism 17
Matthew 10:16 210
Maturin, Charles: *Melmoth the Wanderer* (novel, 1820) 98–99
medals, religious 5, 209
medievalism 8
Men of Boys Town (film, 1941) 196
Mill, John Stuart 214
Millions (film, 2004) 4, 11
The Miracle According to Salome /O Milagre Segundo Salome (film, 2004) 91–92
Miracle of Our Lady of Fatima (film, 1952) 4, 85–86

miracles 5, 11, 13, 222, 229, 284
Miraculous Fatima/Fatima Milagroso (film, 1928) 83–84
The Mission (film, 1986) 256
money 17–18, 21, 22–24, 25, 26–27
monks 7
monster 52, 53, 57, 59–62
Monty Python 29–30, 37–39
Motion Picture Production Code 9
Murnau, Friedrich 99, 107, 108
music 97–98, 105–112
The Mysteries of Udolpho (novel, 1794) 7
Mystic River (film, 2003) 269

nativism, American 8, 9, 121–122
Nelson, Victoria 10, 136–137, 139
New Age 44–49
Nicene Creed 179
Nicholas of Myra, Saint 18, 22–23
Nietzsche 169
Night of the Living Dead (film, 1968) 170–171
nihilism 169, 171, 172, 258
Nosferatu (film, 1922) 99, 107, 108
nuns 7, 10

Olmi, Ermanno 219, 221, 228–230
The Omen (film, 1976) 55, 268
One Hundred Nails (film, 2007) 229–230
Orthodox Christianity 6, 186, 187, 188, 192, 193
other/othering/otherness 8, 152–159, 252–253, 280, 284
The Others (film, 2001) 14, 275–286

paganism 5, 6
Palin, Michael 30
paracinema 67, 72
Pasolini, Pier Paolo 219, 221, 225–228
Paul, Saint 65, 142–145, 149–150, 172–178; Epistle to the Corinthians 172–178
Paul VI, Pope 65–66, 67, 69, 74, 76
Peter, Saint 24–25, 190
Pialat, Maurice 232, 233–234, 237, 239
The Pietà 32–33
Pius XI, Pope 193
Plague of Zombies (film, 1966) 159
Polanski, Roman 171, 232
polytheism 5
Portugal 81–92; Fatima 81–82, 92; New State Dictatorship 81, 87; Republican anti-clerical idealism 81–82
predestination 31
pre-Raphaelites 8
priests 5, 6, 7, 53, 55, 56, 58, 62, 196–208, 210, 212, 222–223, 224–225, 228, 232, 243, 244–253, 256–267, 268–275
Protestant Reformation 6, 98, 118, 121
Protestantism 99, 101–105, 109, 110, 111, 198; *sola fide* (faith alone) 31–32; *sola scriptura* 101

294 Index

Psycho (film) 207
Purgatory 203, 285

race 152–164
Radcliffe, Ann 127, 138; *Mysteries of Udolpho* 7, 98, 126–127
radical poverty, ideology of 19, 24
reality/realism 4, 11, 20–21, 24
reason 7
Reconciliation, sacrament of 13, 196–208, 261–262, 272
redemption 14, 272
"religion of the image" 145, 150
resurrection 5, 13, 169, 170, 171–178
Return of the Exorcist (film, 1975) *see Exorcist III: Cries and Shadows*
Revelation, Book of 189
Rice, Anne 100, 106, 107
ridiculous 3, 4, 8–10, 11
Rodney, Kevin 161
Roman Catholic Church 4, 6, 7, 8, 9, 161–163, 220, 222, 224, 227–228, 230, 232, 246, 253, 254; evil and 241; sexual abuse scandal 9, 268–29, 270
Romero, George 170, 174, 175, 176, 177
Rosemary's Baby (film, 1968) 171, 232
Russia 183–195; Catholicism and 187, 188, 191, 192, 193–194

sacrament 13, 43, 276, 277, 278–279, 282
"sacramental imagination" 277, 281
sacramentality 42–44, 48–49
Sade, Marquis de 244–245, 247, 248–252, 253
saints 4, 5, 6, 8, 10, 11, 13, 233
Santería 161–163
Satan 55, 58, 65–66, 68, 69, 73, 75, 99–100, 103, 110, 233, 235, 236, 238–240, 241
Schrader, Paul 140–141, 145–151, 157–158
Scream films 142
Second Vatican Council 9, 65, 69, 201
Señora de Fátima (film, 1951) 85–86
sex 149; de-sexualization 145
Seytan (film, 1974) 72–74
Sign of the Cross 6
sin 142–145, 146–147, 149, 150, 198–199, 222, 262
Son of Dracula (film, 1943) 120
Song of Bernadette (film, 1943) 4 21
Soviet science fiction 184, 189, 193
Soviet Union *see* Russia
Spain 247–248
spectacle 5–6, 7, 10, 11, 12, 13, 14, 66–67, 71, 72, 74, 76
Star Wars (film, 1977) 268
Stations of the Cross 2, 13
statue, religious 281

Stigmata (film, 1999) 55
Stoker, Bram 99, 103, 105; *Dracula* 98–105, 107, 114, 116, 119, 121, 125
Sugar Hill (film, 1974) 159

technology 33–34, 35
Theorem (film, 1968) 226–227
Therese of Lisieux, Saint 228
13th Day (film, 2009) 92
The Thorn Birds (TV mini-series) 232
Time Bandits (film) 30–33, 35
Todorov, Tzvetan 3–5 10, 20, 52–53, 58, 59–60, 220–221
Tolkien, J.R.R. 8, 41–44, 46, 47–49; *The Lord of the Rings* 11
Tourneur, Jacques 146–147
Tracy, Spencer 196
transubstantiation 6, 263
Truffaut, François 198, 205
12 Monkeys (film) 34, 36
28 Days Later (film) 171, 174
28 Weeks Later 171

Ugandan martyrs (saints) 18, 19, 23
uncanny 3–4, 6–8, 9, 10, 12 14, 284
unheimlich *see* uncanny
United States 7–9
Un urlo nelle tenebre (film, 1975) *see Exorcist III: Cries and Shadows*
utilitarianism 214

The Vampire Bat (film, 1933) 119, 120–122, 124
vampires 4, 8, 10, 12, 97–112; Catholicism and 97–112, 114–125; Eucharist and 4
Vatican 5
Vatican II *see* Second Vatican Council
verisimilitude 52–63
Vertigo (film) 207
Villette (novel, 1853) 8
Virgin Birth 5
Virgin Mary *see* Mary, mother of Jesus
Vodoun/Voodoo 158–161, 170, 180, 259

Walker, Peter 256, 257
Walpole, Horace: *The Castle of Otranto* 7, 126
Waugh, Evelyn: *Brideshead Revisited* 12, 126–139
White Zombie (film, 1932) 124, 170
Without a Trace (TV series) 269

X-Files: I Want to Believe (film, 2008) 269–270

Zizek, Slavoj 44, 142–143, 248, 250–252
Zombie (film, 1978) 170
zombie(s) 4, 8, 13, 169–182; Catholicism and 4, 169–182; Eucharist and 13, 178–180; resurrection of the body and 13, 171–178

www.ingramcontent.com/pod-product-compliance
Ingram Content Group UK Ltd.
Pitfield, Milton Keynes, MK11 3LW, UK
UKHW041926140426
5217IPUK00014B/331